Contents

Preface

There has never been a more appropriate time for us to consider the role of planners in the provision of educational services. As much as the 1960s and 1970s were characterised as periods of quantitative expansion and optimism so the past two decades, and I believe, well into the next century, will be viewed as a time of challenge, austerity and what is euphemistically called, 'adjustment'. The language of educational development is now very much less optimistic with calls for 'doing more with less' and concern for the quality of what is provided. Much of this concern will fall upon the shoulders of those charged with the responsibility for the planning and administration of schools and colleges, be they hard-pressed educational planners working within a central ministry or headteachers in outlying primary schools to whom many of the traditional planning decisions have been devolved and decentralised.

This book will be of use to these professionals and others interested in the educational planning process. Sibrino Forojalla draws on a wealth of personal experience in the writing of this book – from the heady days of the oil boom in Nigeria (when we worked together as young lecturers in education at one of the new universities) to the challenging environment of the Sudan, where he labours well under very difficult circumstances.

Whether one wants to learn more about the nature and scope of educational planning or to evaluate examples of good (and less good!) practice from a variety of national contexts, this book will prove to be of value. Professor Forojalla is also to be congratulated for persevering with this project: it is itself a cause for quiet optimism.

David Stephens

Acknowledgements

I am particularly indebted to Mr P.R.C. Williams, former Professor in the Department of Education in Developing Countries, Institute of Education, University of London, and now Head of the Human Resources Development Unit in the Commonwealth Secretariat, London; for instilling in me the love for the subject of education planning. My thanks also go to Mr Augustino Amuzie formerly of the Department of Education, and Ms Margaret Ayodele for their painstaking efforts in typing the manuscript. Last but not least, I thank my dear wife Mariana Asha, for her patience and encouragement to complete the work.

S.B. Forojalla

Introduction

In 1961, the First Conference of Ministers of Education of Independent African Countries was held in Addis Ababa, Ethiopia. To the African countries then just emerging from many decades of colonial rule, educational expansion was seen as a catalyst for economic development and a leveller of social inequalities. This role and ability of education to bring about such changes was buttressed by research findings in the 1950s in the advanced Western countries, which demonstrated the crucial part played by education in their socio-economic advancement. It was on the basis of such evidence that the conference resolved that all African countries should attain Universal Primary Education (UPE) by 1980; 30 per cent of children completing primary school should be enrolled in secondary schools; and post-secondary enrolment should be provided for 20 per cent of those completing secondary education (Thompson, 1981). Further impetus was given to the drive for educational development by Philip Coomb's book, *The World Educational Crisis: A Systems Analysis* published in 1968, which emphasised that change, adaptation and disparity lay at the heart of the worldwide crisis in education. Thus the book stated that:

Since 1945, all countries have undergone fantastically swift environmental changes, brought about by a number of concurrent worldwide revolutions – in science and technology, in economic and political affairs, in demographic and social structures. Educational systems have also grown and changed more rapidly than ever before. But they have adapted all too slowly in relation to the faster pace of events on the move around them. The consequent disparity – taking many forms – between educational systems and their environments is the essence of the worldwide crisis in education.

Some of the disparities referred to were: first, the growing obsolescence of the curriculum content in relation to the advancing state of knowledge and the actual learning needs of students; second, the mismatch between education and the development needs of societies; third, the growing imbalances and maladjustments between education and employment; fourth, the serious educational inequalities between various social groups; and fifthly, the growing gap between the rising costs of education and the funds countries would be able and willing to invest in it (Coombs, 1985).

A close examination of the causes of disparities revealed the following as the main ones: the sharp increase in popular aspirations for education; the acute scarcity of resources; the inherent inertia of educational systems 'which caused them to respond too sluggishly in adapting their internal affairs to new external necessities, even when resources have not been the main obstacle to adaptation'; and the inertia of societies themselves, 'the heavy weight of traditional attitudes, religious customs, prestige and incentive patterns, and institutional structures – which has blocked them from making the optimum use of education and of educated manpower to foster national development'. (Coombs, *ibid*).

The publication of this book by Coombs, with its dire predictions, further spurred African countries to place more efforts into the development of education with the consequence that by the mid-1970s student enrolments in most countries had increased three to four-fold and expenditure on education had risen so fast that it was consuming between 20 to 30 per cent of the annual budget or up to 4.3 per cent of GNP in most countries.

The preceding analysis by Philip Coombs has been further strengthened by subsequent factors which have all conspired to obstruct the smooth development of education as mapped out by the African leaders at Addis Ababa in 1961. These factors include population growth, political instability, and changes in the economic sphere, which in the 1970s and 1980s have all had the cumulative effect of undermining confidence in education itself, as we show below.

Demographic dynamics

Demographic changes constitute a set of powerful forces that impinged heavily on education in Africa in the 1960s, 1970s and 1980s and is likely to continue to do so in the 1990s. It is now quite clear from hindsight that the education officials who set the targets for educational expansion for Africa for the following two decades at Addis Ababa in 1961, were well wide of the mark. In fact, within the decade of the 1960s the educational systems in Africa found it difficult simply to maintain their existing school participation rates in the face of the rapidly growing school-age populations and harder yet to make a little headway toward their adopted school participation rates. This race between education and population growth, which continued at a hectic pace throughout the 1970s and 1980s, shows little let up in sight for the next two decades. According to the 1989 UNICEF report, the population of Africa, now with the fastest growth rate in the world, will be double its 1975 size by the end of this century, having risen from 406 million people in 1975 to an estimated 828 million by the year 2000. Figures from the Economist (1990) *Book of Vital World Statistics* (Hutchinson) are 725 million in 1988 and an estimated 1379 million in the year 2000. If present long-range projections prove correct, Africa's population will have grown to 2 billion by the year 2100. The trend of population growth is indicated in Appendix 3. Besides the rapidly growing school-age population, political instability is another serious problem which has affected education.

Political instability

Right from the outset, the independence of many African states was accompanied by political instability and eruptions. In some, these initial disturbances soon died down once freedom was attained, as in Kenya and Zimbabwe. In many others, however, the instability assumed new forms and continued throughout the decades of the 1960s and 1970s and is continuing in the 1990s, as in the Sudan, Chad, Mozambique and Angola. In yet others, the eruptions started well after independence, often with a *coup d' état* which then led to civil wars, as typified by Ethiopia and Uganda. Whatever form these political instabilities assumed, the ultimate result was economic disruption and this in turn resulted in the dislocation of the educational system. The causes of the political instability ranged from cultural collisions and protests against repression and extreme poverty to popular demands for participation and greater equality. In many instances in Africa, students and teachers were frequently in the vanguard of these protest movements, including outright civil wars and revolutions. Consequently, as active participants in these disruptions, the schools and higher educational institutions were expected by society to undertake a disproportionate responsibility for curing whatever was wrong.

Yet another result flowing from the political instability that has added further burdens on the school systems of some countries, has been the unprecedented flood of refugees and other migrants between countries. The host country not only must provide the 'new guests' with food, shelter and other basic amenities, as well as jobs and possibly land, to enable them to support themselves, but must also meet the urgent educational needs of their school-age children. Often these are expected of governments and host populations besieged by severe economic and political problems of their own. This is typified by the case of the Sudan which, in 1986, had about one million refugees from Zaïre, Uganda and Ethiopia (Eritreans and other Ethiopians), in the midst of its own civil war, which had been ravaging the country since the period of independence in 1955. The result is overstretched resources and over-burdened education systems. However, changes in the economic sphere have presented by far the greatest obstacle to the improvement of education in Africa over the past two decades and is likely to continue to do so in the 1990s and most likely beyond.

Economic changes

In Africa, the majority of countries attained independence in the first half of the 1960s. At the time of independence most countries had limited provision of social services and infrastructure: health, education and communication and transport networks, and few manufacturing industries. It was therefore incumbent upon the political leadership of each newly-independent country to embark upon the establishment of modern industries and expansion of social services for their populations. By the mid-1970s, however, the output from the expanded educational systems, particularly at the secondary and post-secondary levels, had caught up with the backlog of post-independence manpower shortages and even begun to outstrip the creation of new jobs by the economy. The result was the new phenomenon of educated unemployed, firstly amongst secondary school leavers and then among post-secondary graduates, creating widespread anxieties for the students and their families and worrying political problems for governments and educational systems (Coombs, 1985).

A second change, evolving out of the rapid expansion of the education system, was the outward flow of manpower at the graduate level from the non-oil producing countries in Africa to the oil-producing countries initially within the continent, such as Nigeria, Gabon and Libya and later further afield to the Middle East countries of Saudi Arabia and the Gulf states. African governments, in relation to the African and Arab states, did not view this transfer as a brain-drain but as a lucrative form of export – in many instances negotiated on a government-to-government basis. For example, countries like Egypt, the Sudan and Tunisia instituted this arrangement, which resulted in valuable remittances home of hard currency and which often helped

lessen the potentially politically volatile problem of the educated unemployed at home.

The third economic change which had a severe impact on education throughout the continent and intensified the problem of the
educated unemployed in most countries, was the sudden sharp rise in
oil prices and severe worldwide recession and accelerated inflation
that started in 1973 and continued throughout the rest of the decade
into the 1980s. In Africa, this stagflation was accompanied by severe
price fluctuations which saw sharp falls in the prices of cash crops
such as coffee, cocoa, tea and sugar, as well as minerals – copper, iron
ore, diamonds and tin, which continue to this day. This stagflation
affected the education system in Africa in two important ways: first, it
reduced employment openings for new graduates from post-secondary
institutions; and second, it played havoc with educational costs and
budgets. As Philip H. Coombs, a seasoned observer of educational
developments in developing countries shows, it was indeed a trau-
matic experience for most African countries:

their export earnings declined, their terms of trade worsened, their oil import
costs skyrocketed, unemployment mounted, and extreme poverty spread to an
ever increasing number of families. Their public budgets, already heavily
burdened with a large accumulation of external debt, became seriously
overstrained. Their educational systems, whose budgets had by now become
a much higher percentage of the Gross National Product (GNP) and the total
budget, inevitably bore a sizeable share of the consequences (Coombs, 1985).

The fourth economic factor with the greatest long-term consequences for education and employment, was the further segmentation
of the labour markets in the 1970s and 1980s. In spite of the fact that
the previously dominant percentage share by agriculture of the GNP
continued to decline, the share of the labour force employed in agriculture failed to decline correspondingly. On the other hand, in some of
the countries where the share of the GNP accounted for by the urban
modern sector, with its capital-intensive technologies and much higher
productivity and wages, had grown substantially, there was no corresponding growth in the share of the national labour force. As a result,
it became increasingly difficult for young people with a modern education to find a stable and secure job in this modern sector. In Africa
this situation was exacerbated by the fact that the modern manufacturing sector was heavily dependent on imported raw materials. This
resulted in the closure of many modern factories or their working very
much below capacity once foreign exchange earnings began to decline,
as happened in Ghana in the 1970s and in Nigeria in the 1980s, giving

a clear indication of the fact that the approach to industrialisation in many African countries was based on a 'false start'.

A fifth economic factor which added to the existing woes of the African countries was the impact of the series of natural disasters which afflicted large parts of the continent in the decades of the 1970s and 1980s, commencing with the first Sahelian drought in 1975/76 which devastated agricultural and livestock production of the populations in the sub-Saharan countries throughout the Sudan belt. This visitation was repeated in 1984/85 and this second round extended further southwards to encompass such countries as Zambia and Zimbabwe and even as far afield as the Republic of South Africa, and was followed in 1988 by heavy flooding and the outbreak of a locust invasion in more or less the same areas of the Sahelian region. This series of disasters resulted in large-scale deaths of people and livestock and the mass migration of the surviving victims to other countries. The result was economic disruption in both the afflicted countries and those receiving the displaced populations. However, that was not the end of the story.

This economic situation of the African and other developing countries has continued to worsen in the second half of the 1980s, as a recent report by UNICEF (*The State of the World's Children 1989*) shows:

. . . for most countries of Africa, Latin America and the Caribbean, almost every economic signal points to the fact that development has been derailed. Per capital GNP has fallen, debt repayments have risen to a quarter or more of all export earnings, share in world trade has dropped, and the productivity of labour has declined by one or two percentage points each year throughout the 1980s (UNICEF, 1989).

Elsewhere the report states that:

two elements have dominated the deterioration of economic prospects over much of the developing world in recent years. They are rising debt repayments and falling commodity prices. The fall in new commercial lending and the inadequate and static levels of official aid complete the four walls of the financial prison in which so much of the developing world has been incarcerated during this decade.

The solution, as prescribed by the IMF and the World Bank for the indebted developing countries, is the adoption of adjustment programmes by these countries as a way out of their economic crises. Unfortunately the present policies for coping with the debt crisis are manifestly not succeeding in restoring economic growth to most of the indebted nations. For example, per capita GDP in sub-Saharan Africa declined by 3.6 per cent in 1980–85, by 0.5 per cent in 1986, and by 5.1 per cent in 1987. And the future looks equally bleak. According to the UNICEF report, latest World Bank projections to the year 1995, for example, show zero per capita growth in sub-Saharan Africa. Similarly, the World Economic Survey 1988 of the United Nations, points out that per capita incomes in Latin America and Africa had fallen again that year and were expected to fall still further in 1989. In many nations, average incomes in 1995 are expected to be below the levels of 1980 and in some countries even far below that.

Thus the long-term cumulative financial effects on education of population growth, political instability, world inflation as a result of the oil crises and poor economic management in Africa since the mid-1970s, which have been exacerbated more recently by debt repayments and the impact of Structural Adjustment Programmes (SAP) of the World Bank, are likely to continue into the 1990s and even beyond. These have been summarised by a recent World Bank Report as follows:

The advances (in education) since the 1960s are now seriously threatened – in part by circumstances outside the control of education. Africa's explosive population growth greatly increases the number of children seeking access to schools and the number of potential illiterates. If the growth of educational places is to keep up with the growth of the school-age population, more schools, teachers, books and other inputs are required each year. This requirement comes at a time when the recent economic decline has necessitated significant cutbacks in public spending. Public spending on education in Africa has not been spared, declining from \$10 bn in 1980 to \$8.9 bn in 1983 (World Bank 1980, 1981 and 1988).

The painful adjustments now occurring in many African countries is a daily fact of life on the continent. Hence the emphasis in the 1990s and beyond, as far as education is concerned, should be on policy options that will be employed in mitigating the restrictions on education. In addition, rigorous planning, applying the methodologies and techniques presented in this book, will play a crucial role if the education systems of Africa are to be rehabilitated and expanded to cope with the school-age populations of the coming decades.

Cost recovery and reallocation of resources

The rationale in applying any cost recovery programme is that it should be directed towards those levels of education where potential savings are the greatest and where the impact on student and parental welfare will be least felt. The two main levels to which this could be applied are secondary and higher education. For instance, in sub-Saharan Africa, the cost of providing education at the primary level is roughly one-fiftieth of that needed to finance a university student, and only one-quarter of that needed for a secondary school student (World Bank, 1986). These cost differences largely reflect the fact that many higher and secondary students are boarded at no or little direct cost to themselves. In addition, in some countries, higher education students, besides receiving free tuition and boarding, also receive allowances for out of pocket expenses.

Yet it is quite clear that in many countries both students and parents are willing and able to finance education if necessary, as clearly indicated by the growth of the private sector in education in many countries since the 1970s. Moreover, the available evidence shows that, at present, the majority of students in post-primary education come from homes which could quite easily afford a bigger contribution than they are currently making (World Bank, 1986). Based on the available evidence, it would be quite in order to reduce the allowances enjoyed by all students in higher education and restrict it to low-income students, to be followed by charging tuition to those who can afford to pay in order to recover at least part of the cost of providing higher education. Given the excess demand for higher education, these charges would generate substantial revenues without reducing enrolments. Depending on local conditions, a policy of cost recovery in secondary schools along similar lines might justifiably be effected. However, for those who are least able to support themselves, government could formulate systems of support to ensure that such cost-recovery programmes will themselves not generate social inequity by excluding such groups from education.

The fiscal resources generated through such policy measures as elaborated above, will allow a substantial reduction in recurrent expenditure on those levels of education. A proportion of such savings could then be allocated to the primary level which has been grossly underfunded for decades in most African countries. Nevertheless, while capital spending on primary schools ought to raise the morale of parents, teachers and pupils alike, the maintenance of the existing secondary and higher education sectors to function properly should not be neglected, as the long-term cost of ignoring this can prove to be prohibitive.

The justification for reinvesting such fiscal resources within education itself is that the social returns are highest. Retaining the resources in the education sector would also make the most sense politically as cost-recovery policies are generally unpopular with the public. Unless the political costs are balanced by the prospect of more funds for education, ministries of education would probably be reluctant to accept such policies. In conjunction with cost recovery, there is a need to re-examine the approaches to manpower policies.

Manpower

From the 1960s up to the mid-1970s, greater investment in public secondary and higher education in Africa has been justified in terms of the manpower requirements of the economy. This has usually meant manpower for the urban-oriented employment – to formal industrial/ administrative sectors and their development generally. Despite massive investment in these levels of education, the proportion of the labour force not employed in agriculture (the mainstay of most African economies) increased by only five per cent between 1965 and 1980, while the labour force itself grew by 30 per cent during the same period (World Bank, 1988a). In other words, in spite of the priority accorded to post-primary education for decades in many countries, the structure of employment in these countries has changed only marginally.

Therefore the imposition of structural adjustment on many African countries, should be seen as an opportunity to reassess the true manpower needs of these countries in terms of rural employment and training programmes, the expansion of technician level training, either-on-the-job or via post-primary educational institutions. Moreover, studies carried out in several developing countries have shown that the private rate of return to higher education and secondary education can exceed the social rate by as much as 80 per cent and 25 per cent respectively. While this is, on the one hand, an indication of the degree to which these services are poorly supported by their beneficiaries (Psacharopoulus, 1980, and Psacharopoulus and Loxley, 1985), it is, on the other hand, a demonstration of the fact that the cost of the traditional post-primary education compared with its benefits to society can no longer be justified, especially in the context of the prevailing economic climate of these countries. Hence there is as much a moral as an economic case for reassessment of manpower policy and how to finance it in African countries in the 1990s and beyond.

Resource management

In education, the largest area of recurrent expenditure is that related to staff salaries. It is, however, inconceivable to suggest that teacher salaries should be cut in any way unless as a part of a policy that applies across the board to all sectors of recipients of state funding. One source of potential savings, however, lies in the improvement of incentives to teachers in rural areas, aimed at reducing teacher attrition with its resultant high costs of severance pay, additional recruitment and replacement training and the loss of experienced staff. Yet the stability of the primary teaching force can be easily ensured by such devices as improved school buildings, more in-service training and less staff turnover, all of which contribute to work satisfaction and boost morale in primary education. The importance of the stability of the primary teaching force cannot be overstated since it enables the provision of a better service to the pupils and in the long run, generates savings by avoiding the loss of substantial numbers of employees.

At the level of secondary education, serious attention needs to be paid to consolidating the skills and experience of staff through more in-service training. In collaboration with manpower needs assessments, the training could also include the development of the individual teacher's portfolio in more subject areas. This would offer more flexibility in the current teaching force, and so avoid the greater expense incurred through additional recruitment. In areas of shortage, improvements of salaries could provide the necessary incentives while other subject areas could be allowed to operate within the legal requirements of the curriculum. The adoption of such an approach would enable the realisation of a closer relationship between teacher supply, demand and the graduate labour market. In higher education, where subject specialism is often essential, the prohibitive costs of re-training could be avoided by using salary differentials in favour of the areas of priority in manpower policy. Any other subject areas not central to manpower policy needs should be limited to the private demand for such education, thus the costs, benefits and risks become the responsibility of the potential users of the service.

The introduction of these measures at the post-primary level are intended to do two things: first, to bring into operation some elements of price mechanism into these levels of education so ensuring that the potential beneficiaries of the service take responsibility for its provision. Second, to redress, to some extent, the large inequities that currently exist amongst the different levels of education.

Another source of potential recurrent cost savings is in the area of production and distribution of educational materials. In many countries of Africa, these functions are centralised under the control of the ministry of education, and are justified on the economy of scale required to manage such enterprises. But this bureaucracy often turns out to be insensitive to the needs of the more remote areas and the inflexibility inherent in such centralisation rarely allows for the tailoring of course materials to local needs. Moreover, there is no reason why government should not encourage the development of local enterprises geared towards materials production and distribution.

To overcome problems of inefficiency and inflexibility in the present arrangements, it would be better to establish partnerships at the primary and secondary levels between individual schools (or groups) and local publishers, as a basis for greater efficiency in both production and distribution, while at the same time allowing local teachers to contribute directly to the specific needs of their own area.

A further potential source of recurrent cost savings is through school production, as conducted in Zambia. Production in the Zambian case is used in a broad sense: 'to mean those activities whereby goods or services are produced that have economic value, and which are either exchanged for cash or contribute to the self-sufficiency of the institution' (Hoppers, *IDS Bulletin*, Vol. 20, No. 1, 1989). The impetus for schools to produce in Zambia started with President Kaunda's proclamation in 1975 that all educational institutions should become production units. Since then, schools have embarked on production efforts, particularly in agriculture, resulting in the cultivation of maize and vegetable gardens as well as the occasional keeping of livestock or growing of fruit. Other production activities have emerged from practical subjects in the curriculum: the processing of fruits, vegetables and field crops and food production as part of home economics; woodwork, metalwork, building craft, handcraft and leatherwork in upper primary schools. The result has been the introduction of a range of practical skills in the schools which is now being gradually utilised for a variety of purposes: maintenance and repair of furniture and buildings, the production of simple tools and utensils, construction of toilets and participation in community projects for the erection of teachers' houses and classroom blocks, baskets and belts. While the aggregate value of goods produced through the production units is low and makes a negligible contribution to the national educational budget (it was just over K1.5 m in 1986, Republic of Zambia, 1987), the benefits for an individual school can be considerable during a time of economic difficulties.

Finally, apart from the exorbitant costs of boarding, post-primary institutions incur large staff costs as compared with primary schools. This is derived from very high staff-student ratios. Thus, whereas the typical ratio in the secondary school sector in Africa is between 1:15 to 1:19, that in the industrialised market economies is 1:25 (UNESCO, 1987). The introduction of new class-size norms into post-primary education should contribute substantially to recurrent cost savings. At the higher education level, one further area of greater internal efficiency is to increase the rate of throughput by consolidating syllabuses in the degree courses into modes of study which require one year less in formal education. This then brings us to the area of management.

Administration

To realise the measures suggested above requires that a much greater degree of autonomy should be given to all three sectors of education. It is therefore crucial that at the primary and secondary levels, individual local authorities are allowed ample freedom to decide on such issues as staffing, capital expenditure and the provision of incentives/ penalties regarding the structure and utilisation of the teaching force, as they are likely to be more responsive than the central ministry to such local factors as population changes, enrolment profiles and staff turnover.

In this way, wasteful duplication of planning efforts between the central and local education authorities could be avoided. The ministry would only then be concerned with the monitoring function provided by the inspectorate of schools. Such decentralisation is justifiable at the primary, junior and senior secondary levels, provided that at the latter level there is no variation in the syllabus as the final examination at this level is normally national in character. In higher education, although such restrictions are much less common, nevertheless, to contribute to the development of enterprise, independence and more efficient management in the higher education sector, it is necessary to allow individual institutions a greater degree of autonomy in student recruitment, revenue raising, planning and staff recruitment.

Thus the survival of the education systems in African countries will depend not only on the application of systematic planning but also on the greater contribution of each community toward the development and maintenance of their local school. No longer can we afford to foster the attitude of expecting schools, and other services, to be provided on the basis of 'manna from heaven'.

PART I
PLANNING IN EDUCATION
AND DEVELOPMENT

I

Education and
national development

Education in the context of development planning

The concept of planning assumes that human societies can be made to change in desirable ways through deliberate action. Implicit in this is the belief that such change will lead to progress or 'development'. Hence the emphasis on development planning, including the planning of education, in African and other Third World countries. But what in fact is development?

Development, unfortunately, is a fairly elusive or ambiguous concept that assumes different meanings depending on the context in which it is used. Common to all, however, is the implication of highly valued or positive change in a specific direction. The range of meanings attributed to the concept has derived from the wide diversity of theories advanced over the ages, from the classical period to the present, to explain the how and the why of change, which we today refer to as development. They are the classic cyclical theories, evolutionary theories, structural-functionalism, Marxist theories of development, dependency theory and liberation theory, which in the literature are generally categorised into two paradigms: equilibrium and conflict paradigms (Kuhn, 1962; Gouldner, 1970; Foster-Carter, 1976; Fägerlind and Saha, 1983). Unfortunately, most of these theories of development tend to focus on only one dimension of the process.

The notion of development has also come to be bound up with education and with planning, as nowadays no sound development can occur in the absence of a proper planning system and an equally sound

1

education system. Hence the case for the inclusion of education in national development plans.

Three fundamental reasons are advanced to justify the inclusion of education in national planning. These are: the role of education in production; in human resources development; and the proportion of national resources devoted to education. Let us examine each in a little more detail.

The relationship between education and production is that education generates knowledge, transmits it and enables its application to the task of national development. National development planning involves the setting of objective economic growth targets which are themselves affected by such factors as the availability of manpower, the extent to which productive investment can be increased, growth in labour productivity, etc. (Poignant, 1967).

The major role education plays in production and economic growth is in what is known as technical progress. This is an additional factor to such production inputs as physical capital, labour and natural resources. According to Solow (1957), technical progress could account for as much as 90 per cent of production. Education therefore provides not only knowledge, skills and the incentive needed by a modern productive economy, but also the necessary technology. A second role of education is in human resources/manpower development which is discussed in detail in Chapter 6.

The third reason for the inclusion of education in national planning is the fact that the educational system of any country is a big industry, involving large numbers of personnel, building programmes and the use of material resources. As a result, in most countries, a large proportion of the Gross National Product (GNP) is spent on education. The necessary funds are derived from government and private sources as budgetary allocations, fees, community and individual contributions. The level of budgetary allocations to education in African countries is particularly high, often above 30 per cent of annual budget totals. For instance, in Nigeria, 13.5 per cent of the total investment of N2 billion in the Second National Development Plan 1970–74 was allocated to education, while a sum of N2,500 million in the Third National Development Plan (1975–80) was devoted to education (Third National Plan, 1975–80, vol. 1). Hence such an important sector cannot be left out of the national plans without serious dislocation occurring in the planning system. Thus the factors of manpower provision, productive activities and the proportion of national resources devoted to education indicate the importance of systematic planning in education.

This chapter first explores the meaning of development and its different dimensions. This is then followed by the discussion of the links between education and each of the dimensions in turn – economic, social and political. The final section of the chapter provides a critique of the education-development hypothesis as a whole. The chapter is then brought to a close by a summary of the main points of the discussion.

The meaning of development

The notion of development carries the implication of highly valued or positive change in a specific direction. Thus Professor Dudley Seers, focusing on the economic view of development, defined the concept by posing basic questions when he asserted:

The questions to ask about a country's development are therefore: What has been happening to poverty? What has been happening to unemployment? What has been happening to inequality? If all three of these have declined from high levels, then beyond doubt this has been a period of development for the country concerned. If one or two of these central problems have been growing worse, especially if all three have, it would be strange to call the result 'development' even if per capita income doubled (Dudley Seers, 1969).

However, while economic progress is an essential component of development it is not the only one. For development is a multi-dimensional process involving the re-organisation and re-orientation of the entire economic and social system. Hence, according to Michael P. Todaro:

In addition to improvements in incomes and output, it (development) typically involves radical changes in institutional, social and administrative structures, as well as in popular attitudes and sometimes even customs and belief (Todaro, 1982).

The definition provided by Gunnar Myrdal, the Swedish economist, probably captures best what is meant by development, when he states: . . . by development I mean the movement upward of the entire social system . . . (Myrdal, cited in Fägerlind and Saha, 1983). Hence, development at its most general level is multi-dimensional in both conceptualisation and reality.

Furtado's criteria

Our comprehension of the concept of development can be further extended by a brief examination of its different dimensions on the basis of the three criteria used by Furtado (1977) to analyse it. These are:

a) an increase in the efficiency of the production system of a society;
b) the satisfaction of the population's basic needs;
c) the attainment of the objectives sought by various groups in society, which are linked to the use of scarce resources (Furtado, 1977).

The most common measure of increased growth or the efficiency of production in a society has been the Gross National Product (GNP). These measures are, however, useful only in so far as development is defined in terms of economic growth. The general assumption underlying these measures of economic growth is that as levels of development, they are indicative of the life conditions of the general population of a given society.

However, the use of economic indicators as representing a single dimension of development has been criticised on the following grounds. First, apart from the inaccuracies of such indicators, they provide only a partial explanation, as a high level of economic growth is quite often accompanied by a deterioration in life conditions. As Furtado (*ibid.*) puts it: 'We cannot rule out the possibility that the deterioration of the living conditions of the population at large is due to the introduction of more "efficient techniques"'.

Moreover, it is possible for living standards to rise without any change in economic growth or increase in efficiency of production, for example, when there is a discovery of natural resources such as oil or other minerals. The difficulty with the rise in living standards resultant upon such discovery as an indicator of development, is that it could be short-lived, as illustrated by the copper booms in Zambia and Zaïre in the mid-1960s and early-1970s; the oil booms in Nigeria, 1975–80, Libyan Arab Jamahiriya 1969–1980 and Cameroon 1980–85. Apart from the factor of the irreversible process of the depletion of such non-renewable resources, a more serious factor, noted in recent years, is the serious fluctuation and deterioration of the prices of such minerals on the world market.

Thirdly, since the 1974 Declaration of Cocoyoc (Mexico) with its notion of basic human needs (food, water, energy and shelter as well as education, security, recreation and communication), it is now generally recognised that the living conditions of a population may be a better indicator of the level of development than the economic indicators. Thus, the concept of basic needs, though not incompatible with economic growth, nevertheless stresses the distributive aspect of society. In other words, it is indicative of the extent to which a society shares out its resources and thereby raises the level of the quality of life of its population as a whole.

Furtado's third dimension is concerned with domination and power. The idea is that besides focusing on economic growth and the equal distribution of the society's resources in meeting human needs, societies are more developed to the extent that there is greater participation in the decision-making process, with no one group completely dominating another group. Here, the focus is, therefore, on indicators of political development such as political participation, access to political positions, and the development of national integration and cohesion.

A careful examination of the various dimensions of development reveals that education cuts across the most important dimensions – the economic, the social and the political – as education is essential to the well-being of each. For as W. Williamson has observed:

Devising plans for the modernisation of educational systems is not simply . . . a technical matter of finding the optimum mix of scarce resources . . . . It involves choices not only among competing priorities but amongst different social values and models of development. Thus the central problem of planning in education is the political one of who shall benefit most from changes which are implemented rather than the technical one of what changes need to be brought about. In other words, whatever the direction of change, the complex equation to be solved remains who benefits and who bears the cost?

We shall therefore now examine in turn the link between education and each of the different dimensions of development: economic, modernisation, and political mobilisation and national integration.

Education and economic development

The link between education and economic development is a controversial one. While some argue that historically economic development always preceded educational advancement, others maintain that the contrary is the case.

Historical perspective

According to Shipman (1971) at the early 'take off' stage of industrialisation in England (1780–1850) schools were never seen as being related to economic advancement. This was probably because the simple level of the skills and knowledge demanded by the first factories were about equal to those required for successful farming. Historians are therefore generally agreed that the occurrence of the Industrial Revolution was not due to British scientific and technological superiority. As the English historian, Hobsbawn (1977) put it: 'English education was a joke in poor taste' at the time. However, as the pace of British industrialisation quickened, pressures began to mount for the improvement and expansion of the educational system to reinforce factory discipline and teach respect for authority. On such evidence, it could be legitimately claimed that the expansion of formal education in Britain was more the result, rather than the cause of industrialisation or economic growth.

The history of industrial development in Japan on the other hand, shows that formal education can play a more direct and causal link in economic development. The developments in Japan after World War II are generally regarded as the classic example of the deliberate use of education as a factor for rapid industrialisation and economic and social development (Fägerlind and Saha, 1983). As Stone (1970) and Shipman (1971) have shown, schooling in Japan was regarded from the outset as essential for economic growth. As a consequence, the Japanese example has come to be regarded as representing for the first time, the over-commitment to the belief and practice that education can make a direct contribution to economic growth and advancement. By the end of World War II, this conviction was widespread throughout the world. The result was that in the developed countries, education came to be considered as a crucial component of the factors for the transition into the post-industrial stages, whilst in the developing countries it was seen as an essential engine for the 'take-off' into industrialisation. This is because, according to Hobsbawn (1969), education in the case of a developing society, can assist with the inculcation of what may at first appear minor, but are in fact fundamental skills and habits, for the growth and continuation of an industrial society: literacy, a sense of punctuality and regularity, and the conduct of routines.

Human capital theory and educational expansion

Thus by the late-1950s and early-1960s there was a general consensus amongst politicians, educational and social planners, and scholars that education was a key agent of change for moving societies along the development continuum, as evidenced by the proliferation of books and collection of articles which attempted to demonstrate the direct link between education and development (Anderson and Bowman, 1965; Adams, 1977). This belief was to manifest itself in two ways: firstly, in developing countries, the attainment of a literate population through universal primary education (UPE) became a policy priority. Secondly, in both developed and developing countries there was an explosion in educational enrolments and expenditure (Coombs, 1968).

The theoretical framework for the wholesale adoption of education and development policies, known as human capital theory, was based upon the work of economists, primarily Schultz (1961), Denison (1962), Becker (1964), Harbison and Myers (1964). Human capital theory attempts to prove that formal education is highly instrumental in improving the productive capacity of a population. In other words, an educated population is a productive population.

Education is said to play a major role in economic development through the provision of skills and techniques designed to improve competencies. The direct contribution of education to economic development is therefore in terms of the quantity and quality of occupational skills because labour is a vital component of the factors of national output (see Chapter 6 for a detailed discussion).

To the theoretical formulation of the economics of education was added the works of economists such as Rostow (1960) with his stages of economic development which suggested that developing countries could realise shortcuts to industrialisation and economic development by the widespread provision of education which would raise the level of scientific knowledge – an essential factor in economic 'take-off'. In Africa, the effect of this prevailing economic thinking was the mass expansion of educational systems, fuelled by a series of UNESCO-sponsored conferences in the 1960s. Thus at the Addis Ababa Conference (1961) of independent African States, a consensus was reached to provide universal primary education and secondary education for 30 per cent of the relevant age-group by 1980. Unfortunately, only a few countries have been able to attain the first and even fewer have begun to approach the second target. A second effect of the prevalent economic opinion was the formulation of ambitious plans of the 1960s, concentrated largely on education, as a causal relationship was thought to exist between high levels of schooling and economic growth. A third effect was the enthronement of manpower planning, evolved by P. S. Parnes (1962) as an essential part of development planning in Africa and almost everywhere else in the developing world.

However, since the mid-1970s, the enthusiasm about the causal link between education and economic development has come to be viewed with more scepticism, as the massive effort towards the development of education in Africa and in other developing areas, has not resulted in the expected economic growth. Rather, education has come to be viewed as an important background factor in economic growth, and an essential human right.

It is true that studies have shown that the returns to society from investment in education are generally positive. Even in rural areas, it has been shown that educated farmers have a higher productivity than less educated ones. It was, for example, found that with four years of schooling, farm productivity increased 7.4 per cent (World Bank, 1980). Studies have also shown that the average social returns to primary education were 26.2 per cent (Psacharopoulos, 1973).

Negative features of education

This apparent contribution of education to economic growth, however, has been complicated by other factors such as the increasing levels of unemployment amongst the educated in many African countries which had paralleled educational expansion. For example, Anosike (1971) shows that in Nigeria worsening job prospects occurred alongside a shortage of workers with particular skills even when Nigeria had made great strides in educational expansion. (Universities expanded from four in 1962 to 13 in 1976 and to 23 by 1983.) This suggests an inappropriateness of a certain kind of schooling during periods of rapid educational and social change (ILO, 1971). It was also, perhaps, more indicative of the dichotomy between economic and educational development planning in Nigeria and other countries of Africa.

At the individual level, the belief that more education leads to better jobs has been a principal motive for young people to stay longer in schools. For until recently, there was a direct relationship between years of schooling and occupational attainment. With expansion in education, however, this relationship no longer holds true, as the number of educated persons has outstripped the absorptive capacities of most African economies, resulting in armies of educated unemployed.

All these problems of educational expansion, including qualification inflation in Africa and other Third World countries, were summed up by a World Bank Report (1974:20) as follows:

Serious imbalances are observed between the skills generated by education and actual needs of most developing countries. In some areas, the number of graduates surpasses the absorptive capacity of labour markets, while in others, critical shortages of skills continue to create problems. These discrepancies

... are caused by a complex set of social, cultural and political conditions and aspirations which condition the response to countries' needs (and) is accentuated by the fact that educational institutions have been borrowed from developed countries and have not acquired an indigenous character.

It was in the light of such experiences that the OAU conference of heads of state and government held in Monrovia in 1979, made the following declarations:

Placing science and innovation in the service of technology by strengthening our countries' autonomous capacities in this field; training personnel at the local level in the skills required to manage enterprises; and developing the technical manpower and the technological resources needed to enable our peoples to take a greater part in the action taken to attain our development objectives at the individual and collective level (OAU, Monrovia, 1979).

Hence, whereas a general level of basic education may be conducive to economic development, it is probably not the prime cause. In addition, as Dore (1971) has pointed out, schooling in African countries often does not teach useful skills: 'it encourages conformity rather than innovativeness and an unthinking acceptance of the need for qualifications rather than the application of useful knowledge' (Blackmore and Cooksey, 1980). This therefore requires that traditional Western models of education need to be modified to suit the economic requirements of the individual country. For example, where a country's economy is agriculturally oriented, the numbers of years of schooling may not be necessary for the vast majority of the population for maximum productivity, nor the expansion of the levels of education – primary, secondary and tertiary – to the same extent as in an industrialised, developed country. School and work programmes may be more relevant. Likewise, schools for rural development, apart from stressing skills related to agricultural technology, could also be instrumental in inculcating the values, attitudes and behaviour related to rural life. This is important as economic growth would require an increase of productivity in the primary sector and it is only reasonable, therefore, that the education system promotes the skills and individual motivation appropriate to the sector. The large-scale deaths from starvation in many African countries from 1985 to the present attests to this.

Nevertheless, such attempts at matching schooling with manpower needs would also require changes in the social and economic structure, so that the gap between the living conditions of the industrial and agricultural sectors is reduced. Otherwise, such phenomena as rural-urban migration, low response to those schools leading to jobs in the less advantaged sectors, and possibly frustrations and criminal hostility due to perceptions of blocked opportunities (Evans, 1975), will be with us for a long time. This then brings us to the issue of modernisation and education.

Education, modernisation and development

Modernisation is the second dimension of development. However, before we can usefully discuss the links between modernisation, education and development, it is necessary to state the fundamental conceptions of modernisation itself as embodied in its theory.

Modernisation theory

Modernisation theory evolved in the 1950s largely as an intellectual response to the events of World War II, and its origin has been attributed to, amongst others, Itosetiz (1960), Rostow (1970), Parsons (1971) and particularly McClelland (1962), a social psychologist, who in the 1950s and 1960s, attempted to explain the differential levels of social and technological attainment between societies. McClelland attributes this difference to the level of what he called the need for achievement (n Ach) factor in the population. Advanced societies are therefore those with high proportions of individuals of the personality type or trait with a high need for achievement (e.g. European societies in the first half of the eighteenth century), while less advanced societies contained lower proportions of such persons (McClelland, 1961). The latter would include all Third World countries.

The characteristics of the (n Ach) personality traits are willingness to take risks and start new forms of enterprise, trade or industry and being open to change, assume responsibility and have the determination to achieve change. Thus McClelland's emphasis is on the individual characteristics rather than societal ones (Blackmore and Cooksey, 1981).

Alex Inkeles, who studied the same phenomena from a sociological perspective, focused on attitudes, values and beliefs rather than psychological traits. He developed what has come to be known as the Modernity Scale (CM scale). The scale seeks to measure the extent to which individual members of a given society hold what are considered modern values. Inkeles and his followers contend that to modernise is to develop. Hence, socio-economic development can only occur when the majority of a population are socialised into modern attitudes, values and beliefs through social institutions such as the family, school, and factory (Inkeles and Smith, 1974).

Modernisation theory in this context was thus based on the notion that there is a direct causal linkage between five sets of variables, namely modernising institutions, modern values, modern behaviour, modern society and economic development, as illustrated below (Fägerlind and Saha, 1983).

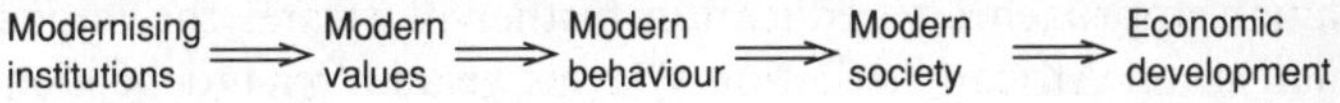

Modernising $\Longrightarrow$ Modern $\Longrightarrow$ Modern $\Longrightarrow$ Modern $\Longrightarrow$ Economic
institutions   values   behaviour   society   development

Fig. 1.1   The process of modernisation

However, of the links shown in the figure, only that between the first two sets of variables has been well established in research, while the links between the others are more problematic. For instance, developing countries with higher exposure to modern media, do not necessarily manifest higher levels of modern values or indeed, economic development (Delacroix and Ragin, 1978; Sutchcliff, 1978).

Criticism: theoretical perspective

Five fundamental criticisms of modernisation theory as presented by McClelland and Inkeles have been advanced. The first centres on the causal linkage between variables as indicated in Fig. 1.1. The second is directed at the underlying assumption of modernisation theory, which is that modern attitudes and values are incompatible with traditional ones. But Gusfield (1967) argues that this is not the case, and gives the example of Japan where traditional labour commitments seem to have been a contributory factor to economic growth. The third concerns the assumption in the theory that modern values and behaviour by individuals necessarily lead to socio-economic development at the societal level. As Portes (1973) and others point out, since a society is not simply the sum total of the individuals within it, this causal link does not necessarily hold. Fourthly, the assumption of modernisation theory about the end of the modernising process is ideologically biased and ethnocentric. If such criteria are used to measure modernisation, then for a society to become modern, it must also become Western (Hoogvelt, 1976). Fifthly, Blakemore and Cooksey (1981) contend that perhaps the greatest weakness of the modernisation approach, particularly in relation to Africa, is its neglect of the impact of colonial rule. Modernisation theory explains lack of change in terms of the failure of African societies to produce modern individuals with a high need for achievement, or by the bondage of traditional values in African societies. This argument sorely neglects the conserva-

tive effects of colonialism on societies, with its maintenance of traditional rules or the invention of others where none previously existed.
By the failure to consider the consequences of colonial rule, modernisation theory would tend to lay the blame for lack of development
entirely on supposed inadequacies and faults of African and other
developing societies. Williamson's (1979) study of the Ghananian and
Tanzanian approaches to education further illustrates the impact of
colonialism on African education systems years after independence.

Following such criticisms against the earlier definitions of modernisation, which equated it with industrialisation in the Western
sense, and as a single linear process shared by all societies, it did not
meet with universal approval. As a result other researchers have tried
to offer non-ethnocentric definitions. Thus Black (1966) sees modernisation as a form of human adaptation and the increasing use of man's
rationality and knowledge in mastering his environment. Apter (1965)
regards it as the liberation of a human population from environmental, political and cultural constraints which place obstacles to its
freedom to choose its destiny. Moore (1979) extends this line of
thought further by his contention that the process of modernisation is
not characterised by particular technologies or institutions, but, rather
it is fundamentally the process of becoming more rational.

Seen in this light, societies of differing circumstances and economies can become more modern to the extent that they become more
rationalised. The secularisation of beliefs, for example that fate or
destiny is within the reach of men and not wholly in the hands of the
gods, is an essential condition for rationalisation to occur. This then
brings us to a consideration of the relationship between modernisation
and education.

Modernisation and education

Modernisation theorists have throughout been concerned with the
process through which modernisation occurs. As already mentioned,
the agents of modernisation vary widely, but schooling or education is
considered to play a special role as perhaps the most important agent
for transforming traditional societies into modern ones. Education is
said to have a pervasive effect on values, attitudes and behaviour, thus
acting as a key agent in the development of all dimensions of modernity. This thesis was supported by a considerable body of research
evidence in the 1960s and early-1970s in both developed and developing countries (Lerner, 1964; Almond and Verba, 1965; Kahl, 1968).
The basic finding of the studies is that exposure to schooling or level

of school attainment, is directly related to modernity-linked orientations: the raising of educational and occupational aspirations, less adherence to traditional customs and beliefs, and an openness to new experiences.

In Africa, Armer and Youtz (1974) in a study of 571 Nigerian 17 year olds, found a direct relationship between exposure to Western-type schooling and individual modernity. They argued that it is fundamentally the curriculum of the Western-type school which accounts for modernity, because when students from a Koranic school were included in the study, an inverse relationship was found. They therefore concluded that it was the formal schooling, based on the Western model, that was responsible (Fägerlind and Saha, 1983). (See Table 1.1).

Table 1.1   Western education and percentage of 'high' individual modernity among Nigerian 17-year olds

	Western educational level								Total
	No education	Primary education				Secondary education			
Years	0	1–3	4–5	6	7	1	2	3	4+	
High individual modernity	37.8	42.0	56.9	57.7	64.7	75.0	80.0	90.9	94.1	49.4
(N)	(312)	(50)	(58)	(52)	(51)	(20)	(20)	(11)	(17)	(591)

Source: Adaptation by Fägerlind and Saha (1983 p. 100) from Armer and Youtz (1971 p. 613).

N = Number in sample

Inkeles and Smith (1974) in a study of five developing countries (Argentina, Bangladesh, Chile, India, and Nigeria), in which they sought to discover the comparative influence of schooling and other factors, came to the conclusion that schooling represented the strongest and most viable policy-related individual modernisation agent, far out-weighing the other factors in importance.

But if modernisation is Western-oriented, then its desirability must be seriously questioned as a by-product of schooling, particularly in those societies which choose not to follow the Western model of development. Delacroix and Ragin (1978) seek to reassure us that the school is able to modernise without Westernising, though this would require further substantial empirical support to be convincing.

In a nutshell, the power of education as an agent of modernisation in the Western sense cannot be over-emphasised: education develops skills and knowledge crucial for technological and industrial change, provides individual opportunities for upward mobility, broadens perspectives and mental horizons, and instils new values and beliefs supportive of the goals and programs of modernity. Furthermore, education breaks down static ways of thinking and systems of social stratification and differentiation. Nevertheless, criticisms of the modernity and education thesis abound.

A *critique of education-modernisation linkage*

Criticism of the education and modernity linkage is based on two fundamental issues: first, the claim that the effect of education is independent of modernity. On this Armer (1977) contends that the standard measures of modernity, as contained in the OM Scale of Inkeles and Smith, include knowledge items which are in fact the result of exposure to Western-style schooling. He therefore concludes that the education-modernity relationship is not wholly true.

The second underlying assumption concerns the direct causal link between exposure to schooling and individual modernity. In almost every society, schooling is a selective institution. As a result, in spite of the abundance of evidence showing that there is a relationship between schooling and modernity, no concrete evidence can be claimed which shows that schooling itself actually causes modernity. It may be that the factors which contribute to school attainment also contribute to individual modernity, hence those students staying longer in school may already be predisposed to modern values and belief. Irrespective of the lack of clear-cut evidence on this, however, it is difficult to dismiss totally the strong association between Western-style schooling and modernity as presently measured.

A more crucial question perhaps than the issue of the link between education and individual modernity, centres on the relationship between modernity and development and it is to this that we now turn.

Modernisation and development

The modernisation hypothesis rests on the general relationship between modernity, modernisation and development. As already noted,

Inkeles and Smith contend that for socio-economic development to occur, a society must have 'modern citizens'. The statement rests on two assumptions: first, that only one kind of development is valid, namely the Western industrial model, and second, that the process of modernisation which takes place through schooling will result in modern behaviour.

On the basis of the first assumption, any society which chooses to follow a different development strategy, for instance one which places emphasis on agriculture as in Tanzania, would not be aided by a school system which produced adults who aspired to non-agricultural or industrial jobs and city lifestyles. Criticism of the modernisation-development hypothesis has also focused on the presumed dichotomy between traditional and modern societies. Gusfield (1967) contends that no such incompatibility exists and buttresses his points by listing seven fallacies of the differentiation between traditional and modern societies (Fägerlind and Saha, 1983). He argues that in certain contexts, the traditional and the modern can in fact co-exist. Portes (1973) extends the argument further by contending that some traditional values are more supportive of socio-economic development than many modern values. He also rejects the notion that the social organisation of traditional societies forms an obstacle to the improvement of agricultural or industrial productivity. He cites the case of Japan where traditional values of the family have been fused with highly productive technologies in the factories.

Further criticisms of the modernisation-development thesis rest on those instances where modernisation has had detrimental effects on the socio-economic development of a country. For example, it may create a large segment of highly-individualistic and highly-trained manpower whose behaviour patterns become harmful to the best interests of the country, as exemplified by the migration of highly-skilled and trained manpower from developing to developed countries (the 'brain drain') or even from one developing country to another developing country. For instance, large numbers of Sudanese professionals and other skilled workers went to Saudi Arabia and the Gulf states and Ghanaians went to Nigeria and Côte d'Ivoire in the 1970s. More recently (February 1987) there were dramatic attempts by Ugandan professionals to leave the country, forcing the government to condemn the action publically and close the borders with the neighbouring countries.

This movement is usually explained in terms of the achievement motivation, which encourages the educated to place their individual success above that of a society as a whole. Portes and Ross (1976), in their study of Argentinian physicians who migrate in large numbers to the US, illustrate this conflicting role of the modernisation process and the interests of a particular society when they state:

... if we were to analyse who 'stands to gain' from premature modernisation of the medical system (of Argentina) we would have to rule out the frustrated professionals, the financially exhausted state, the neglected population and choose, almost exclusively, the receiving countries which add substantial contingents to their professional manpower at little or no cost. . . . (Portes and Ross, 1976).

It is clearly the case here that the modernisation of the health-training facilities has not added fully to the improvement of health-care in Argentina.

Almost the same criticism of the modernisation process and the role of education has been made by the former President of Tanzania, Julius Nyerere. He stated:

The educational system introduced into Tanzania by the colonialists was modelled on the British system, but with even heavier emphasis on subservient attitudes and on white-collar skills. Inevitably, too, it was based on the assumption of a colonialist and capitalist mankind, instead of on his co-operative instincts. It led to the possession of individual material wealth being the major criterion of social merit and worth (Nyerere, 1967).

A similar sentiment was re-echoed in Kenya, by the Report of the National Commission on Educational Objectives and Policies (Government of Kenya, 1976) when discussing Western culture and education. It declared:

In the long run this education has produced weakened family systems, white collar mentality and narrowly-based materialistic education leading to individualistic tendencies. As a result, the fundamentally valuable ethics of African society have . . . been abandoned.

The commission therefore called for a change for the better which 'can only be achieved if the values, aspirations, motivations, beliefs and choices of the core society are taken into consideration, in the national development process. According to Portes and Ross, this negative impact of modernisation manifests itself most often where there is differentiation in society with one segment modernising more rapidly or in isolation from other segments, resulting in serious disjunctures or even contradictions.

On the issue of rationalisation and the assumption that decision-making in traditional societies like those in Africa are not rational, Hutton and Cohen (1975) argue that the resistance by African peasant tribes to economic change, is a highly rational response to economic threat. They contend that resistance to change where there is threat to one's economic interest is in fact part of the development process, in so far as the peasant farmers must protect their own vested interests when faced by new, and potentially damaging, economic structures. Thus Hutton and Cohen question some of the basic assumptions of the modernisation and development thesis when they state:

We are not likely to be helped by attitude surveys and cultural studies designed to test receptivity to modernisation. Rather, we need some understanding of the ways in which particular economies, social structures, and cultures are tied together, and the impact on these of the experience of colonisation and incorporation into a wider economy . . .

We should not then ask how we can change peasants' attitudes to more appropriately modern ones before we have answered the question, why do people hold the attitudes towards development which they do have?

Finally, even where there is openness to change, this will not guarantee that modernisation will proceed unimpeded. Eisenstadt (1970) argues that breakdowns are likely to occur, particularly when there are no comprehensive institutional structures developed to meet the needs of rapid changes in the different social and demographic spheres of society. He gives the example of the Sudan, Indonesia, Pakistan and Burma where considerable progress was made in health and education but without the establishment of commensurate political institutions to overcome the ascription-based elite structure of earlier traditional society. The result was that it was quite easy to block and even reverse the political modernisation of these societies by dictatorial regimes. The lesson of these cases is that the modernisation of some sectors of a society does not automatically guarantee that all sectors of society will be modernised.

Thus while modernisation may for the most part contribute to social and economic development, it is extremely important to specify both the kind of modernisation and the kind of development, for much of the content of modernisation theory has been shown to be inappropriate to developing states (Bray *et al.*, 1986). The result is that more recently the strategy of the United Nations and its organs has shifted to the human needs approach to development. The human needs approach was first suggested by Jan. Tinbergen to the Club of Rome in relation to a New International Economic Order, when he stated:

(There is a) . . . need for new development strategies – national and international – defined and designed, not merely to meet the criterion of private or state profitability, but rather to give priority to the expression and satisfaction of fundamental human values. Society as a whole must accept the responsibility for guaranteeing a minimum level of welfare for all its citizens and aims at equality in human relations . . . . It follows that the problem of development must be redefined as a selective attack on the worst forms of poverty (Tinbergen *et al.*, 1976, cited in Fägerlind and Saha, 1983).

Further dimensions of the needs concept include those of equality and social justice. The concern with equality in the human needs approach is for the distribution of goods among individuals in such a way that the range of variation between social strata is reduced (Galtung, 1976). For this reason alone, some would argue that even if the satisfaction of human needs makes no contribution to economic growth, it nevertheless represents a viable strategy for the development of a society.

Moreover, the strategy of the human needs approach to development parallels the many notions of modernisation and individual modernity already discussed in the preceeding sections, as both focus on people. Both approaches are not only concerned with the improvement in the general quality of life but both place considerable emphasis on education as part of that improvement. Thus while modernisation stresses the social-psychological change, the human needs approach focuses on changes in the physical and political conditions. This then brings us to the third dimension of development.

Education, political mobilisation and development

There is a general consensus amongst social scientists, social philosophers and educationists, that formal education is both determined and a determinant of the political system. This is illustrated by the ancient common sense sayings about the school and the state: 'As is the state, so is the school', and 'what you want in the state, you must put into the school', (cited in Coleman, 1965).

Our task, therefore, is to attempt to answer three basic questions: first, to what extent does education promote the mobilisation of, and participation in, political activities, i.e. national integration? Second, what is the nature of the link between education and political development? Third, to what extent does the political system affect and control what goes on in schools? However, before tackling these questions, some comprehension of the conceptual and operational meaning of political development is necessary.

The meaning of political development

The notion of political development is broad and as a result not easily amenable to definition. The most widely accepted definition is perhaps that provided by Coleman (1965), in which he states that political development is:

. . . the acquisition by a political system of a consciously-sought and qualitatively new and enhanced, political capacity as manifested in the successful institutionalisation of (1) new patterns of integration regulating and containing the tensions and conflicts produced by increased differentiation, and (2) new patterns of participation and resource distribution adequately responsive to the demands generated by the imperatives of equality.

The main concern, therefore, is with integration and participation. Integration is concerned with the extent to which a society is able to create unity and solidarity amongst its diverse peoples and foster a sense of national identity that extends beyond the family and tribe, village or region. In almost all countries in Africa, and probably in many other parts of the Third World as well, the problems of integration are invariably a legacy of the colonial system, which created national states whose boundaries did not take into account the ethnic or social identities of the people, and created educational and/or economic disparities between regions of a country (Fägerlind and Saha, 1983). The underlying assumption in the concept of participation is that a situation in which there is extensive political mobilisation or political awareness in a population, as demonstrated by interest in political matters, is preferable to one in which the masses are politically inactive or stagnant. This has been the dominant perspective of political development and falls within the structural functions paradigm.

The conflict perspective sees political development in terms of conflicts of political interests within the society. It recognises struggles for power as a normal part of the everyday scene of political processes. Conflict theory is therefore concerned with the extent to which these processes occur in an open and equitable context. Dependency theory considers political development in terms of political liberation from either neo-colonial or neo-imperialistic influences from outside the country. The components of the dependency perspective therefore include political integration and participation, self-determination and autonomy. All these perspectives are within the Western capitalist system. Socialist ideology views political development basically in terms of the class struggle and greater working class control over the forces and means of production.

With these definitions we now turn to the question of the extent to which education leads to greater political participation.

Education and political development

The effect of education on political development is basically of a conservative nature. '. . . all national educational systems indoctrinate the oncoming generation with the basic outlooks and values of the political order' (Key, 1963, cited in Zeigler and Peak, 1971; Fägerlind and Saha, 1983). It is, however, also generally accepted that education contributes to political development or change (Coleman, 1965). Thus, education, through the mechanism of the formal school, is regarded as serving three main functions:

1) as the main agent for the political socialisation of the young into the national political culture,
2) as the primary agent for the selection and training of political elites, and
3) as the main contributor to political integration and the building of national political consciousness (Fägerlind and Saha, 1983).

We shall now consider each role in turn.

1 Political socialisation

Massialas (1969) defines political socialisation as 'the process by which a person internalises the norms and values of the political system'. The three most important factors responsible for the continuity of political values and behaviour between generations are the family, peer groups and the school. However, the school, because of its institutional autonomy, is regarded as the prime vehicle for political socialisation. Though the empirical data supporting their contention are rather controversial, Hess and Torney (1967) claim that 'the public school is the most important and effective instrument of political socialisation in the United States' (also Torney et al., 1975).

Regarding the situation in developing countries, such as those in Africa, Fägerlind and Saha (op. cit.), basing their arguments on the findings of Levine (1965) and Almond and Verba (1965), concluded that the possibility of political socialisation through the school is likely to be much greater for two reasons: first, the possible impact of alternative socialising agents is not as great, simply because their participation in the political culture of the new nation-state is not as extensive. In the second place, the political culture and a sense of nationalism may even have to be created through the schools by breaking down the values and orientations based on local ethnic or political structures.

2 The selection and training of political elites

Historical evidence abounds to support the claim that in all societies, the stability, survival and effectiveness of the political system depends on those who constitute the elite and hold positions of power. Our concern, therefore, is twofold, firstly to determine the extent to which schools contribute to the recruitment and training of political elites, and secondly, to show that these elites have a direct impact on the political and economic development of a society.

In the developed countries, there is abundant evidence which shows a positive relationship between education and elite recruitment. The empirical documentation indicates that either the level of schooling or the type of schooling differentiate the elite from the masses (Warner et al., 1963; Frey, 1970; Bourdieu, 1973; Higley et al., 1979). Nevertheless, it is also recognised that there are other avenues to political power, such as religious, economic and military ones (Massialas, 1969).

However, in African countries and elsewhere in the developing world, the patterns are more contingent on cultural and historical factors. It is, for example, invariably the case that after independence or a revolutionary war, the elite are likely to be recruited from among those who were in leadership positions in the struggle for independence. In such a situation, it is possible for those with relatively less education to hold leadership positions. But Massialas (1969), contends that over time, the characteristics of the elite in developing countries begin to approximate to those in the developed. Where such changes occur it points to a more open political system indicative of a participatory democracy, and thus political development arises.

Milkias (1976) concurs with Massialas in suggesting that the pattern of elite recruitment under the African traditional system of education as existed in Ethiopia well before European penetration was similarly based on the type and level of schooling. He goes on to show:

... that this educated class remained a formidable force in the Ethiopian body-politics for over a millenium (which) is manifested by the roles it played in the doings and undoings of monarchs and dynasties. One such outstanding case in traditional history is the role played by a member of this class in the overthrow of the Zagwe dynasty in the thirteenth century.

Nevertheless, he also showed that education can equally serve to maintain a totalitarian and backward political regime, as was the case in Ethiopia before World War II under Emperor Haile Selassie, where the ruling nobility were less educated than the scribes who constituted the educated elite (*op. cit.*). It was in fact not until the 1970s, with the production of large numbers of secondary school graduates, that the educated elite began to challenge the political elite, which eventually culminated in the fall of the Emperor and his regime (Wagaw, 1979, Sjöström and Sjöström, 1982).

Political integration and the nurturing of national political consciousness

A third contribution which education makes to political development is in the development of the nation-state itself 'by legitimating the process of centre-formation and the creation of a national culture'. A fundamental requirement for the formation and stability of a nation-state is the establishment of consensus regarding political values and the conformity of the population to it.

Formal education, and more particularly schooling, has been regarded as the social institution capable of breaking down local identities and forging national identities and loyalties in their place. As Tuqan (1975) writing about the integrative potential of the school states:

Most parents in the underdeveloped society, especially rural areas, socialise their children for participation in the local authority system such as the family or tribe rather than for roles in the broader societal framework. Because this is inimical to the imperative of nation building, and because of the absence of appropriate agencies other than the schools, the latter were declared to be the tools for resocialising the child.

The formation of national consensus is particularly important in the developing states such as in Africa where intra-societal tensions and divisions are rampant. Most social scientists therefore see the role of education as a crucial one in consensus formation in the new nation-states.

It has, on the other hand, been argued that 'the tolerance of diversity of interests and values may, in the long run, strengthen the national bond', and that, '. . . regardless of the perspective from which it is approached, widespread conflict is imperative for the vitality of democratic political systems' (Fägerlind and Sahan, 1983; Zeigler and Peak 1971). Hence, viewed from these perspectives, the current ethnic and cultural diversity in most African societies may prove, in the long run, preferable to forced homogeneity and also for the further reason that coercion is incompatible with political development. This, however, still leaves the issue of the contribution of education to political integration and the consolidation of the nation-state.

Nevertheless, as already stated elsewhere, education serves as a legitimating agency for establishing the legal jurisdiction of state authority and above all for bestowal of citizenship (Fägerlind and Saha, 1983; Cohen, 1970). Hence the reference to the education system, and in particular mass education as a baptism 'in a national history, a written language, national culture, and the mysteries of technical culture' (Meyer and Rubinson, 1975).

The role of education in political integration in Africa

Some evidence from Africa, however, would tend to call into question the ability of education to serve as a viable integrating and consolidating agent. Chukunta (1978) argues that in Nigeria the legacy of the colonial education system has tended to exaggerate and aggravate ethnic differences, particularly between the Muslim north and the Christian south, with the result that the impact of education could be said to be disintegrative rather than integrative.

The strategy of British colonial rule was to educate the south, largely through Western-oriented missionary schools incompatible with Muslim culture. The result was the south came to have a larger number of educated Nigerians who later formed the basis of the political elite at the start of Nigeria's independence. As Chukunta puts it:

This disparity was later to become a disintegrative factor in Nigerian society as corrective measures in employment had to be taken, which drew charges of discrimination by the south (Chukunta, 1978).

The long-term effect of colonial education policy was the outbreak of the Biafran war, six years after independence. Even today, despite various efforts through the education system, there is little evidence that integration is occurring. On the contrary, it could be argued that it is in fact the education system which helps to maintain and exacerbate these regional differences. As Chukunta (1978) observes, it is:

. . . the increased availability of educational opportunities that makes it possible for a Nigerian to obtain all of his formal education – even up to the doctoral level – without leaving his state of origin and, thus, without interacting with a larger number of other Nigerians.

A similar example of the disintegrative effects of education can be found in the Sudan with its origin in colonial policy, which has bedevilled the country's stability and political development since a

year before independence in 1955. As in Nigeria, the colonial education policy favoured the northern Sudan, as some of the southern
tribes were continually in rebellion against British rule until 1934
(Collins, 1981). Consequently, while a proper foundation was laid for
educational development in northern Sudan, largely through government schools and finances, education in southern Sudan was left
almost entirely in the hands of a severely restricted number of missionary societies, with meagre government financial assistance. Thus the
extent of the educational disparity can be discerned from the fact that
while Gordon Memorial College (later to become Khartoum University) was opened in 1934, as a post-secondary institution, the first
secondary school in the south was not started until 1948. The result
has been a very marked educational disparity between the two halves
of the country. The northern elite have used their educational advantage not only to dominate completely and manipulate and maintain
complete political control of the country, but also dominate completely its civil service. The so-called continual rebellion in the south
since 1955, is in fact regarded by southerners as a war to bring about
equality against this sectional domination of the country's affairs. The
result of the continual conflict has been to mark the Sudan as one of
the most politically unstable countries on the African continent.

A third example of educational disparity leading to a disintegration effect is the case of Kenya where there is an uneven distribution
of services such as medical doctors. Thus, whereas there is one medical
doctor per 84 people in Nairobi province, Nyanza province had one
doctor for 2,219 people. The result is considerable variation in political attitudes concerning government policies in the allocation of national resources amongst the students in the different regions of the
country (Court and Prewitt, 1974). Commenting on this situation,
they state: 'when the number of elite roles begins to fall behind the
output of qualified candidates, and individual mobility is correspondingly curtailed, collective concern with regional equality of opportunity is likely to increase' (1974). Evans (1977), who made a study of
Kenyan Secondary School students, came to a similar conclusion, that
increasing unemployment among educated Kenyan youth with high
occupation aspirations posed a potential source of political instability.

Thus these three African examples tend to suggest that the role of
education in potential integration and nation-building may be problematic. It would appear that as education expands to include various
interest groups both in and outside the existing political elite, the
challenge to the established political system may come precisely from
amongst the educated. The frequent student activism and demonstra-

tions against governments in many different African countries since independence in the early-1960s, attests to this. This is, however, contrary to the theoretical model put forward here, that the more educated should be the most integrated into the national culture and its political values. The evidence found in all societies would tend to suggest that education at any level may be dysfunctional to national integration and nation-building. This empirical fact therefore poses a serious dilemma for policymakers. For while on the one hand, political development, in terms of greater political participation and national integration, cannot occur without an educated population, on the other hand, the educational process itself sows the seeds of disintegration and can place obstacles to further integration and thus to political development. Nevertheless, it would be erroneous on these grounds to regard education as inherently destabilising. It can, however, equally not be regarded as a panacea for political stability and development without considerable qualification.

The qualifications one would suggest here are as follows: firstly, that as the educational system expands from the centre to the periphery, however this is defined, the political system must equally adjust to accommodate the 'have nots' outside the prevailing power structure, whether through decentralisation of the national political and administrative system, fair sharing of national finances and high level office appointments, or recruitment into the national instrument of governance (or 'coercion) such as the armed forces, the police and related organisations. Secondly, there should be equitable distribution in the allocation of economic activities and social services – agricultural development schemes, manufacturing industries, banks, power plants, road and air networks, as well as educational institutions at all levels and health facilities of all grades. Finally, above all else, the proper management of national affairs, including a clearly stated political vision to guide national development efforts, particularly the economy, is imperative. However, the effect of education on the political system is only one side of the same coin. We therefore now turn to a brief examination of the other side, that is the impact of the political system on education.

The influence of the political system on education

As we have seen in the preceding discussions, the education system has a significant impact on the political system. In fact, the relationship between the two is a reciprocal one. That means, the level of political development is to some extent dependent on the level of harmony between it and the education system.

The case of the US and former USSR

The type of political system, however, is important in determining the nature of its impact on the schooling process. This is clearly illustrated by an investigation of childhood and schooling in the US and what was the USSR by Bronfenbrennar (1974). He found that while schooling in the US oriented the child to a competitive, individualistic tendency suitable for the demands of a capitalist system (Bowles and Gintis, 1972, 1976), Soviet schooling, being geared to life in a socialist system, was more collective in outlook with less emphasis on the individualistic and competitive aspects. However, in terms of the selection process, both systems reflected the stratification system of their societies. Thus whereas the American system defended its middle and upper-class bias on the grounds of tests (Bowles and Gintis, 1972), the bias in the Soviet system was justified in terms of '. . . the selection of those who will be able to make the greatest contribution to social and economic development' (Dobson, 1977).

Cases from Africa

In Africa, two examples will suffice to demonstrate the influence of the political system on education. The first is the abolition of race as a criterion for the provision of education in East Africa and Zimbabwe immediately after independence. The second is the curtailment by the government of academic freedom through autonomy and the introduction of a quota system as a basis for university admissions and staff recruitment in the University of Zaïre.

Abolition of racial education in East Africa and Zimbabwe
In colonial times, educational provision in Kenya, Uganda, Tanzania and Zimbabwe was based on racial separation, with separate schools for Europeans, Asians and Africans. Educational expenditure similarly reflected this racial approach to educational development, with the European child enjoying the highest per capita expenditure while the African child, despite his numerical superiority, the least. This was also a true reflection of the existing society in these countries, where the Europeans as the ruling group, were at the apex of the society, followed by the Asians as the business class and the Africans as the subservient group, at the bottom.

However, as each of the countries in turn attained independence (Tanzania 1961; Uganda 1962, Kenya 1965, Zimbabwe 1980) there were dramatic reversals of this policy, with the emphasis on the equality of educational opportunity for the individual child in the community. This in turn has entailed the introduction of educational planning concepts such as school location planning (SLP) so as to ensure that there is a school within easy reach of each child. Educational expansion has therefore been facilitated as educational plans are no longer predicated on the narrow premises of colour but rather on the basis of need.

Government and education in Zaïre.

The assertion by the Zaïrian government of its will over the National University of Zaïre (UNAZA) in the matters of academic freedom and autonomy and the admission of students and recruitment of teaching staff on a quota basis, also illustrates the influence of the state over the education system.

Zaïre, formerly the Congo, became independent on 30 June, 1960. After five years of serious and protracted colonial crises Mobutu Sese Seko took power in a bloodless *coup d'état* on 4 November 1965. He then set about, adroitly and unremittingly, to implement a policy of centralisation and concentration of power in his hands (Coleman and Ngokwey, 1983, which was also later to affect the University of Zaïre.

Historically, until World War II, the colonial government of the Congo assumed virtually no operational responsibility for African education (Turner and Young, 1981; cited in Coleman and Ngokwey 1983). What educational institutions operated were opened and staffed by Catholic teaching orders (Hailey, 1957). This was also the case with Zaïre's first and main university, Louvanium, founded in 1954 (La Croip, 1972). In 1971, this university, together with the official university of Congo in Lubumbashi (created in 1955) and the Free University of Congo established at Kisangani in 1963, as well as all other post-secondary institutions in the country were nationalised and amalgamated into a single monolithic National University of Zaïre (UNAZA). In 1981 the whole system was broken up with the institutes separated from UNAZA and returning to their former constituent universities.

In the meantime, these structural changes and reversals were accompanied by equally dramatic developments in the school system in the form of explosive expansion in school enrolments, at the secondary and university levels in particular, as a result of uncontrollable social demand (see Table 1.2).

PLANNING IN EDUCATION AND DEVELOPMENT

Table 1.2 Enrolment increases in the Republic of Zaïre (1950–79)

	Number of students				
	1950	1960–61	1965	1971–72	1977–79
Secondary level	4,004	38,000	118,078	297,556	643,675
University level	–	419	1,107	9,558	13,399

Source: Coleman and Ngokwey, 1983, p. 59 in Thomas, R. M. (ed.) Education and Politics

An additional development was the affliction of the school population of Zaïre by Dore's 'diploma disease' by which is meant that each level of the education system was perceived as a ladder for the next, with the university as the ultimate objective (Dore, 1976). Unfortunately these developments were accompanied by the decline in the quality of education at all levels.

University autonomy and academic freedom

As already noted, in spite of the fact that Zaïre became independent in 1960, its university did not attain formal independence until the creation of UNAZA in 1971. This was so even though 80 per cent of the operating costs of the constituent Universities of Louvanium, Lubumbashi and Kisangani were being covered by the Zaïrian government by that time (Coleman and Ngokwey, 1983). The government's reluctance to interfere much earlier with the functioning of the University in Zaïre, as elsewhere in Africa, can be attributed to a number of factors.

The universities, while acknowledging their obligation to respect the new state, maintained their own individual charters and external links from the colonial days. This ensured that the institutional autonomy and freedom from government intervention which was prevalent under the colonial regime was reasonably respected by the new independent state in the earlier years. It also ensured academic freedom for faculty and students. Besides this inherited or emulated pattern of university governance, further factors such as the close metropolitan dependency relationships, especially in expatriate staff recruitment and in developmental assistance, the singular concentration on the Africanisation of the Civil Service reinforcing the Eurocentric orientation, and the domination of the senior academic and administrative positions by expatriates influenced autonomy and academic freedom (Coleman, 1977). These factors together not only made the universities conservative in outlook, being largely concerned with the primacy of universalism and the maintenance of international standards, avoidance of involvement with or threat to the new regime, but also made the government on its part assume an indifferent, if not reverential attitude toward the universities (Coleman and Ngokwey, 1983). Despite this, however, the early radicalisation of the Zaïrian University students at the main campus of Louvanium in the 1960s was to lead inexorably to increased state intervention and control over the University, the students themselves, and ultimately complete loss of institutional autonomy and academic freedom.

The starting point of this process was a week-long strike in March 1964, organised by the General Association of Zaïrian students of Louvanium (AGEL) during which they called for the Africanisation of the university and student participation in university governance. The strike was repeated in 1969 and 1971. As has been noted by Ilunga (1978), the 1964 strike served to open the door to the eventual loss of university autonomy.

Things changed after the student strike . . . The academic authorities, who for a long time had taken refuge behind the principle of university autonomy and maintained a haughty attitude of isolation and independence, were forced by events to seek the backing of the national political authorities, who were the only ones capable of protecting them from the student challenge. All too willing to be called to the rescue of an institution which they little understood . . . the Zaïrian authorities gradually took advantage of the situation to extend their control over the university.

The events of 1964 resulted in the promulgation of an *Ordonnance Loi* of 1969, which stipulated that the Rector and the Vice-Rectors of the universities were to be appointed by the President of the Republic and professors by the Minister of Education. The event of 1971 provided the *coup de grâce*, in the form of the radical nationalisation into a single University of Zaïre under the complete control of the central government. By using various subterfuges, the government gradually came to dominate completely the running of the university.

This nationalisation and political subordination of the universities can, however, also be seen as the culmination in the educational sector of a general process of secularisation, centralisation and concentration of power, as in all sectors in the country, in the hands of the President.

Nevertheless, there were at least three additional factors which provided the rationale for the government to embark on the creation of a monolithic, multicampus, single faculty, nation-wide system of higher education. The first was the political opportunity provided to transfer the radicalised students of the faculties of social sciences and humanities away from Kinshasa, the vulnerable political centre of the country, to Lubumbashi, 1500 miles away. The second factor was the opportunity that the wholesale restructuring of the system provided for economising and rationalising the development of the Zaïrian higher education, which the government had been trying to do since 1968, but without much success. The third factor was the growing realisation that the European-oriented education being imported at all the three national universities was largely irrelevant as it did not cultivate the skills, knowledge and attitudes required by a developing society. Only drastic surgery, it was reasoned, could bring about that necessary re-orientation.

The result of all these factors was not only the radical nationalisation of all three universities and their amalgamation into a single University of Zaïre under the complete control of the central government following the student strike of 1971, but by using all kinds of subterfuges, the complete government domination in the running of the university.

Regional imbalances and the introduction of a university quota system

A second area which shows the influence of the political system on education is in the application of a quota system for enrolment of students into the University of Zaïre. The application of the quota system for student enrolment into the university was aimed at the correction of the existing regional imbalances in educational provision between the different regions of the country as shown by Table 1.3.

Regional imbalances in educational opportunities originated from the uneven penetration of colonisation, particularly of missions, and the differential response of local populations. This uneven penetration was in turn governed by geographical, demographic, economic, cultural and linguistic factors. Differential response of the local populations was in terms of the reactions of local communities for whom the new institutions such as schools were intended. The reactions would, however, have been influenced by cultural factors such as the community's means of production, its socio-political organisation and/or by the values held by its members (Feltz, 1980). On the other hand, missions were not even present everywhere, nor equally effective everywhere.

Whatever the causes, over time these initial ethnic and regional imbalances had a cumulative, self-producing effect, with the result that the educated elite element of the emergent Congolese society was

Table 1.3 Regional imbalances in education in Zaïre

	Per cent of total (1975)	Per cent enrolled primary school (1974–75)	Per cent enrolled primary T/Train. (1973)	Per cent enrolled for state exams (July 1981)	Per cent profession faculty of economics (1978–79)	Per cent profession faculty of social science (1977–78)
East Kasai	7	100	19	22	30	26
West Kasai	8	52	8	9	10	13
Lower Zaïre	7	85	12	7	20	10
Bandundu	14	76	11	14	13	13
Shaba	13	71	12	10	11	14
Kivu	17	50	8	11	10	16
Upper Zaïre	15	49	13	4	3	3
Equator	12	46	7	6	3	5
Kinshasha	7	–	10	17	–	–

Source: Coleman and Ngokwey, 1983, p. 67.

dominated by a few ethnic groups (Table 1.3). The policy of regional quotas for admission into the university with the creation of UNAZA in 1971, was introduced to remedy these imbalances.

Besides the political goal of minimising and/or defusing the inter-ethnic or inter-regional conflict that might be caused by gross inequalities in educational development, the quota system was also justified in terms of an overall political philosophy of educational democracy and justice, offering equal opportunity to all, a constant theme in President Mobutu's speeches and Party resolutions and directives at the time (Manifesto, 1967). Regional quotas were therefore applied not only to the admission of students into the university, but also to the recruitment of teaching assistants and the award of scholarships for graduate study abroad.

In spite of all the efforts at ensuring equality of opportunity, the predominance of the advantaged groups such as the Bahiba of Kasai, the Bakingo of Lower Zaïre and the Kikongo-speaking groups of Bandundu is bound to continue for some time because of their initial advantages which enable them to circumvent the quota system (Coleman and Ngokwey, 1983).

The case of Cuba

Cuba provides another dramatic example of the impact of politics on education. The economic and political goals of the Cuban revolution after 1959 were to increase productivity, eliminate economic, political and cultural dependency, particularly on the US, destroy the rigid capitalist class structure and create a 'new socialist man' who would accept work as a creative activity (Bowles, 1977).

There were basically three educational reforms initiated in support of these programmes of socio-economic and cultural regeneration. First was a programme of mass literacy, involving a quarter of a million *alphabetisation* or literacy teachers, made up of students and professional teachers. By the end of the campaign in the early-1960s, the Cuban illiteracy rate of 3.9 per cent was the lowest in Latin America. The second reform, known as the *escula al campo* or 'school to the country' programme, emphasised the educational value of productive labour. As part of the programme students from urban areas went to work for up to 12 weeks in the rural areas. Apart from augmenting the agricultural supply, the scheme aimed at breaking the urban-rural social and cultural dichotomy. A further extension of the integration of schooling and work programme was what were called *circulos de interes* or 'interest circles', which aimed at encouraging students to participate in extra-curricular activities in the sciences and technology, as a means of inculcating interest in those fields. A measure of the success of this effort was that by 1973 there were 300,000 students involved in 20,000 circles. The third aspect of the reform process was the expansion of the educational system at all levels, with the intention of breaking down elitism in education. The result, according to Carnoy and Wyathein (1977), was that the participation rate in secondary and university education had risen from 6 and 2 per cent in 1953 to 20 and 10 per cent, respectively, by 1973.

What is apparent from these examples is how the goal and programmes of a political regime can dominate the structure and content of schooling. Hence, the conclusion to be drawn concerning the relationship between education and political mobilisation is that 'the political impact of schooling corresponds to the prevailing ideological goals of the political system, whether those goals be overt or covert, that is, part of the official or hidden curriculum. In other words, school most certainly does contribute to political mobilisation and development. However, the specific form and content of that mobilisation and development is contingent upon the ideology of the particular political system.

Education and development: a critique

The ever escalating cost of education was the first factor to give the lie to the global belief in education as an agent of development. The increases in costs were not confined to expansion but also included the costs of maintaining the system at all levels. As Coombs (1968) observed: . . . each year, *ad infinitum*, an educational system needs more finances simply to accomplish the same results as in the previous year' (p. 47). The basis for such increases are rising costs of teacher salaries and capital expenditure, both being subject to inflation. For example, the average public expenditure on education in the developing countries rose from 11.5 per cent to 15.1 per cent in the period 1960 to 1974 (World Bank, 1980a). What made this situation unbearable was the painful realisation that many countries had reached the limits of their ability to pay, the doubtful quality of the educational output, and the apparent inappropriateness of the education being provided. All these have made people question the wisdom of such expenditure and its contribution to the social and economic development of society. What becomes obvious is that it would appear that the cost of education is counter-productive to development, as the high levels of expenditure on education would tend to deprive other sectors of the economy such as health, agriculture, welfare, transportation and so forth, of funds.

The second criticism of the education-development link centres on the relationship between education and the prevailing labour market crisis. The underlying assumption about the link is that education creates the necessary skilled and viable workforce. Hence, the contention of both human capital and modernisation theories that an educated population is a productive population. Although considerable research evidence in the 1960s and early-1970s tended to confirm the assumptions (Psacharopoulos, 1973), these soon became untenable after the mid-1970s for two reasons. First, economic planners at the time appeared to be uninformed about the economic ties binding countries together globally so that the high fuel and energy costs of the 1970s, combined with the increasing competition for the sale of certain manufactured products in both the developed and developing countries, resulted in the present worldwide economic recession. At the same time educational planners failed to recognise the rigid nature of the education system which prevented it from responding quickly to changing national, social and economic needs. As a result, while on the one hand there were rising costs of production and a decline in economic expansion, on the other hand there was increasing production of skilled and qualified manpower from the education system which led to a worldwide crisis of unemployment.

The issue of unemployment in turn resulted in the growing scepticism about the relevance of schooling for specific types of work and the use of educational credentials as a screening device for job recruitment and selection (Dore, 1967; Berg, 1971; Foster, 1965). In the case of African countries, part of the reason for the growing level of educated unemployed has been attributed to the fact that schooling has produced students for the wrong kinds of jobs, thus creating a workforce with inappropriate skills for the demands of a Third World labour market. Anosike (1977), gives the example of Nigeria, where despite the large numbers of unemployed graduates, an appropriately trained labour force continued to be imported from abroad for certain sectors of the economy. This disjuncture between educational attainment, aspirations and labour market opportunities calls into question the contribution of education to this aspect of economic development.

Further challenges to the education and development hypothesis have come from the radical and neo-Marxist camp. Neo-Marxists, while accepting that education can contribute to economic growth, contend that in the developed countries economic growth has mainly served the interests of those in power and perpetuated the existing social system. For example, they argue that in such countries as Britain, France and the US, schooling tends to reinforce and reproduce the class structure of these societies by producing a docile and compliant workforce (Bowles and Gintis, 1976). This contention has been buttressed by empirical research by Pierre Bourdieu in France, in which he shows that schools provide the dominant classes with 'cultural and material capital', thus giving them the advantage of full participation in the social system and its rewards (Bourdieu, 1973). Hence, while the positive role of education in the production of skilled manpower and aspects of economic growth is acknowledged, it is criticised for its continued fostering of social and political inequality.

In the developing societies, such as those in Africa, schools can be criticised on a number of grounds. First, the schools being modelled on the imported models from the Western industrial societies, continue to serve the same dominant social groups as did the colonial system as a whole. As such, according to Carnoy (1974), schools in developing countries such as those in Africa, are simply a part of imperialism and neo-colonialism and continue to serve the interest of the elites of the former colonial countries. The basic mechanism for the performance of these functions is the selection system and the curriculum structuring. The result is the production of the 'Lumpen-proletariat' (Frank, 1972). These are local elites who choose to serve overseas interests in preference to those of their own people. Clearly on this thesis, the mode of education which has been bequeathed to African countries does not serve her development interests but rather serves to contribute to continuing underdevelopment. It is, however, important to understand that the rejection of the education and development hypothesis is a rejection of its capitalist model and not a rejection of education *per se*.

This then brings us to views regarding the role of education in development in socialist countries. Generally, in the old socialist countries (the USSR and Eastern European countries) as in the new socialist-oriented countries (China, Cuba, Tanzania, Guinea Bissau, Mozambique, Angola, Ethiopia and Nicaragua) education is considered as an essential part of the strategies for social and economic advancement. As a result, all aspects of education have been in the forefront of policy, planning and expenditure (Fägerlind and Saha, 1983), with the elimination of illiteracy always forming an important part of educational policy, as it is regarded as detrimental to development.

Starting with the USSR following the Revolution, and the pattern being consistently repeated in all the socialist oriented countries, literacy campaigns have constituted a first major effort in educational strategy. As a result, in the USSR the literacy rate increased from 32 per cent in 1920 to about 98 per cent by 1959. Similarly, in China and Cuba, the literacy rates had climbed to 70 and 96 per cent respectively by 1975 (Fägerlind and Saha, 1983; A. P. Morales, 1981). Likewise the illiteracy rate in Nicaragua fell from 50 per cent in 1979 to 13 per cent by 1980 (Cardenal and Miller, 1981). Recent developments (1991) in the former USSR and in Eastern Europe raise additional and intriguing questions about the continuation of these policies. One wonders whether a move towards a more free-market economic policy will in turn lead to changes in educational policy.

Literacy campaigns have also been launched in the socialist-oriented African countries of Tanzania, Guinea Bissau, Mozambique, Angola and Ethiopia with equally remarkable successes. All these efforts were based on the belief that literacy is a key requisite both for economic advancement and social and political restructuring of a country. It would appear, therefore, that in socialist societies, as was the case in the 1950s and 1960s, development policy planners regard education as the key agent for the control of social, economic and political change. As such, its potential contribution has gone largely unquestioned, until recently. However, the emerging evidence from socialist countries seems to indicate that similar questionable aspects of education as those in capitalist societies are also present. Thus, Court (1976) in Tanzania and Dobson (1976) both report the reproduction of the social structure and the pervasiveness of unequal access and attainment in the socialist countries. Economic and political reform witnessed in the 1990s will no doubt accelerate these changes.

On current evidence it would appear that doubts on the potential role of education in development seem to cover the different political and economic systems and are not confined to the capitalist one alone. Hence the ability of education to act as a means for controlling social change still requires deeper probing than has so far been undertaken.

Conclusion

As is apparent from the preceding discussions, the relationship between education and its various dimensions defies over-simplification and is contingent on the development of the goals of a particular society. In spite of the various difficulties revealed in this relationship, however, no country can pretend to advance in the absence of an efficient education system. Efficiency can only result from a proper approach to the planning of the system. Hence the imperative for African countries to attempt to improve the existing systems to serve them better. It can also be argued that efficiency, i.e. better planning, will lead to the realisation of the goals of the system. In the 1990s Africa will need to tackle major issues of poverty, the introduction of multi-party democracy into political life; and in education calls for a better quality of education, particularly at the basic level. Questions of health, for example the fight against AIDS, will also put greater demands on policymakers and planners. A systematic planning approach provides the most valuable tool toward the realisation of such goals. The chapters that follow offer a comprehensive guide on a wide range of issues in education planning toward the understanding of the background of the issues in planning education on which to build future advances.

Exercises

1   Outline what you consider as development?
2   What are the links between education and the following two aspects of development – economic and modernisation?
3   Discuss the relation between political development and education.
4   The historical evidence from such developed countries as England and Japan offers contradictory support for the role of education in economic advancement. Can you give examples from Africa?
5   In your opinion, has education assisted African countries to develop or not?
6   Which issues, in your opinion, will educational leaders need to address in the 1990s?

II

The nature and scope of educational planning

The role of educational planning

One of the main developments in the post-independence period in Africa is the widespread belief by governments and people that education is a key factor in the process of economic and social change. Education is seen not only as a means of understanding, controlling and developing the natural environment, but also as a tool for the enhancement of life and enrichment of the human spirit. In order to do this efficiently and effectively, educational planning has come to be accepted as one of the essential elements of overall comprehensive socio-economic planning. This chapter first attempts to define the nature of educational planning, and then outlines some of the reasons that have given impetus to its development as a discipline and profession. The basic emphasis in the rest of the chapter is on the fundamental features of planning in general and the special characteristics of the planning of education.

Educational planning defined

Educational planning can be defined as the process by which an analysis of the present condition of an education system is made in order to determine and devise ways of reaching a desired future state. It basically aims at the co-ordination and direction of all the different parts of an education system towards the achievement of long-term goals of a country or region/state within it. This involves the assessment of the existing situation, including institutional structures and financial and human resources, and the evolution of a strategy of action. As a management tool, educational planning is a continuous process of acquisition and analysis of data from an empirical base for the provision of information to decision-makers. They need to know how well the education system is accomplishing its goals, including in particular, suggestions for the improvement of cost effectiveness of programmes and specific projects.

Definitions of education planning have been offered by amongst others, Gareth Williams, who simply states that: 'planning in education, as in anything else, consists essentially of deciding in advance what you want to do and how you are going to do it' (Williams, G., 1971). Arnold Anderson and Jean Bowman define educational planning as: 'the process of preparing a set of decisions for future action, pertaining to education' (Anderson and Bowman, 1967). Elsewhere Philip Coombs says that: 'Educational planning, in its broadest generic sense, is the application of rational systemic analysis to the process of educational development with the aim of making education more effective and efficient in responding to the needs of its students and society' (Coombs, 1970).

Thus a central task in educational planning, as in other forms of social planning, is to recognise in present conditions inadequacies that point to the desirability of change. Dissatisfaction with current goals, programmes or activities encourages planning as a way to achieve improvements: planning is needed to prevent or find solutions to problems and to give the organisation its forward momentum.

Characteristics of educational planning

The essential features of planning in general and of educational planning in particular can therefore be identified as follows. Planning is concerned firstly with the future, with development. Starting with an understanding of the present, it goes on to consider the likely future conditions. It embodies the skills of anticipating, influencing, and controlling the nature and direction of change.

Secondly, planning deals with the consequences of active intervention, that is, with actions that will change the present into something better in the future. As no organisation is free of change, effective planning ensures survival and growth. Planning helps prevent an organisation from being the helpless victim of change; instead it gains a measure of control and influence over its destiny. In this way, planning is not just forecasting or predicting the future, it involves taking such policy measures that will direct future development towards more desirable ends. It is, of course, recognised that it is often very difficult for planners to achieve this rational objective in times of great change, particularly if those changes are brought about by economic or social forces beyond the control of planning and policy units.

Thirdly, planning is closely linked not only with policymaking but also with making decisions. The purpose of planning is fundamentally twofold: to determine appropriate goals, and to prepare for adaptive and innovative change. That is why planning and policymaking are closely related; it is through planning that decisions are translated into systematic programmes of action for implementation. Because of this, the planner has a dual role: through his function of exploring the likely consequences of existing and alternative approaches, he is fully involved in the development of policy; and once policies and decisions have been made by the executive (political authority) he is responsible for translating these into programmes of action. This explains the close working relationship which invariably develops between the planning unit and the minister and the most senior civil servants in a ministry in Africa and elsewhere in the developing world. Nevertheless, it is important to emphasise that the role of the professional planner is not to make new policies, but merely to interpret and to consolidate policies decided by the responsible political authority. In relation to the other units within the ministry, the planner, because of his access to a wide range of information, is well placed to co-ordinate the efforts of his colleagues in these units for the realisation of the overall aims of the ministry.

However desirable it is to entrust a special unit with the responsibility for planning in a complex organisation such as a ministry, planning is in fact a joint or corporate function that should involve all the different units and sub-units of a ministry both at the headquarters as well as in the field. Removing the planning from the actual work activity tends to rob the work of interest and meaning to the individuals involved. In fact, planning is done most effectively by involving those who are to carry out the plans (Lyons, 1968). Hence, the Province or District Education Officer, the headmaster or principal, and the class teacher must all plan for the efficient performance of their individual and joint tasks, for they are also concerned with the use of resources for carrying out decisions and policies. Planning should thus never be the exclusive preserve of 'experts' in the ministry headquarters.

Problems of planning in Africa

Such a participative approach to planning is, however, not always feasible in large parts of Africa. The difficulties of communication mean that the planning authorities at the ministry headquarters in the capital city are not fully aware of the objective conditions obtaining in the remote parts of the country. When a ministry of education official in Khartoum (Sudan) for example, describes the state of education in the country, he is in fact only stating the situation as it exists in Khartoum or at best only in those most accessible parts of the country. He has very little idea of what actually obtains in, for instance, Bor, Pibor or Tali in the southern Sudan and other equally inaccessible parts of the country. Similarly, the teachers and headmasters in such far-flung areas have little notion of the ministry's plans and their part in it. African governments, for political reasons too, generally favour a more centralised control of the planning process.

Apart from the problem of communication, the lack of know-ledge and understanding of planning by most of the officials lower down the rungs of government bureaucracies in Africa is also a serious obstacle to the practice of participative planning. One can, however, take consolation in the fact that in some of the countries serious attempts are being made to improve the situation. Provincial education officers are being encouraged to provide regular statistics and suggestions for incorporation into annual budgets of the province. In Kano state, Nigeria, for instance, the administration of the state education system, including some aspects of planning, has been decentralised by the creation of zonal education offices. Whether power has actually shifted away from the centre to these offices (rather than purely administration) has been argued elsewhere (Stephens, 1985). Having discussed the nature of educational planning we must now turn our attention to its emergence as a discipline.

Although educational planning as such is not an entirely new activity, its current practice is definitely a peculiar feature of the twentieth century, a manifestation of the need for overall planning to cope with the complex demands of economic, social, political and technological changes.

The emergence of educational planning

Historical evidence shows that certain elements of fairly systematic planning were applied to the development of education in some of the outstanding civilisations of the past, such as Plato's Republic in Ancient Greece, Ancient China during the Han Dynasty and Peru under Inca rule. In more recent times Le Chalotias' idea of education for the common man in 1763, Diderot's plan for the government of Russia under Empress Catherine II, Rousseau's plan for providing education for every Polish citizen, and the Prussian comprehensive national system of state primary education in 1808, can be cited. There is thus a gradual evolution in man's ideas about the systematic planning of educational development (UNESCO, 1964).

These planned conceptions of education do not coincide, however, with planning in the modern sense, largely on two counts. First, although they resemble present day planning in as far as they outlined goals, they failed to take proper account of the time dimension. Second, the need for future changes to suit changing times and circumstances was not adequately recognised. Hence it is fair to say that the contemporary practice of educational planning in the context of economic, politico-cultural and social development only really dates back to the end of World War I with the publication in 1923 of the first Soviet plan of socio-economic development, including the development of education. This first systematic approach to the problem of education development along modern lines has become renowned for its successful implementation of extensive programmes for the promotion of literacy and professional training.

Although some modest attempts were made in educational planning between this Soviet plan and the outbreak of World War II, educational planning as a specialised profession and discipline, with a growing body of theory and literature of its own, is even more recent. It was not until the end of World War II, particularly in the 1950s and 1960s, that a qualitative turning point in educational planning was reached. The then recently established socialist countries of Eastern Europe, seeking their development model in the planning methodology of the Soviet Union, systematically embarked upon the planning of new education systems.

Countries in Western Europe, similarly faced with the problems of economic reconstruction and re-orientation, slowly also came to acknowledge and accept the need for consistent and continuous socio-economic growth through planning. At the international level, the International Institute of Education Planning (IIEP) was founded by

UNESCO in Paris in 1963, which acted as a stimulus to the establishment of educational planning units in ministries of education, particularly in the developing countries. In the developed countries it stimulated the establishment of educational planning as an academic discipline at many universities. It is therefore pertinent at this juncture to identify some of the main reasons that gave impetus to this quickening of interest in educational planning.

Reasons for the growth of educational planning

First, the great economic slump of 1929 and its aftermath, followed by the problems of economic reconstruction and orientation which confronted most countries after World War II led to the general recognition of the need for consistent and continuous growth. To ensure this there was a call for continuous systematic planning. The result, as we have already seen, has been the steady growth of overall planning not only in the socialist world, but also in the capitalist countries. A decisive factor in the development of this planning mentality in most countries is the extremely important part that the state has come to play in the economy (Tibi, 1969). In practice, in almost all countries today the state is responsible for the provision of all the infrastructures, including a large share of the investment in education amongst other things. The running costs of these services represent a large proportion of the gross national product (GNP), with much expenditure going on the maintenance of the bureaucracy required to administer these services.

The result is that the power and responsibility of government has increased to embrace a wide range of functions. Consequently, governments are now expected by the citizens not only to promote economic growth and social welfare, but also tackle such problems as inflation, unemployment and poverty. It is in this context that the concept of planning has come to assume a central position, because to handle most of these difficulties effectively calls for co-ordination of resources between priority tasks and the programming of future activity in a sequential manner.

However, to achieve any planned objective, education has a central role to play as the main supplier of trained manpower to all sectors of the economy (government ministries and the private sector alike). Education also claims a major share of government expenditure in most countries. This is particularly the case in Africa. For example, in its first budget, the civilian administration (1980) in Nigeria allocated education the biggest share amounting to ₦ 1.2 billion or 15 per cent of the total budget. Hence as development planning is not possible without educational planning, its spread inevitably called for the introduction of a planning approach to educational development.

Second, in the case of the developing countries, the enthusiasm for planning has been largely buttressed by the policies of both bilateral and multilateral aid agencies. According to Peter Williams, developed countries, including those that claimed to be free-enterprise economies, always demanded that a developing country wanting aid should draw up development programmes as a condition for receiving such assistance. Yet others advocated its planning in terms of manpower requirements. All these emphases on cost analysis and measurement of the value of educational output have made for a more rational approach to the development of educational systems through planning.

Third, stimulated by world economic recovery after World War II, followed by the attainment of independence by many dependent territories particularly in the 1960s in Africa, there was an unprecedented rate and scale of universal growth in education (Coombs, 1968). This made forward planning for the provision of physical facilities and teachers imperative to avert crisis situations. Moreover, the greater part of this expansion, especially in the developing countries, occurred at a time of financial stringency, so that the competing demands for expansion and for economy meant that more consideration was given to planning than would otherwise be the case. The ministries of finance have consequently been the foremost advocates of the idea of educational planning.

Lastly, at the personal level, increasingly the chief determinant of the level of the job, income and status of individuals in any developing society is dependent on education. Educational labels such as certificates, diplomas and degrees, are becoming increasingly the only yardstick by which employers assess potential employees. This in turn has resulted in greater public demand for education and concern with its policy, particularly the distribution of educational opportunities among individuals and social groups.

Thus the reasons and stimulus for the growth of educational planning in Africa and the rest of the Third World has emanated from a variety of sources: economists, aid agencies, ministries of finance and the general public. Williams gives the example of Britain which as early as 1940 was demanding that its colonies should prepare development plans as a pre-condition for obtaining Colonial Development and Welfare Assistance, though the country itself did not practise planning at home until the mid-1960s (Williams, P.R.C., 1974). Similarly, world bodies like UNESCO, OECD (Organisation for Economic Cooperation and Development) and the World Bank (IBRD) have made significant contributions to the practice and theory of educational planning by establishing research institutes in Europe as well as setting-up educational planning institutions in many developing countries. It is, for example, largely through the efforts of UNESCO by providing technical assistance to governments, complemented by training fellowships at the IIEP, that most African governments have been able to establish educational planning units. UNESCO has also been instrumental in organising the regular planning conferences of the OAU Ministers of Education where common policies and strategies for educational advancement for the African continent are mapped out. It was, for instance, at the first of these conferences at Addis Ababa in 1961 that a recommendation was made to implement Universal Primary Education in all African countries by 1980.

The tremendous interest shown by American and British economists in the 1950s and 1960s in the assessment of the contribution of education to economic growth, has also helped to focus attention on educational planning as an academic discipline. The economists not only introduced such economic notions as productivity and efficiency into the planning of education but were also concerned with measuring its costs and benefits like any other economic enterprise.

In socialist countries the need for planning has always been embodied in the political philosophy. In the developing countries of Africa, although the pressure exerted by the former colonial powers and the international aid agencies was the *raison d'etre* for embarking on planning, its usefulness as an instrument of rapid socio-economic development was quickly appreciated by the ruling elite. As a result, planning has since been incorporated as an essential component of the operations of government.

Sequence, consistency and probability in planning

In planning, whether one is concerned with overall strategy or with individual projects, the three concepts of sequence, consistency and probability are crucial.

Sequence

Sequence basically seeks to order tasks for the achievement of a planned programme in such a way that the time needed for its overall completion is reduced to the minimum. An example will make this clear. Suppose it was planned to increase primary school enrolments in a given province of the southern Sudan from a present total of 152,000 to 175,000, that is roughly by 15 per cent in three years. Concern for sequence will dictate that the first requirement is to programme the provision of an adequate supply of teachers to man the additional classes and new schools that will have to be created. This will be followed by programming for the construction of the actual physical facilities of new classrooms and teachers' housing. Finally will come a programme for the supply of new furniture and other equipment for the new schools. Although this looks fairly obvious, instances from developing countries, including Africa, abound to show that it is frequently ignored with disastrous results.

As the planning machinery of a country or organisation improves, more refined techniques of network analysis such as the Critical Path Method (CPM) and Programme Evaluation and Review Technique (PERT) may be employed in the preparation of time schedules (see also Chapter 8). CPM and PERT are basically concerned with two things: the order in which actions are taken to achieve a given result, and the ways for saving time so as to reach goals as early as possible.

Consistency

In addition to sequence, planning demands that all the decisions and areas covered by the plan are consistent and satisfy the following conditions.

First, consistency in a plan requires that the policies of the different sectors must be in agreement. This means that the total of all the activities and programmes planned should not exceed the actual availability of the resources of the country. For example, in planning its building and other construction programmes, the ministry of education must take into consideration the demands of the other sectors and the capacity of the ministry of works and private contractors to execute them successfully. It is likewise of little use for all the post-secondary education institutions with a capacity for 3,000 new entrants to demand that candidates for admission into their courses must obtain three credits when experience shows quite clearly that the annual output of the entire school system that can meet this requirement is at best only 1,500.

Second, the goals of an education plan must agree with the goals of the overall plan. Hence educational policies must promote the fulfilment of the wider goals of the plan.

Third, consistency is equally important within the education system itself. For instance, the development of teacher training must be firmly based upon proposed developments of primary and secondary education. It would be a gross waste of resources, particularly in a developing country, if the number of trained teachers exceeds the requirements of the schools, thus resulting in teacher unemployment.

Furthermore, apart from these internal consistencies, a plan must also have external consistency between what is assumed about the future behaviour of key factors and the actual experiences of the situation in the recent past. It would, for example, be quite unrealistic to expect that 70–80 per cent of a ministry's planned total capital budget would be realised when the annual pattern of actual fund availability from the ministry of finance has been in the region of 10–15 per cent for the past five years. Therefore to have a good plan it must be firmly based on the proper appraisal of existing socio-economic realities.

Probability

Probability, the last of the three important concepts in planning, refers to the likelihood of events occurring as planned. In a situation where the sequence of events can be predicted with a high degree of confidence, planning is not only facilitated but the formulation of detailed plans covering a fairly long time can be undertaken. However in planning many factors, both human and natural, can introduce a great deal of uncertainty. This is especially the case in the developing regions of the world such as Africa, typified by the severe drought which for the past five years has played havoc with economies of many African countries ranging from the Sahelian countries in the north, Ethiopia and Somalia in the east and extending south as far as Zambia and Zimbabwe.

Similarly, the exports of most African countries, consisting largely of primary products as they are at present, are subject to sudden price fluctuations on the world commodity markets. This can have adverse effects on even the most carefully prepared plan. This situation is exacerbated if increases in the price of a vital import such as oil coincides with such factors as inflation, as the experiences of most African countries has shown over the last five years. What this suggests, therefore, is that the planner in a developing country not endowed with a commodity which can command a high price on the international market, should not only weigh his options carefully, but also make adequate allowance of time and resources against any turn of events for the worse. As Williams has stated: 'In the face of uncertainty, flexibility must be the watchword' (Williams, P.R.C., 1974).

Finally, even when all other factors have been given adequate consideration, the success of a plan will hinge on what has become known as the human factor in planning (Mcfarland, 1979). Experience has shown that the success of a plan can be affected by whether or not those who will be expected to participate in its implementation have been sufficiently involved in its preparation. In many cases the success of a plan will therefore depend in no small measure on how much time and energy is spent on discovering the views and objectives of different groups who are likely to be affected by the plan.

Special characteristics of the planning of education

The preceding discussion has largely dealt with planning in general terms. Let us now turn to the particular characteristics of education that both facilitate and hinder its planning.

Redeeming features

The first factor which favours the planning of education is its organisation on the basis of a structure providing for an ordered sequence, with students moving vertically through specified stages and at rates decided in advance. Advancement or progress through the system is formally organised allowing for no omission of any of the stages. This means that it is normally not possible for anyone to enter a secondary school without first having completed a primary school course or its equivalent. What this means also is that the enrolments and outputs at any level of an education system are largely governed by the outputs and enrolments of the level immediately below it. Forecasting under these conditions is relatively easy. The implications of such a close relationship is that in education the past, present and future are closely bound up.

A second notable feature is the fact that educational institutions form an interlocking system. The leavers or graduates from one type of level of education invariably form the inputs for the next; the qualifications obtained from one course become the entry requirements for another. The flow of students likewise proceeds one way, from nursery through primary and secondary and then to higher or tertiary education, with a return flow of part of the outputs from a higher to a lower level, largely in the form of teachers. Thus, for instance, while the secondary stage receives its student inputs from the primary schools, it in turn provides the latter with teachers.

Lastly, this complete reliance of educational levels or sub-systems upon each other and the fact that the system produces most of its own major inputs not only distinguishes education from other sectors but ensures internal consistency, which in turn promotes its planning. Richard Jolly, for example, calculated that in 1963 some 59 per cent of all those Ugandans who had even completed school certificate were still in the education system as students or teachers (Jolly, 1969).

Complicating factors

Although it has been pointed out that some characteristics of the education system are supportive of the planning effort, equally, some features of the system complicate its planning.

Firstly, the long period required for a cohort of students to pass through the education system from primary school to college or university, means quick changes are not possible. A new approach to the curriculum or even a change in a subject syllabus may take anything from two to four years to reach the classroom. Thus the introduction of a new secondary school science curriculum for East Africa in the 1960s took at least four years to complete (1964–68). Another instance of the long period needed for any real change to occur in a school system is provided by a UNESCO financed curriculum project currently being undertaken in the southern Sudan. In 1976, the World Bank and the Sudan government concluded an agreement for a loan for the establishment of 30 Integrated Rural Education Centres (IRECS) throughout the rural areas of southern Sudan. 'The IREC, as its name implied, would be a community education center for all the people in a rural area; a base for a complex of organisations provided by the various technical ministries such as health, education, cooperatives and rural development and agriculture, with the common objective of improving rural life' (Forojalla, 1975). The idea was to attempt a comprehensive socio-economic effort in the selected rural areas to serve as a model for eventual adoption throughout this part of the Sudan if it was found to be successful. Four years later, however, the project had only reached the stage where the proposed curriculum for the centres was being tested in selected primary schools in and around the town of Maridi in the Western Equatoria Province of southern Sudan.

A related aspect of this same problem is that educational administrators and planners have invariably to live for a long time with the consequences of past decisions. For instance, the introduction of the Universal Primary Education in Nigeria in 1976 meant that for the next twenty years or so the administrators and planners had to grapple further up the system with the problem of trying to find extra places for the additional enrolments into the primary schools that year. Hence the advantages of inbuilt sequence and predictability is counterbalanced by the disadvantages resulting from the rigidity of the system.

Secondly, the high degree of interdependence of education systems tends to make the whole system rather self-contained, hence the charge which has been labelled against school systems as self-serving monopolies by the de-schoolers (Illich, 1971; Freire, 1972; Goodman, 1964; Reimer, 1971). Philip Coombs on the same account distinguishes between the efficiency and effectiveness of education systems. A system is described as efficient if it achieves its own objectives with the least possible input of resources, even if such objectives are limited in their outlook. Effectiveness, on the other hand, is judged on the basis of criteria external to the educational system, that is in terms of the relevance of the education to meet the needs of contemporary and future society by inculcating in its outputs such useful qualities as good citizenship, productivity and talents of various kinds which will make them contribute to the development of society.

Thirdly, the problem of planning education at the national level is the uncertainty about the intended aims of education, as very few countries in Africa and elsewhere have developed a well-defined philosophy to guide the planning of education. The existence of such a philosophy simplifies the planning of education. Tanzania is probably the only country on the African continent with a coherent national philosophy that sets out the goals of society and the role expected of education in their realisation. Policy documents, like the Arusha Declaration and Education for Self-Reliance, declare the objective of creating a socialist society as the fundamental aim of the country. It has since been joined by other countries, notably Nigeria (with its National Policy on Education, 1977).

In those African countries without such clearly stated national aims, education planning is conducted on the basis of a social demand approach. This means educational development aims at satisfying the demands of the users of the system – parents and pupils. There are a number of drawbacks to this approach however. First, to base policy on public demand easily leads to the manipulation of the level of demand by public policy itself. Secondly, it tends to result in conservatism in the planning process, especially as in most countries of Africa governments have a monopoly of educational provision. The danger in such situations is that educational planning is easily reduced to mere calculation of expansion rates and the resources needed for its implementation but without effecting any qualitative improvement of the actual content.

Moreover, the social demand approach to educational development in reality works essentially to satisfy private demand for education. But as has already been pointed out, education in most countries of Africa is heavily subsidised from public funds, this means private demands and private benefits far exceed the social benefits of educational expansion. In addition, a simple response to private demand often favours those social groups or areas that are already privileged as they are invariably more articulate and better organised, thus increasing social inequalities. However, the purpose of educational planning on the contrary is to attempt a reconciliation of private and social interest for the good of society.

Finally, yet another complicating factor in educational planning even if it were possible to define all possible aims of education, is how to identify the exact relationship between inputs and outputs in education. The major input in education (the learner), experiences many influences apart from school ones, such as his family, the mass media and playmates from the neighbourhood, to name only a few. The problem confronting educational planning is how to identify which of these influences makes the most impact on the product (output) of an education system and eventually makes the person what they are, either a good and responsible citizen or just a lazy layabout. In fact the problem is even more complicated than that. Even if it were possible to know the requisite educational inputs to produce the right kinds of persons, the learner is an independent or autonomous participant in the learning process, and can therefore reject what he is being taught even if he is physically present in the classroom.

Hence, although the continuity and interdependence of the education system greatly facilitates its planning, other characteristics of the system such as its rigidity, the fact that education basically deals with people and the fact that many poor and often small countries have little control over the world's economic forces, means that planning in the broadest sense is often clouded by complication and uncertainty.

Exercises

1 Define educational planning in the light of your knowledge of your local educational systems.

2   Discuss some of the reasons that gave impetus to the emergence and spread of educational planning in modern times.

3   What in your opinion are the fundamental constraints to educational planning in any one country of Africa?

4   Discuss the special characteristics of the planning of education.

5   Using concrete examples, illustrate the importance of the concepts of sequence, consistency and probability in educational planning.

III

Objectives for educational planning

Aims and objectives: their importance in planning

When people ask about aims of education they are often thinking of a multiplicity of tasks which they expect the education system to perform, tasks which themselves are often as different as the interest groups whose views they reflect. The debate among thinkers, philosophers and educationalists alike on issues like conformity with traditional values versus progress towards modernity, the distinction between the intrinsic non-instrumental concept of education suggesting depth and breadth of understanding which transforms a man's view of life, and the extrinsic, instrumental view of learning as providing relevantly trained manpower, jobs and social mobility – these are all reflective of the variety of expectations individuals and groups may have of the education system. National aims for education, though couched in different terms, are common to all developing countries: the two main objects are the shaping of man for life in a particular kind of desired society, and the achieving of the highest growth rate (linked with variable social and political imperatives and depending on the physical and human resources available, and in the light of technical, political, administrative, economic and social constraints). In UNESCO's *World Survey of Education* (UNESCO, 1971, Vol. 5), there is, at the beginning of each chapter, a statement of the fundamental aims to which government policy in education is directed. Sweden refers to the need *to develop a critical spirit* (authors' emphasis). Many African countries aim at ridding themselves of the attitudes of colonisation and renewing the strength of their indigenous cultures.

To the educational planner statements of educational aims and purposes and the various tasks expected of the education system are remarkable, if only for the high level of generality at which they are expressed. The very generality of such abstractions about the quality of human beings and human societies that people hope will be produced by education makes it difficult for the planner to ascertain exactly how the educational means are to be related to the stated ends, and how he or she can set about trying to see how far the ends are being achieved. The means that will be adopted to achieve the ends and therefore the forms of planning, in the final analysis, differ widely. Since educational planning is a purposeful activity involving choices and decisions about future action, choices between alternative ends and alternative means to achieve them, it seems logical to conclude that not only is a definition of aims necessary, the planner must also be able to translate aims into concrete terms as objectives. 'Aims', therefore, must be distinguished from 'objectives', the former referring to the direction of educational policy, reflecting societal values and norms, and the latter referring to more concrete and specific targets.

Discrepancies between the aims and objectives of education expressed at the national level and the actual working of the education system are often so pronounced that statements on aims appear as a futile exercise. (This issue will be discussed at greater length later in this chapter.) However, it is only in this way that planners and governmental leaders can find and give direction to their efforts and establish criteria by which they may judge how well they are doing. Here lies the importance of defining aims and objectives; by moving away from the generalities of aims and concretising them into objectives, planners and school personnel at all levels can operate within a given framework to arrive at an output in conformity, with the stated aims and objectives being achieved.

Interest groups and motivations in education

In developing countries education is seen as the master-determinant of national, social and personal development, and provides the criteria for selection into the political and social elite. In countries which have experienced colonial rule and a colonial (Western style) system of education, education has given rise to a class of educated elite which still occupies and controls powerful political, professional and administrative positions. Much of the political struggles and instability in the Third World are due, at least in part, to the determination of old incumbent, not-so-highly-educated ministers, on the one hand determined to remain in power at any cost, and the aspirations and ambitions of the younger, mostly highly educated people, on the other, who see themselves as having a more legitimate claim to these influential positions. Discontent is felt in government ministries where the presence of these 'old heads' effectively nullifies promotional prospects for the young. In some African countries it is not only the present old incumbents who are the cause of discontent. Ministers of education in the educationally backward states encourage younger inexperienced men to remain in government service by promoting them to positions of authority and decision-making rather than forego the loss of their services for those years which further education at a university would entail. The discontent will be more acutely felt in the future (and in fact has already started) as the rate of expansion of the education sector far exceeds that of the economic sector, thereby making an increasing number of qualified people compete for fewer and fewer jobs. These elite enjoy privileged positions and would wish to retain them for their children. A proposal for expanding education to all, any proposal to abolish private schools (as was the case in 1981 in Lagos State, Nigeria), any attempt to encourage or force their children to attend schools of an innovative and dubious nature, would meet with resistance.

In the UK the debate over comprehensive versus grammar schools underlies the difference in interests and social ethics between the Labour Party and the Conservative Party. In Nigeria, the problems associated with the implementation of universal primary education have been attributed, in part, to the deliberate efforts of vested interests to 'sabotage' the programme. We have not found any concrete evidence to substantiate the claim, however.

There are also many other interest groups whose views are likely to influence the objectives set and determine their success or failure. It appears that when *parents* send their children to school they do so not only for love or for the nation or the elevated aims of national consciousness, but for their own good and the good of their children. They do, however, value the custodial function of schools in looking after their children while they go to work. They expect schools to perpetuate their own cultural tradition and social values, but in the main, Third World parents regard education for their children as the royal road to a good job and upward social mobility. *Students and pupils* generally regard education as the surest means of acquiring the knowledge and skills necessary for high economic and social status. Education is still the way to heaven here on earth even if many aspirants to that happy state know they will never get there and that in trying, will perhaps pass through many stages of hell – hopes dashed, failure and destruction of self-images, and so on. *Employers* value education in so far as educational certificates provide them with the cheapest and most reliable means of assessing the ability and competence of prospective employees. Certificates provide them with the necessary credentials. *Politicians* may wish to secure a power base and convince the nation that their governments provide the best of all possible worlds. They may seek to do so by responding to popular demand for education (for example UPE) or by insisting upon the introduction of certain subjects or values into a national curriculum.

Teachers, too, may have a dual regard for education. They may be attracted by the opportunities it offers as a source of income and employment. In some cases the material benefits education brings (car loans, government house, etc.) are so obvious and alluring as to appear to overshadow the non-instrumental aesthetic and spiritual values of education. Within the school situation many of our teachers in the Third World show a remarkable indifference to or ignorance of aims of education. The situation is gradually improving with increased training facilities and more careful selection of candidates for the teachers' colleges. However, from a professional viewpoint teachers must address themselves to the perennial problem of discipline and the extent to which they must act *in loco parentis*, assume personal responsibility and become involved with the social and educational problems of their students.

These and many other groups would wish to have their views reflected in an education plan. A clear recognition of goals to be achieved is essential if planning is to mean anything. Everyone involved in educational development, from the permanent secretary of education to the teacher in the classroom, from the employer to the employee, should in principle know the aim of his particular activity. The difficulty is that, in many cases, these aims are not constant and cannot all be recognised in an educational plan. Successful educational planning involves strong and effective administration at the centre and often group and individual interest must be sacrificed in the interest of national good.

Aims and objectives at national and regional levels

The question of who should determine the national aims and objectives of education or what these should be is dependent on a country's political structure and on its social and political ethics. Since education is a close personal concern of almost everyone in a society, it is important for planners to try to act in accordance with opinions and this means there should be ways in which societal wishes can be relayed to them. At one level the president or prime minister or minister of education, as a politician, has to be susceptible to the opinions within and the values of society and may consider it his duty and in the interests of his party to enuniciate those basic values which he regards as essential to the survival of his government. In a simple developing society, where the societal aims are readily identifiable, or in a one-party, socialist or military state, it is possible to speak of aims of society and consequently it is possible to have a national declaration of goals or a national policy on education such as the 1977 Nigerian National Policy on Education or the Arusha Declaration in Tanzania and Common Man's Charter in Uganda. But in a two-party or multi-party state practising 'democratic planning', the very structure of the society and the diversity of political parties is, in a sense, a reflection of the different values held by different groups and individuals, and this makes it difficult to state national aims except in very broad terms such as national unity, democracy and tolerance, social equality, and so on. M. A. El Ghannan defines it in these terms:

Democratic planning means, first of all, that public policies and their co-ordination in a plan should emerge from a democratic political process and be implemented by a government whose power lies in a popularly elected parliament. Democratic planning also means that planning should involve the masses not only in supporting the plans, but also in their preparation and implementation. It finally means that public participation should emerge voluntarily so that state policies can be carried out without regimentation or coercion (El Ghannan, 1970).

In other countries it might be the case that it was not so much the minister of education or the president who issued directives or determined objectives, but was, for example, the Central Planning Commission. Ideally, detailed targets should then be prepared in two phases:

a) a phase of discussion which should allow all parties concerned (administrators, representatives of economic, social, political

(a)

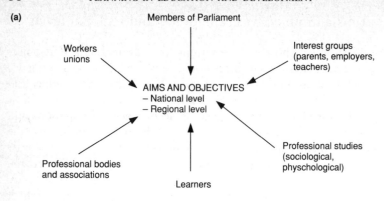

(b)

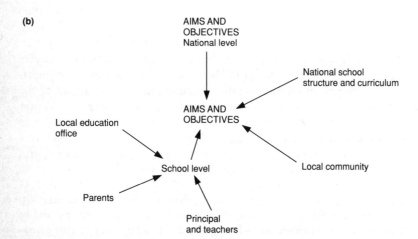

Fig. 3.1   Sources of educational aims and objectives

groups, technicians, etc.) to participate in the common tasks by
expressing their preferences and their views;

b) a phase of arbitration and decision, which will ensure that the
targets thus set in the different sectors are compatible with each
other and with the resources available.

Whoever the objective-setters may be, it is necessary to remember
that it is not the role of planners to determine goals; it is their task to
establish goal feasibility which will achieve what the goals dictate.

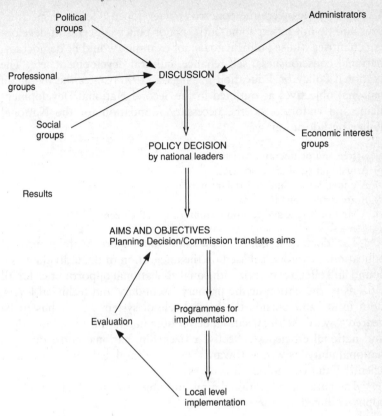

Fig. 3.2 Obtaining aims and objectives

National educational goals

A useful list of policy concerns or national educational goals was compiled by OECD in a document entitled *A Framework for Educational Indicators to Guide Government Decisions* (OECD, 1973). These included:

- Transmission of knowledge.
- Equality of opportunity and social mobility.
- Meeting the needs of the economy.
- Individual development.
- Transmission and evolution of values.
- Effective use of resources in pursuit of the above.
- Policy objectives.

These objectives were the concerns of developed, independent countries and do not reflect some of the major policy concerns of developing countries whose political goals, for example, would be democracy, national consciousness, self-reliance, cultural development, etc. The National Policy on Education in Nigeria (1977) states the five main national objectives as outlined in the Second National Development Plan, and endorsed as 'the necessary foundation for the National Policy on Education' as:

a) A free and democratic society.
b) A just and egalitarian society.
c) A united strong and self-reliant nation.
d) A great and dynamic economy.
e) A land of bright and full opportunities for all citizens.

The document goes on to state that Nigeria's philosophy of education, therefore, is based on the integration of the individual as a sound and effective citizen with equal educational opportunities for all citizens of the nation at the primary, secondary and technical levels, both inside and outside the formal school system . . . it has to be geared towards self-realisation, better human relationships, individual and national efficiency, effective citizenship, national consciousness, national unity, as well as towards social, cultural, economic, political, scientific and technological progress.

The national educational aims and objectives to which the philosophy is linked are therefore:

1   The inculcation of national consciousness and national unity.
2   The inculcation of the right type of values and attitudes for the survival of the individual and the Nigerian society.
3   The training of the mind in the understanding of the world around.
4   The acquisition of appropriate skills, abilities and competences, both mental and physical, as equipment for the individual to live in and contribute to the development of his society.

Two points need to be stressed. Firstly, with their high level of generality many of these aims and objectives are in the realm of pious hopes and their lack of precision has been the despair of many planners and administrators. One may argue that the interpretation of political targets in terms of practical educational objectives is by far the most important professional planning function of the ministry of education. Politicians who prefer targets that fire popular imagination must remember that targets must be translatable into workable propositions. They need to consider questions like: What specifically are 'the right types of values and attitudes', the 'appropriate skills' the students need to be taught to achieve states of self-reliance, national consciousness or self-realisation? Is the educational system sufficiently equipped with relevant material and human resources to realise these objectives?

Is there, or will there be a selection of specialised vocational curricula, specialised and technical secondary education? What are the likely financial implications? What educational structure will carry out the policies laid down?

Secondly, many of the aims and objectives are sometimes not consistent with each other or with established educational practices. 'Individual and national efficiency' may not be easily reconciled with equality; inculcation of a love for the land and respect for the dignity of labour may not square with the common practice in schools of punishing students by sending them to labour on the land. In countries like the Sudan and Nigeria where there is a wide gap in the level of educational achievement between the north and south, equality of educational opportunity can only widen the gap in educational development and lead to regional discontent. It is important, therefore, for policymakers to establish their priorities carefully. It is not surprising that Nigeria, which emerged from years of civil war in the 1960s and hopefully from military rule, is now giving priority to the creation of a 'free and democratic society', a united, strong, and self-reliant nation, with 'national consciousness' and 'national unity', even though the 1960 Ashby Report put most of the stress on education as an investment for economic growth and on the production of high level indigenous manpower to fill key positions occupied by expatriates.

National and regional priorities

In those countries of the Third World divided into states or regions each enjoying a large measure of independence in decision-making and where the financing of education is the responsibility of the central government, the regional or state plans which are expected to be drawn up within the framework of the national plans and embrace the national objectives, do not always reflect national priorities. Disparities between states which have achieved different levels of education take-off make it imperative for the less fortunate ones to occupy themselves with those policies which aim at redressing the imbalance. In 1971 the primary enrolment ratio in Nigeria was as in the table following:

Kano State	7.8%
North-Western State	9.8%
North-Eastern State	12.0%
Benue Plateau States	28.0%
North-Central State	20.0%
Kwara State	28.0%
South-Eastern State	61.5%
Western State	66.4%
Rivers State	62.5%
East-Central State	79.5%
Mid-Western State	86.0%
Lagos State	96.4%
Nigeria Total	44.0%

Source: 'Education Profile: Nigeria', The British Council, (mimeo, 1974, p. C9).

It is no wonder, therefore, that in the 1975–80 Kano State Education plan nowhere in the outline of objectives is mention made of national unity or national consciousness. Under the section entitled 'Policy Objectives', the plan reads: 'The broad policy of the Kano State government during the 1970–74 development plan was a general expansion of institutions and facilities, especially at the primary school level, with a view to increasing enrolment at all levels. This objective remains valid for the 1975–80 Development Plan . . . '

Pitambar Pant (1962) explains this regional problem in the following terms:

It is very difficult to carry conviction to people whose interests are at stake with the simple argument of national interest where thinking is confined to a short horizon of time and the alternative of letting the project go is to have no project for the region at all. In an educational plan, such disputes arise regarding the location of prestigious institutions and facilities, e.g. universities, colleges, central science laboratories. But the proposition would be seen in a different light if the needs of different regions were to be clearly anticipated in a perspective plan of say 15 years so that people of every region are able to find their own place in an overall and region-wise design of development with activities spelt out in space and over time. There could then be a reasonable chance to persuade them to await their turn in respect of their own share of projects which would be both to their benefit and to the benefit of the nation, instead of clamouring for others manifestly unsuited for their region. In this way region and national interest could be reconciled (cited in Guruge, 1969).

It is important for policymakers and planners to have a clear idea, at the commencement of planning, of the solution of those regional problems likely to arise. Education confers power and influence on individuals, as well as on regions within a nation, and education can and often is used either to maintain a balance of power between regions or to tilt the scale in favour of one region or another. Rowley (1971) argues that the concentration of Western education facilities in the southern and eastern parts of Nigeria during the colonial period gave special advantages in this kind of education to the Ibo people.

It was a factor which led to the employment of large numbers of Ibos in the bureaucracy serving in the northern regions and in areas that were far less prominently represented in the public services. This situation, he suggests, was probably one of the factors which led to the civil war of the 1960s. It is therefore important for policymakers to note that unless the discussion of a special approach to the problems of a region is absolutely necessary (i.e. when the development of a backward region is emphasised or the rehabilitation of a particular linguistic, racial or cultural group is considered to be of national importance), the plan should deal with the national picture.

Aims and objectives at the school level

Educational institutions must seek to establish their aims within a framework of national objectives or policies, a national curriculum or a national school structure. Some of these aims are universally applicable, including:

Primary level:
• Literacy, numeracy and communication skills.
• Character and moral training.
• Citizenship education.
• Manipulative skills.
• Ability to adapt to a changing environment.
• Learning to learn.

Secondary level:
• Preparation for higher education.
• Fostering of national unity.
• Understanding and developing national culture and national consciousness.

- Inspiring a spirit of achievement and individual worth.
- Imparting academic knowledge and skill, etc.

Different levels of education (i.e. primary or secondary levels) may embrace different objectives and with varying degrees of emphasis depending on the national structure of education and the opportunities available for further education at higher levels. For example, high level manpower may normally be produced by institutions of higher learning (universities, technical colleges, polytechnics, etc.). Where and when facilities at this level are either scarce or not available, the goals of primary and secondary education may have to be widened to provide basic skills in certain areas. Thus Tanzania's President Nyerere in his *Education for Self-Reliance* (1968) pointed out that since only a few of the country's primary school leavers would have the chance of going on to secondary school, and only a proportion of these would have the opportunity of going on to university, even if they could benefit from doing so, 'the education given in the primary schools must be a complete education in itself. It must not continue to be simply a preparation for secondary school . . . . Similarly, secondary schools must not be simply a selection process for the university, teachers' colleges, and so on. It must prepare people for life and service in the villages and rural areas of this country' (Nyerere, 1968).

However, what educational institutions do in practice may have little relationship to their stated objectives. Whereas the village head teachers may concern themselves with broad issues of relating the schools to the community they are intended to serve, the teachers who are confined within the four walls of the classroom, may define their aims in terms of the learning and the personal development they want their pupils to achieve – 'covering the syllabus' or 'passing the exam'. They have this obligation to the child and to the parent. There may be considerable discrepancies, too, between stated objectives like equality of educational opportunity, 'developing a sense of individual worth' and the hidden aims of a common syllabus. A school which for reasons of equality, lays down the same syllabus and theoretically the same educational treatment for all children leads, in spite of this, some may say because of this, to very unequal results. Failure to complete primary or secondary school may result in lowered self-esteem and a sense of failure on the part of the dropouts, or more appropriately, 'push-outs'. Because of the accepted legitimacy of the system, blame for failure may be imputed to oneself and be internalised, having a deleterious effect on self-images. Paulo Freire (1972) has described the way in which the schooling process impairs the self-confidence of students in generating new ideas. 'Almost never do they realise that they, too, "know-things" they have learned in their relations with the world and with other men . . . they distrust themselves' (Freire, 1972).

Other reasons for the discrepancy between the statement of objectives and educational practice might be explained in terms of the teachers in the system. C. E. Beeby (1968) has suggested that often a particular educational technique may fail largely because teachers are not qualified to implement it. He argues that 'there are two strictly professional factors that determine the ability (as distinct from the willingness) of an educational system to move from one state to a higher one. They are: a) the level of general education of the teachers in the system, and b) the amount and kind of training they have received'. J. S. Bruner (1965) has hypothesised that any subject can be taught in some intellectually honest form to any child at any stage of development. The vital question that must be asked in this context is, can it be taught by any teacher? When one comes down to the nitty gritty of classroom realities, when teachers operate and attempt to 'teach to the goals' they may arrive at a common conclusion that the goals or objectives themselves need review or modification or that they are impossible to implement. New Maths failed to be introduced successfully into Nigerian schools in the mid-1970s because the teachers were not qualified or trained to implement it, and equally important had no experience, as pupils, of such an approach to mathematics.

There is a prevailing dogma, too, that objectives at the school level must not only refer to intended changes in the learner; such changes, it is said, ought to be *measurable* as well. This view has been criticised on several counts, principal of which are, firstly, objective-oriented education may teach only those things which can be measured and ignore important aspects which are not measurable or difficult to measure. Some behavioural changes attributed to schooling are not always immediately observable but manifested only much later in the adult life of the learner. Second, the view ignores the individuality and autonomy of the learner. The student has a mind that questions, interprets and thinks, and the whole point about questioning, experimenting, researching, is that one can never predict in advance what the outcome might be. In a normal classroom lesson the ends in view, as Dewey rightly points out, are constantly changing as one gets nearer to them, the original goal is often transformed long before one reaches it.

Exercises

1 Discuss the role of interest groups in the planning of education in your country. Give some examples.
2 Differentiate between aims and objectives in education.
3 Distinguish between aims and objectives at the school level.
4 Discuss some of the factors which must be taken into account when considering aims and objectives at the different hierarchies of the education system.
5 Discuss the process of obtaining aims and objectives for the education system in your country.

IV

The process of
planning education

According to Y. Dror, planning is 'the process of preparing a set of decisions for action in the future directed at achieving goals by optimal means . . .' (Dror, 1963). This applies equally to all aspects of socio-economic planning including educational planning, as it embodies a functional analysis of the process of planning, plan formulation and implementation. In education, the fundamental task of planning is to organise the rational, efficient and economic use of a country's resources. However, this presupposes the adequate and clear definition of the planning environment. In this chapter we shall therefore outline the conditions, administrative requirements essential for planning, and the planning process itself. Finally, a brief analysis will be made of the factors affecting educational planning in Africa today.

Conditions for planning

Contrary to the misconceptions of most administrators and planning technicians, the power and ultimate authority to plan is the prerogative or exclusive privilege of the highest political authority in the land. Even where a separate planning ministry exists, decisions on priorities and alternatives are the responsibility of the highest authority. This applies to education planning as well as the planning of other sectors of socio-economic activities.

Once the decision to plan has been made at the highest level, however, this is passed to the central planning organisation which in most countries is usually a department of planning within the ministry of finance and economic planning or a separate ministry of planning or a national planning commission. The functions of such a central organisation are basically fourfold (Guruge, 1970):

1   It acts as the final co-ordinating authority amongst the different competing ministries, by preparing a macro-economic plan, indicating:
    i) The allocation of resources (money), men and materials available to the various units including education, during the plan period.
    ii) Investment objectives and their recurrent implications.
    iii) Developments in other sectors which will have a direct influence on education, for example agricultural and industrial expansion and the employment chances these will offer.
    iv) Likely claims by different sectors on the construction industries and others involved in such areas as the making of furniture, fittings and apparatus, and the capacities of these industries to meet such claims.
    v) The likely effects on education of restrictions on imports of materials.

2   It ensures the preparation by a competent body of a fairly comprehensive report on manpower requirements. Such a report, to serve educational planning purposes, should contain:
    i) Forecasts of manpower needs in the long, medium and short terms, at the national and possibly regional levels too.
    ii) Employment opportunities survey showing the types of skills and specialisation requirements.
    iii) Determination of the imbalances between present educational output and actual needs of the labour market.
    iv) Finally, giving general guidelines on the minimum educational qualifications that could be expected for the different types of jobs.

3   It constantly consults with educational planners to ensure the co-ordination of the education plan with those of other sectors.

A proper understanding of the role of the executive as shown above and the central planning organisation in educational planning is vital for the educational planning officer in the ministry of education.

4 It urges the government to take policy decisions relating to:
  i) The employment of expatriate personnel.
  ii) The trend of replacing expatriate personnel.
  iii) The emigration of trained personnel (i.e. brain drain).

Ministry of education planning organisation

The administrative organisation for educational planning in the ministry of education is usually of two types: a planning organisation and a planning unit. Between them, they are designed to perform the following two primary functions in planning:

  i) The orientation of policies relating to goals, targets and means of implementation.
  ii) The collection, processing and analysis of data required to guide decision-making (Gurunge, 1969).

The planning unit found in the ministries of education in most countries in Africa is in fact an internal administrative arrangement being limited to the collection, processing and analysis of data required to guide decision-making functions. Thus as an operational unit, it depends on policy decisions and directions passed down to it from above. It does not exercise any authority over the other units of the ministry but assists their planning efforts. It does not normally actively participate in the implementation of the plan, which is the responsibility of the administrative unit. It is thus basically a service unit.

However this must not be taken to mean that planning and administration are two distinct and separate functions. On the contrary, according to the International Conference on Educational Planning held in Paris in 1968:

The educational planning function must be integrated with the administrative structure; and the planning approach must permeate the whole operational service. The body responsible for educational planning must serve and not control; it should work parallel to, and through, the operative administrators. It is not its role to make decisions, but it should influence them, with an assessment of their implications (UNESCO, 1968).

However, if educational planning is to make an effective contribution to development, a more effective organisation is needed to supplement its efforts. Such a body should have a nationwide prestige and recognition conferred either by legislation or indirectly by the appointment to it of competent people. The functions of this organisation should be:

i) The formulation of educational development plans.
ii) The formulation and revision of regional plans where regional planning offices do not exist.
iii) The formulation of policies and instruments of policies with the ministry of economic planning measures needed to mobilise financial, material and human resources for the implementation of the educational plan.
iv) The evaluation of the progress of the plan periodically aimed at identifying factors retarding progress and suggest measures for dealing with them (Gurunge, 1970).

Two administrative pre-conditions are necessary to effect the above responsibilities: first, the planning organisations, in addition to constitutional and legal authority, should also possess sufficient political and social influence. Second, the operational services of other ministries which perform educational services should also be involved in the planning progress and represented on the planning organisation. It is worth noting, in passing here, that such a process might well operate in a more decentralised way, with teachers at school level involved in particular, in the implementation of policy planned at the centre.

African education planning bodies

The ideal organisation for educational planning fairly commonly found in African countries is an educational planning commission or board. The membership of such a commission is usually as follows:

i) The minister of education as chairman and his permanent secretary as deputy chairman.
ii) Senior officers of the ministry of education and other ministries associated with the national educational effort, representatives of professional bodies, teachers, parents and other interest groups.
iii) The planning unit of the ministry as its secretariat with the head of the unit as the secretary to the organisation.
iv) Other units of the ministry that normally provide support to the planning units such as the statistical, documentation, research, financial, supply and building and construction divisions will be expected to render similar support to the commission or board.
v) It normally also maintains fairly close liaison with the academic or educational services of the ministry and the central organisation/ministry responsible for planning.

In some countries, the role of such an organisation tends to be advisory to the minister of education. Thus the Regional Ministry of

Education Board in southern Sudan merely advises the minister on educational matters but has no legal or constitutional powers. Similarly, in Nigeria, the Joint Consultative Council (JCC) performs this role by advising the ministers of education of the Federation before they take decisions on educational policies and developments.

Apart from the central planning organisation in the ministry of education, planning to be effective, should take place at every level of policy and decision-making. A hierarchy of administrative organisations for planning, with clearly defined limits of authority and responsibility and extending right down to the institutional level is necessary.

Planning at the local level

The main obstacle to the implementation of such a process of participatory planning in most African countries, however, is the level of the educational qualification and experience of local and institutional administrators. Thus, local government councillors and officials are more often than not without any concept of the rudiments of planned national development, although this is rapidly improving. Nevertheless, a number of measures can be taken to guide planning at these lower levels by:

i) Familiarising all administrators with the essential concepts and techniques of planning.
ii) Providing a careful definition of functions, authority and responsibility of each planning organisation.
iii) Preparing and issuing clear-cut terms of reference and guidelines, especially in relation to national objectives and limitation of resources, and the detailed formulation of programmes and projects as a basis for planning at the local level.

It is only by the use of a hierarchy of planning organisation as suggested above, that planning can cope with the wide objectives of education.

Planning for planning

Once established, the educational planning organisation, that is the commission or board, has as a priority to plan for planning. Three areas should receive its attention:

i) A budget for the planning commission and the planning unit.

ii) Administrative limitations.

iii) The collection and processing of basic data.

Each of these areas must receive proper attention if educational planning is to be conducted on a proper basis.

Planning a budget

The size of the budget requirement of a planning organisation depends on the size of the educational system it handles. Apart from this, however, the recruitment and training of staff, the purchase of equipment and the organisation of surveys and studies so as to produce a satisfactory plan will require a fairly large budget. Nevertheless, such initial expenditure when properly utilised, will not only minimise costs but also contribute towards the maximisation of the efficiency of educational services.

Elimination of administrative obstacles

The main administrative limitation to educational planning is that of structural problems resulting from different agencies of the government being involved in education. For example, it is quite common for different ministries to handle some types of professional, technical and non-formal education. In addition, there could also be a system of private schools and colleges or even independent universities. In such a situation, to have a comprehensive education plan, the planning organisation has to be given powers to co-ordinate the efforts of all agencies involved in education, both governmental and private. Apart from being given such authority, if it is accepted that private agencies can run schools, then two issues must be resolved. Firstly, a way must be devised to ensure their adequate representation in the planning organisation. Secondly, a means must be found by which private agencies can participate in the planning and plan implementation processes. This is the area which presents the most obstacles to comprehensive educational planning, especially in situations where a number of fairly strong agencies have grown up. Fortunately, in most African countries, where the government has the major control over the educational system, the situation is less complicated.

Further operational barriers which the planning organisation needs to tackle as a prelude to planning include such factors as personnel, materials, methods and information, both legal and political. The organisation and modernisation of educational administration is therefore a process of dealing with these factors. This in turn will result in the creation of an atmosphere of change and innovation in which administrators would then undertake tasks for the overall improvement of the education system.

Data collection and processing

The collection and analysis of relevant statistical information concerning the educational system and related socio-economic factors forms the third phase in the preparation for planning. Such information provides the necessary foundation for the assessment of the existing situation of the education system and can also be used for making projections regarding the future development of the educational organisation. The types of data required for educational planning can be classified into three: those external to the education system, those internal to the ministry of education, and those obtained by analysis from the previous two types for specific planning purposes.

Types of data

1 *Data external to the education system.*
These comprise of:
  i) Information supplied by the central planning organisation (ministry of planning) on the macro-economic plan, and manpower requirements.
 ii) Demographic data from the census department.
iii) Information affecting the expansion of educational facilities, for example, the availability of land for buildings; the capacity of the building construction industry to meet the requirements of the education system for buildings; and the limitations of suppliers pertaining to the supply of educational equipment.
iv) Information collected from researches on traditional values, social and cultural prejudices and preferences, as well as political awareness and ideologies, relevant to education.

2 *Data internal to the ministry of education.*
This consists largely of statistics on:
  i) Schools and other educational institutions by level, accommodation, condition and expandability.
 ii) Physical plant and facilities, laboratories, libraries, playing fields, and athletics tracks.
iii) Pupils – age, grade and distribution according to levels and specialities.

iv) Class – size, location, distribution, etc.
v) Teachers – sex and age, qualifications, distribution and retrainability.
vi) Administrators – same as for teachers.
vii) Costs – by type and level of education, salary costs, building and costs of equipping.

The collection and analysis of such statistics are expensive in terms of time and energy spent in acquiring them. This can only be justified if they can be used in making decisions more realistically.

3 *Data obtained by analysis from (1) and (2) above for specific planning purposes such as:*
 i) Enrolment, drop-out, repetition and promotion rates, and age-grade analysis of pupils.
 ii) Excesses and shortages, training and re-training facilities for teachers.
iii) Distribution, adequacy and actual condition of school plant and facilities.
iv) Translation of forecasts of manpower in terms of educational qualifications and relating manpower needs to educational output.
 v) Unit costs and analysis of educational expenditure.

It is necessary, however, to stress that the collection, analysis and projection of such data are expensive undertakings and do not in themselves constitute planning, but are only tools for it. Hence the expenditure incurred on them can only be justified if they can be used in making decisions more realistically. Thus, John D. Chesswass has commented that:

The collection and processing of statistics consumes time and money, and statisticians are usually in short supply. Their services should therefore be confined to the purpose of producing material which is essential for the planning purpose (Chesswas, 1967).

This is still the case in most countries of Africa, especially as better paid jobs are usually available for such talents in the private sector.

Data requirement in established school systems
In an established education system the concern of educational planning and hence statistical data requirements centre on such factors as:

 i) National school-gap; enrolment ratios between different regions or states of the country, and further between local governments or zones within a state and even districts within the zone or local government area. Thus School Location Planning (SLP) and the statistics needed for it assume important roles (see Chapter 10).

ii) Statistics required for the analysis of educational financing, in terms of – government, external assistance, parental and other contributions.

iii) Data required for the analysis of costs in terms of unit costs by level and type of school, costs per unit of space by level and type of school, and by geographical area; teacher costs by level and type of school, qualification and experience and possibly geographical location.

iv) Statistics dealing with equity and efficiency aspects of educational planning. In a developing country, such as those in Africa, the main concern is with the equalisation of educational provision between and within regions of a country. To tackle this requires obtaining state-wide/region-wide statistics on:

   a) Recurrent grant allocations from the central government in terms of per capita and per pupil allocations.

   b) Average size of catchment area for primary and secondary schools between regions of the country.

   c) Participation rates between regions or states of the country in terms of distribution of enrolment and participation rates: by level of schooling, sex, and at the second level by type of school.

Thus, as a country starts on a firm foundation of its educational system, the focus of statistical data collection, as of planning, has to be on the even distribution of educational expenditure and educational facilities between regions/states and within them. This is important because national stability, cohesion and even orderly development in a developing country can only be assured when existing contradictions, ambiguities and lack of parity in educational provision and practices in different parts of the country, can be removed.

The planning process: formulation, implementation and evaluation

Once the necessary planning machinery, suitable administrative structure, and the collection, analysis and interpretation of data have been attained, we can then turn our attention to the actual process of producing a plan. This consists of four basic stages:

i) The formulation of education objectives for the plan.
ii) The determination and phasing of the targets to be achieved.
iii) The choice of strategies and policies to suit the targets.
iv) The establishment of guidelines to assist technicians in the arithmetical formulation of the plan.

These are the responsibilities of the educational planning commission/board/committee. In conducting the exercise, they have to take into account not only the statistical aspects but also the insights to be gained from the collection of more qualititative data, e.g. opinions and insights of teachers and parents, case studies from the field, etc.

Preparation of a draft plan

On the basis of the decisions of the planning committee/board, the planning unit then proceeds to prepare the *first draft* of the plan. This will basically be an elaboration and logical arrangement with the objective of:

i) Ensuring that programmes and projects planned have a measure of international consistency.
ii) Showing, through systematic costing and cost analysis, whether the resources allocated to education by the ministry of economic planning and finance is adequate or not.
iii) Suggesting an order of priority and pattern of phasing of various activities such as building construction, equipping and teacher training which normally precede the actual start of an educational programme.
iv) Demonstrating the economic feasibility of the plan and of specific projects within it by the application of such techniques as cost-benefit and cost-effectiveness analyses.

The first draft would be a confidential document meant only for the committee to enable them to revise targets, strategies and policies in the light of the work of the planning technicians. The task of the planning unit here is therefore twofold: to pin-point some of the issues to be decided; and in those cases which demand reconsideration because of such problems as feasibility, inadequacy of resources and consistency, suggest possible alternative approaches. The case for consistency in the plan is an important consideration, as has been forcefully argued by Anderson and Bowman.

Certainly, consistency is a requisite, if we mean by planning a realistic appraisal of alternatives and of possibilities and the development of strategies and tactics that are mutually supportive (Anderson and Bowman, 1967).

Besides the internal statistical consistency, the consistency of ideological goals and external consistency in relation to the macro-economic (overall) plan of the country are equally important.

In developed democratic countries, the *second draft*, incorporating the necessary revisions of strategies and policies, would be produced with the intention of informing and involving the general public, and all those in anyway likely to be associated with or affected by the plan.

However, the practice in most, if not all, African countries differs quite considerably from this. In a situation where the planning process has become established, and the education plan is being formulated as part of a national plan (for example, 5–7 years) the initial discussions and consultations over the first draft take place largely between the central planning organisation, (usually the ministry of planning, national planning committee, etc.) the cabinet, the ministry of education, and other ministries that will be intimately involved in the eventual execution of the plan such as finance, public works and the department of lands and survey. In such a case the education plan forms only one part of a number of other sectoral plans which have to be fitted into the overall national plan. Nevertheless, the detailed formulation of the education plan as a specialised activity, like similar sectoral plans in other fields of governmental activity, is normally left in the hands of planning technicians and administrators who are intimately conversant with the subject.

In those countries that practise a parliamentary democracy, once the first draft has been revised, the general public are usually informed on the presentation of the second draft of the plan to parliament for debate. In the countries that have one-party rule, it is the party's parliamentary caucus that first debates the plan prior to its presentation to the national assembly for formal approval. Under either system, public support for the plan is largely sought at the implementation rather than the formulation stage.

In the ensuing debate within parliament and outside it, that would normally accompany the presentation of the second draft, the role of educational administrators and planners as those officially involved in preparing and formulating the plan, is to provide an objective exposition of a number of factors:

a) The reasons for the choice of a particular alternative in preference to another.
b) The factors that prevent the adoption of a proposal which appears attractive at first sight.

c) The reasons for giving priority in a programme to particular activities and not others (Gurunge, 1970).

In addition, planners need to rectify any errors in data, wrong impressions and misunderstandings by members of parliament as well as supply further background information which may assist better comprehension of the plan.

As this stage is crucial to the overall plan of the government, there will be considerable lobbying involving members of parliament, political parties, members of government and those special interest groups who may be directly affected by the plan, such as the teachers, parents and even students. Other pressure groups, for example ethnic groups, who may feel that they have been neglected by the plan, especially in such areas as the location of projects, will also bring pressure to bear through their representatives as the plan passes through parliament. As a prelude to this, however, it is the responsibility of the planning unit to identify not only the principal points of controversy, but also suggest alternative solutions as well as indicate limitations imposed by resources, feasibility and the need for consistency. It is at this stage that various formal and informal discussions with different organisations and groups, including the chief executive or head of government, take place.

Consequent upon the discussion of the second draft by parliament and the attendant lobbying by pressure groups, the preparation of the *third* and *final draft* will require a new set of guidelines. These consultations form the most important part of the planning process. The aim in the third draft is therefore to produce a technically and politically acceptable document for which the prior concurrence of everyone concerned – pressure groups or lobbies, members of parliament and the government – has been informally obtained. Once this is done, then the final approval of the plan by parliament, either by itself or as part of the national plan, is more or less purely a formality.

Implementation

Once the plan has been formally adopted as an act of parliament, it now passes from the planning technicians to the administrators for implementation. The priority function of the administrators in the process of implementation is to organise an efficient system of information. As has already been pointed out in the preceding sections, in most African countries the generality of the population are not really involved in the formulation of development programmes, rather their co-operation is enlisted at the implementation stage. Education administrators need to educate the population on the objectives and targets, as well as the rationale behind the choice of priorities, so as to enlist their support and generate enthusiasm for the successful implementation of the plan. It is important to pay particular attention to innovations which are likely to affect children and allay the fears of parents over them. Frank and informed discussions with the parents of their fears and anxieties can be of great help. If the plan is well conceived and its formulation guided by sufficient consideration of popular aspirations, it should not prove too difficult to attract public support.

Public information

The head of the government, the minister of education and his senior administrators, should all be involved in the information campaign. It is also vital to enlist the support of traditional rulers and local public administrators throughout the country, in explaining the aims of the plan. All these agencies should utilise to the full any opportunities offered by the mass media, such as television and radio discussions, to assuage fears of the people and to highlight the advantages of realising the targets of the plan. Meetings of educational decision-makers and local people on such occasions as speech days at local institutions offer good opportunities for asking questions freely and answering them convincingly.

Participation of other organisations

Another important aspect of plan implementation is the question of the determination of ways and means through which the participation of local, religious/denominational or private agencies controlling education is to be ensured in plan implementation. In countries where a private school system operates parallel to, or in conjunction with the state system, a number of means ranging from laws giving the government, through the ministry of education, the power to approve and inspect schools and withhold grants-in-aid and so forth, is applied. Through such means it is possible to compel such agencies to adhere to the requirements of the plan.

Process of implementation

The third administrative function in plan implementation is to organise the process of implementation itself. In a situation where more than one governmental or non-governmental agency has a special role in the realisation of plan targets, then a machinery for co-ordination and liaison among them should be organised. However, where the situation proves too complex, then the application of modern management techniques such as the Programme Evaluation and Review Technique (PERT), Critical Path Method (CPM) and others, should be encouraged. These will be discussed in Chapter 8.

To ensure that plans are implemented in some countries, for example the Sudan and Nigeria, an implementation unit is created within the planning department to monitor the progress of the plan. In most other cases each unit of the ministry is responsible for the implementation of its projects.

Plan elaboration

The fourth administrative task in implementation is plan elaboration. This is normally a joint task involving the planning unit and the administrators as it entails a lot of detailed work. It basically consists of reducing the plan into component units for action by carrying out the following functions:

a) Programming.
b) Project identification and formulation.
c) Detailed time sequencing of project activities.

Although there are no readily acceptable definitions of what is meant by a programme or a project, according to Ananda A. Gurunge:

it may be convenient to view a programme as a group of projects which have to be accomplished simultaneously or in succession for the achievement of a specific objective or that it may be necessary to look upon a project as a conglomeration of related activities whose performance simultaneously or in succession is required for the accomplishment of a unit of work contributing along with others to the fulfilment of that specific objective (Gurunge, 1970).

Thus, for example, while the development of higher education may be a programme, the building of a university may be considered as a project which will involve a number of activities such as locating and siting the university; acquiring land and payment of compensation to the occupants of the piece of land; drawing architectural designs, costing and estimating, calling for tenders and selecting contractors, scheduling work, technical supervision, payments and equipping and furnishing it.

The activities envisaged in the plan have sequential and spatial distribution. While some can be carried out simultaneously, others cannot be started unless those that come before it are completed. Some activities have also to be undertaken on a national scale while others are organised on a regional basis. Thus plan elaboration for implementation entails not only the detailed analysis of the time sequence but also the regional distribution of activities.

Moreover, for implementation to be effective, it is necessary not only to delegate certain aspects of it to regional organisations and institutions, but this has to be accompanied by the delegation of authority and responsibility. This is normally best effected by the provision of a budget under the direct control of the regional offices or officers responsible for the execution of the particular activities assigned to them. In most countries in Africa, the traditional budget is the means of effecting this. Unfortunately, the traditional budget suffers from the defect that although it is prepared on the basis of programmes and projects, it normally shows only the spatial distribution of activities and not their time sequence. Consequently complications are often experienced in situations where there is under-expenditure during a particular year on a particular activity caused by delays in accomplishing another activity which was supposed to precede it or when the money is not released on time from the treasury. Except for certain capital expenditures, for which re-votes are usually made, the practice in financial budgeting is that all unspent balances in the budget lapse at the end of the financial year. To avoid such complications, it is necessary that a budget shows not only the spatial distribution of activities but also their time sequence and its preparation should be the function of the planning unit. Fortunately this is now becoming the practice in many African countries. The application of a Planning-Programming-Budgeting System (PPBS) could be introduced as an improvement in budget preparation, but this requires a certain level of sophistication in data collection and processing which many African countries have as yet not attained.

A more easily applied method, and an equally effective complement to the budget, is the construction of network models such as PERT and CPM (see Chapter 8). These could be constructed to show the responsibility, inter-relations and rate of progress of programmes, projects and activities. They should be constructed for the programmes and the projects under each ministry. It is, however, important that networks for administrative action should be modified and simplified and should indicate the administrative unit responsible for each activity. Similarly, modified networks could also be applied to the solution of such problems as the strength of staff required for each unit, identifying shortages in particular types of skills, equipment and materials which could contribute or cause delay in the project or programme. Thus the PERT or CPM, provided it is well modified and presented, has a great deal to offer.

Evaluation and revision

The review and evaluation of a plan forms the final and essential function in plan implementation. Such evaluation can be considered in terms of internal output and external efficiency. Internal output or productivity looks at the rate of progress made in realising the targets set in the plan. For example, if a local education department in a state of Nigeria were to make plans in the national development plan for the establishment of five junior secondary schools, then the evaluation of the internal output would consist of a review of progress made in various activities such as building and equipping the schools, recruitment and training of teachers and then the selection and enrolment of pupils in relation to the planned targets of these schools. In addition, the efficiency of the work done will be considered in terms of such factors as minimum cost, maximum utilisation of facilities and maximum benefit to the public. This is, however, confined to the examination of the efficacy and efficiency of administrative function performance rather than the objectives or targets themselves. This could in fact be considered as an efficiency measure and is similar to that for auditing accounts. The practice in some African countries is to entrust this to an *ad hoc* internal committee of the ministry itself, including the planning unit. The evaluation includes not only quantifiable targets but also such aspects as making decisions on changes in approach and quality.

Cost is an effective criterion of evaluation when alternatives in approaches are assessed against quantifiable targets. This is especially useful when considering the training of a few but specialised personnel, for example, ten science teachers annually. The decision whether to train them locally (if facilities existed) or abroad, would be weighed largely in terms of cost, but such factors as the quality of training and the benefits of being exposed to a beneficial foreign environment are equally important.

A second quantifiable criterion is the number of beneficiaries from a particular programme, project or activity. For instance, if it is planned to retrain teachers to tackle a new curriculum, or new aspect of an existing curriculum, then the decision whether to train them through weekend or vacation courses, or through a full-time course at teacher training colleges, or at university, would depend on the number of teachers who would be trained within the available funds.

This review of progress and evaluation of effectiveness of method and approach assist plan implementation in two ways: firstly, it is used to revise and adjust targets and strategies of the plan; secondly it helps in the preparation of measures to meet unforeseen problems or contingencies that might arise. It is characteristic of all plans to make allowance for revision and adjustment as implementation proceeds and new problems become apparent. Better solutions may also reveal themselves. It is therefore vital that such changes are anticipated and provision made to accommodate them. It is consequently important that the responsibility for making revision and adjustment in particular aspects of the plan be assigned to the appropriate administrative level at the outset of implementation.

The experiences gained in the implementation of one plan can be applied in the preparation of the next. This, however, requires that an effective feed-back system is established between the planning organisation and the operational level.

The above analysis shows fairly clearly that planning and plan implementation are closely related. It is therefore essential that planning officers and administrators understand each others functions and process of working.

The benefits of a plan document

A variety of advantages have been attributed to the production of a plan document (Williams, P.R.C., 1975). The production of a national, state or regional plan avails the country with the opportunity to set out the main national development objectives for a specified period ahead. It is also the time for the analysis of the available resources and the bottlenecks likely to impede the realisation of the desired goals.

First, the plan document may not only contain a statement of national goals, philosophy and values but more important, may provide a national sense of direction. Secondly, the preparation of the plan can be a period for the review of national performance and assessment of national resources potential and those already developed. Thirdly, by establishing quantitative targets for achievement, these become milestones of progress against which performance can be measured. Fourthly, in the process of plan preparation, greater realism begins to develop as the gap between aspirations and actual possibilities become apparent when costings of programmes are made. The usual promises of schools to crowds at public rallies by ministers and other politicians begin to fade away as the magnitude of the costs involved are shown in real figures.

Lastly, an overall national or regional plan shows clearly the relationships and interdependence of efforts and policies between sectors. The result is better co-ordination and ordering of priorities. Potential inconsistencies between policies in the different sectors are also more easily noticed. For instance, if the education sector plan stresses the ruralisation of the curriculum aimed at retaining the children and youth in the rural communities, while other sectors such as rural development and agriculture do not make commensurate efforts, then it is obvious that the education policy will be a failure.

All the above are useful benefits and explain why most governments in developing countries produce a plan document, although these theoretical advantages do not indicate the practical problems of implementation.

Factors affecting educational planning in Africa today: political, administrative and economic constraints

The foregoing discussions have tried to show the process of educational planning. However, the realisation of all these aims is not dependent simply on legal, staffing or technical conditions alone. Political, administrative and economic factors also bring considerable influence to bear on educational planning.

To start with, educational planners in Africa as elsewhere, have no power over the organisation of the national economy, neither are they responsible for establishing broad educational aims and objectives, nor wholly responsible for the actual implementation of objectives once they are set. The former are the prerogatives of the politician and the latter largely that of the educational administrator. As already explained, the role of the planners comes inbetween that of the politician and the administrator. Their concern is mainly the technical formulation of educational programmes for systematic implementation, according to priority, for the realisation of national educational objectives. The lack of proper comprehension of the respective roles of the politician, the educational administrator and the planning technician in the systematic development of education, have tended to affect educational planning in many countries.

Political constraints

In the political arena (Ruscoe, 1969) constraints on the success of educational planning arise from two basic factors: the lack of clear national educational aims and policies; and the failure to distinguish between the political and technical aspects of educational decisions.

Educational aims in many African countries are uncertain because no coherent national philosophy, setting out the goals of society and the role of education in it, has been worked out. What there is amounts to vague general statements dealing with manpower development and the fostering of national unity. This absence of explicit statements of national aims or overall national ethic, has meant that educational planning in reality has come to be based on what is known as the social demand approach. This demand, as already pointed out elsewhere, works essentially to satisfy private demands for education. Where education is free there is therefore heavy public subsidisation of education and the private benefit to individuals may in fact far exceed the social benefits to society at large. The result is to increase social inequalities as rich people and privileged areas are usually in a better position to take advantage of any educational expansion.

Another area in which political constraint is experienced in educational planning, is where there is a lack of distinction made between the political and technical aspects of educational decisions. This is the case especially where there is no separation between political and technical decisions, but both are in the hands of an individual or a small clique or group. They in turn ensure that many of the top appointments are political in nature, even though these positions would require technical competence.

Although there are no glaring instances of this nature in Africa, there are situations that come close to it, especially under military regimes with one-party structures. Where this occurs, then the development of the education system is hindered as many of the most competent and experienced personnel are forced to leave through frustration. Uganda under Idi Amin provides a good illustration.

Such fusion of political and technical decisions affects the educational planner in not only determining his area of competence but also the ways in which his work is to be used. This is best illustrated in the formulation of school expansion programmes. Under such circumstances, the location and siting of schools is not based on technical grounds, as for example the factors of school location planning – school-age population of an area, location and size of schools, and transportation facilities – but rather decided on the basis of political patronage. Schools are therefore located where a particular community, or its leader, is known to sympathise with the government even though the population size may not warrant a school. School resources, both human and material, could be similarly disbursed. These practices could easily distort and frustrate planning attempts at equity and the systematic approach to educational development.

Administrative constraints

A second major constraint upon educational planning is in the sphere of administration (Ruscoe, 1969). Educational plans for improvement and expansion are normally executed by the administrative division. This requires that the administrative system has the resources and capabilities to undertake the task successfully. Before it can implement the new programmes, however, it must show that it is capable of administering the existing system. This is where the administrative system in African countries constrains planning efforts. A number of reasons can be cited for this: first, in a number of countries, there was little knowledge amongst administrators about the workings of the planning unit and vice versa. This was particularly so because in the 1960s planning was then a fairly new subject. Its characteristics and requirements were consequently quite unfamiliar to many administrators. Planners who may have been recruited from the ranks of the younger teachers, or even fresh graduates, for training were largely ignorant of the realities of implementation in the field. In addition, the fact that planning technicians were largely confined to the headquarters, tends to divorce them from the prevailing situations in the rural areas. This lack of the proper appreciation of each others methods and problems results in constraints on planning.

Second, some education administrative departments may suffer from the lack of firmly laid down criteria for recruitment and promotion, such as , for example, competence. The promotion of individuals may consequently not reflect any high standards of competence but rather such factors as ethnic affinity or political loyalty. The result is that the system becomes staffed by lethargic and unimaginative officers, who concentrate on routines but do not make any attempt at innovation. They may also become drunk with their new found authority and power. Therefore plans which call for the initiation of changes and development are most unwelcome and have little chance of success.

Economic constraints

The third major constraint on educational planning and perhaps the most telling in its effect, is the economic constraint. The economies of most African states are at the mercy not only of world market price fluctuations but even such natural phenomena as the weather. The oil price escalations of the last decade have adversely affected the implementation of the socio-economic programmes of almost all the non-oil producing countries in the continent. The effects of the oil price hikes have been compounded by the fall of prices of such commodities as sugar, coffee, tea and cotton which form the bulk of the exports of African countries. For example, according to President Julius Nyerere of Tanzania: 'Tanzania had to sell 38 tons of sisal or 7 tons of cotton to buy a 7-ton truck in 1972. In 1980 that truck required 134 tons of sisal or 28 tons of cotton' (Newsweek Magazine, 1981: 40). Thus, ironically, while the price of oil was reaching unprecedented new levels, that of commodity prices was plummeting. This, and the major issue of debt repayment to international loan bodies such as the World Bank and IMF has led to drastic cuts in spending on a wide range of programmes, including education. Plans for the expansion of the existing education systems have had to be curtailed, while any plans for the introduction of major schemes, such as universal primary education, have had to be shelved indefinitely. Although this situation is no longer common in education systems at the national level in most African countries, it still exists at regional/state and local government or provincial levels where the education system is at a fairly early stage of development.

Furthermore, the administrative difficulties are compounded in ministries which are organised in such a way that sub-divisions or departments within the ministry are entrusted with handling some vertical and horizontal aspects of education, while no proper provision is made for co-ordination amongst the divisions. For example, a ministry may be so divided that primary and primary teacher education form a department which is almost autonomous, having the responsibility for the curriculum, administration, examinations and supervision of such schools. The effect of such organisation is that any changes that might be introduced into the primary curriculum cannot affect the system as a whole, as these changes are not allowed by appropriate changes in secondary schooling which is under a different department. This was the pattern of organisation in the Regional Ministry of Education in the Southern Region of the Sudan (Southern Sudan) from 1972–76. Once the shortcomings of the system was realised, there was a complete reorganisation in July 1976, aimed at ensuring proper vertical and horizontal co-ordination of the different departments of the ministry as well as the individual institutions. In Kano State, Nigeria, a new reorganisation was carried out in 1980, which went a stage further by combining administration, planning and finance all under the same directorate. This means planning, administration, and budgeting and finance are brought into close relationship, thus facilitating maximum co-ordination.

Exercises

1 Discuss the essential conditions in the process of planning education.
2 'The body responsible for educational planning must serve and not control . . . It is not its role to make decisions, but it should influence them, with an assessment of their implications' (UNESCO, 1968). Discuss.
3 Elaborate on the four basic stages involved in the production of a plan.
4 Discuss the process of plan implementation once the draft plan has been passed.
5 Discuss the essential factors that are said to affect educational planning in Africa today.

V

The role and functions of education strategies

The concept of strategy

In Africa, the development of education has assumed centre stage. Political leaders and quite a significant proportion of the masses of their followers, clearly appreciate its role in the development of a modern society. Consequently, the right to education is no longer considered the privilege of an elite or even a particular age-group. The aim is to reach more and more the whole of society. However, to realise the educational aims and objectives of the governments and individuals, requires that it is planned on a more rational and scientific basis than in the past. This demands: first, the deduction of educational objectives from aims approved in overall political policy and the harmonisation of educational objectives with those adopted in other sectors of national activity. Second, translation of policy objectives into operational terms which will result in concrete goals, and resources to be allocated. The success of this approach depends on a clear understanding of the relationship between policy, strategy and planning. The chapter therefore starts with a brief discussion of this relationship. It then goes on to explore the characteristics of educational strategies in developing countries, including Africa, in the recent past. Lastly, an attempt is made to analyse the obstacles to the development of effective strategies in the continent and suggestions made for the future.

Planning, policy and strategy

Change and its implications are now more or less fully accepted by the whole of society in most developed countries of the world. In these societies change has become simultaneously more rapid and more familiar than ever in the past. As a result, most institutions, be they government departments, private firms or welfare agencies, recognise the need for the deliberate contrivance of change, carried out through a rigorous process of anticipating change, plotting its course and shaping the change for the purposes of the organisation (King and Cleland, 1978). Thus terminologies such as 'long-range planning' and 'strategic planning' which denote approaches through which the future impact of change is assessed and integrated into current decisions, are in common usage.

In the developing societies, such as those of Africa, although governments are making strenuous efforts to orient society generally towards the understanding and acceptance of change, outstanding success cannot as yet be claimed for the effort. Moreover, such strivings are also hampered in many cases by the lack of proper comprehension by the decision-makers themselves and some of their immediate subordinates, of the logical relationship between policy, strategy and planning. An attempt will therefore be made in this chapter to elucidate this relationship, particularly in the field of education.

Policy and objectives

In the process of educational development as much as in other spheres of socio-economic development, policy formulation normally precedes the adoption of strategy; policies occupy the initial phase in the planning process during which fundamental choices are made by the responsible organs or individuals such as a political party, the cabinet or the ruler of a country, to guide national development efforts. Policies which in fact designate objectives or desired future states or 'destinations', can be stated in either qualitative or quantitative terms. They are usually broad or timeless statements as opposed to specific quantitative goals or targets. This is necessarily so because educational policy should reflect a country's political choices or options, traditions and values and its vision of its future. These cannot be reduced to merely quantitative targets.

To be useful and facilitate planning, policies should possess the following characteristics (UNESCO, 1972). First, they must ensure that the educational objectives selected fit in with the overall objectives of society; second, they should ensure that educational objectives are derived from aims approved in the overall political aims of the governing group, be this a political party, or a 'Revolutionary Council'; finally, it is essential that the chosen educational objectives are in harmony with those adopted in other socio-economic sectors of the country, or region/state in a federal structure.

Educational policy in order to satisfy the above conditions must be comprehensive and cannot be reduced to the proclamation of a few guiding principles. Its objectives must be specific and should include the following.

General objectives

General objectives, of a spiritual, philosophic and cultural nature, should reflect a society's idea of mankind. In black Africa, the best example of an objective in this category is the philosophy of *Ujaama* as expounded by President Nyerere's *Education for Self-Reliance* (Nyerere, 1968) for Tanzania.

Political objectives

Political objectives should reflect a country's major options for laying a firm foundation for its stability and future evolution. Nigeria provides a good example in this respect. The country's major concern, derived from the experience of the civil war, is to foster the development of a nation through the democratic process. Thus five main national objectives that provide the guiding principles in all spheres of national development have been stated as follows:

i) A free and democratic society.
ii) A just and egalitarian society.
iii) A united, strong and self-reliant nation.
iv) A great and dynamic economy.
v) A land of bright and full opportunities for all citizens (Federal Republic of Nigeria, 1981 (revised)).

The major obstacles to the attainment of these goals have been identified as the existence of uneven political and socio-economic development within the country. The creation of more and more states is one strategy being used to redress the existing imbalances. This, it is hoped, will assist in generating an even socio-economic and political development over all parts of the country. In addition, political and administrative posts at the federal level are, as far as possible, shared in such a manner as to reflect the federal character of the country. A similar approach is adopted in the location of industries and large-scale agricultural schemes such as the River Basin Authorities. In the education sphere, the launching of the universal primary education scheme in 1976 and the adoption of the National Policy on Education, are attempts to close the existing educational gap between the regions of the country.

Socio-economic objectives

Socio-economic objectives identify goals to be attained according to a certain idea of society and development. The Arusha Declaration of Tanzania, African Socialism of Kenya and the Humanism of Zambia are attempts in this sphere. The underlying aim in all three declarations or documents is the equitable sharing of the nation's wealth so that the population as a whole benefits. Interestingly too the documents illustrate the personal vision of the political leaders concerned.

Educational objectives

Broad educational objectives are those which aimed at objectives to be attained by the educational system, far exceeding its normal scope. The Nigerian case again illustrates this. According to the National Policy on Education, instruction at all levels of the education system has to be oriented towards the inculcation of the following values:

  i) Respect for the worth and dignity of the individual.
 ii) Faith in man's ability to make rational decisions.
iii) Moral and spiritual values in interpersonal and human relations.
 iv) Shared responsibility for the common good of society.
  v) Respect for the dignity of labour.
 vi) Promotion of the emotional, physical and psychological health of all children (Federal Republic of Nigeria, 1981:8).

Similarly, in Uganda, the national aims of education are to cherish and develop:

  i) Ethical and spiritual values based on self-discipline, integrity, service to others, personal sense of responsibility, and belief in the spiritual worth of man.
 ii) National unity, and the concept of the unity of mankind – respect for the rights of others; and acceptance of those with different religious, ethnic, racial or cultural backgrounds.

iii) Social and civic responsibilities of citizens and of government.
iv) Skills and knowledge for full participation and productivity in civic, social and economic affairs.
 v) Skills and knowledge for self-development and personal responsibility for continued learning.
vi) National, scientific attitudes and skills for the understanding of natural and social phenomena.

Lastly, the more strictly educational objectives are those approved for the different types and levels of institutions within the education system. Examples of this type are common in all countries. In Nigeria, for instance, four fundamental aims have been identified for higher education.

a) The acquisition, development and inculcation of the proper value-orientation for the survival of the individual and society.
b) The development of the intellectual capacities of individuals to understand and appreciate their environments.
c) The acquisition of both physical and intellectual skills which will enable individuals to develop into useful members of the community.
d) The acquisition of an objective view of the local and external environments (Federal Republic of Nigeria, 1981: 22).

When objectives have been determined and arranged in order of priority to form a co-ordinated whole, we then move from the policy stage to the strategic phase in the planning process.

The role of strategy in planning

That strategy is important in the planning process cannot be understated. Strategy defines the basis for all the further action steps in planning after policy formulation and objective setting. It can be thought of as the overall approach which an organisation selects to move it towards its objective. According to King and Cleland:

A strategy is a general direction, and even if the direction cannot be explicated precisely, it is most often greatly beneficial to have even an imprecisely defined general direction rather than none at all. This is so because even an imprecise, but well-understood, general direction can be translated into tactics or programs to move the organisation in that direction (King and Cleland, 1978).

For instance, an educational institution whose objective is to provide opportunities to population segments not now being served at all, for example, nomads, might do a number of things: introduce programmes designed to appeal to the specific segment, (nomads); open branch campuses in the areas of the particular population; or change admission standards to increase the likelihood of admitting members of the particular population group. Each of these would be a strategy, or general direction, in which the institution might choose to proceed.

The concept of strategy embraces three basic elements: integration of discrete aspects into a coherent whole; allowance for chance occurrences in the future; and the will to face and try to control that chance. Thus, strategy can be thought of as making the best use of the forces over which we have little or no control by using the forces which we do control. As such it can be developed at any level in an organisation. Hence under any set of conditions, strategy attempts to optimise the available effort or resources to gain some objective.

Strategy development is largely related to long-term objectives and macro-forces. Consequently, a specific strategy is usually followed over a long period of time, frequently years. Changes in strategy are normally only contemplated when some critical macro-force is significantly changing, e.g. a school system changing from a 6-5-2-3 to a 6-3-3-4 format; that is, the school system changing from one to six years primary, five years secondary, two years higher secondary, and three years university to one of six years primary, three years junior secondary, three years senior secondary and four years university.

The role and objective of strategy is to translate policy into conditional decisions, thereby determining action to be taken in dealing with the different situations as they arise in the future. Such transcription of policy objectives into operational terms assists in revealing concrete goals and resources likely to be needed as well as throwing light on the policies themselves.

The role of strategy in education

This role of strategy equally applies in the field of education. Hence before an educational system can develop, it is vital that a clearly thought out and defined strategy is advanced to guide its development. In the field of education, by the term strategy is meant an objective preparation for and regulation of education development. It includes the application and co-ordination of tactical lines of approach resulting in the attainment of ultimate objectives of education development. However, in order to meet educational policy requirements, educational strategy must possess the following threefold characteristics:

a) It must be global, covering all educational forms and levels.
b) It must be integrated into other systems of socio-economic policy objectives in which education has a role to play.
c) It must be reasonably long-term (UNESCO, 1972).

Thus educational strategy seeks to give an answer to the most elementary and general problems of the country's educational level during a given prospective period. It endeavours to provide answers to such questions as:

1 What are the goals of all the efforts in educational development?
2 Who and what hinder the attainment of these goals?

A set of concrete answers to these questions constitutes a strategic plan of education development. Furthermore, once strategies have been developed, they can be analysed for their potential effectiveness by posing such questions as:

1 Are objectives and strategies at cross-purposes?
2 Do the strategies anticipate future trends and conditions?
3 Are resources available to back up the strategy?
4 Is the timing of the strategy appropriate?
5 Is the strategy workable? (Brickner and Cope, 1977).

Strategy and tactics

It is, however, important to distinguish between strategy and tactics in educational development planning. Whereas strategy is a general course of action which an organisation pursues in order to achieve its goals, tactics refers to specific programmes which must be carried out for the successful implementation of the strategy. Moreover strategy, being long-term, is relatively stable and changes only as a result of major changes in the objective situation; tactics is subject to more frequent changes in response to partial changes in the prevailing situation. Tactics attempts to give answers to the question: what kind of procedure should be chosen in a particular given situation? And it is always being subordinated to strategy. Consequently, it is the most valuable tool of educational administrators, as it assists in implementing the goals envisaged in a strategic plan.

Apart from transcribing policies into operational terms, strategy provides planners with the opportunity to think and devise different possible ways to serve policy goals. Thus strategy is the central link in a continuum, starting with the detailing of policy and ending with the methodology of planning.

Programmes

Once the above situations are clarified, the next step is to lay down ways and means likely to lead to the realisation of the chosen objective, while making allowance for uncertainties and the time factor. Programmes constitute the ways and means of resource-consuming collection of activities that an organisation carries out in furtherance of its strategies and the pursuit of its objectives. In education these programmes would frequently involve physical development and other forms of expenditure on training or the purchase of equipment and other materials. Such programmes would then be implemented through specific projects such as the construction of 35 new secondary schools in a four-year plan period. Thus a project is defined as an identifiable activity of pursuing a specific goal with identifiable resources.

As resources are required to operate programmes, resource allocations are a basic choice element of planning. If programmes are to be implemented, money, people with specialised skills, facilities and other resources are required. The levels of these resource allocations to various programmes and to each project within it, must be decided as part of the planning process and stipulated in the plan.

The strategic plan should therefore identify all the varieties of resources required to accomplish strategic programmes. Such resources are ultimately measured in monetary terms and expressed in the form of budgets and financial plans. It is, however, necessary to guard against the danger of financial considerations overshadowing the true strategic aspect of plans. Successful planning therefore requires that there is harmony between policies, strategy and planning. This demands that policies are properly translated into decisions with clear ideas of the ways and means of implementing them. Strategy formulation should in turn be neither confused with policy nor with the planning phase but must have a clear view of the targets to be achieved. There should be a strict adherence to the logical process of moving from policy to strategy and then finally to the planning phase.

Educational strategy in Africa: past, present and future

Educational strategy in Africa has undergone a number of changes in the course of the past two decades. This has ranged from the initial emphasis on linear and quantitative expansion to the present more diversified stage.

In the post-independence period of the early-1960s, national educational strategies in almost all the countries were based largely on linear and quantitative expansion of the existing system. By linear expansion is meant the development of an education system on the basis of its earlier evolution, without qualitative aspects, such as types, levels and structures being affected.

The Addis Ababa strategies

The Addis Ababa conference of African states on the development of education, held in May 1961, laid the basis for these strategies. The conference made the following recommendations for the development of education in the continent for the period 1961–80:

  i) First level education, providing essentially general education and extending over six years, should be universal, compulsory and free.
 ii) Second level education, comprising of three years of general education, followed by three years of more specialised education, should be provided for 30 per cent of the children who complete first level schooling.
iii) Third level or tertiary education, should be provided for 20 per cent of the graduates of the second level.
 iv) In addition, the aim should consistently be the qualitative improvement of education at all levels that takes account of child development, the African environment and cultural heritage, as well as the demands of technological progress and economic development (UNESCO, 1961).

These strategies were basically aimed at the satisfaction of the fervent desire of the people for education and the need to accelerate the reorientation of education to the economic, social and cultural needs of each country. It was apparent to the leaders of education that if these aims were to be realised, then education must be open to all without discrimination. This means that special efforts must be made for the education of such disadvantaged groups as women, nomads and the mass of the adult population.

This broad thinking approach was influenced by research findings on the contribution of education to socio-economic progress in the United States and Europe at the end of the 1950s. In Africa, the report of the Ashby Commission on Education in Nigeria proclaimed these findings (Ashby Commission, 1960). The conference reiterated that:

Education does not have for its primary purpose a greater production of goods and services. The purpose of education is to broaden understanding, so that men may make the fullest use of their innate potential, whether spiritual, intellectual or physical. Education would have value even if it contributed nothing to economic development.

However,

Economists have always recognised that increases in the national income are attributable not merely to the accumulation of physical capital, but also to the improvement of human capacity through research, education, inventions, and the improvement of public health, as well as to better organisation of human relations . . . there is no disputing that expenditure on some forms of education is an investment which more than pays for itself even in the narrowest economic terms (UNESCO, 1961).

As is clear from the above, although the need for the development of education as a social service to be based on social demand was at first given equal weight as that for the development of the economy, nevertheless as the conference proceeded, the balance shifted in favour of economic needs. Thus it was stated that:

Education needs to be planned continuously in relation to economic development. The manpower needs arising out of the development plan should be surveyed and the supply of the skills of various kinds integrated with expected needs (UNESCO, 1961).

This suggested shift in emphasis was based on a number of considerations. First, it was recognised that national development in most countries would inevitably be a long-term process. Hence a necessary pre-condition for modernisation and the eventual establishment of fair societies depended on the development of those skills required for the organisation of a stable society which would lead to the establishment of a firm economic base. It was therefore more sensible to concentrate expenditure, initially at least, on the types of education likely to promote economic growth. This would then in turn eventually facilitate the provision of a widely diffused education as a human right for the spiritual, intellectual and physical liberation of man. Second, it was at this time that the concept of educational planning was rapidly gaining acceptance and aid donors, both bilateral and international organisations, wanted to promote its adoption by the African countries. Thirdly, the concept of integrated development planning, in which educational development is geared to economic requirements through the manpower forecasting approach, was equally gaining ground as the recipe for solving the enormous developmental problems of what was then blatantly termed 'undeveloped' or 'backward' countries.

Although it was stated that every country should aim at universal primary education within two decades, the strategy placed immediate priority upon the development of secondary and higher education.

Economic development is highly dependent upon skills of the sort which are taught in institutions to students of 15 years of age and upwards. It is of the highest priority that an adequate proportion of the population receives secondary, post-secondary and university education; this should be put before the goal of universal primary education, if, for financial reasons, these two are not yet compatible (UNESCO, 1961).

The Tanzanian strategy

The Tanzanian approach to educational development following independence is a classic illustration of this strategy. After independence, the country's interim plan and that of 1961–64 gave priority to the development of secondary and higher education (Ta Nga Chau and Calloid, 1975). The aim, in both plans, was to train the manpower needed for the gradual replacement of expatriates employed in the country and to provide the manpower requirement for economic development. The target was to achieve self-sufficiency in skilled personnel by 1980. Because of the priority accorded to the secondary and higher education sectors, it was not possible within the limited resources available to the country, to achieve any rapid increase in primary level enrolments in the period covered by the two plans. Efforts at this level were concentrated instead on qualitative improvements. This took the form of reforms of the structure of primary education, improvements in the teacher-qualification profiles and a radical change in the curriculum.

Nevertheless, by 1962 the average continental percentage GNP allocation to education was 2.3 per cent, while some countries – Kenya, Mauritius, Sudan and Uganda – averaged over 3 per cent (UNESCO/ED/191,1962). By 1975 the average figure had risen to 4.3 per cent and some of the countries such as Botswana, Zambia, Sudan, and Côte d'Ivoire, to mention only a few, had even reached the target figure of 5 per cent. The result of this brave effort was the development of not only the secondary and tertiary sectors of education, but the rapid expansion of primary education in most countries. Thus by 1976 some countries like Tanzania, Nigeria and Kenya had embarked on the universalisation of primary education. In many countries annual budgetary expenditure on education had risen on average from 14 per cent around 1960 to about 20 per cent in 1975 and even up to 30 per cent in some cases.

However, these glowing figures were not without their undesirable side effects. By the mid-1960s, two factors began to show themselves: the growing competition between school leavers, particularly those less qualified, for paid employment, and the dissatisfaction of rural youth with village life and the resultant increasing rate of migration into the urban centres.

For example, a study conducted in Kenya by the Christian Council in 1960, showed that out of about 150,000 primary school leavers only 90,000 could hope for further education or employment (CCK and Christian Church Education Association, 1966). A similar study in the then Western Region of Nigeria in 1967 revealed that at best only about half of those completing either primary or secondary schooling could hope for non-agricultural jobs (Muhammad, 1975). Nevertheless, the influx of youth into the urban areas continued unabated. The results of these studies began to usher in a growing awareness that the development then being followed, with its concentration upon modern industrial and commercial development in urban centres, acted as a magnet, luring rural youth away from the villages thereby producing disparities and social divisions between these centres and rural areas.

Furthermore, in the early-1970s there was a steady decline in agricultural production, especially after the prolonged drought covering a wide belt of the continent, stretching from the Sahelian region of West Africa to Ethiopia and Somalia in the north-east. This placed additional strains on the towns as many rural dwellers were forced to move there once they lost their livelihood in their rural communities.

These factors forced a change in development strategy. In the economic sphere, there was emphasis on rural and agricultural development which has continued. In Nigeria, for example, the federal government declared first 'Operation Feed the Nation' in 1973, followed by 'The green revolution' 1979, backed by easy credit terms for farmers and the provision of agricultural infrastructures and inputs.

In the field of education, there was emphasis on technical education and various attempts at the ruralisation of the curriculum and emphasis on rural crafts. While technical education was aimed at enabling the graduates to contribute directly to industrial production, ruralisation of the curriculum aimed at preparing and orienting primary school-leavers to accept to live in and participate in the improvement of their rural communities. This was coupled with the development of mass adult education, with stress on health education and functional literacy. Tanzania's rural health education and Kenya's non-formal education programmes provide good illustrations. In Nigeria, there has been considerable effort by some state governments on rural electrification and the provision of clean drinking water aimed at attracting small-scale industries to rural areas and thereby retaining rural youths and adults in their communities through employment in such industries.

Thus African governments and leaders are now acutely aware of the necessity of improving rural areas and the quality of basic education provided there. It is there that the vast majority of the country's population live and it is also there that food and other cash crops are produced for the sustenance of the whole country. Improvement of rural amenities and provision of paid employment are also vital if the present tide of youth migration into the urban areas is to be reduced. This will, however, require a proper comprehension of the obstacles that have resulted in the present limited success of socio-economic development strategies, including educational planning. If quality rather than quantity (see Hawes and Stephens, 1990) is to be a priority in the 1990s and beyond, educational planners will have to begin by taking a fresh look at the obstacles that confront them.

Obstacles to the development of effective strategies

As already discussed in the preceding sections, educational strategies in most African countries have been changing constantly. A number of factors have contributed to this lack of constancy in strategy development.

To start with, it soon became apparent that the inherited colonial education system was grossly inadequate to meet the objectives of economic and social development of a society aspiring to full nationhood. This was, however, to be expected. The existing system, being established with the express objective of providing an elitist cadre of manpower destined for a position of privilege in the lower echelons of the colonial hierarchy, could hardly do otherwise. In addition, the linear expansion approach based on the existing system, invariably adopted in most countries at the initial stages of independent development planning, not only exacerbated the elitist nature of the system, but also turned it into a symbol of prestige and power, associated with the ruling groups that had started to evolve at this time. Soon, a wide gap was created between the educated class and the masses of the people, and similarly between educational aims and national needs.

Second, the targets set in national plans for economic and social development did not reflect national aspirations and needs at the time and hence failed to motivate appropriate response from the education system. Moreover, the development strategies, including educational plans, were frequently developed in isolation, without due regard to the interdependent and interacting relationships of the different sectors. For example, in some countries while attempts were made at the ruralisation of the curriculum, particularly at the primary school level, there were no commensurate efforts at the development of infrastructural facilities and inputs in agriculture, or the provision of basic amenities such as drinking water and health and community centres in rural areas. Consequently, the isolated efforts and investments in the education sector did not produce the expected impact.

Third, within the education system itself, reforms tended to be undertaken in piecemeal fashion without a proper conception of the totality of the goals and state of the educational process. The reforms also lacked coherent integrated educational objectives and were neither hierarchically arranged in a proper order of priority, nor stated in operational terms. As a result, it was difficult to adapt them to suit different environmental conditions, population groups and local communities that made up the country. Such aspects as non-formal and adult education, were either neglected or not given the proper emphasis they deserved. Some of the reforms on the other hand, were often too exotic, unrelated to the needs and realities of the situation and therefore ineffective. The integrated rural education centres (IRECS) suggested by the World Bank for the southern Sudan, immediately after the end of the civil war, based on the development of the Bush school system of the missionary societies in the colonial era, is an apt example.

Eight years after the centres were first suggested, none of them is functional, while in the meantime the cost of establishing them has escalated. This is because the circumstances under which the Bush schools functioned were quite different from those that obtained after the long period of the civil war. Before the war, villages were well established and peaceful, with a proper network of roads linking them to the towns. This was not the case after the war. In these new conditions the implementation of the IRECS as originally envisaged, proved very difficult.

Fourth, the administrative structure of the education system is frequently not based on the proper assessment of the political, social, cultural and economic realities of each country. Most African countries, for historical reasons, have problems emanating from regional differences in traditions, languages and culture and frequently compounded by differential levels of modern development. Yet, the structure of the education system, and this is also true of the political structure, has tended more frequently than not, to ignore such realities. Emphasis on central control and direction, invariably from the capital city, with a resultant over-bureaucratisation of planning, has been the order of the day. The result of this unrealistic approach to the development of administrative structures has been the chain of political instability and often outright chaos that has plagued the countries of the continent. In the field of education this is reflected in the constant failures of reforms.

All these point to the need for a re-orientation of the approaches to the problems of socio-economic development generally, and education in particular. In the education sector, changes in plan-strategies are necessary if a measure of real progress is to be achieved.

The first strategy is decentralisation of administration and planning of the system (Mohammed, 1975). The present largely centralised planning and administrative systems which are a permanent feature of the education system in most African states are not conducive to generating and sustaining community efforts at regional and local levels. These require making suitable and adequate institutional changes, to enable local communities at different levels to participate actively in both planning and performance of those tasks that can be most usefully undertaken at this particular level. The success of such an approach, however, requires that the institutions must be designed to encourage the free and active participation of members of local communities. This would then gradually evolve into effective self-reliance. The experiences of decentralisation in Nigeria and to some extent in the Sudan, indicate that provided that there is a healthy economic base, this approach can bring about real progress and a sense of active involvement.

Second, it is important that national objectives in education should be clearly stated; objectives are a crucial input in the design and structure of the education system. They also determine such aspects as curricula, knowledge, skills, values and attitudes, that the education system is expected to inculcate. Generally, educational objectives, (as we have already seen, cover the areas of personal, economic, social and moral, as well as political development. Where emphasis is placed will depend on the social situation of a particular country. The areas to be emphasised must, however, be clearly spelled out, to make the planning task easier. It is, nevertheless, important to stress that schools acting alone cannot achieve much. Education policy must be backed by commensurate changes in public policy and social environment.

Thirdly, there is a need for a strategy of redesigning the existing structures of the education system in African countries. As already stated, as a result of the worsening economic position of most African countries due to price fluctuations of their primary agricultural exports and declining food production, most countries find it impossible to expand their education systems at all levels. A clear example is lack of realisation of the goal of universal primary education by 1980 as envisaged by the Addis Ababa plan of 1961. It is still, however, imperative to try and achieve primary education on a universal basis on the grounds both of equity and of national interest. It is important that all children should have the opportunity to have, at least, a basic education to enable them to compete fairly for opportunities for further education.

Although the organisation of general education is normally demarcated into two levels on the basis of the traditional division of life cycles into those of childhood and early adolescence, there is no worldwide uniformity in the length of these two levels. There is, moreover, no special merit in having the duration of first level education of six or seven years, which is generally the case in most African countries at present. By reducing the length of first level education, to say four years, it will be possible to achieve the universalisation of first level education.

Fourth, a new strategy of educational restructuring should attempt to include all education of school-age children and those beyond this age within its ambit. This means the system should be multi-dimensional, encompassing a variety of courses, including both full-time and part-time. It should be so organised that movement between full-time and part-time, as well as between study and work is facilitated. The aim should be to achieve a work-oriented education and education-oriented work. Provision should be made for dropouts to join the non-formal education system. The formal system should also provide some part-time courses from which those actively engaged in the labour force could benefit. The success of such a system as proposed here would require the rational and equitable distribution of resources between formal and non-formal, full-time and part-time, education. The two aspects should also be viewed as an integral part of the same national system.

Finally, as far as possible, specialisation should be delayed to the later stages of the third level. In view of the long lead time in education and the comparatively higher cost of specialisation, it is wise that no specialisation should take place at the second level and the first degree stage of the third level. The curriculum at these stages should instead be broad based and diversified. Specialisation, where necessary, should be confined to courses of one or two years. This approach would make it easier for planning to respond quickly to unforeseen changes in manpower demands.

The same approach should be followed in technical-vocational education. Here, the concentration should be on the production of lower and intermediate level manpower rather than higher level manpower. Moreover, the bulk of these should be in agriculture and rural technologies, as agriculture is the mainstay of the economy of most African countries. As with general education, technical-vocational education should also be planned as part of both formal and non-formal education, directly related to the vocational needs of local communities. The strategy should be to make technical education work-oriented and to reach as many people as possible. This means the programme should be concerned with the real-life situation within the locality. In this way, the skills provided in such schools will be placed in perspective.

Exercises

1 Discuss the relationship between policy, strategy and educational planning in your country.
2 Compare the educational strategy of any two African states over the past ten years and say which of them has been more successful in achieving the national educational goals and why?
3 Discuss the contention of the Ashby Commission on Education in Nigeria that 'Education does not have for its primary purpose a greater production of goods and services'.
4 Trace the changes in educational development strategy in your country over the period of the past decade or over the last three national development plans.
5 How far would you say the educational strategy in your country has adhered closely to the strategy laid down by the first conference of African Ministers of Education at Addis Ababa in 1961?

PART II
METHODOLOGIES FOR PLANNING EDUCATION

VI

*Major approaches
to educational planning*

The importance of human resources

It is now generally accepted that it is the human resources of a nation, not its capital nor material resources that ultimately determine the pace and character of its economic and social development. The education system constitutes the principal mechanism for the development of the necessary human knowledge and skills. Thus, in most developing countries, it is strongly believed that the quantitative expansion of the educational opportunities holds the basic key to national development. African countries are no exception. All the countries of the continent have committed themselves to the goal of universal primary education as soon as resources can permit. Though strenuous efforts are being made to expand educational facilities at the secondary and post-secondary levels there is an equally strong commitment to improve the quality of education provided. Towards this end, various educational planning approaches developed in the industrialised countries have been applied in an attempt to make the development of the education system more efficient and effective. These include the concepts of human resource development, social demand, manpower requirements and the rate of return. In this chapter we therefore not only outline the basic characteristics of each model but also examine some of the main problems associated with its application in a developing area like Africa. It has to be borne in mind, of course, that these are only models and serve to illustrate the problems and advantages associated in using them. In reality a government may well take a pragmatic approach, selecting ideas and strategies from all or none of these.

Human resource development

According to Frederick F. Harbison: 'In broad terms, human resource development is the process of building the knowledge, the skills, the working abilities and the innate capacities of all the people in a society' (Harbison, 1973). Elsewhere he has argued that:

Human resources, . . . constitute the ultimate basis of the wealth of nations. Capital and natural resources are passive factors of production, human beings are the active agents who accumulate capital, exploit natural resources, build social, economic and political organisations, and carry forward national development. Clearly, a country which is unable to develop the knowledge and skills of its people and to utilise them effectively in the national economy will be unable to develop anything else (Harbison, 1976).

Although the experiences of the OPEC countries in recent years cannot make us agree with this statement in its entirety, it does not detract from its basic truth. The experiences of three countries, namely the US, the former USSR and Japan, in their development process provide concrete evidence to underscore this statement by Harbison. We shall examine the experience of each country in turn.

The experience of the US

In a study based on the analysis of input-output of investments in education in the US, Theodore W. Schultz calculated that the total investment in human capital formation or the total accumulation of human skills considered as wealth in the US from 1900 to 1956 rose from 9 per cent to 34 per cent of the total investment in physical capital. According to Schultz, the rate of return of this investment expressed as a stock of capital or total accumulation of wealth in 1956 dollars, amounted to $180 billion dollars for 1930 and $535 billion dollars for 1957. Thus the increase in the stock capital was $362 billion between 1929 and 1957 (Schultz, 1963).

Assuming that all of the costs of education were an investment in future earnings, Schultz prepared three estimates of returns on these investments. The lower two estimates showed a return of 9 per cent and 11 per cent. These two rates applied to the increase of $362 billion capital stock or total accumulated wealth, show a growth in the national income from education of slightly less than $33 billion, or $40 billion respectively. This amounted to either 16.5 per cent with 9 per cent as the rate of return or 20 per cent with 11 per cent as the rate of return of the total growth on the basis of an increase of $200 billion in the national product or output.

This finding by Schultz is supported by the studies conducted by Edward F. Denison based on historical comparisons. In his study, Denison found that 21 per cent of the economic growth in the US between 1929 and 1957 could be attributed to education (Denison, 1962). He further confirmed these results for several Western European countries (Denison, 1967). Several studies made in the US in the 1950s lend credence to these findings of Schultz and Denison (Abramovitz, 1956; Kendrick, 1954; Solow, 1957).

The experience of the former USSR

In the former Soviet Union, the rate of return on investments in education largely centred on the work of S. G. Strumilin. According to him: 'In 1960 the total national income in current prices equalled 145 billion roubles. Not less than 33.7 billion, or 23 per cent of this, can be ascribed to the raising of the qualification of the population' (Strumlin, cited in Huq, 1975). This is confirmed by a study of V. A. Zhamin who reported that: 'Approximately 27 per cent of the national income in 1962 can be ascribed to investment of resources in education and the consequent increase in qualifications of labour' (Strumlin, quoted in Noah, 1969). In addition S. G. Strumilin has even calculated the labour productivity accruing to a person as a result of education. According to him:

The labour productivity (or productive capacity) of the persons having had four years of schooling exceeds that of illiterate persons by 43 per cent, the labour productivity of persons having secondary education by 108 per cent and of persons having university education by 300 per cent respectively (Strumlin, 1924, cited in Huq, 1975).

Thus, these Soviet studies concur with those of the US.

The case of Japan

The contribution of education to economic development in Japan has been undertaken by the ministry of education itself. The ministry of education study, based on the analytical study of Theodore Schultz and covering the period 1935–55, indicated a high rate of return on investment in education. According to the study:

Though in 1960, the value of the stock of educational capital was 18 per cent (7,110 billion yen) of the value of the stock of physical capital (39,800 billion yen), it yielded proportionately greater return. During 25 years from 1930 to 1955, the increase in the educational capital was estimated to have contributed 25 per cent of the increase in the national income, i.e. 70 per cent of the 37 per cent increase in the national income (Huq, 1965).

This Japanese study therefore lends further support to the studies in the US and former USSR. The studies together demonstrate the significant contribution of human capital to national development. They also have the following implications for development planning. First, that human capital formed through the agency of education has proved to be an active agent of economic growth. In each of the three countries, the productive value of educational investment exceeded that of physical capital, at least for the periods under study.

Second, although investments in education have been found to be generally productive, nevertheless, it would be wrong to infer that investment in any type or level of education regardless of the socio-economic needs in a developing country would be productive. Moreover, investment in education has to be combined with investment in physical capital in a mutually supportive manner.

Third, the study of the education system of the former USSR demonstrates the value of general education, provided this has a substantial content of mathematics and science. Such an education, provided it is well designed, develops the skills not only to learn other skills but also the ability to analyse and solve problems and cope with a new situation.

Finally, the experience of the former USSR also indicates that it is possible to have a satisfactory fit between education and manpower needs. It is similarly also possible to integrate educational and economic investments in such a way that both sectors can move forward in a mutually supportive manner.

Education and the mobilisation of human resources: a re-assessment

Some of the major researches which underpinned the popularity of human capital theory have been discussed above. In the late-1950s and early-1960s education came to be viewed as a 'crucial' agent for the rapid economic growth of national societies. The theoretical framework on which this view was based came to be known as 'human capital theory'. The human capital theorists argued that formal education is highly instrumental to the production capacity of a population. In other words, increased levels of educational provision would lead to increased GNP per capita. This argument was buttressed by 'correlations between GNP and educational provision across countries and within-country comparisons of educational level, occupation and economic status . . . as evidence for the causal link between education and economic growth'. Furthermore, through residual econometric studies, large amounts of the unexplained increase in national output overtime, when known factors such as improvements in technology and capital investments have been accounted for, was attributed to improvements in the quality and quantity of human capital (Schutz, 1961; Denison, 1962; Harbison and Myers, 1964; Becker, 1964; Bowman, 1980). Thus human and physical capacity were equated as providing the key to economic growth and rapid development. Supplements to these studies were provided by a large number of individual level analyses in which comparisons of lifetime earnings were made with educational levels (Psacharopoulos, 1973, 1980). Hence, on the individual level, more education was associated with more income, while at the societal level, an educated population was considered a productive population.

The reasoning for the arguments proceed as follows: first, for any economic growth and development to occur, there must be improvements and greater efficiency of technology because higher technology results in greater production. Second, the skills and the motivation for productive behaviour in the use and employment of technology are imparted through the agency of formal education. Hence an investment in education, so the argument goes, is an investment in the productivity of the population.

This was buttressed by numerous studies that showed consistent patterns between levels of education and economic levels of development among countries. Thus Harbison (1973) showed that school enrolment ratios at all three levels are considerably higher for the advanced than the less advanced countries. He therefore contended that in spite of the many difficulties and critical issues involved in trying to use education to bring about development, education remains a major component of human resources.

In 1980, Theodore Schultz, one of the originators of the theory, in his Nobel lecture, maintained that: 'a fundamental proposition documented by much recent search is that an integral part of the modernisation of the economies of high and low-income countries is the decline of the economic importance of farmland and a rise in that of human capital – skills and knowledge' (cited in Fägerlind and Saha, 1983). He then went on to emphasise the importance of improving population quality in order to enhance economic prospects. He stressed that 'education accounts for much of the improvements in population quality' (p. 642).

Change in the perception of education in the 1960s and early-1970s

In the late-1960s and early-1970s, however, the role of education to promote economic growth became more difficult to defend, particularly as a result of widespread unemployment amongst the educated in such countries as India and Pakistan. In fact, contrary to expectation, the unemployment rate amongst the educated was higher than for the less educated. For example, secondary level graduates suffered more unemployment than either illiterates or the primary educated or the university graduates (Blaug *et al.*, 1969; Turnham, 1971). This increasingly became a common pattern in most countries of Africa in the 1980s (e.g., Egypt, Nigeria, Ghana, Kenya). The possibility of social disorder resultant from mass unemployment amongst youth cannot be ruled out. The appearance of other phenomena on the scene added to the feeling of scepticism about the benefits of education so glowingly portrayed by the politicians and planners in the early 1960s: 'qualification escalation' in the labour market (Dore, 1976a); rural-urban migration as a result of the rural educated seeking the golden fleece (Caldwell, 1969); the well-known 'brain drain' of high-level qualified manpower from the Third, to the First World countries and later, from the non-oil to the oil producing countries (Godfrey, 1976); irrelevance of the curricula of educational institutions (Hawes, 1979; Lewin, 1981); the fear that the 'hidden-curriculum' of schools tended to produce docile and obedient students to pass exams but was destructive of creativity, initiative and independence in the work place and the political sphere (Illich, 1974: Dore, 1976a; Bowles and Gintis, 1976; Lewin, 1980); and finally, the capacity of the education system to bring about social and economic equality in the absence of fundamental economic restructuring came into question (Carnoy, 1977; Jallade, 1977; Colclough, 1978; Fields, 1980). These widespread doubts about the impact of education coincided with general doubts about the concept of development itself. There was a demand that development should not only emphasise the levels of GNP and economic growth but also the distribution of income. Consequently, the promotion of economic and social equality became a central feature of development and an increasingly important goal of the education systems.

Criticisms of human capital theory

A number of criticisms have been levelled against human capital theory. A fundamental criticism focuses on the underlying assumptions of the theory itself. The theory, for example, assumes educated labour market perfection in which the better educated person would get the better job. However, reality shows this to be otherwise with many graduate unemployed chasing jobs traditionally the preserve of the lesser qualified. A second criticism is that supporters of the theory, despite acknowledging that other factors such as job satisfaction and the reward structure contribute equally to worker productivity, insist that education remains the most important factor and the most amenable to human intervention. Third, human capital theory, like modernisation theory, holds that individual characteristics determine economic growth, thus de-emphasising the significance of the role of social structure in promoting development. The nature of international relations is likewise ignored, thus attributing differences in levels of development between countries, advanced and less advanced, rich and poor, to the internal characteristics of each country.

Fourth, radical critics (e.g. Bowles and Gintis, 1976), while accepting the investment value of education in promoting productivity, point out that education, particularly in capitalist societies, tends to maintain the status quo by creating a docile and adaptive workforce which serves the needs of the existing power structure of the economy. In this way, they argue, it may in the long run turn out to be detrimental to the continued economic growth of society. Fifth, the methodology of human capital theory is not completely satisfactory. Human capital theory uses linear equation models to show that gains in productivity (measured as GNP) over a period of time, can be explained in terms of known factors such as improvements in technology and other forms of capital investment. The unexplained gains in productivity (the residuals), after accounting for the known factors, are attributed to improvements in the quality of 'human stock'. However, the basic fallacy in this reasoning is that the size of these residuals in the human capital theory linear models can be the result of many factors (Fägerlind and Saha, 1983). Nevertheless, there is no doubting that human capital theory has greatly influenced policies concerning educational and development strategies over the past several decades, particularly those of international organisations such as UNESCO, OECD and the World Bank.

Keith Lewin, Angela Little and Christopher Colclough (Prospects, 1983), after reviewing the research evidence on the impact of education on a wide range of development factors such as agricultural productivity, modern-sector productivity, income equality, non-cognitive outcomes, health and fertility, concluded that there was considerable evidence for the positive association between education and these development goals. There was also, however, evidence that education was not always a sufficient condition for change. What is therefore required are integrated investment policies, because there is enough positive evidence to suggest that education interacting with other factors, in combination, produce an impact on productivity, or on attitudes. Thus, despite its waning popularity, human capital theory still has some validity when viewed in terms of education combined with other factors. We now turn to the other relationships of the social demand approach to educational planning.

Basic characteristics of social demand

The social demand approach is essentially responding, as far as resources permit, to anticipated future demand for education from pupils and parents. The method thus emphasises that the essential objective of educational policy is to meet the needs of its customers – the parents and pupils. Hence, although it is called a social demand approach, it is in fact a private demand approach.

The fundamental characteristic of this approach is that the expansion of the education system depends on the aggregate or sum total of demand for places (Williams, P.R.C., 1974). Projected enrolment figures at a preceding educational level consequently provide the basis for forecasts of future demand for places at particular levels. Also, the fact that policymakers are invariably keen to ensure that the 'index of opportunity' or the ratio of moving from one level to the next, is not reduced over time, tends to give the impression of education being based on social demand. In fact where any temporary deterioration occurs as a result of say, introducing universal primary education, serious efforts are made to restore the old level, although this may not always be so easy: secondary education is far too expensive.

The example of Ghana has been given, where a substantial increase in primary intake built up in the period 1961–69 as a result of the introduction of universal primary education in 1961. Thus between 1965 and 1969 the chances of a primary leaver getting a secondary school Form 1 place dropped from 15.8 per cent to 10.9 per cent. It was the timely intervention of the ministry of education which set out a policy objective of restoring the former ratio, backed by a programme of secondary school expansion, that saved the situation from further deterioration (Williams, P.R.C. 1974).

Problems of social demand

The concept of social demand for education, however, is not a very objective one, as it can be quite easily manipulated by the public authority itself. The level of demand can be controlled by such factors as the system of financing education, by variation in the shape of the education structure and the situation of the labour market. By varying the admission procedures or the charges for education, it is possible to diminish or increase public desire for education.

Furthermore, exclusive reliance on public demand as a guide to policy can easily result in a conservative approach to the process of educational planning itself. In a situation such as those prevalent in many African countries where educational provision is more or less a government monopoly, planning on the basis of public demand can easily come to mean 'more of the same'. The frequently expressed concern with 'falling standards' in a situation of rapid expansion may be a manifestation of this. The danger is the reduction of educational planning to the level of simple arithmetical manipulation of calculating rates of educational expansion and the resources needed for it.

In addition, as the social demand approach is basically an approach of satisfying private demand for education, the heavy subsidisation of education, as is the case in most African countries, means that private or individual demand and private benefits will far exceed the social or community benefits of educational expansion. The likelihood will be that the more wealthy members of society and the already educationally advanced areas will benefit even more from the provision of education, as such groups are usually more articulate in pushing their interests. Consequently, this will amount to favouring more those better off areas and privileged social groups, thereby increasing social inequalities.

Lastly, in most African countries, there already exists an historical legacy of differential provision of education. Planning on the basis of social demand would simply amount to increasing the yawning educational gap between the coastal areas and the interior. The West

African region typifies this situation, whereas the opposite is the case on the East African coast. Moreover, the aggregate of private decisions as demonstrated by the school location practices of missionary societies in many countries in West Africa, failed to produce a rational school map. Besides, educational planning involves the consideration of orderly development on a long-term perspective. This cannot be achieved if the development of education is to be based on the unco-ordinated private interests of individuals. Although educational planning in a developing area like Africa should attempt to reconcile private and social interests, nevertheless, the needs of society must always take precedence.

The inadequacy of the social demand approach therefore called for other more reliable methods of gearing educational development to meet the economic and social development targets of a nation.

Manpower requirements and educational planning

The development of planning approaches in education has resulted largely from the interests of economists and policymakers in the contribution of education to economic and social development. Moreover, as we have seen in the preceding sections, the productivity of a workforce depends on the level of its knowledge and skills. Hence the attempt to measure the contribution of education to economic growth and calculate 'the rate of return'. Manpower planning is one such measure.

Manpower planning or forecasting, is basically an attempt by economists to ensure that labour of the right volume, quality, type and combination to meet the social and economic objectives of a country or organisation, as specified by the growth targets, is available. To achieve this demands that the education system is geared to future trends of economic and employment requirements.

Preparation of projections

The normal procedure in making such forecasts may be thought of as consisting of five stages. First, a projection is made of the level of output for the target year(s). Second, projections of the expected level of output per worker are prepared, and this in combination with stage one, are used in the third stage to project the total number of workers required. In the fourth stage, the occupational composition of the expected labour force is derived. Finally, the educational level(s) appropriate to each occupation are identified.

Three main methods for preparing projections of output, employment and occupational structures for each industry or sector of the economy are frequently used. The first of these, which may be referred to as the historical approach, consists of the analysis of data on past behaviour in order to quantify the relationship which existed between aggregate and per capita output on the one hand, and the pattern of manpower usage on the other. The second approach, termed the structural approach or analogy approach, may take one of two forms; one centres on the home economy, the second is related to advanced economies elsewhere. In each case, the approach involves the comparison of the pattern shown by the most advanced sectors with that of other sectors. In projections, assumption is made that in future years the remaining sectors will tend to reproduce the pattern currently displayed by the most advanced firms or industries.

The third or survey approach, calls for the collection of information from various firms or sectors concerning the behaviour, over the forecast period, of the expected output and employment. Information so obtained would then be aggregated and checked for internal consistency prior to being used in the preparation of estimates (O' Donoghue, 1971). These steps will be examined in more detail in later sections.

As we have already seen, the abundance of natural resources and the amount and utilisation of physical capital are not sufficient by themselves for the economic development and prosperity of a country. Hence, the interdependence between the supply of qualified manpower with the appropriate levels of knowledge and skills and economic growth. The result, was the spread of interest in manpower forecasting (Blaug, 1970).

Reasons for the popularity of manpower forecasting

In the developing countries, including Africa, the manpower forecasting approach to educational planning has been popular for a number of reasons. First, it apparently provides definite guidelines and hard data for educational planning. Second, educational planners are interested in linking educational expansion to the manpower requirements of a growing economy. Forecasts of manpower requirements therefore provide an external justification and legitimisation for educational expansion, which then become part of the investment in national development. Education is not, therefore, viewed as valuable in itself but as a producer of skilled manpower.

Third, economic planners believe that setting targets for GNP eventually leads to the translation of the output targets in the form of the manpower structure required for the different levels of output. Fourth, manpower forecasting helps to reveal the existence of shortages and surpluses of manpower in a country. Such an imbalance between demand for and supply of manpower is undesirable both from the individual and social point of view. Individuals without jobs suffer from loss of earnings, morale and status. Economic growth may also be held back by shortages of trained manpower. Fifth, those responsible for manpower deployment, such as the ministry of labour, as well as vocational counselling, value manpower forecasting as providing a scientific basis for their activities.

Finally, national manpower surveys and projections have helped to focus attention on the nation's dependence on expatriate manpower and have therefore provided a framework for speeding up the localisation of many occupations (UNESCO, 1968). But what are the sources of data that are applied in manpower requirements assessment?

Sources of data for manpower forecasting

The basic data for manpower forecasting are obtained through a national census. A properly structured census should provide such essential information as the breakdown of population by occupation, by educational level and by age and sex. A comparison of information from one census and the next, provided these are held on a regular basis, would reveal a clear relationship between education and occupation.

A second source of manpower data is through a sample survey of population. Here skilled census staff select an area of the country and ask census type questions relating to occupation and educational attainment, age and sex of the population.

Establishment surveys form the third method of obtaining information on manpower requirements. This is a routine function of the Civil Service Commission which surveys the numbers and efficiency of the civil service. Personnel in the public service are tested from time to time and on the basis of the results of such tests, decisions are taken on whether to promote, downgrade or even possibly dismiss serving public officers. The role of the Civil Service Commission is thus to assess the numbers and performance of the civil service in relation to national needs, and thereby provide manpower planners with information regarding government manpower requirements.

A survey of manpower in industry is yet another source of information for manpower planning. Businesses are asked to indicate the qualifications of their personnel and the employment structure of their firms and to make known their short-term and possibly long-term requirements. It must, however, be pointed out that short-term forecasts of individual employers tend to be either over-optimistic or over-pessimistic. When business is doing well or booming, employers will say that they need a large number of employees because the assumption is that demand is going to increase and with it heightened competition for available manpower. However, when business is depressed, the opposite considerations obtain. The manpower authorities therefore have to moderate these views in order to get at the true picture of the situation. Apart from data provided by the sources discussed above, a further comprehension of manpower requirements can be obtained through the systematic analysis of the prevailing relation between education and the job market.

Analysis of the existing situation of education and employment

In order to have a fairly accurate assessment of the relation between education and manpower development, the educational planner must have a good grasp of the problems of national development beyond the confines of the educational sector. A knowledge of the problems of population growth, unemployment and underemployment, the issue of incentives in critical skill areas as well as the absorptive capacity of the economy is vital (Sokorov, 1968).

Population distribution and trends: implications for education and manpower

Before embarking on the analysis of the education-employment situation, it is necessary that the educational planner is familiar with the analysis of population distribution and trends. This involves an understanding of such factors as:

i) The annual rate of population growth.
ii) The age distribution of the population and particularly those under 14 years, that is, the school-age population. In Africa the school-age population may extend to include those up to 18 years.

iii) The approximate size of the active population, that is those aged between 15 and 64 years.

iv) The present and future size of the labour force and its growth rates in the traditional (agricultural) and modern sectors, and the factors which determine the participation of various groups in the labour force.

All these factors have implications for education and manpower development. The proper comprehension of the above factors can assist in tackling two problems. First, it can help in the evaluation of occupational needs and the capacity of skill-forming institutions. In other words, manpower requirements can be more accurately determined and appropriate programmes of formal education and on-the-job training devised to meet them. Second, targets set for education and training can be more closely related to the absorptive capacity of the economy. What this means is that education and training, both formal and non-formal, should be provided in those areas which are necessary for national development. This is crucial if the provision of education on the basis of social demand with its resultant redundancy and unemployment amongst the educated is to be avoided.

The relation of formal and non-formal education in manpower planning

A second important area of analysis for educational planning is the relation between formal and non-formal education. A careful examination of the benefits of pre-employment training in technical fields of various kinds in schools and on-the-job training in these skills must be made. As far as possible, private employers should be encouraged by means of incentives to give on-the-job training in specific skills to meet their own requirements. This is cheaper and more efficient. The planning of non-formal education could play an important part in national development in African countries, provided it is geared to specific needs.

At the primary level, the greatest defeat, as far as the link between education and employment is concerned, has been the inadequate harmonisation of primary education with rural development. The primary curricula has continued to produce candidates for secondary schools and urban employment. It has failed to provide basic education that would orientate primary leavers to become efficient farmers. Hence the continual exodus of the young to urban centres in search of modern sector employment. It is, however, hoped that the recent awareness by many African governments of the importance of rural development and the emphasis on the 'green revolution' will at least reduce, if not halt completely, rural-urban migration trends.

University education and high-level manpower in educational planning

A third area deserving of close scrutiny is the relationship between university education and high-level manpower. Although university education is absolutely essential in certain occupations such as university teaching and medical doctors, this is not the case in respect of all jobs. Is it necessary, for instance, that every secondary school teacher should have a degree? Isn't a Higher School Certificate (HSC) plus one or two years in-service training, just as efficient? For example, in Nigeria, holders of the Nigerian Certificate of Education (NCE) largely man the secondary schools in most parts of the country. As Mark Blaug has argued, for each job there is a minimum educational qualification below which the task in question cannot be carried out at all, but above which additional qualifications have no economic value (Blaug, 1970). For instance, it would be a waste of resources in an African country for a graduate teacher to teach in a primary school at present. In many parts of Africa the problem of chasing after paper qualifications has assumed quite serious proportions. The consideration of how much general education and how much on-the-job learning should be associated with each level and type of employment is therefore essential, for both realistic educational and manpower planning.

Incentives, education and manpower planning

Finally, the question of incentives is another important area to consider in the analysis of the relation of education and manpower planning. For although we can estimate the manpower needs for various qualifications, it is not always easy to induce people to prepare for and engage in such occupations. This is because salary scales and other non-monetary incentives in many African countries, have continued to reflect colonial traditions and heritage. Where there has been any serious departure from this pattern, then it has been largely as a result of pressures from organised labour in the form of trade unions. Yet, according to A. R. Jolly, the functions that earnings incentives are supposed to perform in a developing society are to:

i) Attract recruits into the training which prepares them for occupations important for development.

ii) Attract trained nationals into the occupations and places where they are most needed for development.

iii) Help to keep nationals in these occupations and places.

iv) Attract expatriates from abroad to fill key specialist posts until qualified nationals become available (Jolly, 1968).

But the incentives differentials between professionals and sub-professionals and technicians are so great that they do not fulfil the first three functions enumerated above. If anything, they serve to increase the aspirations of sub-professionals and other lower level cadres of qualified people to seek professional, graduate level qualifications. For example, in 1980, HND polytechnic graduates in Nigeria demanded that they should be recognised as engineers on a par with university graduate engineers. This is in spite of the clear differences in entry qualifications, course content and structure. They feared the consequences of being labelled as technicians rather than professional engineers. At about the same time, students of the advanced teachers colleges in the country demanded, and won from the government, the right to proceed to university immediately on completion of their courses rather than serve for two years in the schools as was previously the case, before being sponsored on in-service. The fundamental reason behind this demand was the acute awareness that as NCE graduates they would not enjoy the same level of incentives as their colleagues who were university graduates, even if in terms of competence and productivity many of them were far better. The wide differentials in incentives between professionals and sub-professionals and technicians has therefore given rise, particularly in the West African region, to a serious chase after paper qualifications.

It would appear that in many African countries it is not a person's productivity that determines the level of incentives that he enjoys but rather the qualifications he has. The result is what has been called the 'diploma disease' (Dore, 1976), which is a reflection of developing country reality. In these countries the rule would seem to be: it is not what you can do but rather what you have. This outlook completely contradicts the purposes of incentives as a tool for development as reiterated by Frederick Harbison.

In the strategy of human-resource development, the purpose of building incentives is to encourage men and women to prepare for and engage in the kinds of productive activities which are needed for accelerated growth. To accomplish this, the compensation of an individual should be related to the importance of his job in the modernising society. It should not depend upon his level of formal education, the number of degrees held, family status or political connexions. And the relative importance of his job should be based not on tradition or heritage from colonial regimes but on an assessment of the manpower needs of the developing economy (Harbison, cited in Jolly, 1968).

Estimating future manpower requirements

Gross National Product (GNP) by sector method

The basic assumption of the manpower requirements approach to educational planning is that there is a direct relationship between manpower growth and growth in output. In other words, it is an attempt to estimate for some future point in time (e.g. 1999) the stock of skills of different kinds that will be required to produce the expected or desired level of output of goods and services.

It is possible to make reasonably precise estimates of the numbers of graduates needed at each level and in each field of specialisation provided one knows:

a) The number of persons required in each occupation in the economy for any future year.
b) The present number of persons in each occupation.
c) The annual number of withdrawals from each occupation due to death, retirement, or movement out of the labour force.
d) The annual number of separations from one occupation and accessions to another as the result of job changes.

Parnes MRP method

One of the foremost methods of manpower forecasting approaches is the Parnes MRP method (Parnes, 1962). The method has been widely used and was first elaborated by H. S. Parnes in his work on the Organisation of Economic Co-operation and Development (OECD's) Mediterranean Regional Project (MRP). This was an attempt to produce educational plans for Portugal, Spain, Italy, Yugoslavia, Greece and Turkey in the 1960s. The main stages are as follows.

1 The Gross National Product (GNP) target in the current development plan is taken as a base.
2 The target GNP is broken down by sectors (agriculture, transport, education, health, etc.), and even further subdivided by industries (rail, air, shipping, road haulage).
3 The output of sub-sectors or industries is then converted into labour requirements using an average labour-output coefficient (relationship or ratio). It may, for example, be found that in health, for every £20,000 of services produced, 10 workers (doctors, nurses, orderlies, cooks, etc.) are needed on average, whereas the same amount could be produced by only five workers in some other industry. The calculation of labour-output ratio may be based on the current economic situation of the country which may

be assumed to continue unaltered; or an attempt may be made to estimate changes on the basis of recent trends in the country or on the basis of the experiences of a more developed country at the same stage of development.

4   This is then followed by the division of the labour force for each industry or sector into mutually exclusive occupations (Senior Agricultural Officer, Agricultural Officer, Extension Officer, foremen, clerks, laboratory technicians, etc.) Thus if the agricultural sector output is expected to be £100 million, on the basis of this, we may be able to calculate the total number of employees and how many of each category. Again this can either be based on forward projection of the existing occupational structure or allow for changes on the basis of recent trends or on the experience of other countries.

5   Requirements for all the different industries are then totalled.

6   The numbers required in each occupation are converted into educational requirements by the application of a standard qualification, or level of formal education to each occupation (Blaug, 1970; Huq, 1965).

Conversion of estimated manpower requirements into education programmes

Three further steps are necessary, after stage 6 of the Parnes MRP method, in order to change the estimates of manpower requirements into educational programmes.

1   To start with, our target manpower needs for 1995 have to be divided into survivors from the base year (e.g. 1990), and the balance of new outputs needed in the period 1990–95. These are calculated in terms of the different categories of educated manpower.

2   Secondly, the total output covering the whole plan period has to be phased into a programme of yearly outputs. In calculating this, various factors must be taken into account: wastage from the new outputs and from the existing stock; and the need to ensure balance between manpower requirements and manpower stock. It is equally important to ensure that the flow of new recruits is balanced with the rate of demand by the target date.

3   Thirdly, the required flow of graduates from the education system must be translated into various inputs of the system – courses, buildings, curriculum, materials, teachers and student enrolments.

It is therefore clear that unless the developments have been initiated well in the past, it is quite impossible to make a significant achievement within the short period of five or seven years of a medium term plan. It takes at least two or three years to plan a new course and facilities, and another three years to erect buildings and train teachers, and a further three years before students can begin to graduate from the course. The alternative may be to have a crash programme using makeshift facilities, but even here there is a limit to what can be achieved. A practical option is to retrain existing manpower in certain fields of scarce manpower even if they are due for retirement, or continue to use expatriates in such fields, provided, of course, that funds, in the form of foreign exchange, are available for this.

ILO *classification of occupations*

Manpower surveys in most countries nowadays apply the four major elements of the International Labour Organisation (ILO) International Standard classification of occupations which has 45 occupational categories with a large number of occupations within each category. The four classes of occupations are:

i) Class A: university degree or equivalent.
ii) Class B: secondary education with one to three years of training (non-degree such as a diploma) following Higher School Certificate (HSC).
iii) Class C: secondary plus technical training for one or two years, at certificate level, but below a diploma.
iv) Class D: full primary education plus practical training.

In carrying out these classifications, it is essential that educational authorities and manpower planners have a common understanding of what the classifications mean. Experience from some African countries shows that it is quite possible for sharp disagreements to occur between the ministry of education and manpower surveyors. For example, in Tanzania while the manpower surveyors wanted to place primary school teachers in class C, the ministry of education maintained that these teachers should be in class B. It is therefore always advisable that a particular ministry being surveyed, should, through its planning unit, be fully involved in such surveys, otherwise economists and manpower planners may pass value judgements with far-reaching implications for the education system.

Critique of the manpower requirements approach to educational planning

In criticising the usefulness of the manpower forecasting approach two distinctions need to be made: criticism of the inherent problems in the approach itself; and particular mistakes that may be made in the practical application of the method. Here we shall look at the former.

1 Non-economic approach

In assuming fixed relationships between production levels and skill needs, the manpower requirements approach appears to say that skill requirements must be met irrespective of the cost of producing the skill and of employing it. This does not reflect reality, however, with the production of skills often playing a reduced role, particularly in times of economic hardship. Moreover, the market always adjusts through price mechanisms to surpluses and shortages.

2 Rigidity

Most manpower planning approaches seem very inflexible. The assumption is made, for example, that a fixed amount of labour is used per unit of output in each industry. But actual comparisons between firms show wide differences in labour employed to produce a unit of output. Similarly, they work on the basis of fixed proportions between different kinds of workers within an industry. Again, however, a wide variety of practice is actually observable. The manpower forecasters further assume a rigid relationship between their defined occupations and educational qualifications. The reality is that many jobs are poorly defined in terms of their exact content and precise qualifications for their proper performance.

3 Qualification instead of quality

By concentrating on formal qualifications, manpower forecasts seem to forget that some people are totally unproductive even if qualified. The assumption that one can assess the differences in the productive capacities of individuals purely on the basis of their courses and qualifications without any work experience, and that the problem is quantitative rather than qualitative, is highly questionable.

4 Vocationalisation

The manpower approach tends to emphasise the knowledge and skill content of courses (cognitive domain) rather than attitudes and values (affective domain). The effect in education, if adhered to strictly, would be to undervalue flexibility and diversity that may derive from more general skills and instead concentrate on specialisation.

5   Passive role for education

By making the demand for education to be derived from economic targets, the manpower requirements approach seems to imply a passive role for educationally skilled people who are simply needed to staff economic enterprises and not as the creative people who can manage and develop them. The assumed fixed relationship between output and qualifications seems to deny the possibility that education would actually speed economic growth. Yet this vision offers no wholly acceptable explanation of the relationship between education and productivity that has been even quantified by researches.

These criticisms do not mean that the manpower requirements approach should be abandoned. It is still vital to anticipate the potential manpower shortages that could prove to be an obstacle to the development of a particular industry or sector. In addition, it can assist in advising students of future employment prospects so that they choose those options and courses that can lead to marketable skills.

Problems of manpower forecasting in African countries

Manpower forecasting in any developing country faces many technical problems, amongst which are:

a)   How to obtain adequate data for assessing the present manpower stock and its educational profile.

b)   Making reliable projections of national economic growth, in the face of great uncertainties regarding export commodities and external assistance. The present economic situations of many African countries such as Zaïre, Sudan, Tanzania, Ghana, Liberia and many others is a clear example of this.

c)   Establishing a valid relationship between a given rate of economic growth and the supply of manpower for its realisation.

d)   Assessing the vast area of employment and potential employment, particularly in the rural areas, where the majority of the population live. People in the rural areas are not usually covered by studies which focus on 'high-level' manpower needs as the Nigerian studies show (Tables 6.1–6.4); yet they need to be taken into account in educational planning.

e)   Translating conventional employment classifications, based largely on the experiences and practices of highly-developed countries, into educational qualifications that are relevant and feasible in the context of African countries.

National manpower projections: basis and impact in Africa
Large numbers of manpower projections have been conducted in various African countries. One of the most well-known was the Ashby Report on Nigeria in 1960. The Ashby Report may be considered as the starting point for using the manpower needs as the basis of expansion of higher education in the country. Its impact on the national educational system can be seen from Tables 6.1a, b and c, 6.2, 6.3, 6.4 and 6.5.

Table 6.1a: Primary school enrolment and enrolment ratios, Nigeria 1975/76 – 1987

Year	Primary school age population	Primary school enrolment	Enrolment ratios (%)
1975/76	13,330,651	8,185,547	46.3
1976/77	13,574,583	8,100,324	50.2
1977/78	14,027,307	9,887,961	70.3
1978/79	14,389,449	10,798,550	75.0
1979/80	14,760,828	12,117,483	82.1
1980/81	15,141,926	13,777,973	91.1
1981/82	15,533,043	14,311,808	92.1
1982/83	15,934,311	14,876,808	92.1
1983/84	16,346,060	14,383,487	88.0
1984/85	16,768,032	13,025,287	77.7
1985/86	17,292,187	12,914,872	75.1
1987	19,333,078	11,540,178	59.7

Source: Primary School Enrolment, FME, in Report of Eleventh Conference of Commonwealth Education Ministers Oct–Nov 1990, Commonwealth Secretariat.

Table 6.1b: Transition rate: primary to secondary in Nigeria, 1985–88

Year	No. of primary 6 pupils	No. of secondary Class 1 students	Transition rate
1985/1986	1,721,481	569,461	33.5%
1987	1,433,537	602,199	35.0%
1988	1,480,595	638,738	44.6%

Source: Statistics Section, Federal Ministry of Education, in Report of Eleventh Conference of Commonwealth Education Ministers, Commonwealth Secretariat, 1990.

Table 6.1c: Sectoral growth of enrolment in Nigeria, 1961–78

Sector	Unit		Target/Actual	1961	1965	1970	1975	1978
Primary education	(000's)	a)	Target	2,879	3,669	4,125	8,000	–
		b)	Actual	2,911	2,803	3,516	5,259	10,426
		c)	Achievement (%)	97.4	79.3	85.2	65.7	–
Secondary education	(000's)	a)	Target	59.98	113.74	194.17	–	–
		b)	Actual	60.84	132.98	254.64	445	999
		c)	Achievement (%)	101.40	116.90	131.10	–	–
Higher education		a)	Target	–	5,950	9,400	–	–
		b)	Actual	2,480	7,709	14,468	32,212	49,903
		c)	Achievement (%)	–	130	154	–	–

– Not available.

Source: H. N. Pandit, Research Seminar on International and National Trends in Forecasting Manpower Requirements for Economic Development. Table 2, Department of Guidance and Counselling, University of Ibadan, April 1980.

Table 6.2: Sectoral growth of enrolment in African countries by level of education (in thousands)

Country	Year	1st level		2nd level		3rd level		Total	
		MF	F	MF	F	MF	F	MF	F
Gambia	1960	7.0	2.2	1.7	0.4	–	–	8.7	2.6
	1970	17.1	5.3	5.0	1.2	–	–	22.1	6.5
	1980	38.9	13.0	9.8	3.1	–	–	48.7	16.1
	1990	66.1	24.1	22.2	7.3	–	–	88.3	31.4
	2000	110.0	43.1	40.0	14.3	–	–	150.0	57.4
Liberia	1960	58.6	16.8	3.3	0.5	0.5	0.1	62.4	17.4
	1970	120.2	39.6	16.8	3.9	1.1	0.1	138.1	43.6
	1980	219.0	83.8	56.8	16.3	5.4	1.5	281.2	101.6
	1990	384.8	153.6	126.0	39.8	15.7	4.1	526.5	197.5
	2000	602.5	255.0	246.1	83.9	34.3	9.1	882.9	384.0
Lesotho	1960	136.1	84.5	3.1	1.6	0.2	0.0	139.4	86.1
	1970	183.4	110.0	7.3	4.0	0.4	0.1	191.1	114.1
	1980	243.1	143.3	29.0	17.3	2.1	1.3	274.2	161.9
	1990	336.6	189.6	71.7	40.9	8.5	4.7	416.8	235.2
	2000	441.4	236.7	127.5	67.8	18.3	8.9	587.2	313.4

Table 6.2 (cont'd)

Country	Year	1st level		2nd level		3rd level		Total	
		MF	F	MF	F	MF	F	MF	F
Senegal	1960	128.8	41.7	13.2	3.5	1.4	0.2	143.4	45.4
	1970	262.9	101.7	59.4	16.9	5.0	0.8	327.3	119.4
	1980	416.7	167.1	98.7	33.5	12.2	2.8	527.6	203.4
	1990	763.9	321.3	195.1	75.2	30.3	8.8	989.3	405.3
	2000	1266.8	558.0	376.2	158.0	72.3	24.7	1715.3	740.7
Mauritius	1960	112.4	53.0	23.6	7.6	0.1	0.0	136.1	60.6
	1970	150.4	73.0	45.1	18.0	2.0	0.1	197.5	91.1
	1980	129.6	63.2	85.7	40.6	2.0	0.5	217.3	104.3
	1990	161.9	79.5	94.9	46.5	5.4	1.7	262.2	127.7
	2000	149.3	73.4	118.8	58.0	9.4	3.5	277.5	134.9
Morocco	1960	766.4	218.2	86.1	22.1	4.7	0.7	857.2	241.0
	1970	1175.3	398.0	298.9	84.5	16.1	2.7	1490.3	485.2
	1980	2189.3	810.2	795.8	302.2	100.8	24.6	3085.9	1137.0
	1990	3711.3	1497.1	1755.9	721.9	253.8	75.4	5721.1	2294.4
	2000	5001.8	2144.3	2970.6	1296.4	465.1	153.1	8437.5	3593.8

Source: UNESCO Statistical Year Book 1983.

Table 6.3: Actual and forecasts of annual rates of growth for high levels of manpower in Nigeria, 1960–68

Source	Senior manpower	Intermediate MP
Ashby (1960–70)	8.0	13.0
Employers' forecasts (1963–68)	8.6	9.2
National Manpower Board (1963–68)	22.0	22.0
International Seminar (1963–68)	7.1	11.3
Employer Forecasts (1965–68)	1.5	–2.5
Actual (1963–64)	4.9	8.3

Source: Hinchcliffe (1973), Table 6.10, p. 150, in Pandit H. N. *op. cit.*

Table 6.2 shows the growth rates for other selected African countries, while Table 6.3 brings out the extent of inconsistencies between different projections attempted in Nigeria at different times for the same period, thus showing the problems of manpower forecasting.

Table 6.4: Percentage distribution of trained manpower by industrial sector in Nigeria, 1977

Sector of employment	Percentage
Service	37.21
Construction	25.59
Manufacturing and processing	14.40
Commerce	9.53
Transport and commerce	5.26
Agriculture	3.44
Electrical	3.26
Mining and quarrying	1.31
Total percentage	100.00
No. (in 000's)	388.00

Source: Manpower Survey, 1977, Table 7.

Table 6.4 reveals that while 14.5 and 10 per cent of trained manpower were employed in manufacturing and commerce, respectively, the percentage of such employees was 37.4 in the services sector and 25.6 in construction, while the remaining four sectors shared a total of 13.5 per cent of total trained manpower. These distribution patterns are indicative of national distribution of economic activities.

Table 6.5:   Growth in the high-level manpower in Nigeria 1960–75 (000's)

Year	Source	High-level manpower senior (a)	intermediate (b)	Total	Ratio between (b):(a)
1960	Ashby Report	13.7	11.1	24.8	6.8
1970	Second National Development Plan	45.6	126.9	172.5	2.8
1975	Third National Development Plan	91.5	252.0	343.5	2.7

Source: Pandit, *op. cit.*

The impressive growth in high-level manpower in Nigeria over the period of 15 years is shown in Table 6.5. Thus between 1960 and 1975, senior level manpower grew by seven-fold and intermediate manpower by 23-fold. The two together grew by 14-fold over the same period. Similarly, the ratio between the two categories increased from 1:1 to 1:3 during this same period.

Cost-benefit and rate of return analysis in educational planning

Cost-benefit analysis is a fairly sophisticated technique for applying rational analysis for evaluation and decision-making. It tries to answer the practical question of whether a particular programme or project is worthwhile from an economic standpoint. It is in fact an economists' tool, involving a comparison of the economic costs and benefits of a project with a view to determining its costs. A project is considered profitable if its marginal social benefits exceed its marginal social costs. Prest and Turvey, in a comprehensive look at the subject in 1965, offered the following definition of cost-benefit analysis:

Cost-benefit analysis is a practical way of assessing the desirability of projects, where it is important to take a long view (in the sense of looking at the repercussions in the farther, as well as the nearer, future) and a wide view (in the sense of allowing for side effects of many kinds on many persons, industries, regions, etc.), it implies the enumeration and evaluation of all the relevant costs and benefits (Prest and Turvey, 1965).

Provided the costs and benefits in each case can be properly quantified, it is possible to compare, for example, the economic pay-off from investing £3 million in health as against investing the same amount in information, even though neither service can be sold to consumers in the ordinary sense on a profit-making basis.

In cost-benefit analysis, costs and benefits are normally reduced to financial terms because money is the only satisfactory common denominator that can be used to relate costs directly to benefits (Williams, P.R.C., 1974). Fortunately, the direct expenditures in public-sector projects are usually quite readily identifiable, for example the financial costs of constructing a railroad, a motorway or a hospital. Cost-benefit analysis is, however, inappropriate as a technique, if the benefits of a public project are non-economic in character and cannot be valued in financial terms such as national integration, or the improvement of national morality. These factors, although beneficial as values, cannot be directly compared with each other on a single uniform scale. Where non-economic benefits are derived from a project, the correct evaluation technique is cost-effectiveness analysis. We apply cost-benefit analysis only to cases where measurable economic costs and benefits are being considered, because financial costs are equal to economic costs.

In education, cost-benefit analysis is concerned with the return to expenditure on education, viewed as an investment. The calculations of these returns are usually of two types. The first method is to calculate the returns to an individual's investment in his education, by comparing the costs incurred and the returns or benefits received by him, as a result of this education. The resulting rate is termed the private rate of return. The second method is to derive the social rate of return by considering expenditure on education as a social investment and to calculate the costs and the subsequent returns accruing to society. However, in education some of the costs and many of the important benefits are non-economic and cannot be measured in economic terms. This is the limitation of the value of cost-benefit or rate of return analysis, as an aid to decision-making in education. Nevertheless, once it is recognised that investment in education does produce significant economic benefits, it becomes necessary to analyse the nature and magnitude of these benefits in relation to costs, even though this provides only a part of the overall picture. Moreover, because of the importance attached to economic growth, particularly in a developing society like Africa, it is extremely important to have some reliable means of assessing fairly accurately, not only the economic impact of education, but also what sectors of it to emphasise at a particular point of development. The main benefits of cost-benefit analysis to educational planning are therefore basically twofold: first, it provides vital information about the links between education and the labour market; and secondly, it gives an idea about the economic consequence of alternative educational policies.

The measurement of costs

The costs of an education project to the economy of a country consist of all the resource inputs both physical and human, that go into the construction and operation of the project. These costs are measured and expressed in monetary terms. They include not only the costs to the government agencies and individuals directly associated with construction and operation of the project, but also all of the costs that have to be incurred to produce the intended benefits of the project.

The total costs of an education project can be broadly divided into two: private costs and social or public costs, that is cost to individual students and their families and costs to society, respectively. Each of these can in turn be subdivided into a number of categories.

Individual/private costs

The costs of education to an individual student and his family is of three main kinds. First, there are the direct fee payments for school tuition minus the value of any scholarships. Second, are any payments for books, uniforms, travel, sports equipment, which are necessary to enjoy education fully. These, unlike the first category of costs, do not enter into government accounts or even national accounts as education expenditure. Third, the costs to the individual student of being educated is the value of alternative opportunities he has had to do without or forgo, by being educated. These are known as the *indirect* or *opportunity costs* of education. In a modern economy, with available wage jobs, the opportunity costs of voluntarily attending school is the wage a young person might have earned. However, where there is compulsory attendance up to a certain age, then the opportunity cost over that period is nil to the pupil who is under school-leaving age. Opportunity costs are particularly considerable for those students in upper classes of the secondary school or in higher education. In a developing country such as Mozambique or Malaŵi and most of Africa, the situation is complicated, however, by the fact that the value of the young child's services to his family for fetching water, minding younger brothers and sisters or herding, may be relatively higher in some communities than it is in a developed country. On the other hand, earning opportunity foregone by attending school in the age range 15–25 may be less, because of the existence of a labour surplus, even though the labour contribution of the young person to the family may be valuable (Fields, 1965).

Generally, the private costs of education in labour surplus economies, such as prevail in most African countries, are quite small. The earnings foregone by an individual are governed not only by the wage rate but also by the probabilities of employment, underemployment, and unemployment. A young person with low educational attainment has a fair likelihood of being employed but at low wages. In a labour surplus economy where there are large numbers of unemployed and underemployed in search of work, the chances of employment for a person of school age may be very slim. Hence, foregone earnings in such a situation may be very little indeed. Moreover, in most African countries, until recently, either the entire amount or a large fraction of the out-of-pocket costs of education are paid by the government. In fact, the higher the education level, the more likely this becomes the norm. The out-of-pocket costs of schooling may therefore be very small or even negative in many cases. In short, the private costs of education in most African countries with their labour surplus economies, therefore amounts to very little. Thus, for example, in 1972/73 in Sierra Leone the percentage private costs of education at the different levels were found to be 35, 59 and 28 at primary, secondary and university respectively.

Social/public costs

Similarly, from the standpoint of the whole economy or the social point of view, the corresponding costs are also of three kinds. First, there are the direct costs, which include the value of the capital resources used to construct and maintain school facilities and to train teachers, and the operating expenditure on wages and salaries of teachers and on durable goods and services. Second, there is noneducational expenditure incurred in support of education, such as land or buildings that may be donated free for education or the provision of health services to students. Third, the indirect costs of outputs foregone by employing highly-educated persons in teaching rather than in some other occupation, or the outputs and earnings foregone by having potentially productive workers in schools as students, particularly those in secondary and higher education, rather than in jobs. In addition, in the situation of most African countries where the government budget is more or less fixed, other government projects have to be sacrificed in order to provide students with financial aid in the form of bursaries or scholarships. Thus in the evaluation of education as a form of social investment for the purpose of cost-benefit analysis, this must be looked at in terms of the total resource cost of education to the economy and in doing so, the market value of each item must be calculated.

The various cost elements noted above, when combined, would provide an estimate of the annual cost per student at a particular level and type of education. If we assume that there is no wastage, then this calculation would be sufficient for the purposes of cost-benefit analysis. However, where there is wastage, allowance must be made for it, to avoid giving false impressions on annual costs and the normal length of a course at the different levels of schooling.

The measurement of benefits

In discussing the economic benefits of education we must distinguish between two broad categories of benefits. The first one is external productivity, which is the link between the education sector and the rest of the economy. The basis of this link is that education and training raise the economic productivity of its recipients and thereby increase their contribution to the production of goods and services to the economy. The magnitude of the benefit is measured by the increase in the output of the economy that can be attributed to the additional education or training (Woodhall, 1970; Blaug, 1967; Psacharopoulos, 1973).

The second type of benefit is internal to the education system itself and takes the form of improvements in the efficiency of particular sectors of the system. This category of benefits is referred to as internal efficiency and is measured in terms of the reduction in the unit costs per student enrolled or per graduate. Greater internal efficiency enables the system to produce more education (more students enrolled or graduates produced) for the same amount of money or the same amount of education for less money. The resources saved from the education sector represent the benefit to the economy.

In terms of cost-benefit analysis, it is the first category of benefits that is most relevant. The assessment of the external productivity benefits of education rests on two assumptions: i) that the income of an individual is the best available measure of his contribution to the economy's production of goods and services, and ii) that income differentials among individuals with different amounts of education are at least partly due to differences in their educational attainment, that is to say, more education contributes to productivity above that of the uneducated and this is reflected in increased output and higher earnings. Thus the differential of the lifetime earnings between university graduate and secondary school leaver, and the latter and primary school leaver, is an estimate in each case of the higher productivity of the more educated person.

Evidence from a number of studies in modern economies shows that personal earnings are positively correlated with the educational level of individuals. A number of explanations have been advanced for this positive correlation. These, as stated by Blaug, claim at one extreme that educational certificates merely act as screening devices for the employer; such credentials predict a higher level of performance but make no direct contribution to it. If valid, the implications would be most damaging to the economic evaluation of educational investments. The simplest explanation of the observed high association between education and earnings is that the better educated are more productive than the less educated; probably because of the knowledge acquired through the education system. However, even in cases where their education has not included training in specific skills, educated people are more productive because they are achievement oriented, are more self-reliant, act with greater initiative in problem-solving situations, adapt more easily to changing circumstances and assume supervisory responsibility more quickly as well as benefit more from work experience and in-plant training (Blaug, 1974). The acceptance of this explanation of the higher earnings of the educated is crucial for the cost-benefit analysis of education.

In the analysis of education as a social benefit, the whole of the lifetime earnings differential measured before income tax is the relevant measure, whereas in its assessment as a private investment for the individual, it is the post-tax or actual benefit which is relevant. On the whole, the private benefits from education in labour surplus economies may be very large. Percentage wage differentials between different skill levels in labour surplus economies, particularly in Africa, are much greater than even in the developed countries (see Table 6.6). Expected lifetime income for university graduates may be several times as high as for secondary school leavers. The latter may in turn expect to earn several times as much as primary school leavers.

Measurement of discounted cash flow

Cost-benefit analysis encompasses three major alternative ways of expressing the profitability of investments. One of these is called the benefit-cost ratio, which relates the 'present value' of benefits to the 'present value' of costs. The other is the 'net present value' which is the difference in present value between costs and benefits. The 'internal rate of return' is the third, and is what is used to express the profit-ability of investments in education. All three methods rest on the fact that benefits and sometimes costs too, occur over time, as is the case, for example, in education. Benefits received earlier in time are more valuable than those received later in time, even if there is no inflation. This is illustrated in the table below.

Table 6.6:   Compound growth and present values at 10% rate of interest

Year	Amount to which £100 invested will grow at end of each year	Amount to which £100 promised at end of each year is worth today
1	110.0	90.9
2	121.0	82.6
3	133.1	75.1
4	146.4	68.3
5	161.1	62.1
6	177.2	56.4
7	194.9	51.3
8	214.4	46.6

Source: Adapted from Woodhall, M. (1970) *Cost Benefit Analysis in Educational Planning*, p. 22.

Table 6.6 shows that £100 now is more valuable than the same amount a year or two later as a consideration of the rate of interest will easily show. Thus at 10% interest £100 a year later becomes £110, and £121 two years later. The same example could also be considered in terms of discount rates. As the table shows, £121 in two years time has a present value of £100 if the discount (interest) rate is 10%, but if the interest rate were to be only 5%, its present value would rise to £110, but this would drop to £92 if the discount rate were 15%.

Another way of expressing the above is that if £100 invested now would yield £131 in two years at 15% interest, then the benefit-cost ratio is 0.92. On the other hand, £100 invested at 15% interest now and yielding £131 in two years in principal plus interest, would give a 'net present value' of minus £8. In brief, the higher the discount rate, the lower the present value of total costs, and it is the costs that occur in the more distant future that are affected most by a higher discount rate or indeed by any discount rate.

It is on account of this distribution of benefits over time that future benefits are usually discounted and expressed on a standardised basis in terms of 'present values'. Present values consequently provide a standard measure that can be used to compare the profitability of different types of investments and the technique is known as the 'discounted cash flow' technique (Woodhall, 1970; Sirken, 1979). This simply involves the calculation of the present value at some given or assured rate of interest of the income expected in every future year.

The third measure of profitability of investments is the 'rate of return'. Unlike the benefit-cost ratio and net present value, it is simply a statement of the rate of return or yield that an investment realises. Moreover, unlike the other measures of profitability where the calculations are dependent upon an assumed rate of interest, the rate of return makes no assumptions about the rate of interest. In fact, its objective is to calculate the rate of interest that equates costs and benefits. Consequently, it is possible to arrive at conclusions on the basis of a cost-benefit analysis which shows that the social rate of return to university education is, for example, x per cent and that to primary education is y per cent as illustrated in Table 6.7.

Table 6.7: Returns to education by level (in percentages) in Africa

Country	Survey year	Private			Social		
		Primary	Secondary	Higher	Primary	Secondary	Higher
Ethiopa	1972	35.0	22.8	27.4	20.3	18.7	9.7
Ghana	1967	24.5	17.0	17.0	18.0	13.0	16.5
Kenya	1971	28.0	33.0	31.0	21.7	19.2	8.8
Malawi	1978					15.1	
Morocco	1970				50.5	10.0	13.0
Nigeria	1966	30.0	14.0	34.0	23.0	12.8	17.0
Zimbabwe	1960				12.4		
Sierra Leone	1971				20.0	22.0	9.5
Uganda	1965				66.0	28.6	12.0

Source: World Bank Publications, 1980, p. 84.

Table 6.8:   The returns to education by level (in percentages) in Africa

Region (N)	Private			Social		
	P	S	H	P	S	H
Africa (9)	29	22	32	29	17	12

(N) = Number of countries, P = Primary, S = Secondary, H = Higher.

Source: World Bank Publications, 1980, Table 2, p. 87.

Rate of return patterns in Africa

The rate of return patterns that have been found by researchers (Psacharopoulos, 1973, 1976; Hoerr, 1974; Keten, 1974; Fields, 1975; Heyneman, 1980a) in a large number of African countries, shown in the table above, is similar to those in other parts of the developing world and it is not completely dissimilar to those of the developed countries. In general, from Tables 6.6 and 6.7, the underlying patterns of rates of return to education in Africa can be summarised as follows:

1   Amongst all educational levels the returns to primary education, both social and private are the highest.
2   The private rates are in excess of social returns, especially at the university level.
3   All rates of return to investment in education are well above the 10 per cent common yardstick of the opportunity cost of capital.

Cost-benefit analysis and decision-making

Cost-benefit analysis consists of the identification, measurement and comparison of the economic costs and benefits of investment programmes and projects. Its limitation as an aid to decision-making in education, arises from the fact that some of the most important benefits of education are non-economic and hence cannot be measured in economic terms.

Even where the benefits and costs are measurable, the precise relationship between these benefits and the education programme or project that is supposed to produce them, is not at all clear. Where the benefits take the form of increasing the economic productivity and incomes of people who have received education and training, it is very difficult to determine how much of the increase in productivity is attributable to the education project or programme. Similarly, where the benefits are in the form of improvements in internal efficiency, i.e. a reduction in costs per student or graduate, the same type of difficulty is encountered.

In spite of the difficulties and limitations of cost-benefit analysis elaborated above, since the costs of education have become a very important element in decision-making, it follows that the identification and measurement of the economic costs of education programmes and projects can be a useful aid to decision-making.

Substantial evidence in the literature seems to suggest that cost-benefit analysis is more useful to apply in those projects in which the benefits take the form of improvements in internal efficiency rather than external productivity, i.e. in cost-effectiveness analysis.

Lastly, whether the costs and benefits are measurable or not, the fact that cost-benefit analysis is a rational approach to decision-making is important. Public expenditure decisions based on rationality as opposed to bias or intuition, are likely to be better decisions.

Criticisms of rate of return approach to educational investment

The objections to the rate-of return approach to educational planning abound in the literature (Woodhall, 1970; Blaug, 1970; Thias and Carnoy, 1972; Jolly and Colclough, 1972) and therefore only a few of the main ones will be discussed here.

First, in cost-benefit analysis of investments in education, the difference between the earnings of less educated and more educated persons are considered as the benefits due to their additional formal schooling. However, such incremental earnings cannot be attributed solely to additional schooling. Other factors such as differences in ability, socio-economic background and so on, also play a part. Therefore using additional earnings as a measure of the benefits to investment in education tends to ignore these other factors.

Second, cost-benefit analysis assumes that wages are a valid measure of productivity. However, in many African countries public sector wages and employment policies may be totally unrelated to productivity, rather they may be influenced by colonial legacies and the rules of government salary structures. The nature of much of the work performed by people in the public service and in the informal sector by women is often difficult to assess and value. Trade union pressure may also force pay differentials which may not reflect educational differences.

Third, the use of earnings or wage differentials as the benefits to additional schooling gives no consideration to the impact of unemployment. High levels of unemployment may drastically reduce the rate of return to education at any one level.

Fourth, the calculations of most rates of return studies are in practice based on present day salary structures and education costs. Consequently, the rates may very well not remain valid for further investment undertakings in the future; it is most likely that wage differentials and costs are bound to change over time. This is so because the demand-supply situation in particular trades or professions profoundly influences the levels of wages in the labour market. It is, for example, possible that at the time of planning, certain occupations are in short supply and consequently the wage levels in those occupations would be fairly high. However, with increased educational facilities for preparing people in those occupations and consequential increase in the supply of the corresponding graduates, earnings associated with the particular occupation may be greatly altered.

Fifth, rate of return analysis often appears to overlook the importance of skill formation outside the formal school system, through experience or on-the-job training. Higher pay could be due to additional skills obtained outside the formal education system.

Social demand, manpower and rate of return approaches

These three approaches, although usually treated as alternatives, are in fact quite closely inter-linked. Thus, whereas in the social demand approach, student and parental desire for a school place is the central consideration, such desire is often influenced by the awareness of the rate of return calculations in terms of present costs and future benefits accruing from an education. Usually, the greater the demand for a particular type or level of education, the higher the salaries and non-pecuniary benefits realised by persons with that level or type of education, or the greater the probability of admission to the next level of schooling. In addition, in making judgements about the rate of return, the individual may be influenced by the future manpower supply and demand situation. This in turn will influence his tendency to go for those occupations and industries with the highest demand in relation to supply. For example, in many African countries, the tendency in the more educationally advantaged areas is nowadays towards the study of subjects related to private business management, science and technology and this represents a definite shift away from the arts subjects.

Similarly, manpower planning and rate of return analysis are also in many ways complementary to each other. While the manpower approach emphasises fixed relationships between output, skill inputs and educational qualifications, rate of return analysis takes an essentially economic view. But manpower planning often also makes the assumption that a combination of two or more alternative·skills are possible to produce the same output and the choice of what is suitable may be made on the basis of the maximisation of benefits in relation to the cost of producing the skills. There are equally many cases in which manpower planning is used to supplement the rate of return analysis. The later analysis works on the assumption of an economy with perfect competition in which price is the chief determinant of the balance between the supply of skills and demand for them. There are, therefore, certain times where manpower forecasts can assist in identifying temporary shortages and thereby avoid unnecessary wage rises. Similarly, in a situation where a large-scale investment is contemplated or planned, manpower planning can help to avert a shortage of skills and the subsequent rise in wages, by the timely training of skilled people in anticipation of demand. Thus the three approaches, although they may appear at first sight to represent different views of the world, are in fact useful complements to each other in practice.

In the situation of African countries, the main difficulty in the application of these models as aids to decision-making in educational planning, is the dearth of the necessary level of data that is desirable for realistic appraisal. It is therefore important that the results obtained from the application of any one model should be verified by the evaluation of others in order to assure that what finally emerges is a fairly accurate and useful picture of the prevailing or likely situation.

Exercises

1   Briefly, discuss the main arguments that were advanced in support of the importance of human resources and the criticisms that have been levelled against human capital theory.
2   Distinguish between the main characteristics and problems of social demand and rate of return analysis.
3   'Manpower planning . . . , is basically an attempt . . . to ensure that labour of the right volume, quality, type and combination to meet the social and economic objectives of a country or organisation, as specified by the growth targets, are available'. Discuss.
4   What are the main sources of data for manpower forecasting?
5   Discuss the relationship between social demand, manpower planning and rate of return analysis approaches.

VII

Structuring the education system

Structure is simply the logical pattern or supporting framework for grouping the activities of an organisation and assigning them to specific positions and people, thereby facilitating the realisation of planned goals. This framework is normally represented in the form of a structure chart. This chapter discusses educational structures in terms of their roles in facilitating the achievements of planned educational goals. The chapter thus analyses:

- the purposes of the structure chart;
- the role of structure in organisation structures;
- the political aspects of African education structure; and
- some criteria for the assessment of education structures.

What the structure chart represents

The word structure is applied in different contexts ranging from business organisations and the civil service to the natural and social sciences – biology, physics, mathematics, economics and sociology. When used in organisations, the concept of structure refers to the arrangement of authority, accountability relationships, activities and communication channels within an organisation (Hicks, 1971). In other words, structure is the deliberate patterning of relationships between organisation members aimed at achieving stated goals. Its function is to assist members of the organisation to achieve more than would otherwise be possible through their independent, unco-ordinated efforts as individuals. Structure therefore exists primarily as an instrumental device and not as an end in itself.

Organisation chart

The usual form of depicting organisation structure is the organisation chart. Charts show the hierarchy of levels, the departmentalisation, and interrelationships of the main units, the network of authority, responsibility, and accountability in an organisation. Although charts are normally constructed to depict the entire organisation, additional auxiliary charts giving more details are frequently also provided.

The chart is, of course, merely a schematic, static model or diagram of the process of human interaction. As such it suffers from certain deficiencies, for example, it gives no indication of the variation of work which an organisation undertakes and no time scale is given. Generally, it tends to suggest only unidimensional and vertical relations and there is no indication of the versatility of individuals. As a result, an alternative form of depicting a structure known as the matrix is sometimes used instead. Nevertheless, whatever its shortcomings the chart as a representation of the structure serves as a useful basis for studying organisational structure.

Structure in education systems

In the field of education, the concept of structure can be applied in many different contexts. One can, for instance, talk of the administrative structure or the financial structure of an education system. The expression 'education structure', however, normally refers to the courses and levels/cycles (pre-primary, secondary, tertiary) of education and the way these are linked (Fig 7.1). Structure in education thus describes not the size of a system, but rather its form and the connections between its parts.

The essentials of a country's contemporary education system can be discerned through the study of three basic types of chart. First is the administrative organisation chart showing the distribution of responsibility for education policy and action amongst the different elected and official bodies as well as the hierarchy of command within the ministry of education and provincial and local education authorities (Fig 7.2).

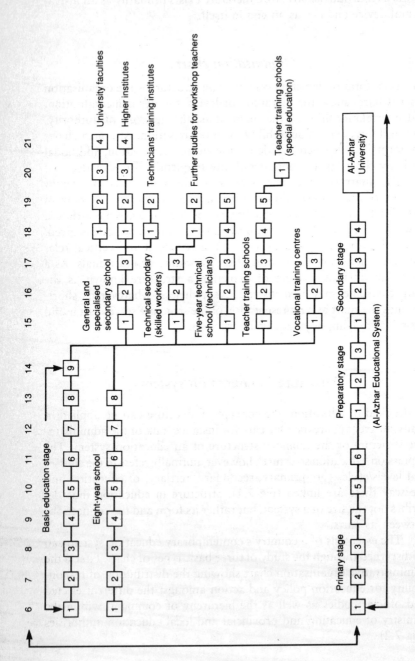

Fig. 7.1   The educational structure in Egypt after 1981/82 (Source: National Ministry of Education, Egypt, Cairo, 1987)

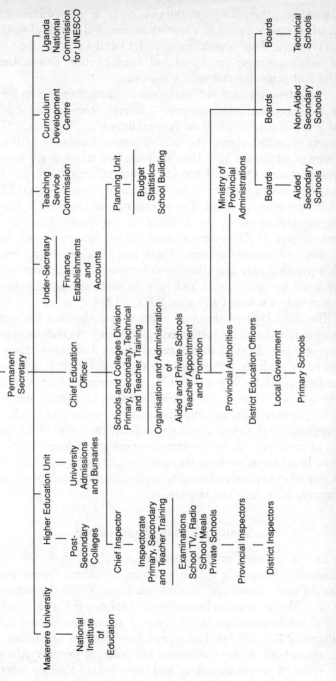

Fig. 7.2 Uganda educational administration organisation chart, showing distribution of responsibility and hierarchy of command within the ministry of education

In Africa, there are basically two types of administrative struc-tures of education systems: a unitary system and a federal system. In a unitary state, there is usually a ministry of education at the national level with supportive provincial and district office. Kenya, Uganda, Ghana and Benin operate such a system.

In a federation such as Nigeria, the constitution provides for three tiers of educational administration – federal, state and local govern-ment levels (Constitution of the Federal Republic of Nigeria, 1979). In addition, in some states, the administrative functions of the state ministry of education have been decentralised to what are known as Zonal Education Offices (Kano state, Nigeria, 1980). The latter have jurisdiction over a number of local education departments (LEDS) in the local government areas. The second type of chart is the diagram-matic representation in the form of an 'education pyramid'. This shows the size of the system in terms of enrolments at each year of schooling and possibly in terms of male and female sexes (see Fig. 7.3). Such a pyramid may also distinguish enrolments in different types of institutions by grade, level and may in some cases, also show the numbers not in school (Williams, P.R.C., 1974).

The third type of structure chart is one showing the different courses that make up the system and the number of grade units in each course or stage and the links between them as well as the routes to be followed by students as they move through the system (Fig 7.1). Thus according to P.R.C. Williams (1974), the structure chart is compara-ble to a road map of the system, showing departure points, the different destinations, and the distances to be covered reaching the destinations. Such a chart could also indicate the width of the 'gate' in terms of percentage transition rates between the different levels of the system. In addition, we have the structure charts depicting the typical structure of individual institutions at the different levels of the system – primary, secondary and tertiary.

Structure and organisation

The first three types of chart enumerated above show the need to distinguish between the structure of an education system and the organised institutional provision of education. Whilst the former con-sists of grades, courses and transfer mechanisms, the latter consists of physical teaching groups in the form of actual schools and colleges (Williams, P.R.C., 1974). Today, in a large number of African coun-tries, the school system comprises six years of primary education, three years of junior secondary and three years of senior secondary

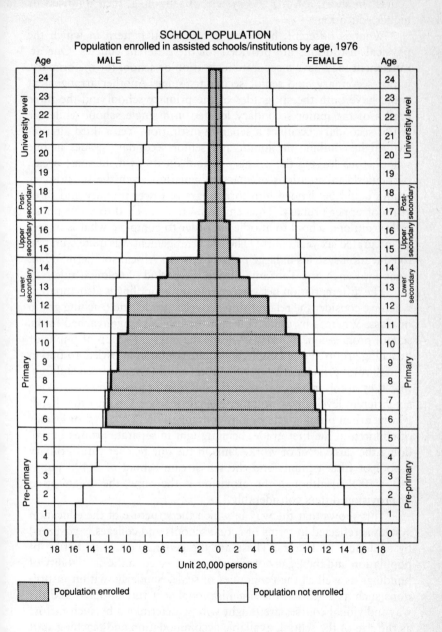

Fig. 7.3 Education pyramid showing system size by enrolment and in terms of sex

course. In short, a 6 – 3 – 3 system of schooling, then followed by higher education.

What is different, however, is the actual pattern in which the physical institutions are provided for the different courses. One arrangement may have a separate institution or school for the primary, junior secondary, and senior secondary stage. Another arrangement could have both the six grades of the primary school and the three grades of the junior secondary located in a single school while the senior secondary occupies a separate institution. Yet a third alternative might combine the junior and senior secondary grades in one school, thus leaving the primary school on its own. In some areas, particularly in situations of sparse population, even the six primary grades could be divided into three years of lower primary and three years of upper primary. Thus children are compelled to move physically from one school to another in order to complete what is in fact an integrated six year course. The last arrangement was quite common to education systems in large parts of Eastern Africa: southern Sudan, Uganda, Kenya and Tanzania during the period of colonial rule.

The differentiation between course and schooling is also apparent when we consider the relationship between 'grade' and teaching group or class. Whereas by grade is meant the level or stage reached in the school progression, by class is meant the physical group of pupils or 'teaching group'. For example, it is quite common in Africa, to find in a small rural primary school with a total enrolment of fifteen children, that they are in fact spread over six different grades and undertaking six different levels of work under a single teacher. On the other hand, a large urban primary school may contain 10 or 12 'classes' or groups of children in the first grade, being taught in separate groups but all doing the same level of work. Thus in the one teacher rural primary school of fifteen pupils and the ten stream school of 2,400 pupils (40 × 10 × 6) although the provision is the same, the organisation of provision differs considerably.

This shows that the way in which the structure of the education system is reflected in terms of actual schools and colleges is governed by a number of factors. These are the geographical distribution of population and the legacy of the past as reflected in the availability of buildings as well as the economies of scale. Similarly, within institutions such as a school, the organisational structure adopted and the way individual courses are taught will be determined by such factors as the size of the school, available accommodation and teaching staff as well as the prevailing educational theory concerning the best way of grouping children. Generally, however, institutional organisations are normally derived from the educational structure, and this in turn is dependent on the socio-economic condition prevalent in the country at a particular time in a nation's evolution.

Key elements of education structures

There are at least three key elements of education structures:

- progression by grades;
- levels, stages and courses;
- transition points and selection.

We shall now proceed to examine each of these in turn.

Progression by grades

The basis for the consideration of education in terms of student progression by grades is the fact that as children grow and mature, their capacity for comprehension of more complex tasks also increases. Moreover, the theory of learning is built on a logical progression from the simple to the more complex. Thus the mastery of the 3Rs is a pre-requisite for any more advanced study. It is on these grounds, i.e. the progressive development of the capacities of the growing child, coupled with our knowledge of the structure of learning which always starts with simple, basic concepts and gradually moves to more refined ones, that the education system has been divided into stages or levels and further, into grades. Thus children of the same age start at the first grade and gradually work their way together up the formal education system. Nevertheless, the acceptance of the logic of graduated steps in learning should not make us overlook the imperfections in our understanding as well as our organisational arrangements.

We are frequently surprised to find that children and adolescents can learn concepts and master skills earlier than normally expected and that our existing curricular sequences are far from perfect. Hence the need for the constant review of our knowledge of child development and the modification of learning sequences.

Levels, stages and courses

Although an education system in theory could be organised so that there is one continuous progression from primary one up to the last grade of the senior secondary school, in practice all systems consist of successive stages of primary, secondary and tertiary. These stages are a reflection of our understanding of the phases in human personal development of childhood, adolescence and adulthood. Teaching styles are also based upon these stages, with more responsibility for individual self-learning being given to the student as he/she moves further up the system. The same logic applies to the needs of different age groups for teaching and recreational facilities. All these are contributory factors for the subdivisions of education systems into stages, and for separation into different institutions and by type, reflecting individual interests and abilities.

The main disadvantage of this outlook, however, is that instead of the education process being treated as a continuous process, there are drastic discontinuities between educational stages. In Africa this is typified by the differences between primary and secondary schools. Thus whereas the primary school is typically built of cheap local materials with a single teacher per class to cover the whole curriculum, this is not the case with the secondary school. The latter is normally at a distance from the child's home and in many cases is a boarding establishment. It is usually of at least several streams with children attending from various communities. The language of instruction in most cases is foreign and the curriculum is subject-based with specialised teachers.

As regards the optimum length of stages, ideally this should not be less than three years, particularly at the primary and secondary levels, for several reasons. Firstly, from all available evidence it would seem that a minimum exposure is necessary for education to be effective. According to Jean Capelle: 'There is a critical mass of educational exposure below which the attainments of schools fade rapidly. . . . I do not believe, from my experience in Africa, that it is possible to go below a four-year period of schooling for children' (Capelle, 1967). This is one of the main reasons for the extension of the duration of primary education from four to six or even eight years. It may also explain the lukewarm reception by governments of the recent call for the adoption of basic education as a solution to the problem of educational provision in developing countries.

Secondly, an educational institution of less than four years duration will mean a very rapid turnover of students and this is likely to militate against the development of a stable educational community with its own ethos, which is especially important for younger children. Thirdly, the question of viability becomes an important consideration in small individual institutions requiring specialised teachers, equipment and plant.

It has consequently been suggested that for a secondary school, the minimum number of classes and teachers should be six and ten respectively: the load of use on specialised teachers and facilities like laboratories and workshops may be too light to justify their provision in a school below this minimum size. The basic drawback to meeting this requirement in many African countries, however, is the low density of population, particularly for schools at the junior secondary stage. Thus in a fairly densely populated country like Nigeria, the Implementation Committee for the New Education Policy (Blue Print, 1978) has suggested a junior secondary with a minimum of three streams. In situations where the minimum population requirement cannot be met the alternative is to combine the junior and primary stages in one school. Another alternative would be to train teachers to be able to teach a wide range of subjects. Unfortunately, it is often in those countries where the population densities are low, e.g. the Sudan, that no effort is made to make the teachers more versatile in their range of teaching subjects. On the contrary, the practice has been to encourage the teachers to specialise in one or two subjects only. The solution adopted instead is to make the schools boarding and thereby very expensive to run. This typifies the rigidities of many African education systems where innovation to suit local conditions is sadly not encouraged. More recently, however, there are changes taking place in response to changing needs.

On the other hand, although combining primary and junior secondary stages in a single school has been suggested as a good arrangement for African education systems, there are strong arguments against making the educational stages too long (Lewis, 1969), particularly where attendance is voluntary. The main argument is that pupils should be able to leave the education system easily, and with some kind of qualification to indicate what they have learnt. Long courses on which performance is judged by a single examination at the end, will place a person who left after five years of a six-year course, for instance, at par with one who never embarked on the course and has therefore five years less education. A better approach at this stage would be to have shorter stages. Short stages also make it easy for employers to match recruits to jobs. These may be some of the grounds that make the concept of basic education as advocated by the World Bank in its Education Sector Review for 1975 appealing. This concept is also the subject of the recent (1991) World Conference on Education for All at Jomtien in Thailand. Finally, from the point of view of financial viability, frequent transition points or shorter courses in the education system provide the possibility of scaling down the size of the system, an important consideration in the light of the present economic situation of most African states.

Transition points and selection

Although selection has come to be regarded as part and parcel of African education systems, it is not always necessary for transition from one educational level to the next.

Where both primary and secondary education are compulsory and of a single type of school, then transfer without selection becomes almost automatic. Three main factors, which are all prevalent in African countries, have made selection a permanent feature of the education system. First, for economic reasons, further education is always highly rationed. Secondly, educational differentiation, with different parallel types of courses at the same level, for example, academic courses and pre-vocational practical courses at the secondary level, has made selection inevitable. Thirdly, even where schools are uniform in the types of courses offered, differences in the quality of individual schools compels the better schools to ration their scarce and highly sought after places. These are usually the old, well established schools, most of them dating back to pre-independence days, that have built up reputations as centres of academic excellence, for example, Rumbek Secondary School in southern Sudan, Kings College Budu, in Uganda, and Alliance High School in Kenya. In West Africa, in Nigeria, we have Barewa College, Zaria, and Kings College, Lagos, Ghana can boast of Achimota College School while Sierra Leone has the Prince of Wales Secondary School and Bo School, and Malaŵi the more recently established Kamuzu College (The Eton of Africa) modelled on the pattern of the English public school.

The basic problem of selection in African education systems as well as elsewhere, is that once a pupil is selected into a branch of the education system, it becomes increasingly impossible as he/she goes up the system, for him/her to transfer to another branch. It is, for instance, hard to transfer from a technical school to an academic school. On the other hand, it is always easier to transfer from general education into a technical stream. Moreover, most technical branches do not always provide access into the mainstream of tertiary education. Even if a technical institution is specifically provided at the tertiary level, its certificates always tend to be regarded as lower in prestige than those of the mainstream tertiary institutions. This is clearly illustrated by the case of the Sudan and Nigeria.

In the Sudan students from commercial and technical secondary schools do not have the possibility of direct entry into the university. This is also the case in Nigeria. Such students go to specialised technical colleges or polytechnics such as the Yaba Technical College or Kaduna Polytechnic in Nigeria, and the Higher College of Commerce, and the Khartoum Polytechnic in the Sudan. Furthermore, in Nigeria, although a polytechnic can offer the Higher National Diploma (HND) and produce graduates with engineering or management qualifications these are not equated with university degrees in engineering, business, or management studies. In Uganda, however, it is possible to study business administration or management at Makerere University on leaving the Uganda College of Commerce.

On the whole, however, the existing structures of the education system in most African countries and the prestige attached to various courses would suggest that the wise course is to stay within the mainstream of the system and it is worth continuing through to university if you possibly can. This sounds a retrograde notion, especially in the light of the serious efforts being exerted towards technical education in recent years. Yet, the reality in many countries is still a long way off from such good intentions. This is because the approach to technical and general education in colonial times has continued to influence the structural organisation of the education system, placing the former in almost a cul-de-sac.

It is important to bear in mind in this discussion that the level to which a country can provide general education to its children in schools of more or less equal standards is largely governed by its wealth. In the developed countries, for example, the tendency has been for some time now to provide a broad general education including theory and practice as long as possible to all. In Sweden and Britain this has taken the form of comprehensive secondary education which in essence is the rejection of institutional differentiation but unfortunately as at present organised, also implies an acceptance of pedagogical differentiation within the school (Psacharopoulos, 1970). However, the idea that children can be divided into 'academic types' needing theory and 'practical types' needing manual skills is not acceptable to many people. What is advocated instead, is a broad general education including both theory and practice for all, for as long as possible.

The situation in Africa

In Africa, although no country has pursued the issue to the extent of the wealthy countries, a serious start has been made to realise similar objectives. The most significant achievements have occurred in the countries of East and Central Africa – Kenya, Uganda, Tanzania, Zambia, Angola and Mozambique – where schools once organised on a racial basis during the colonial period have all been desegregated. This has been followed by the provision of equality of facilities as far as possible in all schools, particularly at the senior secondary level although the introduction of fees in Kenya for private education has affected this.

In Nigeria, within the last two years, some state governments, notably Lagos, have gone even further by taking over schools run by church organisations and private individuals in order to ensure that equal opportunity of entry is afforded to all children to such schools irrespective of religious inclination and parental wealth. All these attempts at structural reform, whether in Europe or Africa, have been conducted on a number of premises.

First, it is felt that for reasons of equality and social cohesion in society, it is unfortunate to continue to categorise children into 'academic' and 'practical' types or on the basis of race. This thinking finds expression in the New Educational Policy in Nigeria, where the curricula for the junior secondary stage in the new 6 – 3 – 3 – 4 educational structure covers both academic and practical subjects for all.

Second, there is less confidence in the reliability on selection procedures now than in the past. This has made the practice of final and irreversible selection at age eleven or twelve increasingly unacceptable. In addition, since later selection means the absence of competitive, externally set and marked examinations, there is a chance for a more relaxed and co-operative atmosphere. This in its turn produces a more creative approach to learning, especially at the primary and junior secondary levels. It is one of the reasons for the advocacy of continuous assessment in Nigeria as a vital component in the new junior secondary schools for the promotion and selection of children into various courses at the senior secondary level.

Finally, the large-scale unemployment amongst the industrial workers of the developed countries of Western Europe and the US in recent years, has clearly demonstrated that there can be no guarantee that the first job a school leaver trains for will last him throughout his working life. This means, therefore, that the initial training of individuals should aim at making them more versatile and adaptable. Hence initial education and training should lay the necessary foundation for life-long education.

The situation in African countries, however, differs enormously from the prevailing conditions in the more wealthy countries of Europe, despite the similarities already cited. Generally, in African countries, the provision of education is restricted by financial pressures. Consequently very few countries have universal primary education. The purpose of selection in such a situation is basically to determine who is able to stay in the education system. Thus in Nigeria it is proposed to restrict the transition rates from primary to junior secondary and from the latter to senior secondary to 40 per cent and 70 per cent respectively (National Policy on Education, 1981).

In the context of contemporary African realities, the luxury of a general education, comprising both theoretical and practical subjects for all students for as long as possible, is an impossible dream. Under these circumstances, selection is a necessity that must operate for the time being. A more important task, however, is to ensure that selection operates efficiently and fairly. By efficiency we mean that the selection instruments are able to identify those who will best profit from the courses for which selection is being made. Fairness in the assessment procedure would entail the fulfilment of the following conditions. Firstly, at the pre-selection stage, there must be, as far as possible, parity of school quality in terms of staffing, school buildings, materials and equipment, so that children have equal chances of developing their talent before facing the selection procedure. Secondly, at the post-selection stage, financial policies can be adjusted through scholarships and bursaries to ensure that no student who passes the selection examinations is prevented from taking up his or her place through lack of finance. By the proper application of school location planning schools can be equitably distributed, well sited in relation to population concentrations and open to all eligible pupils (Williams, P.R.C., 1974). This requires that parents and their children are well informed of existing opportunities in terms of choice of courses and schools.

Thirdly, it may be necessary to modify the selection process itself so that places are given on the basis of quotas to every area or to every school. This would be a sure way of compelling wider distribution of places than is otherwise possible through examination results alone. Although this may temporarily result in lower average attainment of pupils, the long-term political and social advantages will far outweigh such temporary inconveniences. This is particularly important for national cohesion in many African countries, where for historical reasons, wide disparities exist in educational provision between regions and social groups.

Problems of resourcing of schools, particularly at primary level, reducing the number of dropouts (especially girls) and giving greater importance to in-service teacher education are seen by many as three areas of provision requiring attention. Such reforms, though, to be effective, rely upon the existence of strong educational infrastrustures.

The political aspects of structure

The importance and function of structure, as already elaborated, is as a vehicle for getting the work of an organisation done. This means, therefore, that structures are essentially temporary. The critical deter-minant of structural change is consequently the changing nature of the organisational task. The educational system is no exception in these respects.

This temporary or *ad hoc* nature of organisational structures is clearly demonstrated by African and other Third World education systems, which are essentially still at the stage of expansion in an attempt to include all the various societies and corners of the country within its orbit. As such, innovations of structural organisation are essential features of the system and this in turn means existing struc-tures are essentially temporary. Some form of stability can only be attained when the education systems have been transformed from their present elitist nature to a truly mass system.

In the meantime, unfortunately, these structural changes, how-ever necessary from the point of view of the attainment of the aims and tasks of the system, almost always generate happiness in some members and frustration, anger and unhappiness in others. This is because structural changes in organisations for whatever reasons, nearly always enhance the position of some and threaten those of others. Teachers are no exception to the rule that nobody likes exces-sive uncertainty and discontinuity. This is especially so when there is a risk of loss of status involved. The ultimate ambition of many teachers in African education systems is eventually to land a desk job in the ministry or anywhere else in the administrative hierarchy.

Unfortunately, once having attained such a position, any struc-tural changes which could result in their movement out of the ministry headquarters, even if they are still retained within the administrative hierarchy, are usually not welcomed. For instance, the establishment of zonal education offices in Kano state, Nigeria in 1979 aimed at the decentralisation of the ministry and to bring about improved efficiency as well as to serve the rural areas better cannot be claimed to have been a complete success. The fundamental reason, apart from the normal constraints of shortage of trained personnel and finances, hinged on the lack of wholehearted support of the zonal education officers (Ibrahim, 1982).

Many of these officers were senior personnel in the ministry headquarters and felt a loss of status, with no real gain in administrative power, by being posted to a zonal office. In addition, the heads of education department in the local government offices may not wholly welcome an additional ladder of administrative hierarchy between them and the ministry. The overall result is some loss of co-operation between these three levels of education administration. In spite of these difficulties, however, one is happy to note that the ministry in Nigeria has persisted with the implementation of this innovative approach.

A similar problem of readjustment was experienced in the Sudan when, in 1972, the southern Sudan achieved a large measure of regional autonomy over its affairs, including the administration of its educational system. Educational administrators in the headquarters in Khartoum felt a territorial loss. The reaction was to regard the education system in the south as outside the orbit of the ministry. It was consequently deprived not only of active participation in the national education effort but also of its rightful share of national facilities. This attitude has not greatly diminished even after fifteen years, despite some loss of powers by the south.

These examples illustrate the fact that an individual in an organisation always likes to feel that he or she is making a real visible contribution to the organisation (Palsey, 1981). Any structural changes in the organisational set up that in any way give the impression of a diminished status would therefore not be welcomed.

What this means is that structural changes imply the exercise of political art, involving delicate and painstaking work by those responsible for their initiation. This, viewed as a human process, calls for sensitivity and concern; as a political process, it requires persuasiveness and fairness. Both require not only the ability to grasp the critical factors and the skills to articulate them, but also the successful negotiation and implementation of such changes, skills which lie at the heart of good management.

Criteria for assessing education structures in Africa

The structure of an education system can be assessed from either the individual's standpoint or from the social point of view. From the individual's standpoint, a good structure is one that offers the following possibilities. First, it provides courses and schools adapted to the student's stage of development and as far as possible allows the student to learn at his/her own pace. Second, the structure affords the individual opportunities that are physically and financially accessible and with all the options wide open at the different levels of the system, so that the student continues to learn until he/she decides to leave the system. Third, it offers a gradual progression without sharp discontinuities between stages, but at the same time provides convenient exit points so that those who wish to leave can do so with full credit for what they have learned. Lastly, the system should at the upper stages, offer a wide range of differentiated courses to suit individual talents and tastes (Williams, P.R.C., 1974).

Viewed in terms of societal welfare, a good structure is one that should provide the following possibilities. Firstly, it should provide for real learning opportunities to as many sectors of the community as possible and also ensure a wide geographical and social distribution of such facilities. Secondly, it should allow for the establishment of institutions of viable size at reasonable cost and meet the demands for education within available resources. Thirdly, it should provide the requisite numbers, types and qualities of school-leavers for the needs of the economy and society. Fourthly, it should be flexible enough to accommodate change, e.g. innovation, without detriment to its primary functions. Finally, it should identify and develop the maximum amount of talent in the community and reflect the essential values of society such as equality of opportunity and respect for the individual.

Exercises

1 Discuss:
   a) the main uses of a structure chart;
   b) the main types of education structure.
2 Discuss the key elements of education structures.
3 Compare the education structures of any three African countries and state which you consider to have the best structure and why.
4 What do you consider are the major reasons that have given rise to changes in education structures in your country in the recent past?
5 Selection is a permanent feature of most African education systems. Give reasons for this and suggest ways for reducing its importance.

VIII

Planning techniques and models

Educational planning involves intervention to produce a more desirable future. This entails establishing a dynamic perspective on the system, that is, understanding the development of the system over time. Statistical data, particularly for making projections to indicate future trends in enrolment and other developments, are essential in this respect. Unfortunately, time series data on which projections can be usefully based, are most conspicuous by their absence from the statistical tabulations emanating from most African education systems. Yet the most dramatic development of any educational system is in terms of student enrolments and their cost implications. It is on the projections of student enrolments that policymakers rely for making decisions about future expansion: the size of future enrolments is the main determinant of future capital and recurrent financial burden. Hence making a proper forecast of student enrolments and their implications is an important function of educational planning.

Educational planning is equally concerned with the administration of the existing system. For this to be efficient and effective requires that we first understand the way the education system works before we can influence or control it. It also involves the effective management of time and manpower. Management models and techniques evolved elsewhere, can therefore be usefully applied in the management of the education system in Africa.

This chapter sets out to justify briefly the need for forecasting future school enrolment and then discusses some of the models and

163

techniques useful to educational planning and administration. The first part of the chapter discusses the main reasons for the projection of school enrolments. This is followed by a short discussion of the kinds of information needed prior to forecasting. The third part outlines the different types of projections. The fourth part gives a brief account of a number of models and techniques used in planning, with some indication of their application to educational development. When evaluating the 'stocks and flows' model or the approach known as 'management by objectives' (MBO) it is important to remember that these exist not only in relation to each other but also in relation to the context within which they are being used. An educational planner may need to draw on a number of techniques, e.g. PERT, the Gantt and milestone charts, and use them in an approach such as systems analysis, which he/she has decided works best within the particular education system with which he/she is familiar.

Need for the projection of future school enrolment

The projection of likely future school enrolment is an essential component of educational planning. Hence, whatever the dearth of statistics available to the planner, it is desirable to have an idea of what to expect in the future. This helps to avoid the risk of unexpected surprises and impractical policies based on haphazard guesses. Even the day to day smooth operation of educational administration depends to a large extent on the accurate forecasting of enrolments within the education system as elaborated in the following paragraphs.

Generally, the educational planner spends much of his time struggling with the present and future consequences of past decisions on school intake. This is true whether he is dealing with the overall system (the macro-level) or the individual institution (micro-level). At the macro-level the consequences of a major decision on enrolment may reverberate through the system for a considerable time. For instance, in 1961 Ghana launched a universal primary education programme which continued to be a headache to educational administrators throughout the 1960s and early 1970s, particularly in such aspects as the unprecedentedly large groups of examination candidates and applicants for the rather limited secondary school places (Williams, P.R.C., 1975). Right now, Nigeria is grappling with the problems of what do with the products of the UPE scheme which was embarked upon in 1976. Although the plan is to absorb 40 per cent of the first products of the UPE outputs into the junior secondary schools (JSS) of the new educational structure of 6 – 3 – 3 – 4, the current shortfall of revenue accruing to the country from oil sales has made the provision of the necessary facilities an uphill task for many state governments. Some state governments and other commentators have in fact questioned the wisdom of attempting to undertake the task at this point in time. However, as the JSS is only one stage of the new educational policy launched in 1976, it is difficult to see how its implementation could be postponed without disastrous consequences for the whole policy.

Effects of earlier events on later developments

The present consequences of past decisions at the micro-level can similarly be illustrated by the following model of class development for a new three-form entry, three-grade secondary (junior or senior) system (Table 8.1).

Table 8.1: Junior secondary school development

| | Number of classes | | | |
Grade	Year 1	Year 2	Year 3	Year 4
Form 1	3	3	3	3
Form 2	–	3	3	3
Form 3	–	–	3	3
Total	3	6	9	9

Thus as Table 8.1 shows, under normal conditions of development the decision to open the school in Form 1 means a commitment to support nine classes two years later. What this means in practical terms is that once a decision has been taken to open the school, facilities in the form of finance, buildings and teachers will be required in increasing amounts over the period of the school's development. In other words, expansion as it were, is 'built-in' to the system. This is the case even when no further expansion occurs above the first year's intake.

The same effect of earlier events on later development is demonstrated by Table 8.2, which shows a secondary school system that adds 50 classes to the system annually for five years, after which it stabilises for the next two years. However, the system only stops growing in year seven although intake was held constant in year five.

Table 8.2:　Development of a secondary school system

Grade	Year							
	0	1	2	3	4	5	6	7
1	250	300	350	400	450	500	500	500
2	200	250	300	350	400	450	500	500
3	150	200	250	300	350	400	450	500
Total	600	750	900	1050	1200	1350	1450	1500

The situation in a five-grade secondary system would be slightly different, as illustrated in Table 8.3. Here, although growth is held constant at year five, it is not until year nine that the situation could finally stabilise.

Table 8.3:　Development of a five-grade secondary school system

Grade	Year									
	0	1	2	3	4	5	6	7	8	9
1	250	300	350	400	450	500	500	500	500	500
2	200	250	300	350	400	450	500	500	500	500
3	150	200	250	300	350	400	450	500	500	500
4	100	150	200	250	300	350	400	450	500	500
5	50	100	150	200	250	300	350	400	450	500
Total	750	1000	1250	1500	1750	2000	2200	2350	2450	2500

Thus all three tables demonstrate that once educational development has commenced, it seems to grow relentlessly under its own momentum. This demonstrates the need for a fairly accurate estimation of future enrolments.

The influence of population growth

Apart from the influence of past decisions on present and future enrolments, governments in most African countries are confronted by high birth rates in the population, which in turn result in a rapid growth of school-age children. As one of the main functions of educational administration is the provision of adequately trained teachers, failure to anticipate the growth of the school-age population could result in a serious shortage of teachers. Any attempt at raising the educational level would similarly call for increasing the numbers of teachers at a faster rate than the number of school-age children. But as teachers cannot be instantly produced on demand, the estimation of potential school enrolment becomes imperative.

The provision of new schools and buildings and the determination of policy changes

Another area where enrolment forecasting is useful is in relation to the provision of new schools and buildings. Though less time is required for this than for teacher training, the requirements for budget preparations, appropriation of funds, identification of localities for the location of the individual schools, the selection of a site and the award of contracts, all require the projection of enrolments in detail in terms of level of education and type of school. Future enrolment estimates are also necessary to meet planning requirements in such aspects as the provision of accommodation for teachers and students, printing and distribution of school textbooks as well as the organisation of transportation for pupils, particularly in rural areas. Estimates for these purposes would in some cases require to be made in terms of sex, age and grade level of pupils.

Besides its usefulness in the administration of planned or existing policies, projection of future enrolments is equally vital in the determination of future policy changes. For instance, before a government can promulgate a law to make universal primary education compulsory, it would be wise to determine the implications of such a law by making a series of alternative projections of the potential school enrolment and its cost implications for the country. It is only after such an exercise that the government can take a realistic decision based on its feasibility.

Basic information requirements for forecasting

The models illustrated above are 'no dropout' models which hardly apply in reality. Before embarking on forecasting intakes however, it is essential to have proper information concerning the intake situation: whether it is compulsory, selective or voluntary (Williams, P.R.C., 1975).

Compulsory intake

Where intake is compulsory, pupil enrolment is enforceable by law and can be assessed from the total population of those who have attained the age of entry. The numbers can therefore be calculated directly from births in a situation of compulsory birth registration, or estimated from past censuses in the absence of such compulsion.

The problems associated with compulsory attendance are mainly those of the geographical distribution of entrants. The problem in fact focuses on the accurate assessment of internal migration and also on whether compulsion means attendance at public schools only or includes private schools as well. It is therefore important that estimates of the proportion of children needing public institutions must make allowance for private school enrolment where this is allowed. Compulsory intake is hardly practised anywhere in Africa at present, not even in those countries that have introduced UPE. The exception is the Republic of South Africa, where it is compulsory for white children to remain in school from January of the year in which a child turns seven until December of the year in which he reaches the age of 16, or until he passes the Standard 10 examination, whichever is the earlier. This also applies to the 'coloured' and Indian populations, but is not the case for the black majority (Official Year Book, 1977).

Selective intake

In a situation of selective intake, the forecasting of first grade entry is essentially dependent on administrative decision. Selective intake implies excess demand over supply and the assumption is that all available places will be filled. Nevertheless, problems may still arise if the number of places are determined by some indication of demand. For example, the target could be to maintain a fixed proportion in school, such as at least 40 per cent of pupils in the final grade of the primary school to be admitted to secondary school. This is in fact the percentage agreed to, for absorption from the primary schools into the junior secondary stage in Nigeria under the new educational policy (NPE, 1981; Blue Print, 77). Equally, the object might be to maintain a fixed proportion of the age group in school, such as 8 per cent of the age group to enter grade one of the secondary schools. These two cases are not the same, as illustrated by the following example.

Suppose the total primary school age population of a locality is 600,000 children, and only 150,000 of them are in the final grade of the primary school. If enrolment into the secondary school is fixed at 40 per cent of the final graders, then 60,000 pupils will be involved, but if intake is fixed at 8 per cent of the age group then only 48,000 would be eligible. The important point is that in such cases, intake will reflect either the enrolment in the preceeding grade or overall school-age population and will not be an arbitrary decision imposed by the administrators of the system.

A second type of forecasting problem in relation to selective intake arises where selection is made conditional on a candidate's attainment of certain standards. In such a case intake will be governed by performance in examinations. Numbers could be depressed by the failure of sufficient candidates in one case or rise to unexpectedly high levels in other circumstances. Forecasting qualified output from one educational stage is also relatively easy where the final examination is of the straight pass/fail type with no separate subject passes. Probably future rates could be deduced from the records of recent annual pass rates. 'But where a course is broken into subjects which may be taken separately, with multiple grades possible for each subject, and subjects can be repeated in or out of school, then the business of forecasting the number of qualifiers is much more complex' (Williams, P.R.C., 1975). This is the case in the Sudan.

This situation can be compounded even further where individual universities have varying entry requirements. Although hardly any African universities within the same country, conduct what could amount to the equivalent of the Oxford-Cambridge (Oxbridge) qualifying examinations, the practice in some countries of basing university enrolment on what is known as 'catchment areas' as in Nigeria, has quite similar effects. The only difference is that the entry requirements are not solely based on success in the national examinations alone, but are coupled with origin of birth within the 'catchment area' of a particular university. This poses no serious problem as long as universities are evenly spread throughout the country. Moreover, in the particular case of Nigeria, a certain proportion of the intake is based on what is generally referred to as 'federal character'.

In situations where candidates qualify on the basis of multiple sitting of the same examination, forecasting intakes will require access to the records of individual candidates. The alternative is to conduct a survey to determine how many candidates for university entry obtain the minimum qualification at a single sitting and how many are likely to qualify after attempting two or three times. The organisation of a clearing house such as The Joint Matriculation Board (JAMB) in Nigeria would help to ease the situation in such a complex case. But the delays involved in the selection of candidates are a major disadvantage.

Voluntary enrolment

Perhaps the most difficult problems are associated with this form of intake. Here it is almost impossible to say precisely how many children will choose to attend, since this is a matter for individual decision. The level of enrolment would consequently rest not so much on the supply, but rather on the demand for education.

Voluntary attendance at school depends on a variety of factors: organisational, socio-economic, cultural and psychological. On the supply side, such factors as the location of schools and the financial arrangements for attending them, which can be directly influenced by administrative action, are crucial determinants of the level of demand. The type of school provided may equally be important as some parents may not accept the attendance of their children at a co-educational school or in one belonging to a different religious faith, for example. Additional reasons could range from the demand for the economic value of a child's service, to the cultural gap between the school and the home, and the difficulty leavers have in securing a job on the completion of a particular course. In addition, the issue of promotion and repetition within each level of the system is also crucial.

Promotion rates and repetition

There are two components of wastage in the education system: dropout and repetition. Dropout refers to a pupil leaving the education system before the completion of a particular cycle. Repetition, on the other hand, implies spending more than the normal duration required for the completion of a grade, that is, repeating the grade. The significance of wastage can only be assessed by following a cohort of pupils from the initial grade right through to the final grade of the level and noting the dropouts and repeaters at each grade.

As a rule, in an educational system with compulsory attendance, dropout is forbidden until a student completes the years of compulsion. However, in a system where there is no compulsion to attend, voluntary dropout or even compulsory dropout (selection out) may be practised. Nowadays, in most African education systems automatic promotion is generally the norm at the primary level, but at the secondary level and beyond, both repetition and compulsory dropout are practised. Data on dropout and repetition are useful for the computation of various ratios: progression, grade retention/repeater, grade and school retention and output ratios (see following section). Thus the analysis of wastage is essential not only for the assessment of the efficiency of the education system, but also for projection purposes.

What all these various factors point to, is that it is vital to undertake a careful analysis of the factors that influence enrolment at present and then to assess the likelihood of their continuing or recurring, before starting to project past intake trends into the future. In other words, the fundamental requirement of accurate forecasting is to try and understand the factors behind particular changes in enrolment. Has past growth been largely in the cities, or largely males? Has it been average children as a result of the introduction of UPE or the reduction of fees? Could the drops in the past be attributed to a particular occurrence such as civil war, a flood or drought? For example, falling intakes were recorded for Nigeria and the Sudan during their civil wars despite population increases, in Kenya following drought conditions, and in Ghana after the 1966 coup as a result of the non-enforcement of compulsion and the introduction of textbook fees (Williams, P.R.C., 1975). This might also have been the case in Mozambique and Zimbabwe during their independence struggles and could still be the case in Mozambique, Angola and Namibia (South-West Africa) as a result of the continuing conflicts within these countries. However, where school attendance rates reflect deep-seated social and economic considerations, then we can expect only a gradual change with growth largely attributable to population increases rather than to any dramatic rises in demand. Generally, however, voluntary and selective intakes are the most common approaches to enrolment in African education systems.

Methods of forecasting school enrolments

A wide variety of methods of forecasting school enrolments are to be found in the literature on educational planning. These range from the traditional methods dependent upon forecasts of enrolment ratios based on projections of trends and correlations with the demographic, geographic and socio-economic structure of the population, to the more recent models based on individual demand for places. However, in keeping with the purposeful nature of the present book, only those models that can be usefully employed by a wide spectrum of those involved in the development of the education system in Africa will be discussed. It is important to remember when looking at these methods and models that care is taken in their selection and use. An effective educational planner is one who can see the use to be had in using a particular approach and to adopting such methods as may be necessary to meet current and future local realities. Three of these useful methods are the enrolment-ratio method, the grade cohort method or the stocks and flow method.

1   The enrolment-ratio method

This method rests on the assumption that there is some continuing functional relationship between student enrolment and school-age population in defined area or geographical location. However, the ratio may also be that of enrolment at one level in relation to that of another level in the same educational system (Liu, 1966; Chesswas, 1967). The basic data requirements for the purposes of calculation are:

- estimates of population by age and sex;
- school enrolment data by level (from current school statistics) or school attendance data (from census and surveys) in each case by sex and age;
- distribution of school enrolment by grade.

The steps in the computation are as follows:

1   Determine the appropriate age-groups for each level of schooling (e.g. 6–11 primary level, 12–14 junior secondary level, and 15–18 senior secondary level) and then estimate the school-age populations for each age group.
2   If population estimates are given in five year age groups, which is invariably the case in Africa, then estimate single-year school-age population by interpolation (see Fig. 7.3, p. 151 for education pyramid).
3   On the basis of the observations of past trends assume school attendance or enrolment ratios for each sex and age-group.
4   These assumed attendance ratios are then multiplied by the school-age population to obtain the total future enrolment figures.
5   If so desired, the enrolment figures can be broken down in terms of public and private schools or urban and rural schools.

2   *The class or grade cohort method*

This method is sometimes also known as the 'grade survival' method. It attempts to forecast future enrolment variables on the patterns of the past values of the same variables (Liu, 1966; Chesswas, 1967; Williams, P.R.C., 1979; Brimer and Pauli, 1971). No explanations are offered for the cases of change and the relationships and processes at work. What it attempts to do is to adopt the enrolment patterns of the past and extrapolate them into the future. This is done by analysis of what happens to a cohort of students as they progress through all the grades of a level. The computation depends on such variables as current enrolments, estimates of intake ratio, retention and out-put ratios of the school system. Data are consequently required on:

• Enrolment by class for the entire grade of the particular level (six years primary, three each for junior and senior secondary levels, or five for secondary level in countries like Zambia and Zimbabwe).
• Numbers of new pupils and repeaters for each grade by sex and possibly by geographical distribution and according to private and public schools.

Once the various data are assembled, the steps are:

1   With the figures for new pupils and repeaters, compute the progression, retention and repeater ratios between the grades up to the last, e.g. between 1 and 2, 2 and 3 and so forth.
2   After computing the grade retention ratio for a number of years, these are examined for possible trends. If no discernable trend emerges, then the average for the number of years is calculated. However, if a pattern shows, say, differentiation in retention ratios by sex, then these should be computed separately.
3   Compound the class retention ratios (that is, multiply them together one after the other) from the first to the last class to get the school retention ratios. In this way the retention ratios for the cohort after one, two, right through to the final grade are obtained.
4   On the basis of the yearly and average grade retention ratios obtained above, assumptions can be made about future retention levels. In a growing education system these would be expected to improve and approximate towards 100 per cent. These new retention ratios could then be applied for forecasting future school enrolments.
5   By applying the observed intake ratios, the size of the future starting cohorts can be estimated from future school-age

populations. Beginning cohorts beyond primary stage can similarly be obtained by using the intake ratios from the last grade of the lower level.

6 Finally, total enrolment is obtained by applying the assumed school retention ratios to the estimated starting cohorts for future years (see also Table 8.4).

If it is desired to forecast enrolments for rural and urban areas or different types of schools separately, these could be obtained from the totals by the application of past distribution patterns. This can also be considered in terms of a stocks and flows model using simple algebraic expressions.

Table 8.4 Percentage of repeaters in primary education: both sexes, 1980/1988

Below 5%	5% – 9.9%	10% – 14.9%	15% – 19.9%	20% – 24.9%	25% – 29.9%	30% and over
	Botswana (1988) 5%	Djibouti (1988) 10%	Sierra Leone (1980) 15%	Mauritania (1988) 20%	Mali (1988) 30%	
	United Republic of Tanzania (1988) 6%	Rwanda (1988) 10%	Morocco (1988) 15%	Zaïre (1988) 21%	Mozambique (1988) 25%	Togo (1988) 31% Gabon (1988) 31%
	Algeria (1988) 7%	Liberia (1980) 11%	Swaziland (1988) 15%	Tunisia (1988) 21%	Benin (1988) 26%	Chad (1988) 33%
Zambia (1988) 2%		Ethiopia (1988) 11%	Senegal (1988) 16%	Malâwi (1988) 21%		Central African Republic (1988) 34%
Ghana (1980) 2%		Niger (1988) 13%	Burkina Faso (1988) 17% Gambia (1988) 18%		Côte d'Ivoire (1988) 28%	Sao Tome (1988) and Principe 35%
Egypt (1988) 3%	Libyan Arab Jamahiriya (1980) 9%	Uganda (1988) 14%		Guinea (1988) 22%		Congo (1988) 35%
			Burundi (1988) 19%	Lesotho (1988) 22%	Cameroon (1988) 29%	Madagascar (1988) 35% Guinea-Bissau (1988) 42%

Source: World Education Report, UNESCO, 1991.

3   *Stocks and flows model*

This model has been applied in a variety of national contexts, including manpower planning. In education, one of its chief uses is to trace the progress of pupils and students through the school system, as it is concerned not only with stocks but also with flows as shown in Fig. 8.1 (Williams, G. 1975; Open University Press, 1976; Armitage, 1973).

The basic components of the model are as shown in the figure, where the stocks are in the boxes and the flows are represented by lines with arrows indicating the direction of flows. In this case the stocks are the numbers of pupils of a given age who are either in or out of school. In the case of most African education systems at present, with no compulsory stage, it is inevitable that there are more children out of school than in. The exception would be in situations where universal primary education has been in operation for a number of years.

A stocks and flows model as represented in Fig. 8.1 can be set out in the form of statements as follows:

| *Number* of boys (or girls) of given age in school in specified year | = | the *flow* of boys (or girls) who were in school (one year younger) the previous year and who stay on to specified year | + | the *flow* of boys (or girls) who were not in school the previous year and who enter by the particular year when they are of given age |

In other words,

| Total enrolment in primary school in 1980 P1 – P6. | = | Total enrolment in 1979 (minus finalists) i.e. P2 – P6. | + | Present new 1 entrants in 1908 (i.e. P1). |

This updated stock is the sum of the flows within and into the system. We shall, however, concentrate on the stocks within the system. But total yearly numbers or enrolments in the schools will fluctuate on account of two factors: demographic variation of school-age population and wastage, e.g. dropouts, children moving, amongst those already in school. Consequently, the proportion of an age group which gains entry into school is more important than the absolute numbers. Similarly the flow of pupils who stay on as a proportion of those who could have stayed is more important than the absolute numbers. We therefore need to make the following substitution in the above statement.

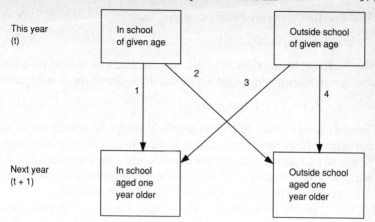

1 the flow of pupils who stay on in school;
2 the flow of pupils in school this year but leave before next year;
3 the flow into school of children who were not in school last year;
4 the flow of children who were not in school last year and who stay outside the following year.

Fig. 8.1 Movements in stocks and flows model

The flow of boys (or girls) who were in school (one year younger) the previous year and who stay on to specified year		the proportion of boys (or girls) who were in school (one year younger) the previous year who stay on		the stock of boys (or girls) who were in school (one year younger) the previous year.
	=		×	

It is now possible to make projections with such a stocks and flows model provided we know the initial stocks in a base year and are prepared to make assumptions concerning the proportions who will stay on as well as the numbers of the new entrants from outside. Hence the provision of inferred transition proportions, based on past experience, for both boys and girls is a pre-requisite for the projection of future enrolments using the stocks and flows model.

All that has been said above can be summarised using simple algebraic symbols.

Let: $N(a, t)$ be the number of those aged a in the total population in year t.

$P(a, t)$ be the proportion of those aged a in the total population in year t who are in school, and

$n(a, t)$ be the number of pupils aged a in year t who are in school.

Thus our first statement will be of the form:

$$n(a, t) = P(a, t) \, N(a, t)(1) \tag{1}$$

Also let f(a, t) be the flow of pupils in school aged a in year t + 1 who were not in school when aged a. Our equation therefore now becomes:

$$n(a + 1, t + 1) = f(a, t) + u(a, t) \tag{2}$$

Thus, we are in effect finding next year's stocks by adding up all the movements from this year's stocks. In fact the convention is to define the age of entrants, not as at time of entry when they will be a + 1, but rather at a year earlier so that they are compatible with the flow of entrants within the system. On this basis we can now say:
Let P(a, t) be the proportion of those aged a in school in year t who stay on to year t + 1 when aged a + 1, and the flows as the products of the proportions and original stocks become:

$$f(a, t) = p(a, t)n(a, t) \tag{3}$$

By substitution, the equation becomes: (2)

$$n(a + 1, t + 1) = p(a, t)n(a, t) + u(a, t) \tag{4}$$

This form of arrangement of the stocks and flows enables projections to be made from initial base year stocks, n(a,t), provided we make assumptions regarding p(a,t) and u(a,t). This allows n(a + 1, t + 1) to be determined. But it also follows from equation (4) that:

$$n(a + 2, t + 2) = p(a + 1, t + 1)n(a + 1), t + 1) + u(a + 1, t + 1)$$

Consequently, if the first calculated value of n(a + 1, t + 1) is substituted on the right-hand side and further assumptions made regarding the appropriate groups staying on and entering, in the next time period n(a + 2, t + 2) can be calculated. Stocks of all ages for all years of interest can be computed in a similar manner.

The systems approach to educational management

The expansion of education systems in Africa during the last two decades of the 1960s and 1970s has reached such a stage now, that the effective management of the system requires the application of more sophisticated approaches. The systems approach, a term encompassing a wide variety of concepts and techniques, offers one such possibility. The purpose of this section of the chapter is therefore to introduce some of the selected concepts and techniques that are relevant for use for the improvement of the management of African education systems. The basic advantage of the systems approach is that it provides the tools for out-come oriented school management, rather than concentration on mere administrative process. It focuses on output and integrates the administrative processes (planning, organisation, direction, co-ordination and control) in a logical and manageable scheme.

Systems concepts

The development of systems thought first originated in the field of biology, and later spread to the natural sciences and engineering. In education, the application of the systems approach to educational administration was largely through the efforts of the American Association of Educational Administrators (AASE). Through its publications, seminars and conventions, the AASE popularised the systems approach amongst practising administrators and this gave impetus to what became known as the 'Systems Approach Movement'.

What is a system?

According to Granger:

A system may be defined as a cohesive collection of items that are dynamically related. The term describes an interrelated network of objects and events or the symbols for such an assembly. Systems are sets of elements or parts which possess some degree of independence or identity, but, at the same time, are an integral part of a larger assembly or whole (Granger, 1971).

While Ackoff says a system is simply a 'set of interrelated elements' (Ackoff, quoted in Landers and Myers, 1977). Kaufman defines a system as 'the sum total of parts working independently and working together to achieve required results or outcomes, based on needs' (Kaufman, 1972). In sum, we can say that a system is a whole that consists of parts and subparts, which have dynamic relationships among themselves and with the whole. Having considered what a system is, we can proceed to examine what is meant by the systems approach.

What is the systems approach?

There is no precise definition of the term systems approach that is universally acceptable. It can, however, be described as a way of thinking based upon systems theory. It involves thinking in terms of the whole problem and its interacting subparts or components, as well as analysing, selecting, implementing and monitoring the optimum alternative sequences of the component parts in order to achieve desired outcomes. Thus Sergiovanni and Carver describe the systems approach to education as follows:

A systems approach is one which relies upon model building and the development of conceptual frameworks which help facilitate decision-making by providing a basis for sorting variables and for showing relationships between and among variables and components. . . . systems thinking, then, is really the generation of intellectual maps with which we are better able to engage in planning problem-solving, and decision-making activities (Segiovanni and Carver, 1973)

Kaufman, who was the first to apply the system approach to education, defines it as 'a type of logical problem-solving process which is applied to identifying and resolving important educational problems.' These six steps as identified by Kaufman are shown in Fig. 8.2. Other planning and problem-solving procedures which we shall consider that are used in educational management are the Program Evaluation and Review Technique (PERT) together with the Critical Path Method (CPM), the Planning-Programming-Budgeting System (PPBS) and Management by Objective (MBO).

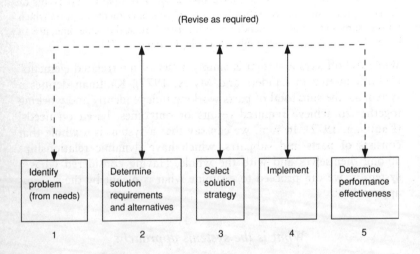

Fig. 8.2 A general problem-solving process
(Five steps identified, the last (revise as required), indicated by dashed lines.)

Task planning and co-ordination

Out of the systems movement has developed a variety of models which have been applied in education, for task planning and co-ordination. This is because operational objectives are the backbone of the individual school plan or the education system as a whole. To realise these objectives such planning questions as 'How do we get there?' 'When will it be done?' and 'Who will be responsible?' should be answered. The process, according to Kaufman, is one in which:

needs are identified, problems selected, requirements for problem solution are identified, solutions are chosen from alternatives, methods and means are obtained and implemented, results are evaluated, and required revisions to all or part of the system are made so that the needs are eliminated (Kaufman, 1972).

System tools and procedures

There are essentially five elements in the systems procedure as shown in Fig. 8.2 (Williams, P. et al., 1982).

1 The first step in developing a system in solving a problem is to identify the goals or needs of the system and then specify or select the problem to be solved. It is important that the real problems of the entire system are specified.

2 This is followed by the translation of such general goals or problems into specific objectives, defined in specific terms that can be accomplished at the subsystem level. What then emerges are specific subproblems or components of the new system.

3 For each objective a number of possible solutions are generated. Out of these feasible alternatives are considered.

4 Methods and means are obtained for implementing the selected solution. The level of success of the solution, however, depends to some extent on the skills of the educational manager or administrator.

5 Results are then evaluated, and required revisions to all or parts of the system are made, on the basis of feedout, so that the problem, or needs are eliminated or the goal achieved.

Researches in other countries have often found that the attempts by education systems to implement planned programmes have often foundered because the necessary procedural details of the various programmes were not clearly spelled out (Wacaster, 1979). The absence of a task plan causes staff to implement, co-ordinate and develop tasks as they went along. The result, as we have witnessed in African education systems time and again, is project failure.

Task planning, in essence, can be defined as the function of:

1) selecting the work requirements to accomplish the objective;
2) developing a work plan or schedule of all work requirements; and
3) controlling to ensure that work activities are completed as scheduled and objectives are achieved (Cunningham, 1982).

Thus task planning and co-ordination involve a systematic attack on an operational objective by breaking it up into parts so as to reach a successful milestone. The trick in doing this is to visualise how a series of actions will progress before starting them. The models that follow are attempts in this direction.

1   *The bar, or Gantt chart and the Milestone chart*

One of the earliest attempts at task planning and co-ordination is the bar or Gantt chart which developed out of making activity lists, or action sequences, normally carried around us of what we have to do. The bar or Gantt technique was developed by H. L. Gantt and Frederick W. Taylor as an aid to administrators faced with tasks requiring many skilled persons and equipment, as well as contractors and material suppliers, all performing a number of different activities that must be done in a prescribed sequence in order for predetermined objectives to be achieved. This requires that the tasks be co-ordinated and scheduled in advance. The conventional method of preparing a plan and schedule in the graphic form as shown in Fig. 8.3 is known as the Gantt or bar chart or network diagram.

The basic advantages of a Gantt chart are that:

i) It makes visualisation of the plan and schedule and task relationships much clearer.
ii) It shows estimated times of each activity.
iii) The total time for the project may be read directly from the Gantt chart by looking at the completion of the last activity.

Although a useful management tool, the Gantt chart has the following limitations:

i) It does not indicate the effect on the project completion time, if some work is behind or ahead of schedule.
ii) It does not show the dependencies or relationships between the various activities or tasks, and as such, cannot help in predicting the effect of a delay in one area over another and on the project as a whole.

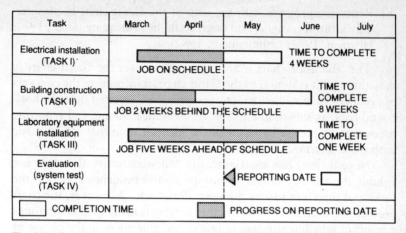

Fig. 8.3 Gantt chart: schedule for a school building project (after Hicks, H. D., 1967, 1972)

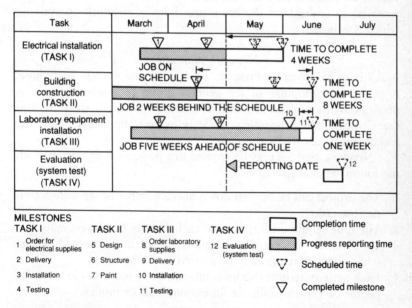

Fig. 8.4 Milestone chart: schedule for a school building project (after Qutubuddin Khan (1985) *Survey of the Evaluation Methods and Techniques of Educational Plans, Programmes and Projects within the Framework of the Implementation of Educational Policies*, UNESCO (ED-85/WS/40), p. 29.

iii) Reporting progress with the help of the Gantt chart is considerably arbitrary, vague, and often could be misleading (Shah, 1971;
Hostrop, 1975; Cunningham, 1982).

The Milestone chart is an improvement over the Gantt chart in
that although it is similar to the Gantt chart, it introduces the concepts
of events or intermediate milestones which are inserted over the horizontal bars, as shown in Fig. 8.4. As a result, planning and reporting
become more precise by virtue of the identification that can be made
with these intermediate milestones.

Nevertheless, like the Gantt, the Milestone chart also does not
exhibit the various interrelationships and dependencies among the
tasks and therefore suffers the same drawbacks. Moreover, the chart
provides no indication as to whether a delay is likely to arise or not as
a result of schedule slippage in one of the milestones in the course of
the implementation of the project.

2   PERT/CPM: *a planning and analysis tool*

Before we embark on a discussion of the PERT/CPM network, it is
essential to understand the basic principles of network analysis on
which it is based.

Network planning

PERT is an acronym for Program Evaluation and Review Technique.
It is the most popular of the general group of models known as
network analysis which includes the Critical Path Method (CPM) and
the Critical Path Scheduling (CPS). However, the basis of all the
techniques is essentially the same.

Network analysis may be applied to a project (or operation) with
the following characteristics:

1   The project can be broken down into a number of *separate* activities (or tasks).
2   The time required (duration) of each activity can be estimated.
3   To complete the project, certain activities must *precede* others,
while some activities may be carried out in *parallel*.
4   Each activity requires some combination of resources in terms of
people of various skills, facilities, materials or money.

Drawing networks

The project is usually represented by a figure consisting of two building blocks: *lines* which represent *activities* and *circles* known as *events*,

which represent *points in time*. An event is a stage in the life of the project when preceding activities will all have been completed and succeeding activities can start. All the activities and events associated with the project are normally joined together to form a single network diagram, which illustrate the logical sequence of activities and events, as shown in Fig. 8.5

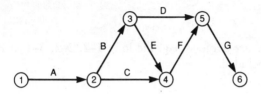

Fig. 8.5   Activities and events in a network

In Fig. 8.5 six activities, labelled A to G, are involved. By convention networks are usually constructed from left to right and a reference number is also attached to each node (event) as shown. For example, activity C is defined by its preceeding and succeeding event numbers as activity 2–4. Thus the network in Fig. 8.5 embodies the following relationships:

1   Event 1 is the starting point of the project.
2   Activities B and C only start on the completion of A.
3   Activities D and E cannot start until B is completed.
4   Activity F can only start when E and C are completed.
5   Activity G cannot start until D and F are completed.
6   Event 6 is the end of the project.

Rules to observe
The following rules must be observed in the construction of a network.

1   No activity is left 'dangling' e.g. activity 2–3 in Fig. 8.6 has no connection with the end event and so must be modified so that activity 2–3 is brought in to a path leading to the end event. This could be done by connecting 3 directly to 6 with an activity which consumes neither time or resources. This activity is known as a 'dummy'.

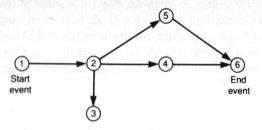

Fig. 8.6

2   Closed loops are avoided, e.g. the loop 1–2, 2–3, 3–1 in Fig. 8.7
    cannot be included.

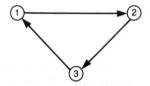

Fig. 8.7

3   Parallel activities cannot have both the same start and end events,
    as this leads to confusion of identity. This is overcome by inserting
    a 'dummy' activity which has zero duration and uses no resources.
    For example:

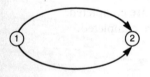

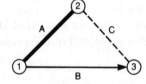

Fig. 8.8

The 'dummy' C is conventionally represented by a broken activity
line. We can now consider PERT in a little more detail.

PERT *as a management and planning tool*
The essential difference between PERT and CPM is that whereas the
former requires three time estimates for each event/activity completion, the latter uses only one time estimate. PERT is a useful technique

for planning and scheduling the systematic analysis and control of activities in a project, which ultimately leads to objective accomplishment. It is particularly useful in situations where the exact time needed to complete a project is not known precisely but could be estimated. This characteristic would make it a useful decision-making tool in African education systems in, for example, the completion of building programmes for the establishment of new schools. Also for the development of new schools for a school system.

The technique was a joint development of the United States Navy Special Operations Project Office and a firm of management consultants in 1957–58 for use on the Polaris Missile Program. Its use was credited with having aided in the completion of the program well ahead of schedule. Since then it has been widely used in business, industrial and educational organisations. PERT is characterised by four main features:

1 A network that graphically depicts the inter-relationship of activities (events) involved in reaching and accomplishing an objective.
2 Three time estimates for the completion of each activity (event) in the network: the most optimistic, the most likely, and the most pessimistic.
3 A formula for calculating the probability distribution of the 'expected' time for accomplishing the activity (event).
4 Identification of the longest expected time sequence through the network which is labelled 'the critical path' since the objective will not be realised until the critical path is completed (Landers and Myers, 1977).

PERT in educational administration

PERT is useful to educational administrators in the management of manpower and time, especially the management of educational projects that involve multiple activities with complex timetabling requirements for their completion. Some areas in which the technique could be applied to advantage are:

1 Budget preparation.
2 Analysing procedures for the purchase of materials and supplies.
3 Planning a feasibility study of administrative organisation.
4 Planning and controlling an educational needs survey.
5 Analysing scheduling procedures.
6 Planning a curriculum evaluation.
7 Analysing media scheduling.
8 Planning and analysing maintenance procedures.

PERT analysis

There are four essential steps in a PERT analysis of a project:

1 Define the project objective.
2 Identify the key activities required to complete the project. This entails the breakdown of the project into its component parts.
3 Understand the relationship between the required activities, i.e. determine the sequence in which activities must be completed, then draw a network to show the sequence by the use of flow diagrams.
4 Estimate the time needed to complete each activity, using any unit of time (days, weeks, months) provided these are kept the same throughout the network.

In PERT normally three time estimates are involved – the Optimistic Time (OT), the most Likely Time (LT), and the Pessimistic Time (PT). The Estimated Time (ET) is then derived from a weighted average of these times using the following formula:

$$ET = \frac{OT + LT(4) + PT}{6}$$

It is assumed that ET is four times more likely than either of the other two possibilities.

Once the times required to complete the project are computed, the critical path, using the critical path method (CPM), through the project is computed. The critical path through the project is a particular sequence of activities in the PERT network which determines the minimum amount of time it will take to complete the project. It is considered a critical path because the completion of each activity along it within the estimated duration of time is necessary in order to complete the project within the estimated time (ET). In other words, the critical path is that path through the network which has the least possible slack.

The network plan or the PERT network, is constructed by drawing circles and arrows in the sequence in which the events and activities are to be accomplished. The network always begins with one event, called the origin, and must always end with another event, called the terminal event. An activity is added to the network when the following three questions have been answered:

1 Which activities must be completed before this activity can start?
2 Which activities must start after this activity is completed?
3 What other activities can be performed at the same time as this activity?

One activity follows another on the network if the one before it has to be completed before it can go on at the same time, if those activities are not dependent on one another and the completion of one activity has no effect on the completion of another. Thus concurrent activities must be independent of one another.

These steps can be illustrated by the example given in Chapter 2 (p. 46) where a provincial authority plans to increase its primary intake from a current enrolment of 152,000 to 175,000 in three years. The first step is to identify and then list the various activities involved in the implementation of the project. Time estimates for the duration of each activity are then made, as shown in Table 8.5 and in Fig. 8.9.

Table 8.5   Estimates for the duration of activities in PERT

Activity description	Time in weeks			
	OT	LT	PT	ET
Determine new classes to be added yearly	0.4	1	2	1.1
Determine number of additional teaching staff	0.4	2	3	1.9
Select junior secondary leavers for teacher training	4	8	12	8.0
Train selected teachers	108	116	128	59.3
Determine location and site of new schools	8	12	16	12.0
Award school building contracts	4	8	16	19.3
Construct new schools	75	108	156	110.5
Furnish and equip new schools	12	16	24	16.7
Post teachers to new schools	2	4	8	4.3
Enrol pupils into new schools and commence teaching	1	1.4	2.4	1.5

The final figure for ET, or the expected time or the weighted average of the other three periods, assumes that ET is four times more likely than either of the other two possibilities and is calculated using the formula already stated.

Another example of the use of PERT is illustrated by the following. Assume that a group of African students in an overseas university decides to publish a journal to be called the *African Voice*, to publicise African viewpoints on university and other issues. They start work on the journal in September 1987 with the first edition expected to be

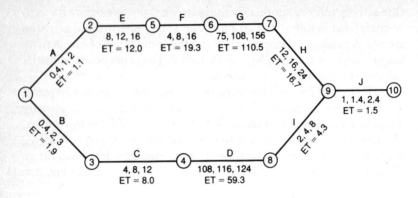

In this example there are basically two paths:

Path	Estimated Times (ET)		Total	Critical Path	Slack
AEFGHJ	1.1 + 12.0 + 19.3 + 110.5 + 16.7 + 1.5	=	161.1	161.1	0.0
BCDIJ	1.9 + 8.0 + 59.3 + 4.3 + 1.5	=	75.0	8161.1	86.1

Fig. 8.9 PERT Network of Activities to be completed before the enrolment of additional pupils for the expansion of the system.

published in September of the following year. To organise their work systematically, the editor decides to apply programme and evaluation technique to the sequencing of their work. The activities involved are itemised in Table 8.6

Table 8.6: Estimated times for activities in production of a student journal

Activity	Time in weeks			
	OT	LT	PT	ET
Conduct opinion poll	0.5	1	1.5	1
Acquire administrative approval	1	2	3	2
Recruit staff	4	8	12	8
Train personnel	2	3	4	3
Solicit advertisements and contributions	4	6	14	7
Assemble student articles	2	6	10	6
Review articles	1	2	3	2
Select manuscripts for publication	0.5	1	1.5	1

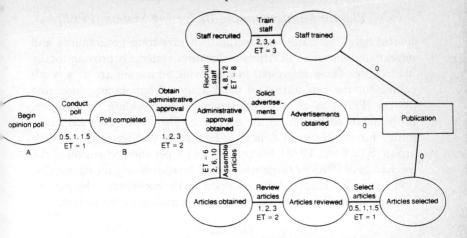

Fig. 8.10 A PERT network of activities in the publication of a student journal (After H. D. Hicks, 1967, 1972)

Uses of PERT *in educational planning and administration*

The first advantage of PERT to the educational decision-maker and planner is that it forces one systematically to analyse any problem under consideration. Thus it provides an invaluable approach in ordering one's thinking and in the organisation and planning of educational projects involving a large number of interrelated phases or stages. Such projects can range from the construction of new schools and the introduction of new subjects into the curriculum or the re-organisation of existing programs to budget preparation and the analysis of procedures for the purchase of materials and supplies.

Second, PERT network sequences can assist in identifying those sub-projects which could be separated from the main project and delegated to subordinates or special sub-groups. In addition, by using the time estimates of the analysis, it becomes easy systematically to construct a calendar of activities covering the whole project period.

Third, once a particular project is being implemented, PERT time analysis serves as a useful guide in monitoring the progress of the project, particularly the critical path.

Finally, the complete PERT analysis is a valuable tool to the educational administrator for communicating with his superiors and subordinates, or anybody else, concerning a project. The network provides a clear picture of the links amongst the various sub-units of the project. All those involved in the project can therefore have a clear idea about how their own tasks fit into the overall scheme.

3 *Planning-Programming-Budgeting System (PPBS)*

Increasingly, the traditional methods of preparing programmes and developing objectives in African education systems is proving totally inadequate. Those interested in improving education are as a result calling for the exploration of the Planning-Programming-Budgeting System (PPBS) as an alternative method for tackling the complex problems of education on the continent. The Implementation Committee for the National Policy on Education in Nigeria is one such group (Blue Print, 1978). But the lack of proper comprehension of the mechanics of PPBS by those who would be responsible for its installation has so far hindered the adoption of the technique. The present effort is an attempt to assist in the understanding of the system.

Definition

The Planning-Programming-Budgeting System is an approach to decision-making which systematically integrates all aspects of planning and program implementation. In planning terms, it is a way of organising information and analysis in a systematic fashion so that the consequences of particular choices can be seen as clearly as possible. Thus by displaying data in a comprehensive format, PPBS assists the decision-maker in analysing and judging all the disparate activities of the school system as an organised whole.

Development

Like PERT, this technique was developed in the US in the 1950s. In 1961, the Department of Defence introduced 'Program Budgeting'. But perhaps the greatest impetus to the development and popularity of the technique was given by President Lyndon B. Johnson when he announced an executive order imposing PPBS on the Federal bureaucracy on 25 August 1965. In his announcement, he described PPBS as 'a very revolutionary system of planning and program budgeting . . .', which indeed it was at the time. 'This program', he went on to say, 'is designed to achieve three objectives: It will help us find new ways to do jobs faster, to do jobs better, and to do jobs less expensively. It will insure a much sounder judgement through more accurate information, pin-pointing those things that we ought to do more, spot-lighting those things that we ought to do less' (Novick, 1965, cited in Alioto and Junghert, 1971).

It was not, however, until 1971 that PPBS was applied to educational planning in the US. Nevertheless, since then its use has become fairly widespread as a planning tool in the educational systems of many other developed countries. PPBS seeks fundamentally to do three things: first, review programmes being undertaken, including testing the validity of stated or implied objectives, and alternative means of achieving them. Second, establishing measures of performance and ways of costing the educational impact of what is being done. Third, evaluating such programmes in terms of priority and consequently either increasing or decreasing the resources allocated to them to ensure maximum effectiveness (Birley, 1972).

Moreover, properly applied, the technique of PPBS could satisfy three basic requirements in education. Firstly, it could ensure program relevance to the needs of pupils, students and the community at large. Thus PPBS attempts to ensure that the objectives of the education system are relevant to the needs of society. Secondly, democratic or participatory decision-making is fostered. The implementation of PPBS requires of necessity a democratic approach and this makes it easier and desirable to involve teachers, representatives of the community, particularly where funds are concerned, and the public at large in decision-making. The PPBS process offers a legitimate vehicle for teachers to participate in the decision-making on priorities and objectives that they and the school system can reasonably expect to achieve. Thus it offers the possibility of joint decision-making between teachers and the administrators. Teachers could therefore be more deeply involved in the development of the curriculum than is the case at present in many African education systems, where their role in this respect is almost peripheral.

Thirdly, cost-effectiveness or value for money, is realised not only by measuring the program costs but also by assessing the success of the existing policies in achieving agreed objectives and making the necessary adjustments accordingly.

Generally, PPBS can therefore assist educational planners in the following ways:

i) Identifying goals and defining objectives.
ii) Designing curricular programmes for the achievement of objectives.
iii) Systematic analysis of the available alternatives.
iv) Providing decision-makers with more and better data.
v) Evaluation of costs and effectiveness of competing programmes.
vi) Extending the time span in planning.
vii) Rational allocation of financial resources to instructional programmes.
viii) Identifying programme priorities.
ix) Promoting innovative programmes and methods.

x) Increasing public understanding of, and support for, the education system. At the present time of dire economic situation of most African countries, it is important to justify public expenditure on education (Alioto and Jungherr, 1971).

The mechanics of PPBS

Any meaningful planning must include as a minimum the following components:

- formulation and analysis of objectives;
- assessment of resources; and
- the preparation of phased programmes to achieve the objectives effectively and economically.

In PPBS this is conducted as a process by stages because the assumption is that meaningful resources allocation necessitates the analysis and review of the whole education system. Hence, the steps in the implementation of a PPBS system are as follows:

1   The first step is to establish a philosophy/goal for the education system. This can be at the national level, or regional/state level or even at the institutional level. Such a philosophy/goal normally takes the form of statements of general educational aims, based on the general expectation of community, students and professional staff. It is therefore general and timeless, that is, not concerned with a specific achievement within a specified time period. National philosophies/goals for education are usually derived from a variety of sources – policy documents by governments, political parties, reports of advisory committees, or the resolutions of representative assemblies. The best examples of this are those contained in such documents as *Education for Self-Reliance* in Tanzania, the *New National Policy on Education* in Nigeria and the *Common Man's Charter* in Uganda. Each of these documents states the goals or purposes which the educational system should strive to achieve. Such statements are, however, only useful to the extent that they provide overall direction for the development of more specific objectives.

2   The second step is the formulation of objectives on the basis of the stated goals or aims. An objective is a desired accomplishment or something toward which effort is directed, which can be measured within a given time frame. An objective attempts to describe the intent of a particular program or activity and this can be stated in terms of performance or behavioural expectations. Achievement of the objective advances the system towards a corresponding goal.

Objectives must consequently be developed that support and contribute to the achievement of the stated goals. Objectives are normally also ranked hierarchically in a PPBS system. This is essential because it is on the basis of the established priorities that resources are allocated. It also serves to direct the efforts of the staff. However, objectives as ends need the means.

3 The third step is to translate the objectives into programmes for implementation so as to realise the end. A program is a group of interdependent, closely related services or activities progressing toward or contributing to a common objective or set of objectives. The first step is therefore the establishment of a programme structure. This is an hierarchical arrangement of programmes which represents the relationship of activities to goals and objectives. The structure would contain categories of activities with common output objectives. The programme structure in a state or region within a country such as Nigeria would, for example, comprise primary education, secondary education and post-secondary education. The programme categories could further be subdivided into programme elements. Thus at the primary level, this would consist of the subdivisions of pre-primary, infant and junior or simply nursery and primary proper. The programme structure is therefore the basis for programme accounting. It provides the framework for programme description, review and analysis.

4 The establishment of a programme structure is then followed by the organisation of a programme budget. The programme budget is in fact a plan that relates proposed expenditures for programmes, within a specified time period, to goals and objectives. In other words, it relates cost information to the categories in the programme structure, thus displaying costs on a programme-by-programme basis. Programmes are usually coded to facilitate the collection of data such as costs and statistics. These data are then used for the purposes of controlling programme expenditures, the evaluation of programme effectiveness in terms of stated objectives, as well as for the analysis of cost effectiveness of alternative programmes. Teachers and principals as programme developers are of necessity fully involved, thus resulting in participatory planning. The programme budget, in addition, includes the proposed revenue sources for financing programmes.

5 The final step in the mechanics of PPBS is the evaluation or assessment of performance and/or impact. Generally, the aim of evaluation of any institution is to obtain information to assist in decision-making. Since the mission of a PPBS system is to obtain

better information with which to make decisions, then the role of evaluation in PPBS is to enable the decision-maker to inform on the question: 'where are we now?' Alioto and Jungherr (1971) have listed the contribution of PPBS as follows:

a) It generates information to determine whether or not, or to what extent, objectives have been accomplished.
b) Additional staff needs.
c) Student transportation.
d) New educational programmes or modifications of existing ones.
e) Needs of instructional support programs.
f) New construction and modifications to existing ones (see Chapter 13 on budgeting for details).

It is important to bear in mind, however, that success in the application of PPBS, as with the old fashioned system in use, is to a large measure affected by the availability of reliable and adequate data.

4   *Management By Objectives (MBO)*

The need for results-oriented management in education in Africa
Up to now no serious attempt has been made to introduce the assessment of professional productivity in the educational systems of Africa. The basic reason for the lack of action in this area is the dearth of knowledge of the tools necessary for carrying out the measurement and evaluation of the effectiveness of classroom techniques and administrative practice. These measures should now be introduced into our education systems for two fundamental reasons:

1   The size and complexity of the schools.
2   The increasing public demand for accountability of the education system to justify the escalations in education costs.

Size and complexity of schools
In all countries of the continent, the size of schools and variety of courses offered in them has increased enormously during the past two decades of the 1960s and 1970s. This has been especially remarkable in the larger countries such as Egypt, Algeria and Nigeria, but equally in some of the countries with small populations like Kenya, Tanzania, Gabon and Côte d'Ivoire. This expansion is perhaps best illustrated by Nigeria. Thus, for example, not only was universal primary education introduced in 1976, but at the secondary level, the institutions provided ranged from the general secondary schools and science secondary schools, to UPE teachers colleges and technical and vocational

secondary schools, and in 1982 the secondary stage was reorganised into junior and senior stages, each of three years duration. At the post-secondary level, an equal array of institutions are also to be found: polytechnics, colleges of technology, advanced teachers colleges, colleges of education and universities (traditional and technological). The numbers of institutions, and thus the enrolments, are large. This means that quality control and maximum effectiveness of the system can no longer be assured using the existing system of organising and monitoring the system. This then leads to the second issue.

Public demand for accountability

The first thing to be noted in this respect is that the expansion of the system in terms of the numbers of institutions and student enrolments, has been accompanied by large-scale cost escalation for developing and maintaining the system. In Nigeria, for example, the Federal and State governments have devoted between 15 per cent and 25 per cent of the annual budget on education. But, in the continent as a whole, there has also been a marked decline in the academic performance of students, especially at the primary and secondary levels. A classic example of this in the Sudan is the fact that many children nowadays leave primary six without a proper command of the 3Rs. And this is continent-wide. Further up the ladder many students leave the universities without a proper command of spoken and written English. There is therefore an increasing public demand for accountability in a system which costs so much and yet manages to produce less than completely satisfactory products.

On the grounds of the increased size and complexity of the education system and the public demand for accountability, there is now time to examine the question of the effectiveness of the classroom teacher. But the administrator cannot demand accountability of the classroom teacher without applying similar measures for evaluating and improving his own administrative effectiveness. The systems approach, which is output oriented, is an ideal instrument. Educational administrators should therefore be given the opportunity to acquire some basic skills in the systems approach, as represented by management by objectives as discussed below. This would then enable them to apply what they learn to their own systems and this should hopefully result in improved performance of the education system.

Management by objectives: Definitions

The phrase 'management by objectives' was first coined by Peter Drucker in his *Practice of Management* (1954), but the most frequently cited definition of MBO has come to be that offered by George S. Odiorne.

The system of management by objectives can be described as a process whereby the superior and subordinate managers of an organisation jointly identify its common goals, define each individual's major areas of responsibility in terms of results expected of him, and use these measures as guides for operating the unit and assessing the contribution of each of its members (Odiorne, 1965).

According to Lander and Myer: 'Management by objectives is a carefully designed, deliberately implemented, and continuously monitored organisation-wide system' (Lander and Myer, 1977).

Cunningham, however, defines the technique as follows:

Management by objectives is a systematic approach to management planning and supervision that establishes common goals and objectives that must be achieved, and gives the authority and responsibility for achieving the objectives to those who must do the work. Objectives are needed to set guidelines for activity within the organisation; they are a source of legitimacy that justifies the existence of the organisation; they serve as standards to assess progress; and they provide orientation by depicting a future situation that the organisation is trying to attain (Cunningham, 1982).

Since Odiorne's 1965 book on the use and importance of objectives in management, the concept has been widely written about (Reddin, 1971; Knezevich, 1973a; Carrol and Tosi, 1973; Bell, 1974; Baldridge and Tierney, 1979) and applied in business, government and education, particularly in the US. The impetus for this wide acceptance of MBO rests on the simplicity of its twin premises:

1 The clearer the idea of what one wants to accomplish, the greater the chances of accomplishing it.
2 Real progress can only be measured in relation to goals and objectives (Cunningham, 1982).

In other words, if one knows where one is going, then one finds the going easier and faster and can also tell when one has arrived. A proper comprehension of the evolution of the MBO system is essential for the appreciation of its usefulness.

The evolution of the MBO process
Management by objectives, like all other systematic approaches to planning and management, is more an attitude of the mind than a cookbook recipe or how-to-do it yourself manual. Its successful implementation therefore requires flexibility and pragmatism.

As noted earlier the initiation of the concept has been attributed to Drucker. He apparently set the ball rolling in his *Practice of Management* (1954) where he discussed the concept of and need for management by objectives, but did not offer a system of implementation (Cunningham, 1982).

McGregor then followed with *The Humanside of Enterprise* (1957), in which he offered a basic view of the MBO process by stating a four-phase process. Odiorne, in *Management by Objectives* (1965) expanded on both Drucker's and McGregor's work and put forward what he called the 'stage's of installation' of an MBO system. These consisted of three stages and sub-steps as follows (Odiorne, 1965):

I Setting goals with subordinates
   1 Identifying the common goals of the whole organisation for the coming period.
   2 Clarify your working organisational chart.
   3 Set objectives for the next budget year with each individual personally.
   4 In the course of the year, check each subordinate's goals as promised milestones are reached.
II Measuring results against goals.
   1 Towards the end of the budgetary year, each subordinate should prepare a brief 'statement of performance against plans' with the copy of his or her performance objectives as a guide.
   2 Set a date for going over this report in detail (and seek for causes of variations).
   3 During such a meeting allow for free two-way communication.
   4 Set the stage for establishing the subordinate's performance budget for the coming year.
III Reviewing organisational performance and defining goals for the coming year.

A further development was presented by J. D. Batten in his *Beyond Management by Objectives* (1966), in which he presented a seven-phase programme, which included the sequence, flow and most important, the dynamics of the on-going process. The components of the programme in outline are:

1 Study of present climate.
2 Development of management philosophy.
3 Development and establishment of objectives.
4 Organisation planning, development, and design.
5 Performance planning and results requirements.

6   2-way communication and motivation.
7   Control.

Drucker (1974), however, disputed Batten's claim that his planning emphasis was beyond what was envisioned as the MBO process. He then propounded six steps which emphasised the planning of service institutions to guide the managers and leaders of such institutions.

Although all these developments were largely directed at business organisations, the education system and the rest of the public sector could not long remain immune to their influences. It was inevitable that sooner or later the attraction of their application to assist in the resolutions of the problems of development in these spheres would call for their implementation. It is to this that we now turn.

The MBO process in education and the public sector

The evolution of the MBO process shows clearly that it originated in the business sector. Once it gained in popularity as a management tool, the US office of education commissioned Stephen J. Knezevich (1973a) to develop an idealised model of the process for use in school systems (Fig. 8.11). The system he developed starts with the identification of organisational aims (goals), leading to the setting of division objectives and then individual objectives consistent with the goals. At step 7 of the model there is an assessment of the feasibility of the performance objective. This may result in recycling back to step 3, if no feasible performance objectives are found in terms of time, money or other constraints. The model then proceeds with the evolution of strategies until step 11. In steps 12 and 14 the management phase is reached, including monitoring to ensure that the organisation stays on target; evaluation and auditing of results then follow. At step 15 the recycling phase is reached and the process starts again.

In terms of the bureaucracy, Chester A. Newland lists the following as the process of MBO and the basic concepts of administration that underlie its initial success.

1   Setting goals, objectives and priorities in terms of results to be accomplished in a given time.
2   Developing plans for accomplishment of results.
3   Allocating resources (manpower, funds, plants and equipment and information) in terms of established goals, objectives, and priorities.
4   Involving people in implementation of plans, with emphasis on communication for responsiveness and on broad sharing in authoritative goals and objectives.

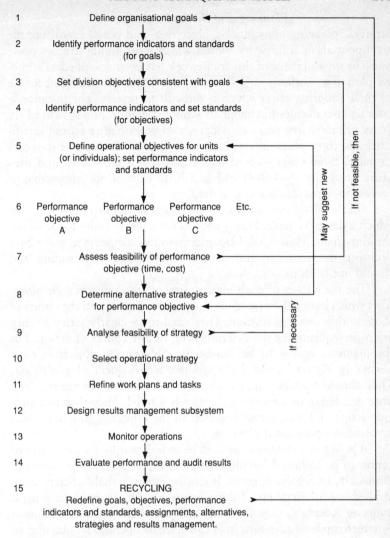

Fig 8.11 A fifteen step MBO model
Source: Stephen J. Knezevich, *Management by Objectives and Results*, American Association of School Administrators, Washington DC, 1973, p. 27.

5 Tracking or monitoring of progress towards goals and objectives with specific intermediate milestones.
6 Evaluating results in terms of effectiveness (including quality), efficiency and economy (Newland, 1974).

Planning and the tools of MBO

Strategic planning aims (goals), objectives, and policy constitute the semi-permanent framework within which most administrators operate. The development of this framework has been described as strategic planning (Anthony, 1965). Such plans are called strategic because of their enduring effect which is difficult to reverse. For instance, a country that decides to change its school system from a system of six years primary, five years secondary, two years higher school certificate, and three years university (6–5–2–3) pattern to one of six years primary, three years each of junior and senior secondary, and four years university (6–3–3–4) will find it difficult, if not impossible to reverse the process once it is started.

Goals (aims) are statements of educational purpose – ends for which a design is made. Future choices are made in order to maximise the aims/goals. Thus, goals help organisational members to make later decisions on what can and should be done and what cannot and should not be done.

The realisation of goals/aims is attained through *strategic objectives* which have a definite scope and suggest direction to the efforts of those within the organisation. They need to be clearly stated as they are a prerequisite for the determination of any course of action. For the planning system to be consistent, the strategic objectives must always be directed toward the ultimate achievement of goals/aims. They should also be capable of attainment and measurement, and once decided upon cannot be drastically altered. They therefore provide scope and long-range direction to the efforts of administrators involved in operational planning.

A *policy* is a statement or understanding that limits the course of action to be followed by administrators in obtaining objectives and ultimately, in achieving goals. It can be either verbal, written or an implied overall guide establishing boundaries that supply the general limits on acceptable organisational action. Policies are the mechanism by which top level administrators can delegate operational planning to lower-level administrators, as they place limitations on the alternatives that may be considered in order to obtain objectives. A simplified MBO system for a regional/provincial state/school system, derived from the Knezevich model could be developed on the basis of Fig. 8.12. As goals and objectives progress from the province to the student level, they reflect both state-related goals and those unique to the individual group.

The set of goals/aims, objectives and policies forms the *strategic plan* for the organisation, and constitutes the framework within

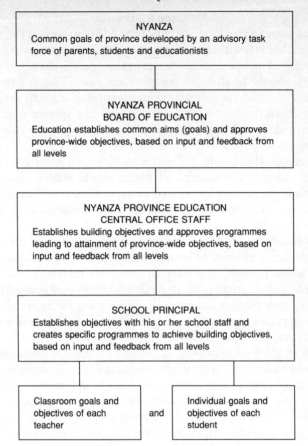

Fig. 8.12 Simplified MBO system for a regional/provincial state/school system

which most operational administrators have to work. The heart of the strategic plan is the definition and establishment of proper goals and objectives. The formulation of organisational aims/goals can be considerably helped by the answers to the following questions:

1 For what purposes does the organisation have the social, human services and expert resources?
2 What is the appropriate role for the organisation?
3 Does the organisation need to be changed to meet new purposes?

Operational planning

The next stage in the development of the MBO process is the translation of goals/aims, strategic objectives and policies into specific operational plans. The operational plan provides specific details as to how the work should be done to complete the task. This is part of the procedure and this, co-ordinated with other tasks, leads to the realisation of school-system objectives and goals. The specific operational plans provide detailed procedures and budgets for the working of departments, units and individual schools.

Operational planning is 'the process by which lower-level administrators ensure that resources are obtained and used effectively and efficiently in the accomplishment of strategic objectives' (Cunningham, 1982). It is concerned with the procedures and methods of completing work.

A *procedure* is a series of related tasks that make up the chronological sequence of work to be accomplished. It is a general statement of the work believed necessary in order to remain within policy contraints and to accomplish strategic objectives and goals. The procedure, or task plan, is the result of determining the approach to the objectives, policies, procedures, facilities available, and total expenditures of time, money and effort.

Before the final approval, the results of the task planning effort are passed back to the central administration for calculations of total costs and benefits as well as checking for any deficiencies that might arise and the relationship between overall strategic plans and other operational plans. As is normal in all forms of planning, as conditions change so must methods, procedures, policies, objectives and goals/aims. As Peter Drucker (1974) has put it, objectives 'are not fate, they are direction. They are not commands; they are commitments. They do not determine the future; they are means to mobilise resources and energies of the business (school system or individual school) for the making of the future.'

Setting objectives

The MBO process requires that specific objectives are derived from general ones so that objectives at all levels within the organisation are appropriate, clearly stated and co-ordinated. Thus whereas strategic objectives usually provide overall direction for the entire organisation, operational objectives are often broken down into objectives for the organisational unit, and performance objectives for the individual.

Moreover, objectives should be achievable within the time span suggested and be sufficiently measureable to check progress at specific intervals within that time span. Objectives should also be set so that outcomes or results (product) can be established and/or specify activities (process).

Objectives, irrespective of their level, have certain components that are crucial for their formulation. These components are usually classified under five major descriptive dimensions.

1 Who – institutional, departmental and/or individual dimension.
2 Behaviour/process – activities/or results dimension.
3 Measurement – qualitative and quantitative dimension.
4 Time and prerequisities – the amount of time and prerequisities needed.
5 Proficiency – specified level of performance.

Objectives based on the above criteria for the school system can be classified into:

a) Strategic objective (for the school system).
b) Operational objective (unit or department).
c) Performance objective (principal).
d) Performance objectives (teacher).

Charles H. Granger (1972) has suggested the following criteria to be applied when developing objectives.

1 Is it, generally speaking, a guide to action?
2 Is it explicit enough to suggest a certain type of action?
3 Is it suggestive of tools to measure and control effectiveness?
4 Is it ambitious enough to be challenging?
5 Does it suggest cognisance of external and internal constraints?
6 Does it relate both the broader and more specific objectives at higher and/or lower levels of the organisation?
7 Possibly, most important, does it suggest desired performance or results?

Nevertheless, while objectives should generally be stated in quantifiable terms, not all objectives can be equally verbal descriptions of the ideal conditions that would exist if the goal were attained. Odiorne (1976) has suggested this rule of rigour that can be applied: 'Measure that which is measurable, describe that which is describable, and eliminate that which is neither.'

In response to the contention that many of the most important outcomes of education cannot be measured, Drucker countered in the same vein as Odiorne:

It is commonly argued that public service institutions aim at intelligible results, which defy measurement. This would simply mean that public service institutions are incapable of producing results. Unless results can be appraised objectively, there will be no results . . . To produce results, it is necessary to know what results are actually being achieved (Drucker, 1976).

Therefore, however intangible and difficult outcomes may be to quantify, there are many indicators that may allow one to determine if the ideal and intangible conditions desired have been achieved.

The review process

Once the objectives have been set, the administrator then plans the needed task activities and takes proper action to see that the objectives are met. He has to decide whether what is being done leads towards the objectives. According to Drucker, administrators: 'must be able to measure performance and results against the goal' (Drucker 1954).

The review process is usually made up of intermediate reviews or evaluations of progress to date and a final review of objective accomplishment. The intermediate review or evaluation serves many purposes.

1 Primarily to determine if organisational units and sub-units are progressing satisfactorily towards the completion of operational objectives and, ultimately, strategic objectives. If not, some corrective action may be needed.

2 Second, to provide information related to performance, particularly personal evaluation. The MBO process provides for the supervision of subordinates by the identification and establishment of individual performance objectives, which the supervisor monitors and then discusses the results of the progress being made. This should never be used for personal domination or intimidation.

3 A third purpose is programme evaluation. According to Cunningham: 'the final review typically involves assessment of which of the operational objectives were successfully accomplished, how well they were achieved, the reasons for any failures, and how well the successful accomplishment of operational objectives contributed to the strategic objectives. This is the application of the MBO to the accountability process' (Cunningham, 1982).

In conclusion, we can say that control is a form of feedback that allows the administrator to move from diagnosis to prognosis and finally to proactive activity, while measurement helps provide direction to effort and vision.

Why use models?

Up to this point, the selected techniques or models for planning have been presented to provide a descriptive view of a situation. In other words, attention has been focused on the way things would happen if we use the technique of Gantt/Miller charts and/or network planning and so forth, as a means of stating in a systematic form the usual or unsystematic practices in developing the education system. Fundamentally, however, the most important benefits of modelling have been stated as follows (Gear and Mello, Open University Press Unit, 15, 1976).

1 It enables the most important factors to be treated in one analysis.
2 The decision-making is more likely to take account of the relevant features involved in a systematic way.
3 Those involved have a common framework, the model, around which their discussions can be centred with a reduced risk of ambiguities and misunderstanding.
4 The model can be used to answer the 'what, if' questions by applying the model to simulate a change in order to observe its effects. This may not be possible in the 'real' world.
5 The model can be further used to simulate the outcomes of particular uncertainties which may be foreseen, and in this way we are enabled to analyse any risks that may be involved.
6 In conjunction with the computer, the model can be used to search amongst the many alternative decisions, in order to find the one which most closely activates the decision-makers' objectives and goals.

However, there are equally telling disadvantages of modelling and these are that:

1 Important factors cannot be included, either by misjudgment or because they were not foreseeable.
2 It is usually up to the decision-maker to decide, on subjective grounds, how much detail to incorporate.
3 Model building can be a lengthy and/or costly undertaking, often involving specialist staff.
4 A model often views factors in an ideal situation and out of the context of the real world of the teacher.
5 A model or method may work well in theory (particularly if developed in say North America or the UK where very different problems and contexts exist) but be found to be difficult to apply

in situations where either change is very rapid or circumstances exist that require rapid adjustment of theoretical principles, etc.

Exercises

1 Define what you understand by the following and state the uses of each in educational administration: PPBS, MBD, the systems approach.
2 Discuss the mechanics of PPBS?
3 Write short notes on the following:
   a) the main features of PERT;
   b) five uses of PERT in educational administration;
   c) the essential steps in a PERT analysis of a project.
4 Discuss the basic information required for the forecasting of school enrolment and some of the main methods of forecasting such enrolments.
5 Briefly state the limitations of the following techniques: Gantt chart; Milestone chart; PPBS.

IX

Planning teacher requirements and supply

The ultimate focus of educational planning and educational administration is the learner and his learning. However, the teacher as the greatest aid to learning is the most important instrument in the school system: the direct personal contact between pupil and teacher remains the linchpin of the educational process. Consequently, the planning of teacher requirement and supply is a central concern in the development and smooth functioning of any education system. Thus teacher planning has come to assume a central position in overall educational plans for the reasons elaborated below.

1 In organising any new, changed or expanded educational programme, securing the necessary teachers for it is one of the highest priorities. But the preparation of teachers requires a long time lead. This is supported by recent studies which show that teacher effectiveness, particularly in developing countries, is associated with the amount of training received. Moreover, just as problematic as the lead time required to produce trained teachers is the even more lengthy time-lag over which poorly qualified teachers may remain in the service with the consequent detrimental effect on the system (Lyon, 1968; Williams, P.R.C., 1979). It was therefore the necessity to think well in advance about teacher requirement that was a major impetus for the development of educational planning.

2 In periods of rapid educational expansion, the teacher-training system may itself come to compete with the schools and other educational programmes for resources. The educational planner is,

as a result, confronted by difficult decisions concerning the optimal allocation of current resources between schools and teacher-training institutions for securing future teacher supply.

3   Teacher requirement and supply are also central to educational planning because of the cost of employing them. Teacher salaries invariably account for a very high proportion of recurrent expenditure on education. This is particularly the case at the primary level. Changes in teacher qualifications or in the pupil-teacher ratios can have enormous impact on the education budget.

4   In qualitative terms, realistic curriculum planning is intimately bound up with questions of teacher needs and teacher supply: the teacher is a key factor in the learning process.

All these factors apply equally in the developed and technologically advanced countries. This points to the necessity for long-term teacher supply. This chapter therefore addresses three fundamental issues. Firstly, it explores the main factors determining the requirements for and supply of teachers. Secondly, it considers possible policy options which the educational planner could use to balance teacher requirements and teacher supply. Finally, it outlines some methods for calculating the requirements and supply of teachers that could be usefully applied in African educational systems.

Teacher requirement and teacher supply

Before we enter into any substantive discussion of teacher requirements and supply, it is necessary to provide some definitions and clarify certain crucial policy issues.

Definitions

Frequently, the term 'teacher demand' is applied instead of 'teacher requirement' when discussing the need for teachers. But 'teacher demand' has several meanings, varying from needs in the layman's sense of what is desirable to the economist's sense of market demand. Hence to avoid possible confusion, the term 'teacher requirement' will be used. This coincides with the instrumental sense of demand and refers to the total numbers assumed, on the basis of given staffing standards, that will be needed in successive future years to service an assumed size of school population. Teacher supply, on the other hand, states the total numbers of teachers assumed, under a particular condition of recruitment and wastage, to be available in successive years to meet this requirement (Williams, P.R.C., 1979; Lyon, 1968; Woodhall, 1977).

From the foregoing, it is clear that the object of teacher planning is to arrive at a supply target, i.e. the total numbers which might be available to satisfy the estimated requirements for teachers. This includes the computation of the necessary numbers of entrants to the training institutions required to ensure the realisation of the supply target.

In short, planning aims at the achievement of a long-term equilibrium between inflow and outflow of teachers such that the stock of teachers can satisfy the projected level of demand.

Factors governing teacher requirement and teacher supply

The assessment of teacher requirement and teacher supply is based on a number of factors. On the requirement side, are the size of the population of maintained schools and staffing ratios, on the supply side, are annual wastage amongst teachers and annual recruitment to the profession (OUP, 1976).

These factors are themselves, however, influenced by the prevailing conditions within the profession. For instance, whereas the supply of teachers is influenced by wastage or loss of teachers from the profession, this in turn can be attributed to such factors as low salaries and poor promotion prospects. Thus the requirement for and supply of teachers is closely bound up with the following important policy issues:

- initial training;
- distribution amongst local educational authorities and schools;
- appointment (and dismissals);
- probation/induction;
- salaries and allowances;
- promotion;
- redeployment and unemployment;
- in-service training and retraining.

However these issues, apart from being policy issues in their own right, are usually built into the calculations of teacher requirement and supply.

Complications: non-regular teachers, language, race and specialisation

Besides these, there are a number of ambiguities that need to be clarified in teacher planning. One such issue concerns who should be counted as a teacher. Should all members of the teaching profession be included or only those involved in classroom teaching? The UNESCO definition of a teacher is a person directly engaged in instructing a group of pupils (students). Heads of educational institutions, supervisory and other personnel should be counted as teachers only when they have regular teaching functions (Williams, P.R.C., 1979). In many African countries, although supervisory personnel are not included as teachers, school heads normally are. The expectation, at least in theory, is that they would participate in some teaching. In practice, however, this is proving increasingly difficult, particularly at large secondary level institutions. In addition, the planner needs to know the extent of his teacher planning, that is to say, is he concerned with teachers in government and private schools in the formal sector only, or is he involved with those for out-of-school courses such as mass education campaigns, as well? The practice in African countries at present is to confine teacher planning to those for formal institutions. Mass literacy and other forms of non-formal education tend to utilise their own specialised teachers or teachers from the formal system on a part-time basis.

Another area of ambiguity to be considered in planning teacher supply is the position of non-regular teachers. Since the interest of ministries of education is to have most of their teachers on permanent service, it is desirable in planning to separate those on temporary employment such as contract staff and part-time teachers and those on permanent basis. If that is the case, then it is necessary to consider those on temporary employment separately from wastage amongst the permanent teachers. Table 9.1 which shows teachers at secondary level institutions of Kano State, Nigeria, Zimbabwe and Malaŵi illustrates what is meant. However, the issue is even more complicated in federated states such as Nigeria and, until 1983, in the Sudan, where each state operates its own school system. In such a situation, for example in Nigeria, how permanent is a teacher of Bendel State origin working in Kano State? If the aim is to provide detailed differentiation in planning, then the more complex the data requirement and the planning problems become. Such detailed planning would entail that apart from planning teacher numbers according to the different levels of the education system (primary, junior and senior secondary) and by employing authority (national, state, local government, religious and private agency, etc.), attention has also to be paid to the classification of teachers in terms of sex, age, qualification, subjects taught and nationality. In the Republic of South Africa (RSA) the racist policy of apartheid further compounds teacher planning (in fact all aspects of education) as teachers have to be further separated on the basis of race – white, black, Indian and coloured.

Table 9.1: Secondary school teachers by qualification, Kano State (Nigeria) 1982/83, Zimbabwe (1985) and Malaŵi (1984/85)

Kano State

Qualification	Numbers ('00)
Expatriate graduates	7.80
Nigerian graduates	3.23
NCE	6.38
HND/OND	.69
Diploma	1.16
Grade I/HSC	.43
Grade II/WASC	4.20
Others	1.57
Total	25.46

NCE: National Certificate of Education
HND: Higher National Diploma
OND: Ordinary Level Diploma
HSC: Higher School Certificate
WASC: West African School Certificate

Zimbabwe (1985)

Qualification	Numbers
Certificated graduate	1,923
Uncertificated graduate	1,115
'O' level plus 3 yrs teacher training	5,488
'O' level plus 2 yrs teacher training	6,600
Junior certificate plus 3 yrs teacher training	52
Junior certificate plus 2 yrs teacher training	63
Standard 6 plus 2 yrs teacher training	72
5 yrs teacher training	17
4 yrs teacher training	226
Others	1,759
Total	17,315

Malaŵi

Qualification	Numbers
Graduates expatriates	267
Graduates local	300
Diplomats expatriate	25
Diplomats local	468
T2, T3 and M Y P	90
Total	1,150

Sources: Statistics Section, MOE, Kano Nigeria; Annual Reports, MOE, Zimbabwe and Malaŵi (1982/83; 1984/5; 1985).

In a situation where several languages are used as the media of instruction at the primary level, as is the case in Cameroon where French and English are the main media of instruction, then the language group of the teacher has also to be considered.

Furthermore, the issue of subject specialisation also deserves serious attention. Generally, it would be expected that the primary level would be the simplest level for which to estimate teacher requirement and supply because of the lack of specialisation among teachers. Nevertheless, in most African countries complications still arise because there is no universal primary education. Even where UPE is in operation as in Nigeria, Egypt and Algeria, the absence of compulsory attendance and fixed age entry means that enrolment ratios in any one year reflect parental attitudes and decision. This results in uncertainties about the exact numbers of additional teachers that would be required each year. And, as already discussed, this is further compounded where teachers also need to be distinguished according to language groups on the basis of the media of instruction in use in the school system. At the secondary level, the main complicating factor for planning is that of teacher specialisation by subjects. However, the countervailing factor in the African situation, is the fact that schools at this level are largely in government hands and are highly selective, which implies that private demand exceeds the supply of places and consequently whatever places are on offer will generally be taken up. Hence, all that is required is to make extra provision for the needs of any private schools that might operate at this level.

Thus detailed planning is required, firstly, to ensure a proper analysis of the present teacher force as a foundation for the planning of new supply according to the different categories. Secondly, to ensure the proper calculation of the differential rates of wastage between male and female teachers, and between teachers by specialisation and level of qualification. Thirdly, it is often the case that although there may be an overall surplus of trained teachers, yet a severe shortage of mathematics, science and applied subject teachers is often experienced.

Lastly, quite apart from the shortage of these specialised teachers, a phenomenon which has only recently manifested itself in some African education systems, is that of the existence of general teacher shortages alongside teacher surpluses. This is best illustrated by the situation in some African countries where qualified teachers are not employed because at the prevailing wage rates for such teachers, and given the present situation of the national or local budget, it is not possible to employ them. Consequently, it is preferable to employ underqualified teachers instead. This is a clear illustration of the economist's use of the word demand, i.e. the 'demand' for teachers is a function of the price of teachers. Thus, the shortage of teachers in this case, is a reflection of the government's unwillingness to offer the market rate for teachers' skills.

Having outlined factors and policy issues affecting teacher requirement and supply and clarified ambiguities involved in teacher planning, we can now turn to a consideration of teacher requirements.

Teacher requirement

The requirement for teachers is here considered as consisting of three components. The first is the identification and discussion of the factors affecting teacher requirement. The second deals with staffing standards and how these are defined. Finally, there is a discussion of the practical planning of the required flow of teachers.

A country's teacher requirement can be considered in terms of the three tiers of its educational organisation: national, local and institutional. In other words, it can be thought of in terms of national needs, the needs of each local educational authority and the needs of each school (Williams, P.R.C., 1979). Although we are here chiefly concerned with the first two levels, it is important to remember that it is the aggregate of the institutional needs that adds up to the national requirement.

Factors influencing teacher requirement

Teacher requirement is basically the product of two factors:

 i) the future school population;

ii) the staffing standards of the school system.

The latter factor is influenced by the available teaching technology in use.

Future school population

The size of the future school population or enrolment is dependent on four key variables.

1   The population of school-going age. This refers to the numbers of the age group that falls within the age range designated by government policy for each stage of the education system, as shown in Table 9.2. It also sets a limit on the level of enrolment in each stage. In addition, the size of the future school-age population is affected by such factors as birth rates and infant mortality.

2   The ages and length of attendance. These are defined by the school structure and the educational laws and regulations of each country. Generally, in most African countries, the age of entry into the primary stage is 6 years. However, the length of grades for each stage of the school system is varied, the commonest being the 6–3–3 or 6–5–2 structures (Open University, 1976).

3   The enrolment ratio. This represents the population of the relevant age group that is actually absorbed into schools. It also reflects the intake and progression rates. These are greatly influenced by government policies. Nevertheless, enrolment ratio reflects equally the response of parents and pupils to the opportunities available for education. In a situation of voluntary attendance, parents can choose for various reasons not to send their children to schools even when the places are made available.

4   Pupil to teacher ratio. The ratio of students to teachers is crucial in planning and is discussed in more detail below.

In African countries, as elsewhere in the developing world, the task of estimating what the future enrolment will be is a complex matter. Most African countries lack reliable and complete population data. Information on the age of existing students is equally lacking. These are compounded by the fact that students have the option of attendance since there is no compulsion.

In summary, there are therefore four vital basic points in the provision of teachers on the basis of future school population. First, government policies play an important role. Second, the best possible projections of enrolment are indispensable for teacher requirement forecasting. Third, in the case of African countries since such forecasts

Table 9.2: Official age-group (primary), ratio in 1980 and 1988, and enrolment ratios of age-groups in selected African countries (1980)

Country	Official age-group	Crude primary school enrolment ratio		Enrolment ratios by age-group (1980)			
		1980	1988	6–11	12–17	18–23	6–23
Burundi	6–11	29	68	17.6	11.9	1.9	11.2
Somalia	6–11	27	15	22.6			
Liberia	6–11	49	35	40.2	45.7	9.1	33.9
Morocco	7–11	83	67	49.3	34.9	14.3	34.9
Mozambique	6–10	99	68	73.5	16.1	2.7	35.8
Zambia	7–13	90	95	69.4	55.5	8.3	48.0
Cameroon	6–11	104	111	76.6	44.5	7.8	47.9
Lesotho	6–12	103	113	66.8	75.2	5.3	52.5
Egypt	6–11	78	90	70.9	45.8	22.1	48.2
Sierra Leone	5–11	52	53	34.9	20.4	2.8	21.5

Sources: Columns 2 and 3, UNESCO (1991) *World Education Report* and UNESCO (1982) *Education and Development in Africa: trends, problems, prospects,* Paris: columns 4–7, UNESCO (1982) *Development of Education in Africa: A Statistical Review,* Paris.

are more likely than not to be unreliable, provision of the greatest possible flexibility in the arrangement for teacher supply is the best insurance policy. The fourth point is the ratio of pupil to teacher which is crucial in planning, and to which we now turn.

The staffing standards

The calculation of teacher requirement from pupil enrolments is based on out-put labour ratio in education, commonly known as pupil-teacher ratios. However, for the proper comprehension of what is involved, it is necessary to distinguish between staffing standards, staffing levels and staffing criteria. Whereas staffing standards are criteria laid down by the education organisation or system, staffing levels are measured. It is the difference between what has been pre-scribed (what ought to be) and what is prevalent (what is). Three components which are used in measuring staffing levels of teacher requirements are: class size, class contact/staff load, and pupil-teacher ratios (Williams, 1971).

1 Class size   This denotes a group of pupils constituting a recog-nised permanent sub-unit of the pupil body in the school. In most African countries, an optimum class size for the different stages of the school system is usually defined by regulation. Thus in Nigeria, the Implementation Committee for the National Policy of Education has suggested an average class size of 40 pupils in the primary and 35 pupils in the secondary school (Blue Print, 1978). In discussing class size it is equally important to distinguish between oversize, maximum or average size. The average class size is normally obtained by adding the total numbers of pupils in the school and dividing it by the number of classes. For instance, if the total pupil enrolment in a single primary school is 228, then the average class size is $228 \div 6 = 38$ pupils. This is not necessarily the average size of the taught class, i.e. the actual number of pupils in a teaching group. However, if the local education authority prescribes a maximum class size of 40 pupils, then the term 'oversize class' would refer to any class above this prescribed maxi-mum size.

Although teachers' unions, administrators and teachers, tend to regard class size as a measure which reflects real standards in that a class of 30 would suggest a higher educational standard than one of 40 pupils, there is no conclusive evidence to support this. However, this can undoubtedly be true if by standards is meant more individual attention and a bigger share of the available resources devoted to each child.

Similarly, the notion of an oversize class suffers from two weaknesses. First, the notion of a fixed maximum is inadequate: the desirable maximum number of pupils in a group can vary widely according to the particular activity or type of pupil. Second, the concept of an oversize class is only one of a complex set of factors which determine the schools staffing requirement and as such its usefulness as a criterion is doubtful.

Even the ideal of the average class size, although it can be a useful measure of comparison for different subjects and stages of the school, ceases to be useful here. One of the main objections to its use for determining staffing requirements is in the case of optional subjects where the average class size results from the arrangement of options offered and the option take up, and can consequently not be predetermined. Hence the usefulness of the average class size does not so much lie in its application in determining the staffing requirement of schools, but rather in assessing the actual provision made, and so the effectiveness of the utilisation of the available resources. Its application has therefore been largely in measuring the actual level of staffing. It would equally be the case in a 'bottom-up approach' to assessing teacher requirements which begins with the classroom and arrives at the total local and/or national need through the process of aggregation.

2   **Class contact/staff load**   This is an approach to planning required teacher numbers on the basis of the time-tabled class contact periods or load a teacher has per week. However, it in no way takes full account of the total work periods of the teacher, which would include the times devoted to lesson preparation and marking (Williams, P.R.C., 1979). It is therefore necessarily an average load, since teachers with marked levels of experience and qualifications as well as of different subjects would have different loads. The part or fraction of the week a member of staff devotes to teaching is known as the 'class-contact fraction' or the 'class-contact ratio', C, and may be defined as:

$$C = \frac{\text{number of periods per week taught by a teacher}}{\text{total number of periods per week}}$$

Thus, if a teacher teaches 42 periods a week out of a total of 50 periods per week, then C is 0.84. The significance of this figure is that the nearer the average value of C approaches 1.0 for a particular school, the nearer the number of classroom contacts per teacher converges to the maximum number. This means the fewer the numbers of contact-free periods available to the teacher. Hence, a high value of C may provide a significant indication of the fact that certain schools are understaffed, which may in turn have adverse effects on the quality of classroom performance, administrative efficiency and job satisfaction. These are issues which concern teachers and their unions deeply. However, the important consideration from the point of view of teacher requirements is that, generally speaking, the fewer periods taught by teachers, the greater the number of teachers required and vice versa.

3   The pupil-teacher ratio (PTR)   The pupil-teacher ratio as applied in teacher requirement calculations, simply relates the number of teachers to the predicted school population, i.e. the ratio is the number of pupils divided by the number of teachers. Generally, the educational authority assumes the teacher ratio for each level of the school system and these are then used in calculating teacher requirements. All that is done is simply to divide the projected number of pupils at each level by the appropriate ratio and the required number of teachers is obtained. Figure 9.1 illustrates the procedure.

There are thus fundamentally two approaches that can be used in calculating teacher requirements using the pupil-teacher ratio. The first is simply by dividing the numbers of pupils or expected enrolment by the pupil-teacher ratio to obtain the required number of teachers.

The second is slightly more complicated and involves the application of the other two components of staffing standards – class size and class contact/staff load in three steps (Fig. 9.2). The starting point is again the number of learners. This is divided by the average class size to obtain the number of classes. The resulting number is then multiplied by the average number of teacher contact periods per week per class. This gives the total weekly time-tabled teacher contact periods per class, which divided by the average weekly teaching load per teacher, results in the number of teachers required.

The following two examples serve to illustrate the two methods described above.

1   A junior secondary school plans to enrol 210 pupils. Given a teacher:pupil ratio of 1:35 for junior secondary schools, calculate the teachers required?
  Solution   Given enrolment = 210
      Teacher-pupil ratio = 1:35
      Teachers required = 210 ÷ 35 = 6 teachers
2   Calculate the number of teachers required for a junior secondary school with a total enrolment of 315, given that the average class

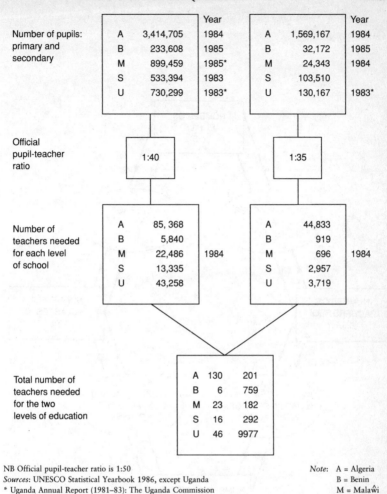

			Year				Year
Number of pupils:	A	3,414,705	1984	A	1,569,167	1984
primary and	B	233,608	1985	B	32,172	1985
secondary	M	899,459	1985*	M	24,343	1984
	S	533,394	1983	S	103,510	
	U	730,299	1983*	U	130,167	1983*

Official pupil-teacher ratio	1:40	1:35

Number of	A	85, 368		A	44,833	
teachers needed	B	5,840		B	919	
for each level	M	22,486	1984	M	696	1984
of school	S	13,335		S	2,957	
	U	43,258		U	3,719	

Total number of	A	130	201
teachers needed	B	6	759
for the two	M	23	182
levels of education	S	16	292
	U	46	9977

NB Official pupil-teacher ratio is 1:50
Sources: UNESCO Statistical Yearbook 1986, except Uganda
* Uganda Annual Report (1981–83): The Uganda Commission
for UNESCO, 39th Session, October 1984.

Note: A = Algeria
B = Benin
M = Malaŵi
S = Sudan
U = Uganda

Fig. 9.1: Teacher requirements for primary and secondary (general) schools, Algeria, Benin, Malaŵi Senegal and Uganda (1983–85)

size is 35 pupils, and the average weekly teacher contacts per class is 60 periods and the average weekly teaching load per teacher is 21 periods.

Solution   Given enrolment of 315 pupils and class-size of 35.
∴   Number of classes = 315 ÷ 35 = 9 classes. But average weekly teacher contacts per class is 60.

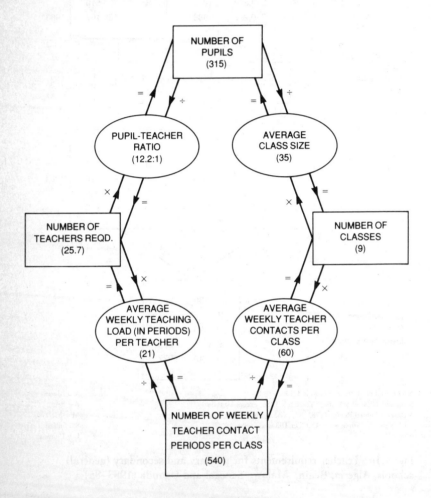

Notes 1 Figures in brackets in the boxes are illustrative

2 Mathematical signs and directional arrows indicate
relationships between neighbouring rectangular boxes
(via oval boxes).

Fig. 9.2 The constituent elements in the pupil-teacher ratio

∴   Number of weekly teacher contact periods per class = 9 × 60 = 540 periods. Average weekly teaching load per teacher is 21 periods.

∴   Number of teachers required = 540 ÷ 21 = 25.7 = 26 teachers.

It is important to remember that the required number of teachers can be arrived at by starting from any point in Figure 9.2.

Dynamic perspective: teacher flow over time

The foregoing discussion has only dealt with the static perspective of teacher requirement. We shall now turn our attention to its dynamic dimension, which deals with teacher flow over time. Here we are concerned with those determinants of the rate of teacher recruitment involving the following three main factors.

Development demand

By this is meant the resultant changes in the size of the teaching force due to the growth or decline in enrolments, or from policy changes concerning how teachers are used in the education system. For instance, population growth and increase in participation rates in education as well as improved staffing ratios, will all result in an increased demand for teachers. Conversely, a fall in the birth rate or serious financial constraint, could equally result in a decrease in teacher requirement.

The growth or decline in the numbers of learners can be caused by a number of factors:

1   The growth or decline in the numbers of a particular school-age group will have a serious effect on enrolments. Generally, in the developing countries, including Africa, because of high birth rates, it is necessary to envisage an additional 3 or 4 per cent more children annually, just to keep enrolment ratios at existing levels.

2   Increasing or decreasing the duration of a school course, or a change in the entry or leaving age, could equally have a direct effect on enrolments.

3   Similarly, the introduction of any programme of large-scale expansion such as the 1976 universal primary education scheme in Nigeria, will immediately result in a rise in enrolment ratios with consequent demands for additional teachers (NPE, 1977).

4   Furthermore, changes in educational practice, resulting in changes in teacher-pupil ratios can equally affect development demand for teachers. Such changes are usually brought about when new subjects are introduced into the curriculum. For instance, the stipulation in the Nigerian New National Policy on Education for the provision of practical subjects into the junior secondary curriculum will inevitably result in high teacher requirements (NPE, 1981). Similarly, the intention in Zimbabwe to expand the education system at all levels will result in an increased development demand for teachers (Zimbabwe Annual Education Report, 1986).

Special replacement demand

These are special programmes designed by the managers of an education system to replace temporary teachers, such as expatriates, and its own nationals, untrained teachers by trained professionals. More often than not, replacement in the case of unqualified nationals may mean being offered a chance of going to a teacher's college or to enrol on a part-time in-service course through distance learning. In Nigeria, for example, the National Teachers Institute (NTI) based in Kaduna undertakes this task. As a result of the need for such arrangements, the required annual flow of replacement teachers will be dependent on the planned length of period over which such replacement is to take place.

Normal replacement demand

This serves simply to replenish any shortages in the existing stock due to normal wastage through retirement, resignation, illness or death.

It is therefore necessary that teacher requirements policy is based on the separate calculations of these three components of total demand: normal demand, development demand and special replacement demand. Having discussed these, however, we should now turn our attention to the issue of supply as teacher requirement derives from the difference between needed stock and available stock.

Teacher supply

The supply of teachers, like its requirements, may be considered in terms of stocks and flows. Teacher flows has two component elements: out flow/wastage and inflows/recruitment. They are the factors affecting potential supply and are both highly influenced by

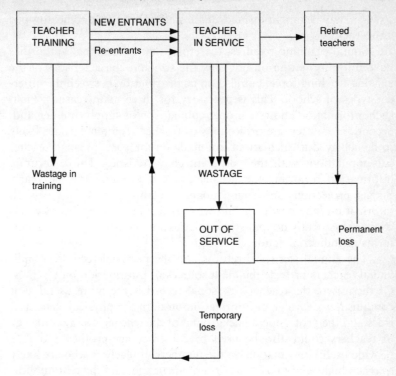

Fig. 9.3   A flow model of teacher supply

government policy. The workings of the various factors are illustrated in Fig. 9.3

Teacher stocks

The teacher force or supply at any moment in time comprises those actually serving in the schools, plus those on the payroll but on release for in-service training or approved leave. Hence it is important to realise that the total supply of teachers does not necessarily equal the demand: schools and colleges could be short-staffed and have vacancies; they could equally be over-staffed above their norms. The fact that teachers are employed is not necessarily proof that there is a real manpower need. Furthermore, although quantitatively, supply might equal demand, the composition of the teaching force may be considered unsatisfactory in quantitative terms. Many of those employed could be unqualified or certain subjects such as mathematics and sciences may be taught by inadequate staff or have even to be dropped altogether.

Sound planning requires, therefore, that educational authorities have full information on not only the size and characteristics of the existing teaching force, but also on its distribution between the different types of school. This is necessary for three main reasons. First, such information allows a proper comparison of supply and demand. Second, more accurate projections of teacher requirements are likely to be achieved if calculations are made on the basis of small teacher sub-populations with their different characteristics. Third, accurate information regarding the teacher stock is essential for the yearly budget projections and sound financial planning. The lack of such information may partly explain why teachers in many African countries are frequently not paid their salaries and have to resort to various forms of industrial action.

The annual statistical returns and the personal records of individual teachers provide the main sources of information on teachers. Of these two, the teacher's personal record is the more useful as it contains a wide range of information on both the physical characteristics and the professional background of the teacher. Data on the age of teachers could also be used to construct age-profiles and thus provide useful information on the numbers of teachers who are likely to reach high salary positions or retirement age, and the cost implication that would be expected. Thus the two types of information when constantly updated, would provide the educational authorities with an accurate picture of the movements within the teaching profession in terms of losses, transfers and re-entry (see Fig. 9.3).

Teacher flows

As the model (Fig. 9.4) shows, by far the majority of teachers in any one year are those retained from the previous year. Like all manpower profiles, teachers are normally not replaced wholesale. Nevertheless, the system is constantly subjected to inflows and outflows of its members. The inflow of teachers, or recruitment, consists of new teachers from the colleges, untrained teachers recruited, and any former teachers attracted back into the profession from other jobs, from various forms of approved absence or from courses. The outflow, or teacher loss, results from such factors as retirement, resignation or death. Thus there is more than one source of both inflow and outflow and these we shall now consider.

1 *Inflows*

Most education systems experience a strong development demand for teachers in order to satisfy their plans for expansion, qualitative improvement and replacement. These together result in a large requirement of entrants. There are five main sources for the annual recruitment for new teachers.

a) New entrants   These are teachers who have completed their initial training from the teacher-training system. They provide the main source of supply to the teaching force. However, the annual input of the potential new entrants to the profession from this source depends on the numbers being produced by the training colleges. This in turn is dependent on the capacity of these institutions and the initial admission into them. The achievement of admission targets into the colleges is itself governed by future policies in the following areas: minimum qualifications for entry; number of student scholarships and bursaries; pay and employment prospects; and in-course and post-training wastage. In most African countries policies on admission levels are taken at two different levels. In a centralised system these are in the hands of the central educational authorities in respect of all institutions on a national scale. In a federal system such as Nigeria, each state ministry of education decides on the policies to be followed in its own colleges within the context of the general national guidelines.

Once the decisions on the numbers to be admitted have been made, the actual output of the colleges, and hence the actual supply of new recruitment, rests on the level of wastage amongst the students as they progress through the course, as illustrated in Figure 9.4 showing a three year primary teachers' course for junior secondary products.

The figure (9.4) shows that from an initial enrolment of 1,500 student teachers who entered college in 1982 only 1,272 or 85 per cent will successfully complete the course in the normal duration and pass out at the end of 1985. This is a loss of 15 per cent (or 12 per cent a year later) out of the original intake. If the plan is to have 1,500 new teachers out of the 1982 intake, then allowance must be made for the 15 per cent failure rate, by increasing the initial admission to 1,765 ($85\% \times 1,765 = 1,500$).

The rate of the failures on the final year examination is quite important in determining the level of teacher supply for the classroom. The practice in African countries varies. In some countries such teachers are allowed to repeat the year in college, whereas in others they are permitted to enter teaching and pass the failed subjects at the end of

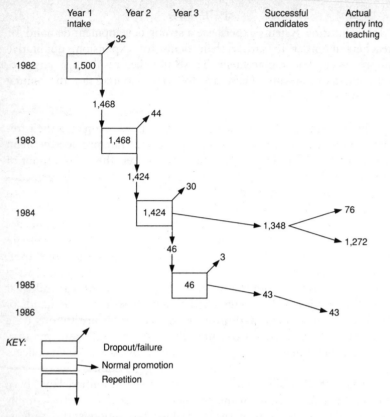

Source: Adapted from Williams, 1979; Brimer and Pauli, 1971).

Fig. 9.4 Cohort progression in initial teacher training

the year. In yet others they are allowed to continue repeating the failed
subjects until they are successful.

b) Re-entrants and returners   Re-entrants are former-qualified teachers who for one reason or another left teaching in the past. They are
hardly significant in African education systems at present. Occasionally, however, they do appear, as was the case in southern Sudan at the
end of the civil war in 1972 when retired teachers were asked to come
back into the service.

Returners are much more significant, as they are those teachers
who are returning to the classroom after a period of in-service training
or secondment. The impact in terms of teacher supply is felt particu-

larly in situations where a programme of large-scale training or re-training is coming to an end.

c) **National service arrangements**   The use of the graduates of secondary or post-secondary institutions to teach as part of their national service obligations to the country has become quite widespread in Africa. Thus National Service Corps are found in Nigeria, Tanzania, Zambia and Ethiopia. The scheme has the dual advantage of mobilising large numbers annually while at the same time lowering teacher training costs as national service corp members are paid minimal salaries.

d) **External labour markets**   In the period immediately after independence, a large part of the teacher supply at the secondary and tertiary levels in most African countries tended to be expatriates, invariably from the former colonial country. At times of rapid or large-scale educational expansion, expatriate teachers have also been recruited to meet teacher supply. This has been the case particularly in the oil-producing countries such as Nigeria, Gabon and Libya. The use of foreign teachers is useful if wisely planned as a stop-gap, providing a country with the opportunity to develop its own national resources of teacher supply. The disadvantages of this system from the linguistic, cultural and political points of view, should not be disregarded, however.

2   Outflows

As Figure 9.4 shows, the vast majority of teachers in any one year are those retained from the previous year. Like all manpower profiles, teachers are normally not replaced wholesale. However, over a period of time the existing stock suffers deterioration and loss through sickness, ageing and retirement. Thus the teaching force suffers wastage, resulting in depletions in its numbers, in three distinct ways.

i) **Retirement**   The retirement rate of the teaching force will be dependent on its profile. In growing education systems such as those of Africa, the average age of teachers is much nearer entry age than retirement age, consequently the rate of retirement is insignificant, something in the order of 0.5 or 1 per cent annually. However, in the more stable education systems, the numbers reaching retirement age would be about the same as the new annual intake.

ii) Death   This is not a serious cause of loss, as an expanding force, like that of Africa, consists largely of young, newly-qualified teachers.

iii) Resignation   This form of teacher wastage is a reflection of the relative unattractiveness of teaching in comparison with other jobs. Before resigning a teacher would consider four basic factors.

a) Conditions of service
   These include pay and such fringe benefits as allowances, pension entitlement, housing arrangements and so forth. How good these are will, to a large extent, govern whether a teacher decides to remain or leave the service.

b) Promotion
   Generally, in most countries, it is the case that the ratio of senior to junior posts tends to be unfavourable in teaching. The only exceptions are in the use of a rapidly expanding school system or as a result of restructuring of the system. The slow pace of promotion can, however, be ameliorated by the prospects of teachers earning promotion through further qualifications and professional competence.

c) Professional support
   Teachers are often posted to remote rural schools and may tend to feel lonely and isolated. A good educational administration can assist in such a situation by making teachers feel appreciated by the practice of fair appointments, promotions, postings and the provision of opportunities for professional refreshment.

d) Economic influence and education
   An additional factor which may affect the general level of retention and wastage amongst teachers is the state of the economy. Wastage is generally lower in a situation of economic recession and scarce alternative jobs. But in a situation of fairly sound economy and serious shortages of manpower, resignation rates may tend to be quite high unless checked by bonding. The educational level of teachers is also an important determinant of whether a teacher stays in teaching or not. It is generally the case that graduates are much more likely to move out of the service than their counterparts who only have certificates.

However, it is important to remember that even where considerable data is available, the estimation of future rates of teacher wastage is always problematic.

Having discussed teacher requirement and supply we now turn our attention to a consideration of how to achieve a balance.

Balancing teacher supply and requirement

The preceding discussions of the factors determining teacher requirement and supply lead on to the consideration of adjustment between them.

Static and dynamic balance

The planners aim in teacher development is to try and achieve a balance not only at a particular point in time (a static equilibrium), but also a continuing balance (dynamic equilibrium). However, a dynamic balance can only be realised in a situation of steady rate of increases in the teaching force and a constant rate of annual wastage. But in the conditions of expanding or evolving education systems such as those of African countries, the contrary circumstances are more prevalent. In such education systems, cases of irregular trends in development demand for teachers are necessitated by policy decisions such as, for instance, whether to increase the enrolment ratios at the secondary level or introduce universal primary education. Both these and many other decisions demand sudden acceleration of outputs of teachers.

Another feature of planning often overlooked is creating the most effective balance between pre- and in-service teacher education. Many governments are looking seriously now at ways to reduce training at pre-service level and increase such provision once the trainee has started work and is, possibly, in a better position to appreciate training.

Besides these internal factors, events in the politico-economic sphere, beyond the control of the educational planner and of even the government itself, can bring about imbalance in the requirement and supply situation. For example, the failure of a country's major export crop due to the weather, or the drastic fall in its price on the international market, can lead to the weakening of the government's capacity to sustain economic and educational expansion. The effects of the fall in OPEC oil prices, accompanied by the decline in the volume of oil exports and the resultant economic austerity measures in mid-1983 in Nigeria and Libya, and in 1985 in Cameroon, attests to this.

Apart from such unexpected events, other social trends can equally upset the forecasts of the educational planner: trends in migration or fertility, wastage rates amongst pupils, examination pass rates, and the resignation and re-entry of teachers. A small positive or negative change in any of these factors can seriously affect the numbers of teachers required.

Furthermore, the educational planner's projections are as significantly dependent on assumptions as on calculations. This means that however good his computational skills, the reliability of his projections will largely rest on the reliability of the assumption built into them. This means that certainty about teacher requirement and supply and therefore the balance between them is most difficult to realise. The realistic option is to prepare for more than one alternative or one possible future.

This, in practical terms, means firstly, that forecasts of teacher requirement and supply should provide for a range of possible values according to different stated assumptions rather than being stated in terms of a single value. Secondly, it is necessary to monitor constantly and to adjust such forecasts. A third approach is to create a flexible capacity into the teacher supply system. In practice this could take the form of training teachers who are, for example, able to teach subjects in different areas such as biology and mathematics or economics and religious knowledge, so that when necessary such a teacher could concentrate on one of them full time. Flexibility could also take the form of structural organisation of courses in such a way that it facilitates student transfer between teacher training and other activities. It could also take the form of the provision of training courses of different durations, say 4 years and 3 years, within the same college. To achieve such flexible capacity requires the avoidance of exclusive concentration on lengthy, single-purpose specialisation in terms of physical facilities, teachers or courses. In short, the best approach to teacher planning in the face of uncertainty is to provide a flexible capacity as an insurance policy against any sudden changes in policy or circumstances.

Measures for attaining balance

In addition to the practical measures stated above, when confronted by actual or an anticipated surplus or shortage of teachers, the educational planner's first course of action should be to undertake a thorough study of all the factors causing the imbalance and then consider ways to tackle them. A variety of policy measures is usually available for dealing with any gaps between teacher requirement and teacher supply: alterations in the size and flow rates of teacher training; upward or downward regulation of school intake and enrolment;

changes in pupil-teacher ratio; new policies on replacement of temporary teachers, and so forth.

A second consideration to take into account in trying to meet a
demand/supply balance is that it is only one objective of educational
planning and as such must be viewed within the context of the overall
objective of a country's education system. As such, it should not be
achieved at, say, the expense of effective pupil learning by lowering
teacher qualifications or increased class size. Thus the balance between requirement and supply can be realised at many different levels
of requirement in terms of levels of enrolment and modes of pupil-
teacher interaction. Similarly, the supply target can equally be attained
by effecting changes in different areas such as teacher training, teacher
wastage and so on.

Third, in deciding on measures to establish a balance in the
demand/supply situation, governments pay serious attention to political sensitivities. For instance, in the event of a teacher shortage, a

Table 9.3: Factors affecting teacher requirement and supply

Requirement			Supply	
School population	Birthrate			Withdrawal on marriage
	Pre-primary school-age children			Job dissatisfaction
	Numbers in schools	Wastage from profession		Early retirement
	Number out-of-school			Death
	Other Factors			Teaching in independent school
Staffing standards	Pupil-teacher ratio	Recruitment to profession		New entrants from training institutions
	Class size			Re-entrants to profession (e.g. married women)
	Class contact			

Source: Unit 8, 'Providing the Teachers', Course E222, *The Control of
Education in Britain*, The Open University (1979).

government may find it unacceptable to cut school hours for pupils or introduce a shift system; instead, an increase in class size might excite less public criticism. This naturally depends on public awareness of the value of education.

A last consideration is the fact that teachers once employed represent an on-going financial commitment, as it is not easy to lay them off. It is therefore important to ensure that not too many teachers are employed who cannot be usefully engaged in the school system. To avoid such situations arising, it is always wise to aim on the low side in planning teacher supply, as it is always possible to make good any shortfalls with temporary teachers.

All the factors influencing teacher requirement and teacher supply discussed in the preceding sections can be summarised as shown in Table 9.3.

Essential steps in teacher projections in practice

The aim in this section is to show some of the practical steps in calculation which a practising planner might use to show the existing situation of teacher supply and future requirement on which to base suggestions for possible policy options that will assist policymakers to make decisions (Williams, P.R.C., 1979). The steps are as shown below.

1 *Projection of enrolments*

The initial step in making future enrolment projections is by first knowing the situation of enrolment. This is followed by making two assumptions. One concerns the level of future enrolment in grade 1 of the particular school level. This is easy to calculate where there is compulsory education, with a fixed age of entry and insignificant rate of repeating. It is problematic, however, in the absence of these conditions. The second assumption concerns changes in wastage rates noticeable in present enrolments and likely to affect future intakes. Likely government policies and the effects of other social factors on intake levels and wastage must also be considered in making future projections. However, where government has no policies or plans for changes in the future, then past trends would be assumed to continue.

2 *Pupil-teacher ratio*

Once enrolment figures are projected, then the required number of teachers can be calculated using a pupil-teacher ratio. In deciding whether to use the existing ratio or alter it in making future teacher projections, the planner will be influenced by several factors. Firstly, whether government policy is likely to change regarding such factors as teacher loads, class sizes and staffing norms for schools. Secondly, factors such as trends in population density and school sizes. Increasing urbanisation may make for higher pupil-teacher ratios, whereas extension of schools into remote rural areas with sparse populations or little enthusiasm for schooling, may have the opposite effect.

3   Total teacher requirement

The total demand for teacher stocks over different times in the future is obtained simply by dividing the expected future enrolments at those times by the pupil-teacher ratio.

4   Stock of acceptable teachers

The definition of 'acceptable teacher' varies with each country. Here it is assumed to be the professionally qualified nationals. The present numbers should normally be available in either records at state/regional or national level. Stocks in future years can then be calculated by the addition of net flows to previous stocks.

5   Net wastage

Net wastage is easily obtained in a situation where comprehensive educational statistics are available. Unfortunately this is not the case in most African school systems. Statistics kept on teacher flows are confined basically to college outputs rather than actual intakes into the profession. In other words, such statistics do not identify the newly-trained teachers who actually take up teaching appointments.

Exercises

1   'The ultimate focus of educational planning and educational administration is the learner and his learning'. Critically examine this statement.
2   Distinguish between teacher requirement and teacher supply.
3   Discuss the factors influencing teacher requirement.
4   Elaborate on the essential steps in teacher projections in practice.
5   Discuss what likely measures you would take to ameliorate the situation of teacher surplus in your education system.

X

School size
and location planning

What is school location planning?

School location planning (SLP) is the term normally applied to the set of administrative policies and procedures that are used to plan the distribution, size and spacing of schools. Its basic aim is to match the distribution of schools, and particularly the student spaces in those schools, to the distribution of the potential population to be served. It attempts to plan the pattern of educational provision so as to allow more pupils to have easier access to schools as well as to allow a more efficient use of current and additional resources (Gould, 1978).

School location planning was originally referred to as 'school mapping' but it is more than simply compiling a map showing the distribution of schools. Such a map is, of course, necessary as the starting point in the process of identifying current inadequacies in distribution and to realise appropriate types and patterns of school provision. However, SLP goes beyond this, and is concerned with the planning and distribution of inputs such as learning materials and teachers for the efficient functioning of the school system. As such SLP can be applied to all levels of education, ranging from kindergarten to universities, but its greatest value is in the planning of primary and secondary education where regularity of access is an important feature.

This chapter first discusses the legacy of the past in the present pattern of schools in Africa. This is followed by looking at the purpose of the school map and then the role of school location in the development of African education systems through an historical perspective. The fourth section discusses the theoretical considerations in school location planning while the fifth part of the chapter deals with the determinants of appropriate school size followed by a consideration of ways of creating viable schools. The final part of the chapter is devoted to the discussion of how the past has impacted on the present planning of schools and how, in turn, the existing school map will influence future development.

In order to understand the present role of school location planning in educational administration it is necessary to look at the development of schools in the past, thus an outline for Africa now follows.

The legacy of the past

In Africa, in education perhaps more than in most areas of public activity, the present is determined by the past, and changes can be made only slowly. An educational administrator is consequently liable to find a mismatch between the current distribution of school facilities and present population distribution. The pattern of schools inherited from the colonial era was determined by several fundamental factors: the spread and influence of Christian missions; the cultural resistance by African peoples; and environmental conditions.

African resistance

Although the orderly territorial spread of European colonialism and rule was sanctioned by the Berlin Conference of 1884 on the Partition of Africa, the actual extension of their influence within the individual territories proved far more problematic. This was particularly marked in the attempt to spread Christianity and schooling. It is important to point out from the outset that African resistance to missionary proselytisation or spiritual influence and education was as universal as the resistance to colonialism in general. However, the degree of opposition was particularly marked and enduring amongst the nomadic and pastoral groups and in areas of early Islamic conquests and penetration. The pastoral peoples of the southern Sudan, Nuer, Dinka, Toposa and Turkana, the Masai of Kenya and Tanzania, the Karamajong of Uganda and the Fulani of West Africa, typify the former while large parts of northern Nigeria exemplify the latter. The result of such resistance in all cases is manifest in the current low level of enthusiasm for schooling to the disadvantage of these communities within their national boundaries.

The missionary impact

In almost every African country, as pointed out above, the impact of missionary activity was unevenly spread within each country. While it was comparatively easy for some areas to accommodate missionary influence and institutions, this proved far more difficult in others. Consequently, the inherited pattern of schools does not comprise a network of institutions each standing at the centre of a good-sized catchment area. The result is that today, in West Africa, the general pattern is that towns which were once economically important and centres of missionary activity have more than their share of facilities. Williams has given the example of Cape Coast, the one time capital and major sea port of Ghana which is still famed for its educational establishments, although its economic fortune has so much declined, while thriving new suburbs of Accra-Tema like Madina and Ashaiman have very poor facilities. In East Africa, the impact of missionary influence is all too obvious. In the southern Sudan for instance, where school location has been heavily influenced by the activity of Christian missions, secondary schools are largely to be found in rural locations on former mission stations, far removed from urban areas and centres of population. The catchment areas of such schools, as Gould has pointed out in the case of Ntare school in the Ankole District of Uganda, is the whole country since the schools were wholly boarding. This was also the general pattern in Kenya and Tanzania. But with independence and the establishment of many more schools this pattern has been greatly modified. Nevertheless, these schools still maintain their premier positions within the country.

Environmental conditions

A third factor determining the pattern of schools is the physical features of parts of a country. A remote or difficult terrain was often a sufficient deterrent to missionary or even governmental activity. This partly explains the thin spread or complete absence of schools in the Sudd region of the southern Sudan inhabited by the Nuer and Dinka. A similar situation was prevalent in the dry Karamoja region of Uganda, the north-eastern frontier region of Kenya and the riverine area of Nigeria. This inaccessibility was frequently accompanied by fierce resistance by the indigenous populations to external contacts and influences. It is therefore equally important to take cognisance of the effect of environmental conditions on the geographical distribution of schools. These various factors from the past have continued to influence the current development of the educational system in most African states. The implications of the past on present and future school planning are discussed later, after we have looked at the theory of school planning. It is appropriate now, therefore, to look at the preliminary definition of school location planning and outline the purposes it serves.

Purpose of the school map

The school map is part and parcel of the educational planning process; consequently, one of its essential functions is to assist in the realisation of the targets set out in the plan(s). School mapping occurs, therefore, at local level once the major educational objectives have been set out by the central or regional planning teams. The best known and the most universally acknowledged of the targets are the following:

1 Giving all children of school age a basic education, and within the limits of the available resources of the country and its economic and social requirements, extending teaching beyond the end of the period of compulsory education.
2 Providing for 'equality of educational opportunity'. Although this target may be interpreted in diverse ways, as far as the school map is concerned, there are two basic objectives: (a) a geographical levelling out of the conditions of supply through the creation of equal intake capacities and an equitable distribution of human, material and financial resources over the various areas, and (b) equal social opportunities for, and access to, schooling through active measures encouraging children to go to school and opposing segregation of schools on the grounds of race or creed.
3 Making systems more effective by improving the ratio between costs and performance. In the process of drawing the school map, efforts will be directed at ensuring that the utilisation rates of premises, equipment and staffs and the length of time they are used are the highest possible within the limits of pedagogic, administrative and political considerations.
4 Reforming structures, curricula and methods: the role of the school map is vital in any attempt to reform education systems. The

failure of education programmes in many countries can be attributed largely to the lack of a school map (Hallak, 1977).

The conceptual framework

As noted by Hallak (1977), the school map is a tool of analysis and serves as a bridge between the initial drawing up of the plan and the detailed working of plan implementation at the local level. In addition, it helps to co-ordinate networks of schools at different levels and types of instruction. This involves at least four steps.

1   A method for the co-ordination of school networks. If the school map is to be organised rationally, there has to be a co-ordination of school networks, since any school in a given level draws upon students in schools at the level just below it (See Fig. 10.1).
2   The regionalisation of the plan, i.e. the breakdown of the aims of the plan by region. This breakdown of the goals of the plan is imperative within the national framework and is always a prior condition for adoption of the school map. This is so because the national map and regionalisation are both expressions of the same reality which cannot be considered in isolation, one from the other. In regional terms the task is to determine homogeneous geographical areas in the light of economic, demographic, geographical, administrative and other factors.
3   Further elaboration of the area goals in terms of the work involved, taking into consideration the structure of the existing education system and the rules and standards laid down for schools.
4   The drawing-up in detail of the local school map, in the light of local requirements, local characteristics and the specific problems of the area. This detailed work on the local map entails:
    i)   a diagnosis of the geographical distribution of supply;
    ii) establishment of: a) criteria for determining schools' catchment areas such as population densities; b) standards for school size, taking account of pedagogic, economic and administrative limitation, and c) standards of floor-space and types of construction, supplies and equipment;
    iii) breaking down of school plan targets by area in the light of each area's development prospects;
    iv) projection of schooling requirements taking into consideration the breakdown of the targets and demographic developments of the area;
    v)   elaboration of proposals for a future map of premises in

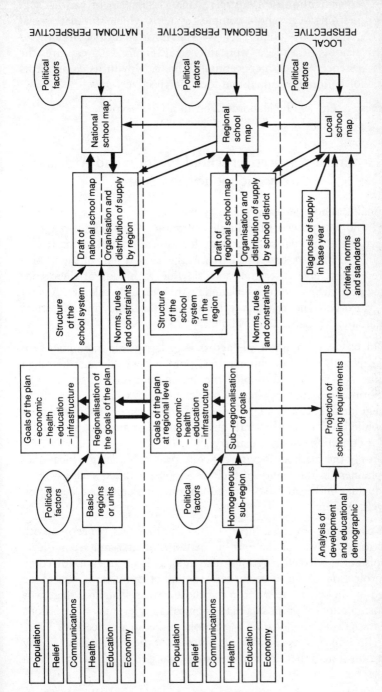

Fig 10.1 The conceptual framework (after Hallak, J. (1977)) *Planning the Location of Schools: An instrument of educational policy*, UNESCO: IIEP, Paris, p. 20)

consideration of a cost/performance analysis of various suggestions (e.g. school complex systems which stimulate social integration – comprehensive system or small neighbourhood schools of a more 'workable' size). Figure 10.1 captures the essence of such a conceptual framework with its components of national, regional and local perspectives.

All these issues will be elaborated on in a later section.

Historical perspective: school location and African educational development

Originally, school location planning was referred to as 'school mapping', and this dates to the implementation of the school mapping project of the International Institute for Educational Planning (IIEP), a UNESCO affiliate based in Paris, in the second half of the 1960s. There were twelve case studies worldwide with four of them conducted in African countries – Uganda (Ankole), Côte d'Ivoire, Algeria and Morocco. The research projects had the following objectives (Hallak and McCabe, 1973; Hallak, 1977):

a) 'Identify and analyse all factors – pedagogical, economic, geographical, social, administrative, political, which must be taken into account in determining the optional location of schools.

b) Formulate a methodology in sufficient detail to make it useful as a guide to educational planning in a wide range of member states, while keeping it sufficiently flexible to accommodate the particular conditions of each country.

c) Apply the methodology to concrete problems facing educational planners in the reality of their development tasks, such as introducing universal first-level education, implementing education reforms, etc'.

Each case study involved three stages. The first was concerned with the critical analysis of the existing network of first-and second-level schools in the selected grographical area(s). This was then followed by the projection of the medium-term potential population size to be served by the school network in the chosen areas. The final stage was the formulation of proposals in the light of all relevant considerations for rationalising the location of schools in the area concerned.

This approach is such a basic function of the management of any education system that one may justly be surprised that it did not claim a prominent place in the educational planning literature until then, particularly as it is a subject which could attract scholars of a variety of interests and bents as demonstrated by the range of specialisations of those involved in the IIEP studies. Three reasons can perhaps be adduced for the lackadaisical attitude (Gould, 1973). First is the piecemeal and gradual approach to the expansion of education systems in the developed countries, often taking the form of adaptations and additions to the existing school system. The level of physical capital investment in the existing school network was such that the cost of change would appear to be prohibitive and perhaps even outweigh the advantages that would accrue from total restructuring. The result was that more often than not decisions on modifications to the school map were arrived at by local politicians and education administrators under them, on an *ad hoc* basis depending on the myriads of different individual situations that arose. There was little inclination to search for general principles. Second, consciousness of the wide differences in levels of opportunities for pupils in different schools and areas has been allowed to develop. Third, some social and cultural groups regarded differential provision, resulting in separate schools for groups on the basis of sex, religion or individual aptitude, as having a positive value.

However, in the early 1960s, with the advent of many developing countries to independence, particularly in Africa, the problems of large-scale changes in the scale of provision and in the existing structure of education systems suddenly loomed large, and these found expression in the series of UNESCO-sponsored continental educational planning conferences in Karachi (Pakistan) 1960, Addis Ababa (Ethiopia) 1961, and Santiago (Chile) 1962. At the conferences, it was realised that the problems demanded a comprehensive plan for each country for supplying and distributing educational services evenly. If expansion and structural reform were to be achieved effectively and economically *ad hoc* adjustments to the existing network of schools were no longer feasible. Moreover, unlike the situation in the developed countries, less physical, financial and emotional capital had been invested in existing schools and colleges. It was on those grounds that the school mapping project of the IIEP was envolved. Since then, interest in planning the size and location of schools in a systematic way in Africa has been sustained with the encouragement of multilateral organisations such as UNESCO, UNICEF, and more recently, the World Bank, and by the demands of equity and efficiency. The result is that African national educational systems have now moved away from the *ad hoc* basis of competitive missionary and erratic government school provision of the colonial era. The emphasis is now centred on equity of provision as a foundation for national cohesion and socio-economic advancement.

School location planning: theoretical considerations

School location planning (SLP) or the school map, is an integral part of the educational planning process, and as such a tool for the practicalisation of the objectives and targets of the overall plan. There are two universally acknowledged goals of educational planning: i) it shall promote equality, and ii) it shall promote efficiency.

Systematic planning of the size and location of schools is vital in furthering equality of educational opportunity. It ensures a better distribution of schools so that every child has the chance to attain initial access to school and does not eventually drop out because his home is not within easy reach of a school. Home-school distance is a greater cause of unequal access, and later of absenteeism and attrition, than is parental socio-economic status in countries where there is no universal education.

SLP is also a major vehicle for improving the efficiency of the school system both educationally and financially by improving pupil-teacher ratios, ensuring better use of space and lowering per capita pupil and graduate costs. SLP ensures that the utilisation rates of premises, equipment and staff are the highest possible, considering pedagogic, administrative and political limitations. The approach at its best, is to integrate the provision of schools with the provision of other social and economic services as part of broader regional development services.

In addition, SLP is also concerned with reforming structures, curricula and methods. Irrespective of the level of development of an education system, it invariably tends to obtain certain schools with peculiarities of their own in terms of either structures, curricula or methods. Therefore whether the aim is restructuring or expansion, SLP facilitates the determination of how the existing schools may be re-converted and premises re-allocated within a geographical area so as to adjust supply to the education system's new characteristics as envisaged in the reform programme. Thus the pursuit of equity and efficiency makes SLP an important technique in educational planning.

Moreover, schools have come to assume such an important place in modern society that school location is not necessarily pre-determined by existing residential patterns: it can itself influence them.

Thus in an education-conscious society the decision to provide or deny a primary school to an isolated rural community may vitally affect the viability of such a community and the willingness of parents to continue to live and work there (Hallak and McCabe, 1973). A school has various useful attributes: it can bring material resources and employment into a community; it ensures the presence of young people; it is itself a concrete expression and separate identity of a particular community with its place in a larger system. School location policy can therefore be used quite deliberately to retain people in rural areas and to sustain rural communities. Even in urban areas, a large and important institution such as a university may create enough employment to become, in time, the main prop of the economy of a medium-sized town (Williams, 1975). The University of Nigeria, Nsukka (UNN) and the Ahmadu Bello University, Zaïre, both in Nigeria, Njala University College, Sierra Leone and the Maridi Education Complex in southern Sudan, are typical examples. Many such instances abound elsewhere in the developed and developing world.

Equally, where it is intended to concentrate population, confining school provision to central locations only will be an influential means to realise this objective. For example, the attraction of the school was one of the main incentives used in the establishment of the centralised *Ujamaa* villages in Tanzania. Similarly, in the case of the location of new towns and industries, the provision of good schools is an important factor for the attraction of skilled workers and their families – in the case of developed countries it is in fact a pre-condition. Even where no such official policy on population distribution exists, the presence of a high-quality school in an urban neighbourhood or district readily attracts those most concerned with the education of their children to live in its catchment area. In Africa this is at present only felt in the largest towns and in situations where boarding has been eliminated. Nevertheless, all this goes to show that in real life school location not merely reflects, but clearly affects population distribution and mobility.

Unfortunately, in most discussions of SLP, little attention is paid to the use of school location policies to influence population distribution and residential patterns (McCabe and Padlye, 1975). Attention is concentrated instead on the way in which population distribution determines school location. Consequently, what is essentially a two-way interaction tends to be discussed as if it were a one-way dependence of school location on population distribution, present and future. Moreover, when population movement in response to school distribution is mentioned, discussion is focused on the travel and transportation of pupils from home to school and hardly in terms of the more permanent shift of parental homes.

School location planning, like planning itself, is a continuous process, focusing on the continuous updating of the inventory of facilities in order to answer the question 'what is where'? An examination of the factors influencing school location that follows will clarify the issues.

The school catchment area

Normally, in deciding on the location of a school, two sets of considerations are pertinent. The first is the need for, and the place of, the new school within the overall network of schools. The second is the availability and suitability of a physical site in terms of the size and shape of the plot, the fitness of the ground for building, accessibility in terms of ease and safety as well as the availability of basic infrastructural facilities like water and light and so forth. In short, for a school to be actually built, a suitable site must be found at a place where a school is needed. Consequently, it is not uncommon, especially in urban areas, for the lack of a suitable site to prevent the location of a school at its most ideal position. Similarly, there are many instances where a school has been established at a physically attractive site but with little to recommend it either in terms of the location of existing schools or in terms of the clientele the school is intended to serve.

However, what is of prior importance is the place of the school in the overall network. A new school should be started on the grounds that there are learners whom the existing schools of the same type serve poorly or even not at all. Hence, the main concern of school mapping is not so much the fitness of particular sites but rather the spatial relationship between schools. The concept of school catchment area is therefore the key factor underlining the development of schools.

Definition

The school catchment area is the administratively defined geographical area served by a school, that is, the area from which the school recruits its pupils. The catchment area for each school is defined partly in relation to the location of the maximum acceptable distance a child can travel between home and school, the size of the school, and the density of school-age population. In a compulsory education system, all the populated parts of the country are divided up into either contiguous or, if choice of school is allowed, overlapping catchment areas. Thus every child's home must fall within the catchment area of a particular school or group of schools. The only exception is in areas where population is so sparse that education is provided instead through correspondence courses or peripatetic teachers, as in the remote parts of Australia. In contrast, in the case of African countries where education is not compulsory, large populated areas are commonly found which are not assigned to the catchment area of any school because no school exists. The only exception is perhaps where universal primary education is in operation such as in Nigeria.

The logic behind rational school location based on catchment areas is that, other things being equal, there will be an appropriate school close to each individual learner and that the learner will, by choice or direction, attend that school. Ideally, therefore, pupils are assigned to schools on the basis of such objective considerations as location of home, age and sex, etc. This also presumes that schools of the appropriate type are equal in quality and there is therefore no question of choice and no need for catchment areas of schools in the same category to overlap. Hence, the easier becomes the task of school administrators.

In theory, the catchment area is based on two factors: i) population requirements; and ii) the range.

Threshold population

In practice, schools and classes cannot be provided everywhere. The threshold population therefore refers to the minimum total population sufficient to establish a school with the minimum acceptable capacity in terms of student spaces or potential enrolment. For example, if a primary school has a six-grade capacity of 240 (6 classes of 40 student spaces) and if the national primary school-age population is 15 per cent of the total population, and there is a 100 per cent enrolment, then the threshold population for the school would be 1,600.

$$\text{If } 15\% \text{ of } T = 240$$
$$\text{Then } T = \frac{240 \times 100}{15} = 1,600$$

Where T is the threshold population.

Hence for a school to have 240 pupils, there should be a total population of 1,600 in its catchment area. If, however, the enrolment above represents only 75 per cent of the primary school age group, then the threshold will be higher since 320 children will be needed in order to have 240 of them in school. The threshold population would consequently rise to 2,133.

$$\frac{(40 \times 6)}{(0.15 \times 0.75)}$$

Similarly, the threshold for a single grade school would be the same as that for a six-grade school, that is to say 2,133

$$\frac{(40 \times 1)}{(0.025 \times 0.75)}$$

Generally, $T = \dfrac{s \times c}{a \times e}$

where T = threshold or total population; s = class size; c = number of classes per school; a = relevant age group as a percentage of total population; and e = target enrolment rate.

Range

This is the maximum acceptable distance children are expected to travel to school each day. In most countries of Africa this must be assumed to be the walking distance from home to school, though in some of the countries, and particularly in the larger urban centres, the bicycle may become important in the secondary grades as a means of transport to school.

If aggregate pupil movements between home and school are to be minimised, catchment areas should be as small as possible. Pupils can then attend a school very close to their homes. This will save the pupils and their parents time and effort, and possibly even expenses. Public authorities may also be saved the effort and expense of organising transport.

In order to maximise convenience and minimise cost, schools should be sited in such a way that the journey from home to school can be undertaken on foot by all pupils (Fig. 10.2). This suggests that the main distance children have to walk should be minimised. It has been suggested that the maximum effective range of a school, that is, the distance it recruits pupils should be 5 km (3 miles) or approximately one hour walking time for secondary pupils, and should be at most 2 or 3 km (2 miles) for the youngest children. Excessive distance between home and school is sometimes the key factor in reducing access and increasing absenteeism, and thereby performance (Gould, 1978). Thus the norm for a maximum catchment area where pupils walk to school would be about 80 sq km (area of circle of 5 km radius or πr^2, is 78.55 sq km). For the younger children, where the effective range is 3 km, as noted above, the catchment is 28.28 sq km (area of circle of 5 km radius or πr^2). This,

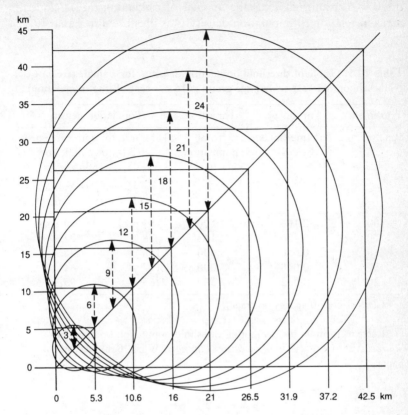

Fig 10.2 Spatial representation of catchment areas (after Hallak, 1977, p. 150)

of course, assumes the absence of any severe geographical impediments to movement within the prescribed area. The range norm would tend to vary within a country depending on the presence of such physical features as rivers, hills or mountains, forests and even railways and motorways, as well as modern traffic hazards. The presence of these factors would tend to reduce the distance it is in practice possible to ask children to travel to school on foot.

Theoretically, therefore, the catchment area of a school to be reached on foot is a circle whose radius is the maximum distance from home to school. But the size of the catchment area of a school is based on not only the most acceptable walking distance from home, but also on the potential school-age population from which the school can draw its enrolments. Thus the manner of estimating the catchment areas in relation to population density is as illustrated in Table 10.1.

Table 10.1   Table of threshold population densities for a single stream 6-grade school (Six-year school age group is 16 per cent of total population)

Enrolment	Enrolment	Threshold	Population density	
Rate (e) %	Rate multiplied by .16*	Total population (f)	Threshold (d) with catchment area (k) of: 28.28 km²	78.55 km²
			(3 km radius) (d)	(5 km radius) (d)
100	0.160	1,500	53 p.s.k.	19 p.s.k.
70	0.120	2,143	76	27
50	0.080	3,000	106	38
30	0.048	5,000	177	64
20	0.032	7,500	265	95

a.   Class size = 40 spaces (average).
b.   School size = 6 grades, single stream = 240 spaces
*   Refer to formula for computing threshold population on page 248
Source: After Gould, *School Location Planning*, World Bank occasional paper, 1978, p. 8.

Circular catchment areas, however, have one major drawback which is that either some areas fall outside any catchment diagrams or some belong to more than one catchment scheme. As a result hexagonal shaped catchment areas as illustrated in Figure 10.3 are more satisfactory. The enrolment numbers are given by the equation $E = 2.589r^2 \times d$, where $2.598r^2$ gives the area of an hexagonal cell, and d is school-age population density.

The assumptions on which such calculations of catchment areas are based include: homogeneous population distribution; equal possibilities of reaching the school from all places within the catchment area; schools with identical characteristics in terms of size, standards, admission regulation and availability of accurate population statistics for every district of the country. In practice, however, things do not work out this way; it is rare indeed to find a district of uniform relief or populations uniformly dispersed over the geographical area in which a school is located.

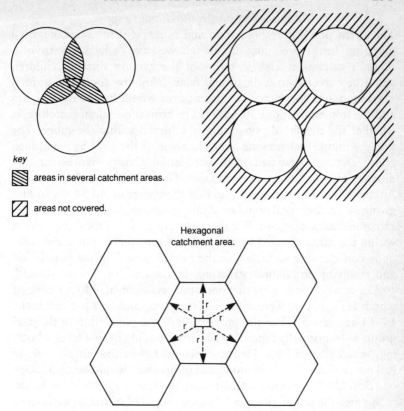

key

▨ areas in several catchment areas.

▨ areas not covered.

Hexagonal catchment area.

Fig 10.3 Circular and hexagonal catchment areas (after Hallak, 1977, p. 151)

Consequently, the issue of whether or not schools can be provided within walking distance of every home depends in practice on a balance between two basic factors:

1 The number of potential clientele or pupils within a reasonable distance of the school. This number in turn is the product of several factors:
   a) the overall population density and structure in the area;
   b) the sub-population to be served, as defined by the structure of the education system and the basis for organising schools; and
   c) the participation rate among the sub-populations.
2 The minimum threshold or the acceptable minimum size of school.

These issues are discussed in more detail in the next section.

Interaction of threshold and range

The interaction of threshold and range norms is at the heart of school mapping. In the preceding discussions we have defined the size of a school's catchment area in terms of the average distance children could be expected to walk to and from school on foot. The normal maximum area for such a catchment area would be about 80 sq.km and the minimum about 30 sq.km. The critical question, therefore, is whether the threshold population is achieved within the range. The average number of persons living in areas of the sizes as mentioned above can be calculated from population density figures for any district, provided these are available. Gould (1973) in his study of Ankole District in Uganda found that there were about 54 per sq.km, giving an average total population (all age-groups) in the average-sized catchment area of 4,240. But the proportion of this total population within the range covered by all grades of the school system will vary quite considerably according to the rate of growth of the population and resultant population structure. In the case of Ankole (Gould, 1973), for example, overall population was put at 4.8 per cent of whom 16.7 per cent were in the 5–9 age-group and 12.9 per cent in the 10–14 age group. Thus the proportion of the population in the age-group 5–14 normally regarding as corresponding to first level schooling, was 29.6 per cent. Hence, it would follow that in an average Ankole catchment area in numerical terms there would be an average of 1,250 (26.9 per cent of 4,240) primary school-age children. In the urban area the population per 80 sq.km would of course be far higher. Nevertheless, what the figures do emphasise is the fact that in determining the numbers of children in a geographical area of a given size, population structure is almost as important as population density.

Education structure is also important, for the longer the primary school course, the higher the proportion of the 5–14 age-groups in a six-grade primary school. In a seven-grade school we can expect the figure to rise to seven-tenths of the age-group. Thus in a given area larger schools are attainable with longer courses. This may be part of the reason informing the decision of the Kenyan government to lengthen the primary grades to eight instead of the present six (1986).

Another fundamental determinant of the size of a school's clientele is the basis of school organisation. If schools are differentiated along say sex or religious lines, so that each recruits not from the total population but from a sub-population then schools of a given size must draw their pupils from further afield. In this regard, the comprehensive school as organised in Britain or Sweden, which takes in all children of a certain age-group is spatially the most efficient. For example, a fully comprehensive school may have a potential clientele of over 1,000 pupils within a radius of 5 km, a specialised private denominational girls art school may have no more than 50 pupils at this distance.

Data on population density and structure, together with information on education structure and organisation, will provide an indication of the maximum potential clientele for a school recruiting from its local catchment area. However at present, in most countries in Africa it is generally the case that schools do not enrol all of those potentially eligible. Consequently, if the range norm is, for example, established at say 3 km, and assuming no barriers to movements such as a hill or river, there will be round the school a circular catchment area of 28.28 km² (or 3.142 × 3 km²). If we assume that the population density exceeds 75 per sq km (say 75.4) and the six-year age-group constitutes 15 per cent of total population and the target enrolment rate is 75 per cent of the age-group, then the threshold population

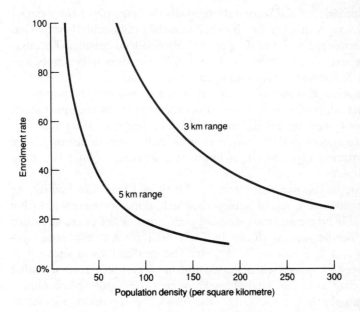

Fig 10.4 Single stream school (240 spaces, 6 grades). Interaction of range, enrolment rate and population density threshold (After Gould, W.T.S., 1978, *Guidelines for School Location Planning*, Washington D.C., The World Bank)

required for a 240 space, six-grade school will be 2,133 (28.28 × 3² × 75.4). If, however, in any area with this age profile the population density is less than 75 p.s.k, the threshold population will not be reached within the range. Hence any one primary school can operate up to capacity in such an area only by the adjustment of one or more of the norms: extension of the range to 4 or 5 km to serve more people; reduction of the threshold population required by having smaller schools; raising the target enrolment rate (Fig. 10.4).

In the majority of African countries, wide variations are found in enrolment ratios between different areas and localities. Generally, much higher participation rates can be attributed on the one hand to the deficiency in demand for education, with parents and children deciding for cultural or economic reasons not to avail themselves of existing places in the school system. On the other hand, where demand for schooling is high, the cause of low participation rates is deficiency in supply. A system of rationing consequently operates because fewer school places can be made physically available than the demand for them. This appears to be the case in some of the larger urban areas in Africa.

Similarly, at the secondary level, the proportion of the primary school leavers that can be absorbed into the public school system has to be restricted to 10 or 15 per cent for financial reasons. This may represent nationally only 3 to 4 per cent of the secondary school age-group. Moreover, since admission to secondary school is often by examination, this means in effect that in any one area the number of students admissible is far lower than the number of the appropriate age-group who would like to attend. The result of such a heavily selective system in the rural areas, with little public transport, is the wide spacing of secondary schools and so these often have to be boarding.

Part of the national effort in SLP should therefore involve the preparation of a set of tables in which these norms vary within acceptable limits, and the threshold population densities are identified as the norms vary as shown in Table 10.1 for a half-stream, two-stream and three-stream intake, etc. The implications of such tables are more clearly seen when accompanied by a graphical representation of the data as in Fig. 10.4. They show that the higher the enrolment rate and the larger the range, the lower the threshold population density needs to be. The preparations of such tables and graphs will serve the dual purpose of having a general application in the country as a whole, and can be used by local authorities for more detailed analysis of school locations at the local levels.

Practical factors influencing the shapes of catchment areas

Our theoretical discussion of catchment areas assumes regularity of shapes of these areas. However this is not the case in practice. Findings of the IIEP case studies (Hallak, 1977) identified a number of practical factors that influence the shape of catchment areas and they include:

1 The 'regulations' factor: catchment areas are generally not very regular in shape, but lack clear-cut boundaries. Most countries do not have strict rules to compel children to attend school where they live. Without such compulsion, the concept of catchment area loses most of its meaning.

2 Infrastructure: the uneven distribution of dwelling-places and the characteristics of the existing road network both result in irregularly-shaped catchment areas.

3 The administrative factor: quite often, the boundaries of catchment areas are affected by the boundaries of existing areas for other administrative purposes such as development districts or local administrative units.

4 Time taken from home to school. The conclusion of IIEP studies is that in practice the main determinant of the shape and size of catchment areas is not so much the distance children have to travel but the time they take doing it. On the whole, the maximum acceptable time taken in getting to school seems to be about 45 minutes at the primary level. Thus the shape and extent of the catchment area is decided not by the maximum distance to be covered, but by:

a) the maximum time spent on getting from home to school;

b) the means of transport used and its speed. Assuming 40 minutes as the maximum acceptable time from home to school and the walking speed as 4.5 km an hour, that on bicycle and motor-transport as 18 km an hour respectively, we obtain a catchment circle with a radius of 3 km for children walking to school, one with a radius of 12 km for those on bicycles, and two axes 30 kms long along the roads, the two catchment areas for children enjoying motor-transport but taking a certain amount of getting to the pick-up point. If on top of this the area is a hilly one, the shape of the catchment area will be still more complex and irregular, influenced by physical relief and by means of communication. Fig. 10.3 shows how the shape of a catchment area is determined by school-home time.

5 The political factor. The significance of catchment areas differs according to the planning systems in force and the goals of the school map.

a) Drawing the boundaries of catchment areas is only useful if children are compelled to attend the school where they live.

b) Boundaries will be drawn in relation to economic criteria: reducing transport costs if the aim is to keep costs down to a minimum level. However, if the intention of the school map is to mix the different social classes or ethnic groups, then the boundaries of the catchment areas will also be different depending on whether there is universal or compulsory schooling. In rural areas with low populations unorthodox approaches to the provision of schools is the most feasible. Where there is sufficient population density to justify minimum size schools, then considerations of means of communication, the maximum low-school time, and the distribution of inhabited places are main determinants of location.

In urban areas, where large schools are feasible, two possibilities are available: the first aims at keeping costs down to a minimum, and the other at providing the greatest measure of mixing of social classes in schools. The two systems are not necessarily compatible, and policy considerations will therefore opt for one or the other.

c) Beyond compulsory education. If admission to schools is dependent on examination results alone then in theory any child can go to any school of his choice and where a large number of the schools are boarding as Gould shows in the case of Uganda, then the catchment area concept loses a lot of its meaning.

6 Private schools. The existence of a network of private schools tends to complicate the drawing of catchment areas, as these invariably do not follow the same admission rules as the state schools. Consequently the boundaries of the state schools can become less clear cut.

Determinants of appropriate school size

Besides the issue of accessibility to the learner, there is also in SLP the question of what constitutes a 'good' size of school. In taking any decisions on this there are at least three factors to be considered. First is the question of pupil and teacher identity in the school. Here the important consideration is whether the school is of such a size that the pupils and teachers can relate easily to each other and the institution. A child starting his first year of primary school may feel quite uncomfortable in his class of 30 or 40 pupils. However, as he moves up the class and gains in maturity, he will not find his entry into the secondary school and university such daunting experiences. He will have learnt to overcome the oppressive feeling of anonymity in a large institution. Nevertheless, even at secondary or higher levels, the big school or institution needs to be structured to provide pastoral care for the individual in smaller groups. However, as important as the need to control the size of school to give pupils and staff a sense of belonging is, it should be sufficiently large to provide variety and interest.

A second but related consideration is the size of institution that can be effectively managed and controlled by the head. This will depend on the style of management and the degree of devolution and authority. A head who delegates extensively to deputies, departmental heads, administrative assistants, teachers and so forth, can effectively handle a larger institution than one who heroically attempts to deal personally with the plethora of administrative problems in an institution – pupil discipline, staff matters, timetabling, community relations, etc. to name a few. Large institutions such as universities and polytechnics are able to handle very large numbers of students effectively only by the devolution of most of the administrative burden to faculties and departments.

The third consideration is economy of scale. This, in simple terms, means that while promoting effective learning by pupils, one must equally ensure that resources in education are used as productively as possible. In a school system, the most expensive inputs are normally teachers, then buildings and fixed equipment, therefore, in a school of efficient size, teachers and classrooms will be used both as intensively and as extensively as possible. This requires that teaching groups will be kept at the maximum efficient size and carry their fully prescribed time load over the school week respectively. It is the case that per pupil costs become exorbitant when teachers, classrooms and laboratories operate with under-enrolled classes or only half-time. Let us elaborate a little on the concept of intensive and extensive use.

In a situation such as that of the primary school where teachers, teaching space and the curriculum are all unspecialised, adequate 'extensive' use of facilities can be realised over a larger part of the school week without many undue organisational difficulties. The problem is more likely one of ensuring sufficiently 'intensive' use by getting adequate class sizes. When numbers in the teaching-group fall below the norm (usually 30–50 pupils), per capita costs or costs per pupil rise. It then becomes imperative to economise on teachers and teaching space by combining parallel or consecutive classes.

But where the curriculum calls for subject differentiation and specialisation, as at the secondary school, then it is only a multi-stream school that can keep class sizes up to the optimum in all teaching subjects. It is by restricting choice to only two subject areas, say arts and science, that a school of only two streams can provide alternatives quite effectively. Hence a wide range of free subject choice to pupils, with teaching groups of adequate size in each subject, is only possible in a large school of say 1,800 – 2,000 enrolments. In most parts of Africa where population is generally sparse, schools of such sizes are rare, and where such enrolments are realised then resort is often made to a double shift system. Second, apart from the intensive use of facilities, through teaching groups of optimum size, it is equally important that the number of weekly teaching periods are sufficiently high in each subject to allow adequate 'extensive' use of specialist teachers and facilities such as laboratories, art and music rooms.

Thus, it is clear from the foregoing, that it is not possible to prescribe absolute rules about maximum and minimum school size. However, the ideal size of an institution in purely educational terms is dependent on factors such as the age of the pupils, the type and breadth of curriculum and the administrative style. Gould, in his study of Ankole, recommended 650 pupils as the ideal or optimum size for both primary (2-stream) and secondary (4-stream) schools. More recently, the Implementation Committee for the New National Policy on Education in Nigeria suggested 360 pupils (3-streams) for the new junior secondary schools (1982) as the ideal size.

From a more practical point of view, though, the size of a school in terms of the total number of classes or teaching groups is the product of two elements. One such element is the course structure or number of years/grades in the course as defined by the educational structure: the larger the length of course in years, the easier it is to form a big school. The other element is the number of parallel streams a school has at each level, which in turn is a function of population density and size of catchment area. To illustrate, an 18-class school can consist of 9, 6 or 3 streams for 2, 3, or 6 year courses respectively. Thus, whereas the policy on course structure is invariably determined at the national level of policymaking, size of intake is governed by local circumstances of population density and structure. Hence, the school mapper's task is to try and reconcile the claims of national educational structure and school size norms with the realities of the inherited patterns of schools, if any, and local population distribution. In other words, the challenge likely to confront the school mapper is how to attain desired school size in the face of perhaps an insufficiency of accessible clients. It is the solutions to this issue which we discuss in the next section.

Creating viable schools

Most school systems encounter at some level the problems of not attaining the school or college size norm within the walking range. As we move up the education ladder, it becomes progressively more difficult to create a viable institution on a purely local basis. This is explained on two counts. On the one hand, is the fact that the desired size of institution tends to get bigger if it is to offer a comprehensive range of studies. On the other hand, the eligible entrants are fewer as a result of at least four factors.

1   In most African countries, as elsewhere in the developing world, population growth has meant that older age-groups are much smaller than younger.
2   Since higher education is not compulsory, many pupils opt to leave formal education as early as at the end of the first level.
3   Financial shortages mean that the state cannot in any case afford to admit all those who might desire it, to higher education.
4   Finally, the majority of higher level institutions by and large, tend to be monotechnic, i.e. offering only one speciality, consequently, they are hardly likely to attract a large proportion of their students from the immediate vicinity than a more broader based or poly-technic institution.

All these factors mean that the basic school mapping problem of reconciling desired institution size with an insufficiently numerous local clientele arises at some point in all systems.

Three basic possibilities can, however, be adopted (Williams, P.R.C., 1975). First, is the enlargement of the catchment area by the removal of the constraint that attendance must be on a pedestrian basis daily from the home. Second, recruitment to the school or college should be of a higher proportion of the population in the catchment area. Third, there should be acceptance of a lower norm for school size. These three possibilities are elaborated below.

1   *Extension of school range by transport or boarding*

The provision of transport or boarding can facilitate the enlargement of the catchment area or remove the constraint that attendance must be on a pedestrian basis. In our previous discussions, the largest catchment area for a school, based on daily home-school journey, was considered to be 80 sq km. This gives a radius of 5 km, considered to be a reasonable walking distance for the average pupil at the second-ary level. If, however, the 80 sq km area is inadequate to produce the required number of pupils for the school of desired size, then the solution is to space schools further apart and enlarge the catchment area. This will consequently entail that pupils from the most remote parts of the catchment area must be conveyed to school daily either by a public transport system or by special school buses. The alternative is for pupils to travel to termly lodging during term either with friends or relatives near the school or in specially provided boarding accommodation at the school. All these solutions, however, may involve extra monetary expenditure by parents and/or the authorities, as well as the expenditure of time by pupils in the case of daily transport. The monetary costs may be offset, partially or wholly, by the creation of schools of a more economic size, i.e. large schools in which the costs of teachers' salaries and maintenance of facilities are spread over a greater number of pupils, thus reducing the per capita costs.

Arguments for and against the boarding system abound. The essential school mapping argument in favour of boarding schools is that they permit the formation of large schools to serve sparsely populated areas and thereby facilitate the provision of equality of educational opportunity irrespective of the location and demographic distribution. Boarding schools can serve a politically useful function in making it possible to provide educational facilities to peripheral areas of political importance, thus ensuring the spread of educational institutions widely among the different districts and regions of the country. Moreover, from the point of view of African countries, boarding institutions, by promoting the mixing of students of different regions and backgrounds, contributes to national unity. This is the *raison d'etre'* for the Federal Government Colleges in Nigeria.

2 *Increase in catchment area attendance*

The second possibility of attaining the desired institution size within a catchment area is to increase the proportion of catchment area population attending school. The most obvious way is to ensure 100 per cent attendance of eligible pupils. Generally, low rates of participation can be attributed to one of two reasons: the lack of supply of school places; or schools existing which are not fully enrolled because of lack of demand from parents – a reflection of social, cultural or economic factors. Where school fees are charged, these constitute a particularly strong disincentive.

Schools can be made attractive to parents in a number of ways.

a) By phasing the school day and school year in such a way as to permit children to be available to help parents with household chores and other activities.

b) By making special efforts to adapt the curriculum to local concerns and to attract indigenous persons in the locality into teaching and thereby increase community confidence in local schools.

c) By remitting fees in whole or in part. In economic terms, where schools are only half full, the marginal cost per place of expanding enrolment is far lower than the average cost per place. Where possible, universal enrolment would facilitate a cheaper day system with shorter journey times. There are obvious economies in unit costs to be gained from increasing participation rates in schools.

Comprehensive recruitment to every school provides a second approach to ensuring that a school attracts the maximum possible proportion of eligible children in its area. In this way the fragmentation of the potential clientele for schools through differentiation for school recruitment purposes on the grounds of sex, religion or ability and thus prevent the chance of any school reaching a viable size, is avoided.

The school structure offers a further approach to the formation of large schools. As already stated, school size is a product of length of course (in year grades) and number of form entries or streams. Where it is only possible to recruit a single class to the first grade of a school, it is desirable to lengthen the coverage of the school in terms of grades. This therefore suggests two things: firstly, that the structure of basic education in sparsely populated countries should be based on a few long stages rather than on many short ones. Secondly, where local conditions allow, the organisation of education should allow for the combination of successive stages in an all-age or an all-through institution. This would make it possible to establish larger schools than is possible with separate stage institutions. Within such an arrangement, it is possible to have a separate primary and junior secondary or a junior and senior secondary section of a school, but sharing some staff and facilities with the resultant economy of scale.

3 Re-examine the potential of small schools of 15 to 20 pupils

Pedagogically there may be every advantage in teachers handling classes of this size, especially if more active learning methods are being used. However, with diminishing size one immediately encounters the difficulties of 'uneconomic' teacher pupil ratios, i.e. the costs of education per pupil rise sharply as the teacher-pupil ratio is reduced, because teacher salaries account for such a heavy proportion of the total school budget. One way of keeping this ratio at a financially tolerably level is for teachers to teach combined grades of pupils in one group or even a single teacher handling a whole school of 30 or 40 pupils spread over five to six grades, i.e. the one teacher school.

Implications of the past

The foregoing aspects of school location planning involving catchment areas, size and viability of schools, have been partly influenced by historical settlement patterns and educational systems – the inherited school map. We now turn to the effect this inherited school map has had not only on the present or existing school map, but on how this existing map will in turn influence future developments.

The historical background to school location planning in Africa was discussed earlier in the chapter. Here we look at two ways in which the impact of the past or the inherited school map manifests itself, first through the unevenness of schooling, second in the differentiation of existing schools.

Unevenness in provision of schooling

The uneven geographical distribution of schools which is quite common in most African states is one effect of past developments. A school map of most countries shows that the amount of schooling provided varies from region to region and even from area to area within the same region. The differential levels of educational provision can be measured in terms of such factors as available premises, participation rates and pupil/teacher ratios. They can be further refined in terms of such comparative measures as repeater and dropout rates, teachers' qualifications, furnishings and equipment, adequacy of premises, and unit costs and budgets.

More important, however, is the effect the existing school map may have on the way the education system develops, that is to say, on the relationship between educational supply and educational demand. This is because, generally, educational provision in most countries tends to follow what is known as 'school demand'. Two indicators of such a demand are the numbers of children in a given age-group which can be used as a basis for the assessment of demand; and the participation rate. Thus the IIEP studies showed that Côte d'Ivoire and Morocco, for example, experienced unevenness of educational provi-

Table 10.2: The influence of supply and demand on primary school enrolment in areas of Kano State, Nigeria

Area	Total population (projected) (a)	School – age population (b)	Actual Enrolment (c) M/F	Total	Enrolment as % of school-age population
Dutse L.G.A.	414,000	58,421	21,796/6,642	28,438	48.7
Kano Municipal	794,000	105,950	67,502/46,797	114,299	10.9

Note: (a) Projected population figures are from the Kano State Statistical Yearbook, 1981.
(b) Figures calculated from (a) above at 4% of total population for Kano municipal, and 2.5% for Dutse Local Government Areas.
(c) Enrolment figures are from Kano State Ministry of Education, Statistical Yearbook, 1984/85.

sion. Generally, what the studies showed is that the relation between educational supply and demand is not a one-way street; supply determines demand and vice-versa. Thus the demand for education influences the development and structure of education supply typified by the greater numbers of schools in urban areas than in rural areas because of the higher demand for education. A comparison of Kano Municipal area (urban) and Dutse (rural) in Kano State, Nigeria shows this clearly (Table 10.2).

Conversely, as the experience of the UPE scheme in Nigeria shows, in spite of the availability of primary schools in many rural areas, such schools can only recruit a small proportion of the appropriate school-age population in their catchment areas because of the low level of demand for modern education in these areas. The primary school enrolment figures for Kano, Borno and Sokoto shown in Table 10.3 illustrate this clearly.

Table 10.3:   Enrolment primary grade 1: actual and projected, 1976/77

State	Projected population	Actual enrolment	Actual as % of projected	Gap between actual and projected
Borno	123,400	88,200	71	−35.2
Kano	237,800	193,100	81	−44.7
Sokoto	186,900	78,700	42	−108.2

Source: Blue Print, Federal Ministry of Education, 1978, p. 54.

On the other hand, the structure of supply can equally influence demand as measured by participation rates. For instance, it is the case that the participation rates at all levels of education are generally higher in those areas with a longer history of educational development with a resultant greater supply of schools at the different levels. Thus, the northern Sudan, with a well-developed school system, has a much higher level of participation than the southern Sudan where educational provision has always lagged far behind as a consequence of government policies. Whereas in 1976 the average enrolment in primary schools in the north was over 50 per cent the figure for the south was only 22 per cent. The gap is even wider at the secondary level, where in the south only 5.5 per cent of the eligible age group were in schools, while 18.5 per cent of their counterparts were enrolled in the north. A similar situation prevailed in Nigeria in 1976–7 where the southern part, because of the longer period of the development of

Table 10.4: Secondary enrolment and population by state, Nigeria 1976–77

Northern States	Population 1976	Enrolment 1976–77	Er/10,000 Pop.	Southern States	Population 1976	Enrolment 1976–77	Er/10,000
Bauchi	3,337,046	8,853	26.5	Anambra	4,936,479	89,243	180.8
Benue	3,331,173	32,630	98.0	Bendel	3,377,767	107,114	317.1
Borno	4,114,180	13,684	33.3	Cross River	4,773,873	60,639	127.0
Gongola	3,575,823	14,684	39.4	Imo	5,040,863	117,950	234.0
Kaduna	5,625,094	35,226	62.6	Lagos	2,172,419	84,985	391.2
Kano	7,926,206	23,753	30.0	Ogun	2,128,760	49,496	232.5
Kwara	2,353,196	39,741	168.0	Ondo	3,746,608	85,444	228.1
Niger	1,639,506	12,875	78.5	Oyo	7,149,390	130,981	183.2
Plateau	2,781,663	22,275	80.1	Rivers	2,360,665	50,000*	211.9
Sokoto	6,229,660	19,638	31.5				
TOTAL:	40,913,547	222,757	54.4		35,686,842	775,852	217.4

Source: Blue Print, Table 4, p. 67.
* Estimate. Source of population data, FOS (Federal Office of Statistics).

modern education, had greater enrolments than the north. This is demonstrated in Table 10.4.

However, the significant difference between the situation in the Sudan and Nigeria was that in the latter case, equality of educational opportunity was seen by government as a vehicle for national unity and thus the implementation of universal primary education in 1976 was a serious attempt to close the educational gap between north and south as well as the less privileged areas within each region. This has been accompanied by the massive expansion of the education system at every level throughout the country. As a result, the less advantaged areas have made rapid educational progress. This has not been the case in the Sudan.

The basic result of uneven schooling between parts of a country, apart from the inequality of educational opportunities, as Ronald Dore has postulated in his essay, 'The Late Development Effect', the later a country embarks on the modern development process, the more exclusive tends to be its dependence on educational qualifications for job recruitment in the modern sector. This means that the less educated groups will be excluded from the better paid jobs and such exclusion in African countries is strongly reinforced by such powerful additional factors as religious and ethnic loyalties and family ties. The result of the combination of all these in the Sudan is the exclusion of the southern Sudanese from playing any active role in the central government to the extent that they have become in reality second-class citizens in their own country. In Nigeria, with the emphasis on the equalisation of educational opportunity and national unity, all parts of the country participate fully in national affairs. This is ensured through the insistence on federal character in job recruitment in the civil service at the federal level as well as in the private sector.

Differentiation of schools

In the preceding discussions of catchment areas and school size, the assumption was that schools for a particular age-range were of a single uniform type. By extension it would follow that all school-going children of the same age would attend the same type of school. In practice, however, there is usually differentiation between schools at the same level commonly based on three types of characteristics: differences in pupils; differences in curricular offerings; and differences in the managing bodies.

The most obvious difference among children of the same age is the one of sex, with schools organised on the basis of male or female gender. This is a reflection of the fact that certain cultures and religious groups strongly object to co-education for boys and girls, particularly during adolescence, at the secondary level. Separate schools are usually also established for children of different measured abilities such as the handicapped and occasionally also the geniuses, although the removal of such separation is increasingly being advocated. It has also been the practice in many African states to find the brightest 10 or 20 per cent being educated at the secondary level in academic schools while the remainder attend schools with less theoretical courses such as technical and crafts schools.

Secondly, schools may be distinguished on the basis of curriculum and content. Thus differentiation amongst schools may be based on the language used as the medium of instruction, with some schools using a vernacular language, while others use a regional or official *lingua franca*, and yet others an international language such as English or French. For example, in Kenya at the primary level, most rural schools operate through the medium of the local ethnic language while those in the urban areas with their heterogenous populations use Swahili or English. At the secondary level, all schools operate through the medium of English. Similarly in the southern Sudan, in the rural areas with their homogenous populations, the local languages are used at the primary level while schools in the urban areas with their usually mixed population use Arabic or English. This approach to language use in schools is quite common in African countries. A second set of differentiation at the secondary or post-secondary level is on the basis of specialised subject content, where there may be different educational institutions specialising in, say, technical science or commercial subjects.

Thirdly, differentiation may be in terms of management and financing. Schools in the public system may be directly under the national or regional government; they may be managed by local authorities; or they may be controlled and managed by voluntary agencies with some financial assistance from the state. Within the voluntary sector, distinctions may be based on religion, with separate systems for Muslims and Christians with sectarian denominations. Thus the Christians may be divided into various denominations – Catholics, Episcopalians, Presbyterians, Methodists, etc. – and the Muslims into Suni, Shia, Ahmaddyya sects and so forth. This is still a common practice in a number of African countries.

Besides the system under the control of the ministry of education, there may be a chain of schools run by the ministry of defence at military establishments – army, navy and air force, in their bases throughout the country. Outside these publicly-financed schools is usually also to be found a system of independent or unaided schools organised by religious bodies, community groups, charitable trusts (Starehe in Nairobi, Kenya) and private entrepreneurs.

Different viewpoints have been expressed concerning the desirability or otherwise of differentiation of schools. Schools for the severely handicapped and for pre-vocational and vocational are probably the most widely acceptable forms of special provision. Most other forms of differentiation are hotly debated. While some argue that schools should stress common values and not differences, others are of the opinion that variety is valuable and differences should be recognised. Thus, for example, the opposition to the take-over of voluntary schools by the Lagos State government in Nigeria in 1981 largely assumed religious overtones, with the stress on the fear of the erosion of denominational values.

However, from the point of view of the school map what is of major concern is that differentiation reduces the size of the potential clientele for any one school. For example, a girls' school may need twice as large a catchment area as a mixed school in order to attain the same size. Similarly, separate Catholic and Protestant schools in the same locality may be below the desired enrolment level, whereas in combination they might form a viable school.

Nevertheless, the argument for choice and differentiation may still hold on other grounds: different media of instruction, different specialisms, or even differences between schools nominally the same but with better staff and excellence of teaching, quality of premises and range of curriculum. All that is being emphasised, however, is that from the standpoint of spatial considerations, other things being equal, a differentiated system of schooling would result in pupils travelling further to school.

All the foregoing discussions show, however, that it is difficult to generalise about the correct approach in these matters for all countries and conditions in Africa. What is necessary, though, is that the same age-group should be as comprehensive in their intake as possible so that schools of adequate size can be formed close to pupils' homes. A system of defined catchment areas is useful as a check on whether every child has a potentially accessible school and to identify those beyond the range of any school. Efforts also need to be made to ensure that each school offers the full course in terms of years and grades, and a comprehensive range of options. The rights of parents to make choices should be respected, especially in situations where there are marked differences between schools in facilities, curriculum or staff. A more reasonable approach should be to restrict choice to a group of local schools, with the option to parents of the private system.

Exercises

1 Define school location planning (SLP) and state the purpose of the school map.

2 Discuss (a) the conceptual framework of school location planning;

(b) the concepts of the school catchment area; threshold population; range.

3 Discuss (a) some of the practical factors influencing the shapes of catchment areas;

(b) the main determinants of appropriate school size.

4 With concrete examples, discuss the impact of the legacy of the past on the attempts of any one country in Africa to implement a programme of school location planning.

5 Do you consider that the present knowledge of school location planning is being sufficiently applied to the development of education in your country? If not, what are the factors that are proving to be the main hindrances?

XI

Planning non-formal education

Education in Africa was traditionally conducted informally, based on daily life activities. The language, values and skills necessary for the growing child were all learned from a range of individuals in the community. As such 'the major learning modes were imitation combined with learning by doing' (Evans, 1981). Formal schooling, however, operated in the ancient empires of Egypt, Nubia and Ethiopia and later in Ghana, Mali and Songhai. But the pattern we know today is largely a colonial introduction which for the past two decades or so, has been under an intensive barrage of criticisms. The criticisms centre on two major dimensions: the pedgagoical and social (Kassam, 1977). In terms of pedagogy, schools are held to teach largely irrelevant and useless knowledge; they mislead many to equate education with schooling, discourage co-operation while promoting competitiveness; they alienate the young from their community and kill the desire to learn; they are examination ridden, thus stifling creativity and the development of an inquiring mind. In social terms, schools have been blamed for creating and/or perpetuating a hierarchy of power and privilege in society. They are also said to promote class stratification and discrimination against the working and under-privileged groups while maintaining the control of the ruling elite. These critics therefore see non-formal education as a possible remedy (along with overall egalitarian transformations of society) to the social differentiation created by formal schooling. However, as Chanan and Gilchrist put it, 'schools are not a source of social ills but rather a faithful reflection of ills stemming from society at large' (Chanan and Gilchrist,1974).

Moreover, in Africa, the promise of economic development consequent upon educational development once held at independence in the 1960s has not been realised. What is more, the formal school system is far from obtaining universality, even at the primary level. The 1961 Addis Ababa targets for universal primary education by 1980 has been implemented in only a few countries (UNESCO, 1981). The financial, human and other resource requirements for the rapid expansion of the formal school system has proved beyond the economic and administrative capacities of most African countries at present. Even more alarming, however, is the fact that in some of the countries where rapid educational expansion has occurred, the phenomenon of educated unemployment, including university graduate unemployment, has reared its ugly head. For example, in the last three years, graduate unemployment in Nigeria has become rampant, in spite of such schemes as the National Youth Service Corps (NYSC) which assists in retaining graduates off the job market for at least a year. Egypt has been confronted by a similar phenomenon for much longer, which explains the large-scale migrations of educated manpower to other Arab countries. Even tiny Swaziland also experiences the same problem.

Furthermore, it is now recognised that there are many educational tasks for which schools are not suited, even where resources are available. Hence an awareness has developed amongst educational planners, that 'education will not make its optimum impact on development unless its various elements – whether formal, non-formal or informal, and the interrelationships between them – are conceived and planned as part of a coherent overall approach (Wass, 1980). In short, a national educational system for development must of necessity comprise both in-school and out-of-school educational processes.

Much has been written on the advantages which may accrue from the implementation of well-designed non-formal programmes, especially in the context of the current emphasis on rural development, employment and equality. The first priority in developing a coherent educational system as proposed in the preceding paragraphs calls for the development of 'a new breed' of strategic planners who will be capable of assessing the overall educational needs for the society's development as a whole (Coombs et al., 1973). This is necessary in the light of the current desire for decentralisation of the development process and the increasing awareness of the importance of participation of local populations in their own development. As a result, some non-formal education programmes centre directly on the client and the process necessary to provide the skills and the motivation for people to become involved in their own development. This is what Paulo Freire has called 'conscientisation' or consciousness raising, and Susan Kindervatter has termed 'an empowering process' which is the need for non-formal education (NFE) 'to enable people to develop skills and capabilities which increase their control over decisions, resources and structures affecting their lives' (Kindervatter, 1979). The planning procedures and the educational and management structures required for these new approaches will, of necessity, be different from those being practised currently in the formal education system.

This chapter attempts to present simply and in outline, the institutional framework for planning non-formal education. It starts with the definitions and characteristics of non-formal education. This is followed by a review of non-formal education in Africa. The third section focuses on the role of non-formal education in development while the fourth part of the chapter suggests a possible organisational framework for planning NFE programmes in Africa and the activities to be carried out at the different levels: national, regional and programme. The final section discusses the limitations of the non-formal approach to educational development.

Non-formal education (NFE): definitions and characteristics

Definitions

In general, non-formal or out-of-school education tends to be defined in terms of negations, that is in terms of what it is not. As a result, the definition provided by Coombs and his associates has come to be widely accepted. This states that non-formal education is: '. . . any organised educational activity outside the established system – whether operating separately or as an important feature of some broader activity – that is intended to serve identifiable clienteles and learning objectives' (Coombs et al., 1973).

In Africa, the best definition is that provided by the United Nations Economic Commission for Africa (ECA). It states:

Non-formal education is a loosely structured educational and training activity not located within the highly structured formal educational and occupational performance . . . system geared towards certain selected clienteles and intended to achieve specific educational objectives. It complements activities within the formal educational and training system by providing extra-curricular learning experiences, by offering opportunities for continuing education and by supplying the educational base for the implementation of certain development-oriented projects, such as *animation rurale*, integrated rural development schemes, etc. . . .

Non-formal education is therefore functional, skill-oriented and geared towards serving the immediate basic learning performance deficiency needs for employment and increased productivity. It functions as a means of providing greater educational opportunity for skill acquisition and upgrading to disadvantaged sections or groups of men and women, such as school-leavers, rural dwellers, lower and middle-level urban workers, as well as workers within the informal sector of African economies. It provides training for the work force for better skill efficiency and extends facilities for employment promotion. Thus the emphasis is on flexibility and adaptability; the administrators and teachers of NFE as such need to be people of imagination and creativity in responding to particular situations.

A more radical definition of non-formal education (deriving from Freire's concientisation process) is provided by Kindervatter, who sees NFE as not only promoting the acquisition of information and skills, but rather as an empowering process. Empowering here is defined as:

People gaining an understanding of and control over social, economic, and/or political forces in order to improve their standing in society (Kindervatter, 1979).

Thus whether related to literacy, vocational skills acquisition, or health, NFE for empowering places importance on how educational processes and relationships affect learners. Programmes are consequently designed to enable people to analyse critically their own life situations and develop the skills required for collaborative action to improve them.

Characteristics of NFE programmes

The above definitions between them cover the main characteristics of non-formal (out-of-school) education. First, non-formal education is loosely structured. Programmes are thus neither conceived of or treated as inter-related parts of a coherent system. Instead, programmes are flexible and adaptable. This requires that the administrators and teachers of non-formal education programmes must be creative and imaginative. Second, NFE programmes are aimed at specific groups or selected clientele in society, with the intention of achieving specific educational objectives.

Third, it complements the formal education system by either offering a continuing education and training or by supplying the same education offered by the formal system as a necessary basis for certain development-oriented rural projects, e.g. *animation rurale*, integrated rural development schemes and so forth.

Fourth, as we noted under definitions, non-formal education is functional, skill-oriented and geared towards serving the immediate basic learned/performances deficiency needs for employment and increased productivity. Finally, NFE is concerned with improving living conditions. It is concerned with equality and functions as a means of providing greater educational opportunities for skill-acquisition and upgrading to disadvantaged sections in society – low-level urban workers, women, rural dwellers and school-leavers. This then brings us to the role of non-formal education in development.

Non-formal education in Africa

In Africa, the period of the 1960s and the early 1970s were times of particularly rapid expansion in the formal education systems. Then, within the second half of the 1970s, limits to this expansion started to manifest themselves in two basic ways. First, the education component of national budgets could no longer be sustained at the same levels. The general situation in most African states has been and in fact still is, that education absorbs a substantial part of the national budget, often as much as 25 per cent or even higher. The prospects of increasing the level of resources to education is slim, especially under the current economic difficulties obtaining in most countries. On the contrary, the inclination in many countries is towards reducing the budgetary allocation to education (see Chapter 14 on financing education). Moreover, the available resources are basically concentrated on formal education, with only a tiny fraction expended on the non-formal sector.

Second, in spite of the substantial increases in the size of the formal system since the 1960s, continued population growth and resource limitations have meant that a large proportion of the school-age population is still not attending school. This is likely to continue as the possibility of introducing universal primary education has now greatly receded in most countries. The result is that a good proportion of the school-age children will have no chance of attending school in the near future. There is similarly less likelihood for the expansion of adult programmes. Furthermore, unemployment amongst school-leavers has appeared on the horizon and threatens political stability. It was therefore out of these pressures that the demand for the rapid expansion of non-formal education was borne.

As a result, African governments and other organisations have evolved a diversity of pragmatic, down-to-earth non-formal education schemes in the different countries. Some of the best-known amongst them are such as the Botswana Brigades and the Kenya Village Polytechnics. Characterstically, most of the programmes start with a small group of individuals working in a small setting, often funded by a private foundation or a religious group. These programmes can be grouped for purposes of discussion into rural and urban types.

Rural programmes

In rural areas emphasis is on agricultural skills, literacy, local crafts and home-making. The more successful of the ventures have been those in response to the unemployment problems of school-leavers. Thus the Botswana Brigades and the Kenya Village Polytechnics were planned to provide productive ways of integrating primary school-leavers into the process of rural development. Both started as small projects at the local level and then grew through a process of trial and error; another feature of the projects was to incorporate productive work as a learning process and as a source of revenue. Moreover, in both cases, although the programmes were non-governmental in motivation, the popularity of the programmes compelled the government to provide support and co-ordination (Evans, 1981).

Other more recent programmes of NFE in Africa are the functional literacy programme in Khashmael-Girba and the Gezira Rural Television, both in the Sudan (Rasheed and Sandell, 1980). The Tanzanian rural health campaign (Sahafa Africa), conducted largely by radio, is a successful national undertaking that is well known in the literature.

Urban programmes

Besides the rural programmes, there is also a wide variety of vocational and skill-training programmes. Most are small and confined to the large urban centres. The small size of the modern economy in most African countries, however, means that there are usually difficulties in placing the graduates of these enterprises. It would appear that it is more the projects that aim at facilitating self-employment that have a better future and will continue to be the mainstay of the non-formal education sector.

Francophone Africa

A slightly different approach to non-formal education is to be found in Francophone Africa, covered by the blanket term *animation rurale*. The approaches presented in these countries are *maison familiale* and *enseignement moyen practique* or rural youth training schemes. Efforts were exerted in two different phases in these countries: the earlier in the 1960s and the later in the 1970s. N. Phan-Thuy (1985) in his review of the impact of the schemes, shows that the earlier attempts were generally civil service schemes often organised on a para-military basis in the euphoria of independence in the 1960s and were launched in Benin, Burkina Faso, Côte d'Ivoire, Mali, Mauritania and Senegal. The schemes have been criticised on the following grounds.

1   They proved to be costly, e.g. in Benin it cost US$1,500 to train and settle a young pioneer in a co-operative village.
2   The content of training programmes was geared more to general and civic education for early school-leavers than training for rural employment.
3   The national armies with their shortage of equipment, qualified technical and supervisory staff could not mobilise and train large numbers of young people. The result was that only a small proportion of the unemployed were taken into these civic services, e.g. only 1 per cent in Benin and Côte d'Ivoire and 3 per cent in Burkina Faso. Moreover, the lack of these facilities meant the restriction of the participants to land clearing and irrigation, using labour intensive methods. There were thus seldom permanent employment opportunities after demobilisation. This was exacerbated by the fact that the government did not secure legal title to land in advance.
4   Finally, most of the schemes were invariably hastily established for political and prestige purposes and as such were not firmly linked to each country's plans for development and human resources. As a result, by the end of the 1960s, the laudable aims of the schemes as a means of giving young people training to enhance their chances of finding subsequent productive employment and integrating them into rural communities had all but disappeared (ILO, 1969; International Labour Review, 1966).

In the 1970s the para-military schemes of the 1960s gave way to special youth employment and training schemes for development purposes, the so-called special youth programmes. The latter programmes are generally multi-disciplinary in nature (intended to provide training in civic, vocational, agricultural, business, etc.) and employment schemes (labour-intensive public works, land settlement, self-employment, farming.) Participation was also voluntary rather than compulsory. They were instituted in Benin, Burkina Faso, Cameroon, Guinea-Bissau, Côte d'Ivoire, Mali and Mauritania. The programmes also went under different names in the different countries (4-D clubs and young pioneers in Benin, training centres for young farmers in Burkina Faso, national community service in Cameroon, Integrated Peoples Education Centre in Guinea-Bissau, community service in Côte d'Ivoire, Rural Promotion in Mali, and Mass Education Facilities in Mauritania).

All the schemes had two fundamental aims: i) to increase agricultural production; ii) to integrate young people into their rural communities of origin after the completion of the project. They were thus located in rural areas and the programme content focused on general civic education and agricultural training. Other characteristics of the scheme were that recruitment into the programme was on the whole on a voluntary basis with priority being given to early school-leavers (1–3 years of primary schooling), or dropouts or those with no formal schooling at all. Participation in the scheme generally lasted one to two years, and the average number of recruits on a typical scheme was about 1,000 each year.

On the basis of their characteristics enumerated above, UNESCO has classified these programmes into three categories.

1 Programmes with emphasis on civic service combined with training and productive works and aimed at the integration of the products into the modernising rural sector (Cameroon, Côte d'Ivoire).
2 Programmes with more emphasis on rural training than civic service, intended to integrate the young into their own rural communities of origin (Benin and Mali).
3 Programmes stressing training and rural development community works (Burkina Faso, Guinea-Bissau and Mauritania) (UNESCO, 1982).

Generally, however, the programmes suffer from a number of shortcomings. Firstly, their effectiveness in combating youth unemployment and rural-urban migration is questionable (JASPA, 1983).

Secondly, the per capita costs in the special youth programmes were much higher than in primary and secondary education. The result was funding problems for governments and very limited extension of the programmes to only 1 per cent of the youth population. Thirdly, there was a discordance between the educational level of the beneficiaries who are either uneducated or primary school-leavers and the training level and the skills they were expected to acquire. Fourthly, difficulties were also experienced in defining the role of expatriate and national staff and in determining how the former could be replaced by the latter and yet maintain the autonomy of the programmes. Fifthly, it has been found that, with few exceptions, the contribution of the schemes to national output and hence to the economy has been insignificant. Lastly, the socio-economic evaluation of these programmes often faces daunting obstacles because of the dearth of base-line data in these countries and the absence of a monitoring system to assess the costs and benefits.

A more recent trend is therefore towards the encouragement of the rural communities to be self-sufficient in terms of production and consumption of their own goods. Unfortunately, many of these efforts have been set back by the long period of drought in Africa.

On the whole, non-formal education in Africa is at an early stage of institutionalisation and is consequently characterised by a rich diversity of models and approaches. Thus the scope for the introduction of new approaches and the improvement of those already on the ground is still immense. The experiences of the revolutionary societies such as Ethiopia and more recently Burkina Faso, would likely serve as a good guide to future developments.

As pointed out by D. R. Evans, the best examples of non-formal education are to be found in countries such as Cuba, China and Tanzania, which have embarked upon a major transformation of their political, social and economic structures. It is important, however, to note that in these countries the changes in the educational system are resultant upon changes in the larger society (Evans, 1981).

Non-formal education and development

In terms of planning methodology, the role of non-formal education in the process of national development must be considered prior to its planning. This is because at the national policy level, non-formal education would be discussed within the overall context of the place of all kinds of education in development. This would be followed by the formulation of some general guidelines concerning such factors as the size, the range of purposes and the distribution of resources between the various approaches to education. All these are decisions which are primarily political in nature and as such are the prerogatives of the political leadership. The planner's role at this stage is to provide the political leadership with reasonable understanding of the various options and the limitations of education of all kinds as a force for development, before decisions are taken. Once the decisions have been made, only then can planning take place.

The meaning of development

National goals generally centre on the kind of society envisaged in terms of its political, social and economic structures. The means towards the realisation of the chosen goals entails the measurement of the existing structures and the development of a change in strategy leading from the present to a more desirable future structure. Planning in education takes place after these two issues have been resolved.

Modernisation and radical change are universally (including Africa) the two fundamental goals of development. First, there is the goal of modernisation. This is the kind of development, capitalist in orientation, as typified by the United States and the countries of Western Europe. The dominant development strategy is gradual change and reform. Such a change is seen as taking place within the context of the existing structure which is regarded as basically suitable. What is required, therefore, is simply a modification of aspects of the structure in order to remove any faults and inefficiencies. The role of education in this context is to supply the requisite numbers of trained manpower to satisfy the demands of the modern sector. The function of the school is one of certification and allocation of students to different societal roles. The spread of education, formal and non-formal, to those not currently reached, is gradual, with the rate of growth dependent on the availability of resources and the absorptive capacity of the modern sector. This is the colonial inheritance bequeathed to Africa, and is firmly entrenched in the majority of African countries.

Radical change

At the opposite end of the development spectrum or continuum are nations in which fundamental changes in economic and social structures are sought. The changes are in terms of the ownership of production, the process of allocation of economic surpluses and the distribution of resources to all parts of society. The former Soviet Union, and the countries of Eastern Europe before 1989, China, several other countries in South-east Asia and Cuba, typify this socialist approach. Some countries in Africa – such as Tanzania and Zimbabwe have tried to follow this socialist path. In these countries of Africa, the colonial educational institutional legacies, both formal and non-formal, are considered obsolete as they were intended to fit people into the existing system of colonial administration and society. As such, they can hardly bring about radical attitudes and activities to produce the required changes for rapid socio-economic development. With the changes in the USSR and Eastern Europe we may well see a reappraisal of these sorts of policies, with new ways sought to achieve national objectives.

Some proponents of non-formal education have argued that certain types of non-formal education can bring about increased awareness amongst populations of the need for substantial social change. Non-formal education which aims at consciousness raising or as 'an empowering process', it is claimed, can constitute an important component of the reform process. Nevertheless, it would be unrealistic to expect educational activities, even of the non-formal conscientisation type, to bring about substantial structural changes in a country on their own.

Basic human needs

As a result of the dissatisfaction in Third World countries with the modernisation approach to development based on the 'trickle down' theory, a new approach has now been evolved. This is the basic human needs approach as categorised here by R. Herbold Green of the University of Sussex:

- Personal consumer goods, e.g. food, clothing, housing, basic furnishings.
- Access to services, e.g. water supply, community medicine, hygienic environment, communications, opportunities for learning.
- Infrastructure (human, physical and technological) and capacity to produce the capital and immediate goods necessary for the provision of those personal consumer goods and essential services.
- Productive employment yielding both high enough output and equitable remuneration, so that individuals, families and communities earn (and/or produce for their own use) enough to have effective access to those goods and services.

- Mass participation in decision-making and in strategy formulation and review as well as in implementation of plans and projects (Lalage Bown, 1980).

This list provides a suitable framework for non-formal education projects.

In Africa, the majority of countries tend to exhibit both the modernisation change goals and the radical change goals, resulting in a mixture of development goals and strategies. The educational goals are, as a result, also a mixture. For example, non-formal education projects aimed at modernisation co-exist with projects which place greater emphasis on liberation. However, as the determination of basic educational policy rests foremost on political and social criteria, this places the planner in a difficult situation as the thrust of national development goals often becomes unclear.

To avoid this situation, the question which both policymakers and planners should seek to answer is simply this: which functions are best suited to formal education and which to non-formal? Examination of the current conditions in Africa and elsewhere in the Third World, have led to the suggestion of several approaches – basic education; merger of formal and non-formal education; and non-competitive non-formal education (Evans, 1980; Simkins,1978; Grandstaff, 1974; Callaway, 1973) – as being suitable, particularly for those countries that have opted for the modernisation approach to development.

Planning non-formal education: national, regional and programme levels

The discussion on non-formal education in Africa shows the diversity of existing programmes. What is required, therefore, is first to bring coherence to these efforts through co-ordination and integration. This means the individual programmes have to be interlinked and their activities defined. They also need to be made genuine complements of the conventional educational system and be integrated into overall development planning. All these factors require a planning organisation with clearly defined responsibilities at the level of the different administrative units – national, regional and programme levels.

Towards an institutional framework

It would seem a contradiction to talk of an institutional framework for planning non-formal education, as the characteristics which underlie its success are precisely those incompatible with large bureaucracies: flexibility of programmes and programme goals; local initiative in programmes tailored to the specific characteristics of local situations; proximity of the decision-making process to the point of implementation, and so forth.

This contrasts sharply with the normal process of government planning, with its need for long-time horizon and the attendent delays for reviews at different levels. It is precisely these contrasting characteristics that have given rise to two different approaches to the organisation of non-formal education in Africa.

In most countries where non-formal education programmes have assumed a national scale, they are usually organised as a part of the ministry of education, e.g. adult education in the Sudan, Uganda, Kenya. In such countries whenever a decision is taken to emphasise non-formal education, then such a programme is provided with a separate budget and a governing council outside the ministry of education. Examples of such efforts are the National Literacy Campaign in the Sudan, called Ten Millions to Light, launched in 1976. However, where non-formal education has taken on the character of a mass education movement it may be organised as a separate entity. This was the case in Kano State, Nigeria under the civilian government (1979–82) when an Agency for Mass Education was established with a separate budget as a parastatal independent of the ministry of education, and the Tanzanian adult education programme (under which the programme *Mtu ni afya* (man is health) was launched.

Whatever the form, the advantages of central management are several: more exposure of non-formal education; a greater claim on central government resources; the possibility of better co-ordination and reduced duplication of effort; and the opportunity to apply systems methods of planning and evaluation. But the disadvantages are equally familiar – a strong tendency for planning and decision-making to be conducted centrally and then disseminated to local users; and strong pressures to extend control over non-governmental programmes with the likely resultant decrease in local participation and initiative.

The alternative is the policy of no central planning. Planning is instead confined to individual programmes. The advantages are all the characteristics of non-formal education elaborated above. The disadvantages are duplication, over-lapping of programmes, competition for limited scare resources, and unevenness in the quality and effectiveness of programmes.

What is required, therefore, is a mixture of systems planning and programme planning. This means at the national level, the focus is on setting general policies, articulation of national priorities and the identification of serious duplications. At the sub-national level (region/ state or provincial levels) emphasis is on co-ordination of non-formal education activities amongst government ministries, and the establishment of informal councils or committees to facilitate the exchange of information, mutual support and planning amongst non-government bodies involved in non-formal education. Programme planning is left in the hands of those directly involved in the implementation of specific activities.

Locus of control

The issue of who controls what, determines the choice of organisational structure for planning non-formal education. Programmes to meet the needs of populations and requiring their active participation need to have a great deal of local autonomy, as do programmes which are intended to inculcate self-reliance, local initiative and increased social consciousness.

Where the locus of control is centred at the national and regional levels, it is not possible to realise such goals at the programme or local level. This then brings us to the issue of planning.

Criteria for the design of planning procedures

Non-formal education, unlike its formal counterpart, is a diverse collection of educational enterprises of divergent goals, methods and outcome. Hence, there is no single planning process encompassing all activities as is the case with the largely homogeneous nature of schooling. What we have instead is a differentiated set of planning strategies or procedures with different methods for different categories of programmes. The developments of planning strategies therefore require some kind of criteria for making choices between alternative approaches.

Evans (1981) has suggested the following five criteria to assist the system planner in deciding on both the amount and type of planning which are appropriate for a particular kind of non-formal education.

1 The geographical spread of the clientele likely to participate. Programmes conceived on a national or regional scale will require careful planning and organisation because of the larger numbers of people and resources, e.g. national public health or literacy campaign. But the planning of a programme for limited numbers at the sub-district level, for example, on nutrition education, would be confined to those directly involved.

2 The ratio of governmental to non-governmental resource inputs required. Programmes which are completely or only partially financed by government would be planned commensurate to the level of such financing. There would be little government intervention in planning of programmes wholly financed from local resources or by private organisations. Thus programme demand on public resources is the determinant of the extent of its planning and oversight of its activities.

3 The amount of scarce technical expertise and expensive equipment needed. Similarly, the scarcity of the inputs required by a programme will determine the level of direct planning. This is because the scarcer the inputs, the higher their value and the greater the cost to society if not used efficiently, e.g. vocational training centres for agricultural or industrial skills.

4 The estimated duration of the need for the programme. Planning is generally more appropriate for needs which are expected to continue for some time while those which can be met by several short activities are not. However, there is also a need for planning when a programme proves unexpectedly popular and spreads rapidly. The village polytechnics of Kenya typify this phenomenon.

5 The risks of non-planning. Like any other activity, planning involves both costs and benefits and the decision to undertake it or not must be weighed in those terms. Planning invariably involves some shift in the locus of control from practitioners in favour of the planners and policymakers. One of the explicit criteria used in designing planning for non-formal education should therefore be the balancing of the benefits of increased planning against the costs in training opportunities.

These five criteria form a good start for making decisions about the kinds of non-formal education activities that should be included in a planning process. This then brings us to the analyses of the range of planning activities which are possible and at what governmental level.

Non-formal education planning at the national level

The discussion of planning at the national level will focus on three aspects: goals of planning, types of planning activities and the institutional location of the planning efforts. Planning for non-formal education at the national level involves 'minimal planning' with emphasis on policy alternatives and on the qualitative aspects of education.

Goals of planning

Five major goals for non-formal educational planning at national level have been identified as follows.

1 The development of an overall educational sector analysis in collaboration with formal educational planners.
2 Articulation or statement and assessment of the costs and benefits of alternative policies for the role of non-formal education in social and economic development.
3 The development of a broad map of the range of learning needs which can best be met by non-formal education in the different regions of the country.
4 The compilation of a general summary of major government-sponsored non-formal learning programmes and the larger private and commercial learning efforts which operate on a national scale.
5 Creation and support of effective planning capabilities at the regional level and assistance in obtaining co-operation from appropriate ministries (Evans, 1981).

Thus the major goal of planning at the national level is basically to work in co-operation with formal education planners, analysing basic policy alternatives in the entire education sector. This involves the assessment of the comparative advantages of different ways of educational provision in terms of technical feasibility as well as social and political perspectives.

National planners can also point out deficiencies in regional programmes. They also are responsible for creating the capacity and competence for planning non-formal education at the regional level. In other words, they are responsible for ensuring that the planners at the regional level are trained: it is at this level that detailed planning takes place and is also the focus of the major efforts at co-ordination of different kinds of non-formal educational activities, especially amongst the different ministries.

Planning activities

In terms of actual planning activities that should be undertaken to realise these goals at the national level, the basic requirement is for the formation of a general policy. This requires two types of information: a country-wide understanding of the content and distribution of learning needs, followed by a fairly comprehensive overview of the means available for meeting those needs. Since only minimal planning is involved, no detailed data are required on programmes and learning needs.

1   The assessment of learning needs entails looking at development goals, the economic and geographic characteristics of various regions, the existing and planned development activities and the present skill levels of the populations. In other words, needs assessment at the national level is of two components: drawing a broad set of learning needs nationally and for each region; and then developing methodologies to be used for detailed analysis at the regional level.

2   The collection of information on large-scale non-formal educational activities in both the government and private sector is the second activity. The information will again be restricted to basic data such as the number of participants, training content, completion rates, and especially data on utilisation of training after completion. The question of which sectors of the population are being served is equally crucial; this will facilitate the identification of the learning needs of those not being served at present.

These two sets of data will enable the national-level planner to prepare a general map, indicating the differences between the priority needs for development and the existing capacities to meet those needs.

3   The third role of planning at the national level is the development of regional level capacities to carry out their own planning. This includes the formulation of plans for organisation and financing of planning at the lower levels, sponsorship of training programmes for regional staff, and the development of manuals or handbooks and planning methodologies. The aim is to enable those at the lower levels to take over their own planning as quickly as possible so that planning at the national level will come to focus on policy formulation and co-ordination of national efforts on non-formal education. This then takes us to the question of the type of organisational structure needed.

Organisational structure

There are three possible approaches to the development of organisational structure for non-formal education at the national level:

1   First, in line with the general approach of minimal planning and integration of non-formal education within the overall education sector, planning for non-formal education could be part of the existing structure of education. This is the case in Zambia where there is both a department of continuing education and an Adult Education Advisory Board. Whereas the former provides educational facilities to youths and adults who want to improve their education or acquire vocational skills through part-time courses, the latter advises the Ministry of Education and Culture and other voluntary organisations on matters pertaining to adult education, co-ordinates the various adult education programmes organised by the same bodies as well as undertaking the appraisal of their programmes with the aim of bringing about a more efficient use of resources, both material and human (Zambia Annual Report, 1981). The advantage here is that it is part of an established and accepted organisation. But the disadvantages would be the likelihood of the predominance of the same techniques and philosophies of formal education over non-formal education.

2   A better alternative is the formation of an inter-ministerial planning group which includes a representative from formal education, the private sector (where heavily involved), to deal with all out-of-school activities in education. This, for instance, was the case in Uganda in 1976 when an inter-ministerial committee was formed to plan and guide the Basic Education Integrated Rural Development Programme (formal and non-formal education). The membership of the committee comprised the permanent secretaries of the ministries of education, planning and economic development, agriculture and forestry, culture and community development, animal resources, information and broadcasting, health co-operatives and marketing, local government and industry (Uganda Education Reports, 1984). In line with the marginal planning approach, such a planning body would be confined to setting policy, with implementation largely delegated to regional level authorities.

3   A third approach is to create a separate planning organisation for non-formal education. This is the approach which has proved to be more effective and successful in parts of Africa as typified by the Agency for Mass Education of Kano State, Nigeria during the civilian era (1979–83) and the adult education programme of Tanzania (see Figs 11.1 and 11.2).

**Fig. 11.1   Ministry of National Education –
new organisation structure: Tanzania (Hall,
B.L 1975, *The Structure of Adult Education
and Rural Development in Tanzania*, IDS
Discussion Paper No. 67: Appendix II**

*This chart shows reporting relationships only and not
necessarily relative status

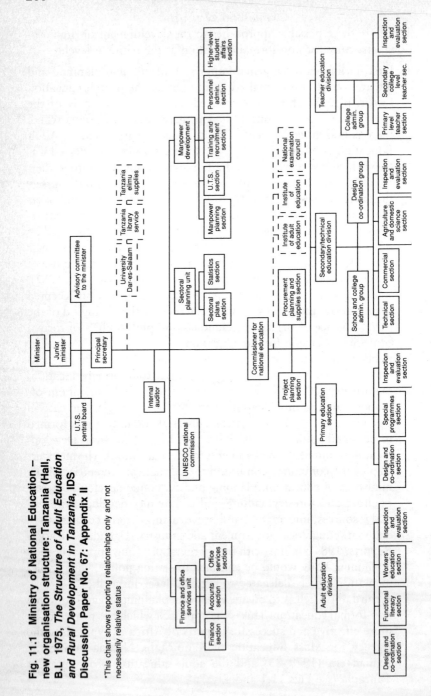

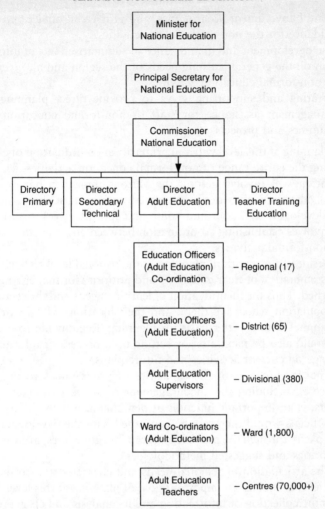

Fig. 11.2 Organisation for adult education in the Ministry of National Education: Tanzania (Hall, B.L. 1975)

Non-formal educational planning at the regional level

Goals of planning

The major goals for regional level planning would comprise:

1 Translation of national-level policies into sets of priorities and guidelines for non-formal education within the region.

2 Co-ordination of non-formal education, including direct supervi-

sion of government programmes, and profferring advice and direct guidance for the non-government activities.

3 The development and maintenance of summarised sets of information on the general learning needs of the region and an inventory of non-formal education activities.

4 Creating and supporting ways to provide direct planning and management assistance for staff of non-formal education programmes and projects.

Planning at this level will aim primarily at co-ordination of efforts covering the entire range of non-formal education activities. This co-ordination will involve getting the various ministries having non-formal education activities, such as education, agriculture, health, rural development, labour and youth and sport, to work together. It also involves establishing co-ordination between government and private non-formal activities.

Besides co-ordination, planning at the regional level also involves the dissemination of clear guidelines and priorities for the region to all concerned. Thus the identification of learning needs and the sectors of the population who have them, and their location, will provide all programmes with a better basis for planning. Regionwide co-ordination would also be facilitated by setting up a process of information exchange on current activities and future plans.

The development of the capacities of programmes to plan for themselves, including the encouragement of active participation by learners, is an important function of planning at this level. Regional level officials would therefore be concerned with the development of this capacity through the provision of training, guidelines, information of priorities and suggested methodologies.

The articulation of regional needs and characteristics to the national level is equally an important goal of planning at this level. This entails the collection of information and its analysis and clear presentation to the national level. Thus the facilitation of the upward flow of issues is a crucial task in non-formal education.

Planning activities

With regard to activities at the regional level, these will depend on the size and extent of non-formal activities. The primary focus of planning is on facilitating effective programmes and not their control and direction.

Co-ordination activities will concentrate on the provision of concise information concerning existing and future needs and facilitating planning efforts. Provision on needs and programmes will centre on the construction of general maps for highlighting the issues for distribution. The purpose is to inform those active in non-formal education in the region about the gap between needs and the provision of services to meet them.

Activities in support of programme planning and management capacities have high priorities and will include:

- the organisation of regular training sessions for staff of various programmes;
- development of manuals on planning and management;
- provision of consultancy to programmes seeking assistance to improve their effectiveness;
- provision of programmes of sample instruments for use in needs assessment, and training in their use;
- assisting programmes in recruiting qualified personnel when vacancies occur.

Organisational structure

A wide range of structures at the regional level can be envisaged, depending on the size of the region. Where a regional planning body already exists, including education, then the permanent staff for non-formal education could be located there. This would facilitate liaison with activities in ministries outside of education. In large regions, most of the activities discussed here should be delegated to the district level, provided there is support from a regional centre.

Non-formal educational planning at the programme level

Our concern so far has centred on system planning efforts. Nevertheless, programme planning also concerns us in so far as a major task of the system efforts is directed towards the development and support of the capacity of programmes to plan for themselves. It is in fact at the programme level that the most meaningful efforts and decisions take place. Traditional programme level planning proceeds along the following steps:

- assessment of needs;
- formation of goals and objectives;
- evaluation of alternative procedures for meeting the objectives;
- monitoring of implementation;
- evaluation of the outcomes.

In designing at the programme level, it is therefore important to bear the following dimensions in mind.

1   Learning objectives

This seeks to answer the question: 'why is an educational programme needed?' Where the concern is with social or political issues, then the basic question is reframed as 'what are the basic programme objectives?' In either case there is likely to be a set of learning goals.

Generally, the most typical educational goal of non-formal education is general education, often today called basic education. The major components of which are normally literacy, numeracy, basic health and nutrition, motivation for change and development, and sometimes consciousness raising.

In addition, there are those learning projects that combine general education objectives with more specific goals. The village polytechnic of Kenya is a typical example, in which the goals are a combination of maintaining and extending the general skills gained by some formal education and providing specific vocational skills that enable the learner to undertake productive roles in society.

Lastly, there are those programmes which aim at providing specific skills: agriculture for farmers, crafts and trades for artisans, family-life skills for young women and mothers, entrepreneural and management skills for small businessmen and/or women.

In devising learning projects, however, planners have to bear in mind one of the basic issues in non-formal education which is the question of how and by whom learning goals should be determined. How this is tackled depends on the characteristics of the clients, which is the second major dimension of non-formal education.

2   Characteristics of learners

Characteristics of learners are major factors in determining their likely learning needs, prospective locations for learning activities, probable limitations on the timing of training and feasible training methods.

In many cases, the target group of learners is identified by political or social factors and this provides the bounds for planning. Goals and other aspects of programmes are derived from the characteristics of the learners. Thus learners may be specified by:

- age and schooling, e.g. dropouts and primary school-leavers;
- sex and role, e.g. young women and mothers with young children;
- occupational role, e.g. farmers, auto-mechanics, carpenters, small businessmen/women or village leaders.

In spite of such characteristics, however, a major strength of non-formal education is the possibility of heterogeneous groupings of people providing ranges across age, sex and previous schooling. Such heterogeneous groups provide a range of possibilities for alternate learning strategies in which group members are used as learning resources for other members of the group.

3   *Organisational structure*

This dimension deals with questions related to the internal structures of programmes and the relationships of programmes with larger organisations. The internal organisational aspects are discussed below under staffing, financing and learning methods. The major external organisational issue is the relationship to the national ministry of education or other ministry.

At the programme level there are advantages to be gained by allowing some programmes to operate outside government administration. Even where the programme is part of a nation-wide government-sponsored effort, responsibilities in such a case should be delegated to local officials and the participants in it. Apart from meeting the need for flexibility and responsiveness in non-formal education activities, this approach, by simplifying supervisory hierarchy and keeping the administration as localised as possible, will cut down administrative costs. Finally, the advantages of close interaction with other organisations such as commercial agriculture, large-scale development programmes like irrigation schemes or village settlement programmes, should not be overlooked.

4   *Staffing*

As is the case with teacher salaries in formal education, staffing in non-formal education is a crucial planning issue because of its impact on programme costs. Hence the frequent resort to the use of volunteer and part-time staff members. Although the use of primary school teachers was a common strategy initially, the lack of proper incentives for them tended to result in nominal execution of non-school duties. A more promising strategy is the use of members of the local community – parents, community leaders, artisans, farmers, older pupils (in- and out-of-school) as teachers. Planning at this level concerns itself with the identification, selection, motivation and support for such staff as the success of the promise of non-formal education to deliver on lower costs hangs on the issue of staffing.

5   *Financing*

Costs for non-formal education are categorised into staffing, facilities, transport and expenses for materials and supplies. The issue of staffing has already been discussed. The use of existing facilities such as a primary school, public halls and so forth, is cost effective. Most of the costs of local materials could be met by local subscription or collection. Transport, particularly for supervisory and support-operations, however, poses a problem. Some economies could be made by using local personnel. The provision of training to such personnel could eventually reduce, if not eliminate altogether, the need for supervisory travel.

The major planning strategy to save the costs is the location of programmes in such a way that costs are minimised. This might entail the use of non-educational organisations and encouraging self-help efforts amongst local communities. Hence it is important always to remember that decisions made in the other dimensions all have a direct bearing on costs.

6 Learning methodology

This dimension combines a wide variety of possible alternatives with the difficult problem of training educational staff to undertake new kinds of educational roles. Amongst the innovative alternatives which have been tried fairly widely are peer learning, discovery methods, programmed texts, learner-centred curricula, community-based learning and a wide range of media-based educational strategies. Any methodology selected has a direct effect on the kinds of staff needed and the internal structure of the learning settings. The three dimensions therefore need to be planned together.

The choice of learning methods will be governed by the decision of whether the intention is to encourage the learner to be a passive or active participant in the learning process. Non-formal education projects that emphasise consciousness raising and the development of active community groups require methodologies which encourage and allow learners to assume responsibility for their own learning process. This then brings us to the issue of control.

7 Locus of control

The issue of control is at the heart of non-formal education and is in part reflected in the issue of the role of the learner in the learning. The fundamental question in this regard is: who makes decisions for whom and through what mechanisms? The issue of the locus of control is also at the root of the concern about appropriation of any planning on the central or regional level for programmes with the goal of local participation. The task for planners is one of balancing national-level needs against the demands for local control by the people themselves, over those programmes which are of direct benefit to them. Concepts

such as decentralisation, participatory structure, and systems of representation are part of this debate.

Although there are other dimensions, the seven discussed above
provide a reasonable framework for decision-making in the design of
non-formal education programmes at all levels.

Limitations of non-formal education

In order to understand the relationship between NFE and social
change, it is necessary to answer two questions: first, what were the
objectives of non-formal education? Second, what reform goals were
sought by non-formal education?

Primary amongst the goals of non-formal education was the
delivery of educational services to the neglected sections of society –
the poor, women, rural communities and adults who did not have the
opportunity to attend school. NFE was to give these groups a chance
of gaining basic literacy and numeracy, the chance to learn productive
skills and the possibility of effective participation in the development
of their societies. Non-formal education was seen, in addition to other
factors, as a strong accelerating factor in socio-economic development
of rural areas. Through the consciousness raising aspect of NFE, the
less-advantaged groups would be enabled to band together and put
pressure for changes on the existing politico-economic structure, thus
leading to the more equitable distribution of opportunity and wealth.

In short, non-formal education was expected not only to reform education but
to have a substantial impact on the structure of society (Evans, 1981).

However, La Belle (1976), in an analysis of non-formal education
projects in Latin America, has suggested several serious limitations.
First, most non-formal education projects were relatively small and
fell far short of the needs of a developing country, confirming the
earlier findings of Sheffield and Diejomoah (1972) and Coombs and
Ahmed (1975), for Africa and Asia. Thus programmes which may be
successful in achieving limited educational goals for the participants,
had insignificant impact on the larger society.

Second, La Belle raised a much more fundamental issue which
was that nearly all programmes, even those inspired by the Freirean
philosophy and method of consciousness raising, were centred around
changing the characteristics of the individual learner. These person-
centred or psychological approaches, as he called them, emphasised
changing the attitudes and behaviours of individuals.

This is a deficit approach, which suggests that changing the characteristics (attitudes and skills) of the individual will enable him to participate more fully in the process of development. The approach derives from two development thrusts. First, the assumption that lack of opportunity has produced a deficit in an individual's capabilities. Second, that a long history of psychological dependence has made the individual incapable of freeing himself from the structure which is the cause of his poverty. The attraction of the individual approach is the practicality of operating it within the existing governmental and social structures, as the causes of underdevelopment are attributed to persons rather than institutions. As such, it is non-disruptive of the existing order and so suits the modernisation approach.

La Belle contrasts this person-centred approach with one which focuses on the system, or a system-centred approach. The latter is based on the belief that inequality of opportunity is a result of the social and political structure of the country. It places emphasis on the links between individuals, institutions and the environment. Improvements in individual lives will result only through the modification or radical alterations in the pattern of relationships in society. It is unrealistic to expect the individual to apply his or her newly-acquired knowledge and behaviour successfully in a situation of unaltered political and economic structures.

The approach thus debunks the belief that education can and should be the prime mover in the development of poor and rural areas. The limitations of the system-centred approach is of its feasibility and practicality. It is unrealistic to expect that the social or economic system of a country can be restructured through non-formal education projects. Any attempt at such changes are bound to generate strong opposition from the beneficiaries of the existing system, who most likely are those in authority within ministries. This therefore helps to explain the predominance of the person-centred approach in non-formal education projects in non-socialist countries.

Bock and Papagiannis (1976) have cited other shortcomings of the impact of non-formal education on its clientele. Non-formal education generally lacks the credentials which give power to formal education. As a result the links between completing training and the likelihood of finding employment are even weaker for non-formal education. The more successful skill-training programmes (extramural) in non-formal education tend to demand some amount of formal education as an entry requirement, thus excluding precisely those sections of the population most in need of training. In this way, non-formal education may tend to reinforce existing inequalities.

A further handicap of non-formal education is that it often functions primarily to socialise learners into the acceptance of a permanently inferior status in the social and economic system. The small improvements in the status of the products of non-formal education, may tend to induce contentment, thus lessening pressure on the existing system to bring about meaningful change. Finally, the provision of vocational training programmes, whether through formal or non-formal approaches, does not in itself create jobs. Better distribution of employment in society requires both job creation and the training of workers. Education alone has little influence over job creation.

The one situation where non-formal education seems to have been effective as a main agent is in revolutionary societies such as Cuba, China and Tanzania, where many of the basic structures of the systems as a whole – social, political and economic – are simultaneously undergoing change. Formal and non-formal education components are fused as part of the overall change strategy. It is in such situations that non-formal education can effectively complement and contribute to the new goals of society.

Thus, the hope that non-formal education could be a prime mover in reforming the education system has proved largely false. Nevertheless, the dialogue about it has helped in several ways. Firstly, it has exposed the limitations of the school system. Secondly, it has brought about the proper recognition of the problems of the large populations outside the school system in our countries. Thirdly, it has helped in the introduction of innovative programmes into formal schools. Finally, perhaps the greatest benefit of all, is the lesson that non-formal education suffers from the same limitations as its formal counterpart and serves essentially the same role as formal education in relation to society. It is the social and political structure of a country, combined with its development goals, that sets the basic framework within which formal and non-formal education function.

Exercises

1 With the help of Appendix 1 discuss possible reasons for the differences in illiteracy rates between the following countries: United Republic of Cameroon and the Sudan; Ethiopia and Egypt; Zimbabwe and Côte d'Ivoire; Malaŵi and Somalia; Sierra Leone and Lesotho.

2 Attempt an explanation of the disparity in illiteracy rates between Botswana and Niger; Zambia and Guinea; Mozambique and Zaïre; Mauritania and Mali; Gambia and Libyan A. J.

3 Outline the planning of non-formal education at the national, regional and programme levels.

PART III
THE FINANCING OF PLANNING

XII

Costs in education

African education systems are today in a state of crisis as a result of the greater crises in the economy that have engulfed the continent for well over a decade. The economic difficulties have arisen partly as a result of natural factors such as the Sahelian drought of the mid-1970s and the worldwide phenomenon of inflation which really began to show about 1975. These difficulties are currently being exacerbated by the revisitation of the drought in the Sahelian region and the Horn of Africa. Part of the economic woes can also be attributed to economic mismanagement by African governments.

The fundamental problem now facing education ministries almost everywhere on the continent is simply how to maintain the existing system at its present levels in quantitative and qualitative terms. To realise this calls for the modernisation of management capabilities in the areas of costing, budgeting and financing. A proper understanding of their inter-relationship is essential for:

a) The development of well-defined and up-to-date objectives.
b) The evaluation of the performance of the education institutions established as a result of the objectives.
c) The discovery of ways to improve the education institutions' efficiency and effectiveness.
d) Planning their future with these changes in mind.

This chapter begins by offering the basic explanations of various concepts applied in costing and is followed by the definitions of the characteristics of educational costs. The next part discusses some of the basic data requirements for cost analysis. A presentation of the methods of educational costing then follows. Finally, a discussion of the relationship of costs and efficiency and costs and planning brings the chapter to a close.

Types of costs

In attempting any meaningful consideration of costs in education, it is necessary to make some essential distinctions in the measurement of costs and the use of cost figures. Perhaps the most basic distinction is that between the use of cost figures for 'accounting' purposes and their use in 'planning'.

Cost in accounting

In accounting, the use of cost figures is concerned with allocating costs that have already been undertaken for purposes that have already been fulfilled. In other words, accounting costs are the outcome of retrospective or historical allocations of resources which have already been used for or allocated irreversibly to particular goals and activities. On the other hand, the definition and estimation of costs for planning purposes cover all attempts to estimate in advance the costs that will be incurred in achieving purposes and goals that have not yet been embarked upon. Thus costing for planning purposes is concerned principally with those resources which are the real subject of choice since they have not yet been finally committed. Nevertheless, frequently some costs derived for accounting purposes are also used as estimates for costs for planning. An example will clarify what we mean.

Let's assume that surplus teaching space has just been added to a teachers' training college. Assume also that the teaching load on the existing staff is at its maximum limit. A given course has been running with 60 students and the costs have been calculated as follows:

1   The cost of academic staff participating in teaching the course is £15,000.
2   The cost of teaching space-hours required by teachers and students in the course. The costs involved here can be calculated from an accounting point of view, from the proportion of total cost of space-hours of teaching premises used by the particular course. This total cost in turn will be calculated as an annual figure for the costs of all premises and it is obtained by spreading the capital cost

of all premises used for teaching purposes over the lifetimes of the premises. Assuming that this amounts to £20,000 per annum, then from an accounting point of view the overall costs of the subject under those two heads amount to £35,000 (£15,000 + £20,000) (Westoby, 1976).

However, from the planning standpoint, the situation is quite different. Supposing that the following three decisions are being considered:

1 to close down the course entirely;
2 to continue it at its present level of enrolment;
3 to double the enrolment on the course.

We must assume also that the staff at present engaged on the course be transferred onto other courses if option 1 were selected. If we wish to adopt option 3, while maintaining the existing teacher-student ratio, then this would entail doubling the expenditure on the staff from the present £15,000 to £30,000 as the existing staff are fully employed. But the existence of spare capacity in teaching premises makes the accounting figure misleading in choosing between the three options. It not only over-estimates the planning costs to be met if enrolment on the course is expanded but also those costs which could be saved if the course were closed down. Capacity on the course could in fact be increased without any additional cost on premises. Thus although the cost of teaching premises will be included in any accounting cost of the course at any particular level of enrolment, it is not a relevant cost as far as planning for the future is concerned. The relevant costs are only those pertaining to teaching staff as they must enter into any consideration of policy alternatives, they can be avoided or transferred if the course is terminated, and must be increased if the course is to be expanded.

Financial and economic costs

A second distinction that must be made is between financial and economic costs. Essentially, financial costing is concerned with the actual cash payments made by the institution in carrying out and expanding its activities. Economic costing on the other hand, is concerned with the use by the institution of productive resources, irrespective of whether these are directly reflected in a cash outflow in the institution's account. If such resources provide services to the institution over a number of years, these are costed on an annual basis, even if the financial cost was all met in a single year. Buildings and accommodation costs provide a good illustration. Supposing a teachers' college purchases a new piece of land, then proceeds to erect on it an additional building as part of its teaching accommodation. It then continues to maintain the building and pay depreciation and maintenance of any heavy equipment installed within it over the lifetime of the building. The financial cost of the accommodation will be extremely high in the first year or so when the land is being purchased and the building constructed. This will be followed by a dramatic fall in financial costs as only the maintenance and insurance (not available in all African countries) costs will be involved. In terms of economic costs, however, all the costs are regarded as spread over the lifetime of the building. Conventionally, the college distributes the capital costs on land, buildings and heavy equipment, together with the interest charges on them, and the depreciation and maintenance costs of any heavy equipment in the building, over the whole lifetime of the building. This reflects the fact that the services the building provides to the institution are spread over its lifetime and not just in the initial years in which the bulk of the financial cost was defrayed.

Opportunity cost

Both financial and economic costs as defined above, are categories which are most relevant in the context of accounting costs. For planning purposes, though, the concept of opportunity cost is also employed. This involves making a choice between alternative courses of action when resources are short or scarce.

The cost of embarking on one course of action is the benefit 'forgone' irrespective of whether this is measured in monetary or non-monetary terms. Thus, in economic terms, rational action is that which is dictated by the maximisation of benefits resulting from the consideration of each available alternative and then choosing that yielding the greatest benefits. Cost in this sense is referred to as 'opportunity cost' as it measures the sacrifice of choice.

Opportunity cost when estimated from the standpoint of the individual or the individual institution, is known as 'private opportunity cost'. However, when considered from the standpoint of the economy as a whole, it is referred to as 'social opportunity cost'.

Therefore the opportunity costs to an individual of being educated to whatever level, is the value of the alternative opportunities he has had to 'forgo' by being educated up to the particular level. In a modern wage economy the opportunity cost to a young person of voluntarily attending school is the wage he might have otherwise earned. In such a situation, the opportunity costs are very considerable in late-adolescence or early-adulthood in the upper secondary stages or higher education. Below the school-leaving age, the opportunity cost is nil as child labour is forbidden by law. In African societies, the service of the young child in minding younger brothers and sisters, fetching water or herding, are of great value to his family. Similarly, although the income-earning opportunities forgone by attending school between the ages of 15 and 25, may be less, particularly in a rural setting, the labour of the young person on the farm or in the family business is no less valuable.

Besides such opportunity costs, there are the direct costs as well: payments of school tuition, for uniforms, sports equipment, union dues, travel and Parent Teacher Association (PTA) levys and so forth. Apart from these private costs incurred by the students, there are also the social or public opportunity costs incurred by the country. This is viewed in terms of the loss to the nation of the production which the resources used in the development and maintenance of the educational system would otherwise have produced. These social opportunity costs like their private counterparts, are of three kinds. First, there are the direct financial costs in terms of expenditure on goods and services (staff, materials and services – meals, health care) and in the education system which have to be paid for, then there is the non-educational capital expenditure incurred in support of education such as the purchase of land, and durable equipment, Finally, there is the question of the earnings which students forgo during the period of their studentship which is also a loss as it represents a loss of national output.

Characteristics of educational costs

The first characteristic common to education costs in most systems is the dominance of personnel costs and teacher costs in particular. This can be attributed to the fact that education is a labour-intensive industry relying on a predominantly handicraft technology (Coombs and Hallak, 1972).

Another common pattern to education costs is the inexorable rise in unit costs. Inflation aside, the real costs of education per student appear to have been on the increase in most African countries in the post-independence period. Two reasons have been advanced to explain this. The initial reason was the scarcity of educated manpower, including teachers, resulting in an abnormally high salary differential between this elite and other workers in the economy. This was then followed by a gradual decline in the salary of teachers until they reached a more viable balance in relation to average wages and per capita income. But the establishment of modern industries and large-scale commercial concerns, with their more advanced technologies and consequently better productivity, resulted in a slight drop in teacher salaries in relation to the wages of people of similar educational qualifications and competencies employed in these concerns. Consequently, in order to retain its share of talent, the education system is forced to pay increasing amounts if it is to produce future talent. One hope for the reduction of costs in education was the possibility of applying innovation in instructional technology to increase productivity to keep pace with the more progressive sectors of the economy (Leslie and Jamison, 1980). This has, however, not yet materialised on any large-scale in Africa.

A third characteristic of educational costs is the prevalence of higher costs at higher levels. As a general rule, unit costs tend to rise with each successive level of education, and science and technical education, at whatever level, is more costly than general education. Linked to this is the fact that non-teacher costs become a higher proportion of total unit costs as the total increases. Both these features are explained by a number of factors: at the post-primary levels there are fewer teaching hours but teacher salaries far exceed those of their primary counterparts; lower pupil-teacher ratios; the need for larger libraries and more expensive equipment; costly board and lodging and student grants. Researches have shown that the maintenance cost of one student per annum at university is roughly 9 and 36 times respectively that of a pupil at the secondary and primary levels (Coombs and Hallak, *op. cit.*)

A further common pattern of education costs is that unit costs tend to decline as the size of the activity expands, until such a point when the economy of scale is exhausted. This phenomenon of declining unit costs provides an important basis for improving the cost-effectiveness of education in a variety of circumstances. The need to achieve efficiently-sized educational units is even more imperative above the primary level because of the broader and more specialised curriculum, more diversified staff and more expensive equipment and other facilities. Generally, the higher the educational level the more scientific or technical the programme, the larger the institution size requirement to realise acceptable costs and a satisfactory educational programme.

Basic data for cost analysis

Before embarking on cost analysis, the analyst needs to amass some fundamental statistics as a basis for analysis. Such statistics should include:

- Total enrolment by levels and types of institution, geographic areas, and if possible by individual grade level.
- Annual numbers of graduates from each category of institutions.
- Yearly numbers of repeaters and dropouts by type of institution, geographic zone, and possibly by grades and geographic zone.
- Total numbers of teachers by institution and levels and by qualification and salary grades.
- Total annual expenditures on each level and types of institution, broken down into recurrent and capital costs. These could be further differentiated into teacher and other recurrent costs, new construction and equipment and repairs, maintenance and replacements (Coombs and Hallak, 1972; Cheswass, 1969; OECD, 1967).

In addition, the following data relating to economic and social trends are equally useful in cost analysis and planning: data on growth and distribution of national income and public revenues; population growth, migration and distribution; manpower needs and employment trends; general price, wages and construction cost trends and changes in the structure of the economy. These data are usually located in various government units (Vasudevan, 1976).

Cost analysis

1 The need for cost analysis

Experience in the development of educational systems has proved two important facts concerning cost analysis: firstly, any measure taken to improve educational quality or opportunity without prior examination of its cost consequence easily proves self-defeating; secondly, costs have little meaning or value unless they are set against educational results and such results are in turn weighed against objectives. In other words, costs are only one side of the equation that links educational resource inputs to educational outputs and benefits. Coombs and Hallak (1972) have identified at least seven purposes which educational cost analysis can usefully serve in the course of the development of education systems.

1 Costing and testing the economic feasibility of educational plans.

2 Evaluating and improving the allocation of available educational resources.
3 Weighing the comparative advantages to pursue the same educational objectives.
4 Determining both the short- and longer-run cost implications of a particular project.
5 Estimating the introductory cost and the likely longer-term cost impacts of a major educational innovation.
6 Conducting a general search for ways to improve efficiency and productivity.
7 Checking the economic implications and feasibility of special policy decisions before they are made.

Educational cost is normally considered from two aspects. First from the point of view of financial consideration (diagnosis). Second, from the standpoint of the projection of the trend of the education system (prognosis).

The discussion which follows will therefore consider both aspects from the standpoint of cost analysis and largely in terms of how to organise the necessary data in order to facilitate the calculations of total and unit costs and their application in expenditure forecasts.

Methods of educational costing

The first step in educational costing starts with the estimation of total expenditure and unit costs. Educational expenditures can be estimated from either the published documents of financing agencies or the accounts of education establishments. Once such estimates have been made, unit costs can then be derived depending on the purpose to which they are to be used (Hallak, 1969; Basov, 1972; Bennett, 1972). This is in principle a simple method, based on the examination of the accounts of different education sources of finance: central government, state governments, local authorities, external aid and private sources. These are best displayed in tabular form as shown in Table 12.1.

Estimation from education establishment accounts

If for any reason, difficulties are encountered in arriving at estimates using documents on the sources of finance, then the accounts of the

Table 12.1 Educational finance by sources (financial year)

Sources of receipts	Budget allocation	Actual expenditure
A *Public sources*		
1 Federal or central government departments dealing with education		
a) Education department	_____	_____
b) Other government departments	_____	_____
2 State or provincial authorities dealing with education	_____	_____
3 County, city, district or other local authorities	_____	_____
Sub-total received	_____	_____
4 Foreign aid (received)	_____	_____
B *Private sources*		
1 Tuition fees	_____	_____
2 Other private receipts from parents	_____	_____
3 Private gifts, endowment, etc.	_____	_____
4 Other sources	_____	_____
Sub-total	_____	_____
Grand total	_____	_____

spending agents or educational institutions offer the best alternative. Nevertheless, this is in practice not a widely-applied method owing to three basic difficulties.

First, establishment or institutional accounts in most African countries tend to be confined to secondary schools and higher education institutions and not at lower levels. Second, such accounts must be kept according to a uniform, functional standard, if they are to be processed at the national level. Lack of such uniformity would render the accounts useless for the purpose of estimating educational expenditure. But as we have noted above, at the primary level not only are there invariably no budgets, but even where there may be, teachers' salaries may not be included in the school budget. Further difficulties are:

Table 12.2 Standard breakdown of educational expenditure by nature and purpose

Nos.	Nature	Tuition	Administration	Transport	Board/Lodging	Health	Total
1	Salaries						
2	Materials, supplies						
3	Maintenance						
4	Operating costs						
5	Depreciation						
6	Recurrent expenditure						
7	Construction						
8	Equipment						
9	Capital outlay						
10	Total (6+9−5)						

Note: A depreciation does not represent actual expenditures, but is a reserve for renewing fixed assets such as typewriters, duplicating machines, etc. Thus it is both a capital and recurrent item and hence the logic of its exclusion from the grand total (item 10).

1 The method of estimating from establishment accounts is likely to prove inadequate on its own for assessment of total and unit educational costs. The establishment of a uniform functional accounting system is therefore a pre-condition, particularly in government institutions.

2 The quality of the information on the financing system will also depend on whether the institution is private or government owned.

3 The statistical techniques to be used will vary with the level of the education system. At the primary level, an exhaustive census would be preferable. This depends on the size of the country and its degree of educational development. In technical and higher education for all African countries, a systematic survey of each institution is necessary, despite an abundance of special cases, and possibly because of the smaller numbers involved.

4 A double-entry table is shown in Table 12.2, which extends the classification of educational expenditure discussed previously (page 307) by breaking down educational expenditure by both nature and purpose, provides a better frame of reference for accounting.

The principle underlying the construction of the table is on the one hand to disaggregate expenditure by nature thus distinguishing between salaries, materials and supplies, maintenance, operating costs, provision for depreciation and capital expenditure. On the other hand, it is necessary to separate tuition from other expenditure such as administration, transport, board and lodging and health. Once we have arrived in this way at the total outlay by nature and purpose, we can then turn our attention to the consideration of unit costs.

The term 'cost' refers to either capital or recurrent cost. As used here, it is applied in the purely accounting sense to mean expenditure. Unit cost in turn therefore means either unit recurrent or unit capital costs. For convenience, unit capital cost is referred to as 'unit cost per student place'. While the term 'unit cost' will designate recurrent cost per student per year. Thus the unit cost in primary education signifies the annual recurrent cost per student in primary education, while the unit cost per student place in primary education will connote capital cost per student in primary education.

In educational planning we are interested in ensuring that unit costs serve practical purposes. Hence it is necessary to break down unit costs in schools of different classes into their components and thereby obtain a number of unit measures such as:

- The total cost per graduate.
- The capital cost per student place.

- The capital cost per occupied student place.
- The average cost per teacher.
- Cost per school.
- Cost per course.
- Cost per square cubic foot.

The selection of the particular unit to use will therefore depend on the particular item with which we are concerned. For example, when costing such items as exercise books, pencils, textbooks required, the individual student would be the most appropriate unit, as the cost here would vary directly in proportion to the number of students. But the requirement for teachers, desks or other classroom equipment would be more suitably costed per classroom.

Although one would expect that there would be uniformity in unit cost at each level of the education system, this is in practice not the case. This can be attributed to a number of factors: higher or lower pupil-teacher ratios between schools; the relative workload of teachers, whether or not their time is fully utilised, and their qualifications. An added factor in African countries is the uneven provision of supplies to schools. In most cases, particularly at the primary level, schools in the urban areas are more favoured in terms of the provision of supplies than those far away in the rural areas. Cost variations at the secondary level are more likely to be due to differentiation in subject offerings in schools. Thus studies of disparities in unit costs are useful not only in projecting education expenditures but also in determining the cost-effectiveness of projects.

Costs and efficiency in educational provision

A system is efficient if it combines inputs in an optimal way, in a given state of technological knowledge, to produce specific outputs. Thus we talk of the effectiveness of an education system which is defined as the relationship between the inputs and the corresponding immediate output of any educational process. Cost benefit, on the other hand, is the relationship between the inputs and the resulting benefits that accrue thereafter. Cost-effectiveness is a measure of internal efficiency, while cost-benefit is a measure of external productivity. Thus whereas there is no disputing the utility of these concepts, the real problem arises in their application in practice because of the special characteristics associated with educational provision.

In a market process, efficiency problems are dealt with by the normal working of competitive forces. Efficiency is normally therefore thought of in terms of minimising the cost of producing any given output. This means that in a competitive climate or situation, firms must strive to achieve cost-minimisation, as failure to do so would lead to competitors selling at a lower price and would ultimately force the inefficient firm out of business (O'Donoghue, 1971).

Similarly, in principle, the question of efficiency could be dealt with in education by the use of a competitive system. In practice, however, the efficiency aspect of education is complicated by the public sector financing or provision of schooling which usually tends to have a multiplicity of objectives. In addition, there will also be some divergence between the private and social allocation of the costs and benefits associated with such education, coupled with differences in the relative valuations attached to various effects. Hence the existence of these ambiguities in the definition and measurement of the output or 'product' in education means that any assessment of efficiency in provision becomes more complicated.

The result is that, for example, expenditures per student or per graduate, because they are measures that are fairly easy to calculate, are often used as measures of efficiency of education systems and institutions. But the pitfalls in this are quite obvious. If the sole objective of the education system was that pupils should have the satisfaction of attending school, then expenditure per pupil attending school may indicate the level of efficiency. But as the objective of school attendance is learning, then cost per student signifies very little by itself. Expenditures per successful graduate might perhaps give a better measure of indication, but even they tend to ignore all the learning output embodied in those who left school early, or failed the examination.

A similar error is frequently committed by comparing schools within the same educational system in terms of expenditure and examination results and drawing up an efficiency table on this basis. But such an exercise can be considered legitimate only if the relative value of initial student inputs can be found. As an American study has suggested: 'the character of a schools output depends largely on a single input, namely the characteristics of entering children. Everything else – the school budget, its policies, the characteristics of the teachers – is either secondary or completely irrelevant' (Jencksetal, 1972). Hence, prestige schools perform better not only because of their better staff and buildings, but also because of their better quality intake. This also draws our attention to the observation of R. S. Peters on the problem of the subject of quality, of whether it is the level of achievement or the extent of progress we think to be important

(Peters, 1969). Assessment of output by the number of pupils passing examinations assumes that all pupils were equal on entry to the system. Thus efficiency only has validity when objectives and outputs are clearly formulated.

Hence the basic approach adopted in tackling the question of efficiency in education and public expenditure in general, whatever the differences in phraseology or nomenclature – cost-effectiveness, systems analysis, output budgeting, etc. – is essentially one that seeks to identify the 'output' or 'objective' of each expenditure programme in a measurable way, and then to determine the cost patterns associated with the attainment of these outputs. It must be emphasised, however, that efficiency in these contexts is thought of as the minimisation of cost for an appropriately defined output, and this should not be confused with cost minimisation in any absolute sense. The aim is therefore not that of identifying the 'cheapest' way of providing a product or service, because the cheapest system might provide an inappropriate and hence inefficient output.

Scope for economies

The question that then arises is how to attain efficiency in education in the sense of producing the same outputs with less inputs, measured in financial terms. The best answer is to cut out any totally unproductive expenditure, i.e. genuine waste, and to stop any losses through misappropriation. Unfortunately, except for misappropriation, shear straightforward waste is difficult to identify as almost any expenditure can be defended as contributing in some way, however indirect, to the achievement of the objectives of an educational institution.

Beyond these, two other possibilities suggest themselves. First, greater efficiency may be attained through the realisation of economies of scale by the intensive use of all of the fixed inputs to education. The 'output' of a teacher, or a building over a year, is a function of the number of hours per week they are operational, and the average number of pupils handled at a time. The 'output' from either factor can often be increased without a proportional increase in expense. For example, a building which represents a fixed cost, apart from the cost of extra light, can be used for 50 hours a week for classes of 45 rather than 30 hours a week for classes of 35, even though the capacity is doubled. In the case of a teacher his salary does not normally vary if he teaches 50 pupils in a class instead of 20. It may therefore be possible to increase his weekly teaching load by 10 per cent without adjusting his pay. It is common for teachers to work for longer terms and even during the holidays without extra renumeration. The essential point here is that if costs per unit of output are to be reduced, one must take advantage of any capacity which can be brought cheaply into extended use. As teachers' salaries and school buildings normally account for the lion's share of the education budget, attention should first focus on using them more intensively.

Another possible approach involves changing the mix of inputs to education by replacing more expensive resources by less expensive ones, while attaining the same· end results. This would involve, for example, the use of teacher assistants to do some of the work of highly-qualified teachers, by allowing the latter to specialise in the more professional aspects of the job. Other more radical proposals involve restructuring by, for instance, training teachers on the job through various courses instead of in college.

In Nigeria, for example, the National Teachers Institute (NTI) runs long-distance training for unqualified primary school teachers, while the institutes of education in the universities organise in-service vacation courses leading ultimately to degree qualifications. But the pre-condition for the effective implementation of any such options requires proper financial management. by ministries of education. Hence the importance of cost analysis and the weighing of alternatives has become a vital function of any ministry of education.

Costs and planning

The role of costs in planning is by the application of unit cost in expenditure forecasts. This is usually needed in the third phase of the planning process when the assessment of unit capital and unit recurrent costs are required for the costing of the education plan in the fourth phase. The great pitfall in the application of present unit costs or even costs per student place, as a derivative of future expenditure, lies in the fact that the past and present standards of educational provision can be unsatisfactory. One way to overcome this problem is to study the past trends in the unit cost for each level and branch of education, disaggregated into its components and in terms of whether it is for capital outlay or for recurrent cost. In the case of capital outlay, unit costs will in practice vary by regions, by size and type of the institution and also in construction cost and unit equipment costs (Hallak, 1969; Vaizy and Cheswass, 1969; UNESCO: IIEP, 1967). For each institution the calculation shown in Table 12.3 is necessary.

Table 12.3 Unit capital costs for a secondary school

1 Enrolment			
Pupils	200	500	1,000
Cost of building and equipment	£5,000	£8,500	£16,667
2 Equipment	£300	£500	£1,000
Secondary school total	£5,300	£9,000	£17,667
Average cost	*Boarding*	*Day/Boarding*	*Day*
of equipment	£400	£300	£200

Table 12.3 shows that it is essential to supply construction and initial equipment costs separately. The necessary information is usually obtained from the building unit in a ministry of education or ministry of works or directly from the contractors. In the case of land cost, this varies according to locality, and only national estimates can therefore be made. The unit of calculation may be the pupil, the class, the institution or square metre, etc.

Recurrent costs

The most expensive item in recurrent cost in African educational systems (primary and secondary) is the salaries of personnel, particularly teachers. Maintenance and upkeep of schools and the provision of the needed teaching materials and welfare facilities tend to be sorely neglected.

In practice, in so far as no radical departures in instructional methods are envisaged, the average unit costs from the most efficient schools in the system can be used in the forecast of educational expenditure. However, as certain factors such as the reduction in the average pupil-teacher ratios or an increase in the proportion of qualified teachers, can also influence costs by the end of the plan period, estimation of recurrent unit costs for the reference year, should include assessment of level of quantitive and qualitative targets. Such estimates entail that distinctions are drawn between the following:

• Unit costs of administration.
• Unit costs of teaching staff.
• Unit costs of maintenance.
• Unit costs of student welfare.
• Unit costs of aid to students.

Thus proper cost projections must flow from the preparations of a fairly detailed set of unit costs relating to sufficiently homogeneous elements.

Exercises

1 Discuss the different types of costs involved in education.
2 Discuss:
   a) the characteristics of educational costs.
   b) the basic data required for cost analysis.
   c) the methods of educational costing.
3 What do you understand by the term 'unit cost' and how is it used in educational planning? Give examples, if you can, from at least one national context.
4 Discuss costs and efficiency in education.
5 Differentiate between capital and recurrent costs in education and show how these influence educational development in your country.

XIII

Budgeting in educational planning

A chief characteristic of planning in African countries is the dominant role of the public/government sector. This is particularly so in educational planning where the growth of government schools is a prominent feature of educational development.

Details of public sector programmes are normally included in government budgets at both the national and lower levels of government such as region/state or local governments. Hence, as educational planning is primarily concerned with formulating educational objectives for action, the budget plays a major role in planning, programming and controlling educational costs during the plan period. Thus whereas a draft plan is only a blue-print for action, the budget is basically operational in nature. This therefore requires that it should be devised in such a way that it highlights the truly operational characteristics, both physical and financial of any given programme.

The annual budget session of any government, irrespective of whether it is a democratic or authoritarian system, is the occasion during which plans are either accepted, modified or rejected. It is at this point that further reality is added to strategic plans by the allocation of resources between various activities required to achieve strategic objectives.

This chapter begins with the discussion of the relationship between the budget and the plan and then proceeds to examine capital and recurrent budgets. The third section of the chapter deals with the different budgeting types, such as line-item, programme (PPBS) and zero-base budgets. The fourth and fifth sections of the chapter respectively consider the use of estimates and unit costs and budget timetabling in budgeting.

The budget and the plan

The budget constitutes the principal instrument with which the authorities of an education system (national, regional, local or municipal government) express their priorities in terms of plan objectives and overall policies. Budgeting also offers management the opportunity to examine in detail both the general situation of the economy and the economic inter-relationship among all the education systems' various activities.

The budget therefore normally accords closely with and operationalises a plan's projects and programmes by allocating financial resources for a fixed period, and appropriating the necessary funds. In other words, budgeting ensures that required resources will be available at the right time in the right amount to be able to complete proposed actions and accomplish planned objectives. Consequently, there is usually more detailed costing in the budget than in the plan. Nevertheless, the plan and the budget together provide a composite picture of what is intended and expected and the means by which the objectives are achieved. This makes the budget a powerful tool in the planning process. Budgets thus control the implementation of the plans through the programming of its costs and ensuring the annual appropriations of funds needed.

However, because budgets tend to be shorter term than the plan, normally one year, this discourages fundamental re-examination, as the amount of change that can be accomplished in a year is limited. Nevertheless, as J. Hallak has stated: 'both as a "watch-dog" and a yardstick for measuring the fulfilment of the planned programmes, the budget is undoubtedly an indispensable complement to the educational plan' (Hallak, 1970).

Capital and recurrent budgets

A capital budget normally finances capital projects such as building and heavy equipment with a long life. A recurrent budget, on the other hand, covers consumable services and goods of short-term duration such as teachers, services, electricity, paper, books and transport costs.

But some light equipment and books with a medium-term lifespan are usually also included in the recurrent budget. Minor capital items such as small buildings or extensions to buildings are also sometimes included (Williams, P.R.C., 1975).

We also need, however, to distinguish between 'development' and 'capital' expenditure. In education, capital spending is often replacement expenditure or making up the backlog of facilities such as provision of classrooms and equipment, for classes already admitted. On the other hand, many expenditures, for example, in-service training or curriculum development which are normally put in the recurrent budget are in fact highly developmental.

Capital-recurrent relationships are also important in budget formulation for other reasons. Often, by attempting to realise savings through quality cuts on capital inputs, we may end up incurring higher recurrent expenditures for maintenance (in terms of any repairs, or printing) or running costs (through heat loss or cleaning). New buildings certainly involve higher interest charges but they may have lower or higher running costs than the buildings they replace.

Finally, whereas a current budget normally has a lifespan of one year only, capital projects are phased over several years. Any funds left undisbursed by the end of the budgetary period are usually returned to the treasury for reallocation. This then leads us to the examination of the different types of budgeting.

Types of budgets

The budget is used to do several things (Cunningham, 1982). First, it is used to plan for cash receipts and expenditures. In most education systems in Africa, the education service, like all other units of government, operates within a fixed amount of budgetary allocation based on plans and needs. This is an appropriation budget. Any additional amounts required above such allocation can only be incurred through a supplementary budget allocation.

Second, the budget is used to plan for debt repayment and the efficient use of cash. The general cash fund in African countries is held by the ministry of finance at the national or regional level or the sub-treasury at the local government level; and its proper operation is the sole responsibility of the finance ministry under the guidance of the national or regional political leadership.

Third, the budget usually covers one academic year and should include receipts and expenditures for both the previous and current financial year (FY) and estimates for the following fiscal years. The budget should also project receipts and disbursement on a monthly, quarterly or half-yearly basis depending on the rate of cash flow and outflow from the reservoir or general fund in the treasury. Methods of revenue estimation are, however, complex and are the province of economic and financial experts. The primary sources of revenue are local, state/regional and national taxes. Other sources of funds include property sales tax, rebates, rents and tuition. In African countries the state is the main source of revenue for education budgets, supplemented by tuition fees. These are also used to cover capital expenditures, although external aid may sometimes be solicited towards this.

There are basically three major formats of budgeting used in planning the flow of funds into and out of the general cash flow available to government:

1 Line-item budget or function-object budget.
2 Programme budgets of planning, programming, budgeting.
3 Zero-base budgets.

These types of budget are not incompatible and can in fact be complimentary. Each is capable of presenting needed information for planning, control and management. Though the plan for classifying expenses is often the same in all three systems, there are marked differences in the organisation of the plans.

The line-item budget

This is sometimes also referred to as the function-object budget. The basic feature of a line-item budget is the breakdown of the budget items or objects – salaries, supplies, equipment, services and so forth – and their distribution or classification according to purpose – administration, instruction, student welfare, adult education, etc. This approach to budgeting is sometimes also referred to as input budgeting, as the budget is prepared on the basis of resource inputs.

The basic components of educational expenditure in many African countries, are generally arranged on this basis under the following three functional sub-heads.

1 Personnel emoluments (salaries, allowances, insurance and superannuation).
2 Other charges or running expenses, which covers a wide range of items.
   a) Travel and transport of personnel; purchase of goods, materials for instruction or administration.

   b) Services – water, electricity, sewage, telephones, postage.
   c) Repairs and maintenance of buildings and equipment.
3   Capital expenditure

Where the responsibility for undertaking expenditure is the concern of autonomous (independent schools) or semi-autonomous (e.g. grant-aided schools) organisation, budget items may simply be listed as grants to X, Y or Z organisation. The items listed above are then arranged in one of three ways: according to educational level; spending institution; or educational objective.

   A properly refined budget should show the 'programmes' and 'activities' established for each function entrusted to an organisation showing precisely the work objectives. The aim should normally be for the programme and performance budget to answer such questions as: What is the purpose of doing a specific thing? What is the cost of doing it, and how far have the programme objectives been accomplished?

Line-item budgeting and planning

In the traditional line-item budget common in school systems in African countries, each expenditure item takes a line with the appropriate sum of money indicated against it for the particular financial year (Table 13.1). The various sub-heads of expenditures are then arranged in one column, followed by actual amounts spent on each item in the previous year in its second column. This is followed by the estimated amount to be spent on the same item for the current financial year in the third. Details of the various activities on which the funds were expended are, however, not shown. In the fourth and fifth columns a growth pattern is shown. Quite often the estimates column would be followed by one for approved estimates.

   The fundamental problem of the line-item budget is the way estimates are planned. One approach, as shown in Table 13.1 is the incremental procedure. Typically budget estimates are made from one year to the next (1987–88) by the addition of a fixed percentage increment to the preceding year's budget. What this means in practice is that heads of department decide on a fixed percentage increase above the preceding year's actual expenditures or even approved estimates. The budget authorities (Ministry of Planning/Planning Commission/Ministry of Finance) in turn take a fixed percentage cut (or addition) in the departmental requests to arrive at a final figure. As one writer has stated:

Table 13.1 Ministry of Education estimates of expenditure, 1988–89

Code number	Item of expenditure	Expenditure 1987–88	Budget 1988–89	Budget 1989–90	Increase/ decrease (%)	Budget 1988–90 first quarter	second quarter
12/010	Secondary schools administration	Ls635,450.07	Ls82,740.00	Ls870,250.00			
14011	Research, planning and development	Ls250,690.95	Ls290,850.00	Ls200,315.00			
14020	Instruction	Ls12,690,160.85	Ls14,490,065.00	Ls16,400,025.00			
14022	Other instructional costs	Ls900,450.45	Ls1,250,400.00	Ls1,650,350.00			
14030	Students and staff health	Ls670,450.75	Ls850,065.00	Ls950,400.00			
14040	Student transport	Ls1,550,900.65	Ls1,755,020.00	Ls1,990,500.00			
14060	Services (operation of school plant)	Ls2,450,815.45	Ls3,350,030.00	Ls3,750,750.00			
14061	Maintenance of school plant	Ls1,250,450.25	Ls1,470,650.00	Ls2,150,420.00			
14070	Fixed charges	Ls1,050,350.49	Ls1,570,250.00	Ls1,950,220.00			
14090	Capital outlay	Ls550,050.15	Ls350,450.00	Ls650,900.00			
	TOTAL SECONDARY SCHOOLS	Ls21,999,770.06	Ls25,460,520.00	Ls30,563,930.00			
	OTHER PROGRAMMES						
14080	Teacher training	Ls150,520.45	Ls285,490.00	Ls245,300.00			
14082	Adult education	Ls155,500.00	Ls175,000.00	Ls195,260.00			
14084	Special education	Ls45,650.75	Ls55,480.00	Ls65,350.00			
	TOTAL OTHER PROGRAMMES	Ls351,671.20	Ls515,970.00	Ls505,910.00			
	GRAND TOTAL	Ls22,351,441.26	Ls25,976,490.00	Ls31,070,840.00			

Source: Modified from Cunningham, William G. (1982) p. 90, Table 6.1.

Educational goals were related only indirectly to utilisation of resources. More often past practices were perpetuated with minor modification. The typical procedure was to record expenditure for a given budget classification for one or two previous years, enter the request for the future year, and note additional amounts requested. Little effort was directed toward justification of increases on grounds other than vague allusions to 'need' (Knezevich, 1973c).

This approach to budgeting, therefore, does not relate required resources to specific objectives. Instead it tends to obstruct the planning process rather than to complement or refine it. It could also be wasteful, as the tendency is to perpetuate obsolete programmes and thus possibly hinder innovations and thereby defeat the overall planning process.

The incremental technique concentrates the decision-makers' attention on the new or changed programmes. Whether last years' programme deserves to be continued is a question that ordinarily does not get much attention (Mann, 1975a).

In spite of these shortcomings and all the criticisms levelled against it, the line-item or function-budget has endured.

This is probably, as recent research has found, because it supports strategic planning and promotes financial control and management (Sharkansky, 1968; Lyden, 1975; Leloup and Morel, 1978). Line-item budgets are in fact based on strategic plans even when the incremental approach to budget planning is used. This may explain why it has remained the most prominent budgeting system in education, especially in Africa.

The programme budget (PPBS)

The programme budget or planning-programming-budgeting system (PPBS) method (to give it its full name) entails setting forth certain major objectives, defining programmes essential to these goals, identifying resources to the specific types of objectives and systematically analysing the alternatives available (Novick, 1975) (Table 13.2).

This means that the programme budget (PPBS) involves an analysis leading to the choice of the preferred mix of a set of proposed projects. Such decisions require, first, a qualitative discussion of some of the more relevant non-quantifiable issues involved in the decision, e.g. political factors, non-quantifiable 'spill over' effects and so forth. Second, a programme budget provides for the determination of the costs of programme goals and objectives. This can be used to compare the costs and advantages of competitive programmes (Cunningham, 1982).

Table 13.2 Programme budget financial statement for expenditures of vocational education

Programme: vocational education (230)

Cost category	Actual 1987–88 condition	Recommended 1988–89 condition	Year to date first half 1988–89	First half 1988–89	Under budget	Over budget
Administration (14010)	Ls263,765.00	Ls325,892.00	Ls245,900.00	Ls250,920.00		
Instructional services (14020)	Ls991,815.00	Ls998,386.00	Ls450,300.00	Ls450,300.00		
Attendance and health services (14030)	Ls63,505.00	Ls67,082.00	Ls33,500.00	Ls33,500.00		
Other instructional services (14022)	Ls22,852.00	Ls34,313.00	Ls33,500.00	Ls33,500.00		
Public transportation services (14040)	Ls33,676.00	Ls45,596.00	Ls20,500.00	Ls20,500.00		
Plant operation services (14060)	Ls53,524.00	Ls60,350.00	Ls25,900.00	Ls20,500.00		
Plant maintenance services (14061)	Ls50,524.00	Ls52,842.00	Ls26,450.00	Ls26,450.00		
TOTAL	Ls1,479,661.00	Ls1,584,461.00	Ls837,050.00	Ls835,670.00		

Source: Modified from Cunningham, William G. (1982) p. 96, Table 6.2.

Thus PPBS differs from the line-item budget, which despite its degree of retirement and sophistication, is essentially no more than a descriptive tool, in that it aims at examining alternatives. Some of the main differences are set out below.

Line-item budget

1 Is not output oriented. No direct links between inputs (workers) and outputs (productive activity). Have personal emolument which does not specify the activities of the individuals enjoying them.

2 Does not show total cost of decisions made. There is usually omission of implicit costs in education such as pupils' time and rentals on buildings.

3 Does not provide sufficient information on future expenses of programmes. Whereas the capital aspect of a development plan may project expenditure for the duration of the plan, the recurrent aspect only defines the expenditure for the current financial year. Consequently, the recurrent implications of capital expenditure in future years in terms of teachers and other staff salaries and the operational expenses of capital equipment tend to be sorely neglected. As a result the line-item is in a way not forward-looking.

4 Tends to give the impression that budget is made on an incremental basis, with no proper economic appraisal of the current budget. Thus the budget shows by how much the proposed budget for the future year differs from that of the current year.

5 Despite its degree of refinement and sophistication, it is still no more than a descriptive tool.

6 Budget costs are presented by the type of item purchased. Concentration tends to be on organisational responsibility and the various elements of expenses.

Programme budget (PPBS)

1 Aims at examining alternative means of reaching the targets.

2 Costs are displayed on a programme by programme basis. There is therefore a justification of items on which expenditures are incurred or their relative efficiency or productivity as measured against the planned objective.

3 The programme budget represents the appropriation of a fixed sum of money to achieve a specific objective or a set of objectives.

4 Does not increase incremently, management has to decide consciously how much to spend on a programme in order to achieve a set of objectives. This involves a comparative analysis of alternative action in terms of costs and effectiveness. It is therefore only

the cost-effective programme that is finally selected to achieve the planned objectives.

5 PPBS analysis generally consists of an attempt to minimise fund allocations required to meet the objectives of the school system. In other words, it aims to maximise the input of a set of programmes subject to the overall projected constraint from estimated revenue or receipts.

6 The overall framework for PPBS analysis is management objectives arrived at by weighing alternatives to be selected on the basis of costs and benefits.

Programme budgeting structure

The single most important task required to change from a traditional line-item budget format to PPBS is the development of a programme budgeting structure. This requires the identification and definition of programmes necessary to achieve the objectives of the education system within the guidelines of financial resources provided by the ministry of finance. This is then followed by a simple budgeting and accounting procedure of matching each programme and its sub-programmes in terms of its financial implications and the expected target output.

A PPBS programme structure adopted from one originally suggested by Harry J. Hortley, based upon grade-level and subject-matter organisation, is as follows:

Code	Programme category
001	Nursery/infant education
050	Primary grades education (1–6)
150	Junior secondary grades eduction (7–9)
200	Senior secondary grades education (10–12)
300	Social sciences and humanities (7–12)
350	Mathematics and science (7–12)
400	Creative arts (7–12)
450	Physical and health education (7–12)
500	Business, vocational, and home economics (7–12)
550	Pupil personnel services
600	Special education
650	Adult education and community services
700	Administration and general support services.

The typical line-item classification would be used under each of the programme areas.

Initially, in trying to convert to PPBS, it may be necessary to maintain the codes of the traditional functions object account code by simply adding the PPBS codes to them. For example, if the traditional code format was as follows (Alioto and Jugherr, 1971):

Fund	Function	Object
General	Instruction	Supervision
A	12020	150

This can be converted into PPBS structure by the addition of the code of the particular programme, e.g. physical and health education thus:

Fund	Programme	Function	Object
General	PHE (7–12)	Instruction	Supervision
A	450	12020	150

In this way the code contains both the traditional programme structure and the function – object reporting system. Thus the traditional financial code A – 12020 – 150 for instructional supervision, becomes A – 12020 – 150 – 450 for cost of supervision in physical and health education (Cunningham, 1982).

Criticism of PPBS

Typically, programmes are organised around broad themes based on outputs and objectives. The result is that such programmes tend to cut across functional responsibilities and traditional budgetary line items.

Moreover, as PPBS expenses are analysed and separated into those for general administration and overheads and those for programmes, difficulties are encountered in trying to group into programmes those outputs of particular organisational demands that support similar objectives. How to allocate fixed overhead costs is one situation where these difficulties are compounded.

Further, because some specific outputs serve multiple purposes or objectives, there is an inevitable overlap (e.g. improve services for the speech and hearing impaired).

Lastly, a programme structure may not always follow an educational authority's established hierarchy. Hence deciding on who should prepare the budget in such a case may not always be clear.

Zero-base budgeting (ZBB)

According to Peter A. Pyhhr: 'Zero-base budgeting in its correct context refers to a general management tool that companies can use to improve planning, budgeting, and operational decision-making. With it, managers can re-assess their operations from the ground up and justify every dollar spent in terms of current corporate goals. Instead of staying within the same budgetary structure year after year, they can make major allocations of resources from one year to the next (Phyrr, 1976).

Thus ZBB does not build upon the previous year's base. Instead, the budget begins at a decreased expenditure or base zero. Functions or programmes can therefore be ranked as to desirability and marginal activities and increments, as well as the identification of activities, new or old, that the organisation can no longer afford.

Theoretically, zero-base budgeting starts from the basic premise that the budget for the next year is zero and that every expenditure, old and new must be justified on the basis of its costs and benefits in relation to the strategic plan. This means that there should be a fresh start each year with little consideration of the past. This is, of course, unrealistic as the past serves as both a guide and a constraint upon the future. In practice, it is not the case that we start at the point zero-base budgeting process.

Zero-base budgeting requires that educational administrators determine the minimum or basic requirements (increments) for running their activities. Any costs above the base increment are identified as added increments that must be justified. Those increments that cannot be justified must consequently be eliminated, resulting in cost saving to the school system. There is thus a ranking process.

Determining increments

The ranking process is at the heart of zero-base budgeting. Through the ranking process, management determines a priority for each programme or decision package in the overall context of school operations. The graphical representation shown in Figure 13.1 best summarises how ZBB works. The assumption in the figure is that the language arts curriculum of a school system is divided into three types of decision-units: 1) primary, 2) secondary, and 3) special education. It is further assumed that each decision unit is sub-divided into four parts (increments) or 'decision packages' (Cunningham, 1982). The ranking order of priority is as shown in the extreme right hand column in the figure.

The highest priority of essential needs constitutes the base package; this represents the barest minimum and must include the essential functions and costs required by law or representing inescapable obligation requirements. Typically, it defines the minimum level of activity below which effort ceases to serve any useful purpose. The operational

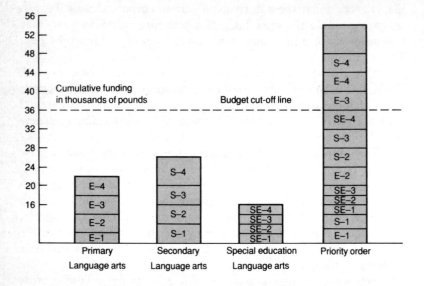

Fig 13.1   Representation of ranking of decision packages for a language arts programme (based on Stonich, P.J., 1977)

administrator or head of unit therefore must determine what are the most important service needs provided by his unit or department in setting his priority. Additional increments of service and cost are then ranked in order of priority. Generally, the minimum level or base, plus one or two increments/units are required to bring the operation of a department up to the current levels.

An alternative used in determining increments under zero-base budgeting is to decide on the minimum requirements for each decision package under normal or standard operating conditions. All costs above the norm are then identified as increments of that particular activity. The base or normal decision package would be excluded from review and only the increments would be considered. This procedure is similar to the traditional incremental analysis used in line-item budgeting.

A second alternative method used in deciding on increments is to submit three decision packages or plans for each activity budgeted. The base increment would be less than 100 per cent of the current funding level. The current increment could include the additional activities required for the continuation of last year's programmes including increased costs; and the new increment would include that required for an expansion of programme objectives.

A third approach is for top decision-makers/management to set a ceiling according to which various plans are then prepared for funding. The ceiling is normally stated in terms of the present financial year, based on estimated funds available for the next financial year. This level would form the maximum that would be approved by top management. The base plan might amount to 80 per cent of the budget, which would enjoy an increment of 20 per cent to raise it to 100 per cent. Then, finally, the ceiling increment, a 15 per cent to 115 per cent of currently budgeted funds would be added.

This incremental analysis is the most important stage in the ZBB process. As has been stated:

The identification and evaluation of different levels of effort probably represent the two most difficult aspects of the zero-base analysis, yet they are key elements of the process (Phyrr, 1976).

As illustrated in Figure 13.1 the base increments indentified as representing minimum activity are (E-1, S-1, and SE-1). Additional increments to bring the activity first up to current levels of effort, and finally to increase the level of effort are then identified.

The ranking process

One of the characteristics of ZBB is the establishment of an adequate review procedure into the process. It is assumed in ZBB that the ranking process will focus attention on the most vital aspects of a programme, generally referred to as a marginal package, that is those parts of a programme just below or above funding level for the projected financial year. This ranking process assists administrators in two ways: first, in identifying functions that have lost their effectiveness and are consequently placed at low priority or eliminated altogether; second in allocating resources away from out-dated functions and making such resources available to more effective functions. Thus it provides a basis for cost reductions or additions as revenues fall or rise.

This is done by listing all the increments identified in order of decreasing benefit to the school system, thus establishing priorities among the operational increments or activities described in the plans, according to the costs and benefits of each increment. Political considerations are equally vital in determining the priorities. Once the ranking has been completed, management can then set the budget amount based on the forecast of revenue. Thus in the example of the language arts programme, the priority order is E-1 and then S-1, SE-1, SE-2 and

SE-3 took priority over E-2 and S-2. Hence, funding the third increment of special education took precedence over the second level of
either primary or secondary language arts programmes. The expenditure levels show that the maximum spending level was £44 million,
which served as a cut-off point in the ranking process. Consequently
S-3, SE-4, E-3 and E-4 and S-4 become marginal increments. These
decisions made in the ranking process are then translated into budgets
used to monitor performance.

A basic problem in zero-base budgeting is the time required to
complete the review process as this can be time-consuming and frus-
trating. The solution Pyhrr suggests (Pyhrr, 1976) is not to concentrate
on ranking packages that are obviously 'high priorities' or 'requirements' and well within expenditure guidelines.

Allocating resources

When the allocation decisions have been completed, detailed budgets
are prepared, simply by adding on all the approved increments to
the base increment to show total allocation for the particular item
in this way. The group of funded increments then constitutes the
coming year's budget. The increments are then arranged under different heads: base increment under 'reduced', base plus the first increment under 'current', and the third increment added to the first
two under 'improved'. Finally, the total increments appear under
'Administration recommendation'. Thus the final format for a ZBB
resembles that of the line-item budget or PBBS.

Estimating and unit costs

Whatever the format of the budget, the preparation of forward estimates is efficiently done on a 'unit' basis. In this way we specify the
number of units of a particular input required per unit of output, since
a unit could be 'per school', 'per teacher', or 'per student' reading a
science or arts subject and so forth. These are, of course, translated
into money equivalents.

Increases in the new budget will be on account of two factors:
1) New services, including such things as a new building coming into
commission; and 2) Old services expanded, improved or modified.
These increases could be in terms of change in total numbers or units,
streams, pupils or teachers, classrooms, etc. through growth or take-
over. There could also be changes in expenditure allowances due to
price rises, adoption of policies of improvement or simply as a result
of change in the composition of units from less expensive to more
expensive. There could also be a whole year's effect of new services

introduced in the previous year but not budgeted for the full year in the last budget. The timetable factor is also important.

The budget timetable

1 The budgetary process starts fairly early in the last year of the lifetime of a particular budget, usually by the issuance of treasury guidelines on the likely amounts by which public expenditure may rise above the previous budget and a target date for submission of estimates through a call circular.

2 A discussion between the ministry of education and the treasury for the clarification of any issues raised in the guidelines would follow. This would normally include other ministries as well.

3 The third step is holding a policy-meeting within the ministry of education with those at the policy and decision-making level to map out the priorities to be included in the budget.

4 This is followed by the invitation of estimates from departments, regions, districts and so forth.

5 Analysis of submissions for the different units and levels and holding of internal budget hearings then follow.

6 Such admissions are then reconciled with available resources to produce a budget that is compatible with both ministry priorities and treasury ceilings.

7 A proposed budget is presented to the minister and the treasury.

8 Budget hearings with the treasury then follow.

9 The treasury reconciles the submissions of all the ministries with available national/state resources.

10 Finally, cabinet/parliament discusses and gives approval and issues the budget. Implementation starts soon afterwards.

Exercises

1 What do you understand by capital and recurrent budget?
2 Discuss the importance of the budget for the plan.
3 Briefly discuss each of the following types of budget:
   a) The line-item budget.
   b) Programme budget.
   c) Zero-base budget.
4 Discuss the main differences between the line-item budget and the programme budget (PPBS).
5 Discuss the type of budget used in your country's education system.

XIV

Financing education in Africa

Educational financing in Africa is today at a cross-roads. The current crises in the economies of most countries, with high rates of inflation and falling revenues, and the threat of famine in areas like the Sahel and now central and southern Africa, have pushed the issue of finance for education to the forefront of any discussions of educational organisation and development. This has become particularly acute as African educational development right from colonial times and the period of Christian missionary control, has been run as a welfare system. Consequently, parental contributions towards the education of their children in the form of fees and other charges has, on the whole, always formed a tiny fraction of the actual cost of total education expenditure. Even many of the so-called independent schools found in the capital cities and other large urban centres under voluntary/private management today, are in fact heavily subsidised by the government. For example, the capital school (primary) and many of the Islamiya schools in Kano State, Nigeria, enjoy substantial government grants.

The main justification for the assumption by government of complete responsibility for the financing of education is on the grounds of ensuring, as far as possible, equality of educational opportunity amongst all its citizens. The present lack of sufficient revenues and the escalating costs of financing the system place most governments in a real dilemma. Any attempts to shift some of the costs of education onto the parents may jeopardise the existing levels of equality of educational opportunity. The haves in society will further increase their present advantages over the underprivileged groups in society and this could endanger the future development of an egalitarian society – the moral basis of the African demand for freedom and independence.

This chapter seeks to provide an understanding of the fundamental principles and techniques of educational finance as well as some of their workings. Thus section one of the chapter briefly traces the history of education finance in Africa from colonial times to the present. Section two discusses the scale of public education expenditure, which is then followed by an examination of the composition of education spending. The chapter concludes with a discussion of the sources and trends in educational financing in Africa.

Brief history of education finance in Africa

Education in the modern or Western sense is a colonial importation into Africa, largely through the agency of Christian missionary societies. Consequently, just as the education system has evolved over the decades, so has the system of financing. Four stages of financing may be identified from colonial times to the present: the pre-government era; the development of mission and government partnership; pre-independence developments and the current pattern.

The pre-government era

At the beginning of the colonial administration, Christian missionary societies were alone actively engaged in the education system. The colonial authorities were too pre-occupied with effecting the expansion of their rule through the conquest or pacification of indigenous power centres to be concerned with the education of the natives. The necessary funds for establishing and running the schools were entirely the responsibility of each missionary society. The missions derived their funds from their parent societies in the metropolitan country and donations from groups and individuals (Graham, 1966); educational activities were considered part and parcel of proselytisation. Educational work was therefore seen as an investment in a secure Christian future. Later, as the mission became established, the local Christian groups and the parents of the children attending schools started to make contributions and a small fee was also charged (Taiwo, 1980). Thus at the initial stage, the missions invariably had complete monopoly over the direction of educational development (Fajana, 1978).

Once the colonial authorities had established a semblance of administration over their territorial claims, then the need for Africans to provide the necessary supportive roles in the lowest rungs of the administration as clerks and artisans started to be felt. This in turn resulted in government interest in missionary educational activities. This interest gradually expressed itself in the provision of subsidies to missionary societies towards defraying some of the costs of maintaining the schools, thus marking the beginnings of government participation. For example, in Nigeria the first government subsidy for education, totalling £30, was made in 1872, 30 years after the establishment of the first mission house in Badagary near Lagos, by the Wesleyan Missionary Society. This sum was shared equally amongst the three missionary societies then operating in the country – the CMS, Wesleyans and the Roman Catholics (Fajana, 1978). In southern Sudan, the first government contribution to education was a sum of £100 given to the governor of Bahrel Ghazal in 1905 to the Roman Catholic Mission, to be used for the Wau Technical School. However, the first grant-in-aid to the school system as a whole in southern Sudan only commenced in 1922, 24 years after the reconquest of the Sudan in 1878, with a sum of £500. Since the grant was confined to post-elementary education, it was not until the Juba school qualified in 1925 that the sum was raised to £1800 (Sanderson, 1981).

The development of mission and government partnership

The next stage in the development of education finance was when there occurred a substantial increase in government grants to the extent that it became a major source of funds. Thus in the colony of Lagos, for example, then part of the Gold Coast Colony, government grants went up from a mere £30 in 1872 as we have noted, to £300 in 1874 and this was doubled in 1877 so that each of the three missions received £200. This level of allocation was maintained for the next ten years. As a result, by the time the government introduced the first education laws to regulate the overall development of the education system in the colony of Lagos, it was contributing about 20 per cent of the total educational expenditure of the CMS and the Wesleyan Methodist Society. 'The promulgation of the 1882 ordinance was significant in that it marked the legal end of the exclusive control of educational policy by missionary bodies and the beginning of government participation in the framing of policy' (Fajana, 1978). Although the ordinance achieved little in practice, it provided a clear indication of government intentions.

In 1886 the colony of Lagos was separated from the Gold Coast. This was followed by the enactment of the first purely Nigerian education ordinance in 1887. This established a board of education with precisely the same composition as in 1882 and provided for the re-structuring of the education system into infants, primary, secondary and industrial schools. More important, it laid down the conditions for grants-in-aid to schools and teacher-training institutes in greater detail. Henceforth, the rates and conditions for grant-aiding were to be based partly on the subjects taught and partly on the degree of excellence in the schools. The rates in sum were 2/- for primary, 6/- for secondary and 25/- in the industrial schools. It was in this way that the principle of payment by results was established. Unfortunately, the strict application of the system meant the missions were no better off financially in 1888 than when the system of block grants was in operation in 1887 as indicated in Table 14.1.

Table 14.1 Distribution of grants in 1888

Mission	Average attendance	Grants
CMS	930	£377.17.0d
Roman Catholic	543	230.7.0d
Wesleyan	350	130.8.6d
St Mary's (Special)		30.0.0d
	Total	£768.12.6d

Source: Fajana, A. (1978), p. 58.

Although the education budgets between 1886 to 1891 further demonstrate unequivocally the financial aspects of the system of payment by results, they also show the increased importance of government in funding education in the country (Table 14.2).

Table 14.2 Education budgets 1886–91

Year	a) Total education expenditure	b) Grants-in-aid	b) as % of a)
1886	£805.6.8d	£800.0.0d	99.34
1888	991.6.8d	768.12.6d	77.49
1889	973.6.8d	800.0.0d	82.19
1890	1,168.0.0d	1,000.0.0d	85.62
1891	1,168.6.8d	1,000.0.0d	85.59

Source: Fajana, A. (1978).

A further advancement in educational financing was the establishment of schools entirely by the government out of public funds. This was the case in northern Sudan right from the on-set of colonisation in 1898. In Nigeria it started with the establishment of schools for the Muslim communities in the colony and protectorate of Lagos in 1896 and was followed later in northern Nigeria in 1909 under the Nassarawa schools of Hans Vischer in Kano.

The Nassarawa schools for boys received financial support not only from the native administrative treasuries of the emirates but also from the central government in Lagos. In the period 1910–11 the Nassarawa schools, comprising schools at Kano, Sokoto and Katsina, received a total of £3,260 per annum from local government sources alone. By 1913 overall government expenditure on education in Nigeria totalled £30,915. Of this total £27,800 was spent in southern Nigeria (£12,500 on government schools and £15,300 in assisted schools) and the remainder in northern Nigeria (Taiwo, 1980).

The situation of educational finance just before the amalgamation of southern and northern Nigeria was the existence of three distinct systems of education operating in the country: government schools wholly financed from public funds; assisted schools established by missionary societies and grant-aided by government; and non-assisted or independent schools run by missionaries and other voluntary agencies with no government jurisdiction over them. In short, what was in operation was a dual system of education, which was a common feature of educational development and financing in all British colonial African territories.

Besides the consolidation of the education system by the promulgation of ordinances and codes, the progression of education finance in Africa owes a great deal to the Phelp-Stokes' Reports on Education in Africa (1922, 1924). It was these that prompted the issuance of the 1925 Memorandum on Education in British colonial territories. The main point in the new policy as far as finance was concerned, was its advocacy of increased expenditure on education and improved status and conditions of service of the education department in the colonial territories in order to attract the best available manpower. Secondly, schools run by voluntary agencies that attained a satisfactory standard of efficiency were to be treated on a par with government schools and be grant-aided. Thirdly, grants-in-aid were no longer to be dependent on examination results. The overall effect of the implementation of the recommendations of the Reports was that in Nigeria by 1929 there was a total of 3,066 schools with total enrolments of 147,753 students, and with government expenditure alone amounting to £154,180

(£99,530 of it as grants-in-aid). In southern Sudan, where educational development was conducted wholly through the agency of missionary societies as in southern Nigeria, but on a minuscule scale, grants-in-aid to education amounted to £7,450 in 1930. The result was that by 1932 there was a total of 52 educational establishments (primary, intermediate and teacher training) with a total enrolment of 4,140 students. These figures, of course, compare most unfavourably with northern Sudan where education was largely in government hands. In the period 1929–30 total enrolment was 43,022 and total expenditure was £179,609 (Bashir, 1969).

Thus the basic features of the period immediately following the Phelp-Stokes' Reports and the resultant British colonial Education Policy in Tropical Africa pronouncement, were threefold. First, there was an accelerated rate of educational expansion, largely through the system of grants-in-aid to missionary societies.

Second, the necessary foundations for eventually unifying the education system in every territory under a single department of education were laid down, e.g. in Nigeria the appointment of E. R. Hussey as the first director of education of Nigeria in 1927 paved the way for the enactment of the Education Ordinance of 1948 which became effective on 1 January 1949, and brought the education of the north and south together. In the Sudan, a director of education was appointed for the first-time for the south in 1926. This was to give direction to the proper development of the education system in line with government policies.

Third, the rudimentary foundations for some of the institutions that would eventually evolve into important tertiary institutions in future years, were laid, e.g. Achimota in the Gold Coast, in 1924; Makerere Technical College 1925; the Yaba Higher College 1932, which later moved to Ibadan in 1947 to form the nucleus of the present University of Ibadan and the Gordon Memorial College, Khartoum 1932 (Fafunwa, 1974; Fajana, 1978; Taiwo, 1980; Sanderson, 1981).

The pre-independence developments

The fairly large-scale and advanced developments in education noted above, eventually led to the initiation of the first national education plans. In the Sudan, the first educational plan spanning the period 1938–46 for both the north and the south was approved by the Governor-General's Council in 1938. The estimated capital cost of the plan amounted to £500,000, out of which £154,000 was earmarked for building a secondary school; £42,000 for Bakhtel Ruda national teachers training college; recurrent expenditure was to increase from £140,000 in 1936 to about £300,000 in 1946. This represented a national budgetary increase from 3.3 per cent in 1936 to 5.9 per cent in 1938. In spite of this huge expansion in expenditure, the share on southern Sudan education out of the total budget only rose from 7.5 per cent in 1936 to 9 per cent in 1946, mainly to missionary societies in the form of grants-in-aid (Bashir, 1969; Sanderson, 1981).

In Nigeria, the first plan for the systematic development of education was the ten-year Morris Plan of 1942. The plan envisaged an initial cost estimate of £26,000 (Taiwo, 1980) involving an annual expenditure of £799,254 in its final year. It was, however, rejected by the colonial office as being shortsighted and financially stringent.

It was therefore not until 1945 that a new plan prepared by R. A. McL. Davidson, which incorporated some aspects of the Morris Plan, was accepted. This plan was more comprehensive and covered the whole country and was open for discussion at all levels and by all those involved in education. It also, for the first time, proposed the involvement of the local communities in the control of education by proposing that the local education committees became the formal committees of the local education authorities when established. It further suggested the separation, for the first time, of education finance into capital and recurrent components. The plan covered a wide range of educational aspects: administration and control, finance, local education authorities, etc. In brief, government expenditure on education in the form of grant-in-aid between 1938–49 was as follows (Fafunwa, 1974; Taiwo, 1980):

1939/40	£106,562	1944/45	£288,281
1940/41	106,071	1945/46	393,759
1941/42	133,210	1946/47	529,264
1942/43	186,864	1947/48	758,700
1943/44	296,948	1948/49	1,250,000

On the whole, educational developments in Africa in the period immediately preceding independence tended to follow constitutional developments. Nigeria perhaps best illustrates this. For instance, the Macpherson constitution of 1951 (Taiwo, 1980) which assigned a large measure of responsibility to the regions with their own legislature, also led to the establishment of a regional education department under a director who became responsible to the regional executive council and not the central director in Lagos. This new constitution was duly embodied in the Education Act of 1952. An important feature of this Act was the amendment of the grant-in-aid regulation to conform with the provisions of the Nigeria (Revenue Allocation) Order in Council, 1951. By this Act, the central government transferred to the regions the responsibility of meeting the cost of the grants-in-aid in their areas in accordance with Grants-in-aid Regulations. The Nigerian director of education (now inspector general), however, retained the right to inspect all grants-in-aid institutions throughout the country and to call attention to any incorrect or ill-advised application of the regulations.

The amount of grants-in-aid in respect of a primary school consisted of teachers' salaries and contributions towards other expenses at a specified rate, less the assumed local contribution. The latter was invariably in the form of parental contribution in the form of fees. But any rise in the cost of teachers' salaries would automatically result in an increase both in the grant-in-aid and assumed local contribution – the latter implying higher fees.

In order to alleviate parents of the heavy burden of fees, a levy of local rates was collected by the native authorities and local government councils. The 1952 Education Act therefore provided for the establishment of local education authorities and local education committees. Thus the total financial burden of primary education came to be shared between the central, regional and local governments as well as the local communities and the parents.

Then, in January 1955, the government of the Western Region declared a policy of free universal primary education, which was an event of enormous magnitude. The capital costs of the scheme on buildings, excluding the contributions of various agencies – native authorities, voluntary agencies, local communities and parents, was £6,944,600 (Taiwo, 1980). This in turn gave rise to increases in recurrent expenditures from £2,223,390 in 1953/54 to £7,884,110 in 1957/58. In percentage terms, the increases in this period ranged from 30.7 per cent to 39.9 per cent of the total recurrent expenditure. In addition, the share of contributions from the Development and Welfare Fund were £276,760, £252,940 and £307,910 in 1953/54, 1954/55 and 1955/56 respectively. A similar scheme of universal primary education was launched in eastern Nigeria two years later, in 1959. Such high levels of budgetary allocations to education were a common feature of the immediate post-independence period in most African countries.

Thus educational financing in Africa has evolved through a number of stages. Initially, educational funding was entirely in the hands of voluntary agencies. This was soon followed by the *ad hoc* provision of funds by the government for specific purposes and this later gave way to the system of grants-in-aid by the colonial administration to voluntary agencies. Some schools were at the same time financed entirely from public funds. Finally, in the immediate pre-independence period, education financing came to be included in development plans. This has continued to be the pattern in the post-independence period to this day.

Definition of terms

Before proceeding to a discussion of the scale of public education expenditure, it is useful to explain some of the common approaches to and terminologies used in education finance.

As a rule, before a government decides whether to raise more money for education and how much, it will want to know the level of present expenditure on education. Official estimates of national education spending, however, often understate some expenditure and overstate others. Because of the difficulty of data collection, private spending on fees, books and supplies is commonly understated. Understatement also occurs regarding expenditures on education and training by other ministries such as agriculture, health, defence, rural and community development, and labour. The result is that education spending by these ministries seldom shows up in estimates of national education expenditure.

Education expenditures can equally be distorted in the other direction through overstatement of expenditures as a result of faulty bookkeeping. This is usually through double counting of transfers of funds between different levels of government and from government units to individual educational institutions. Governments have, however, become aware of these deficiencies in the estimation of education expenditures and have instituted measures to correct them.

Once a reasonably reliable estimate of a country's expenditure on education has been made, the authorities have then to decide whether they can spend more. To arrive at this decision requires a comparison of present and future levels of spending with what the country can and will afford. But since there is no formula for determining how much a nation can afford to spend on education any more than there is one for deciding how much it can afford on any of its other responsibilities, this becomes a matter of political choice.

Two indicators commonly used to compare national education expenditures externally with other countries and internally (over time) are the GNP ratio and the budgetary ratio. The *GNP ratio* is the ratio of total education expenditures, both public and private, to the Gross National Product or National Income. The *budgetary ratio* is the ratio of public expenditure on education to total public expenditure or revenues. Thus, whilst the GNP ratio provides a measure of education's share in the entire nation's total expenditures or income, the budgetary ratio measures how much the public as distinct from the private sector, is spending on education in relation to its total expenditure or revenues. The two ratios between them indicate what the economy as a whole and the public sector in particular, are spending on education. They are therefore more meaningful than total or per capita expenditures for purposes of inter-temporal and international comparisons.

In terms of which of the two ratios provides a better measure of what a country is spending on education in relation to what it can afford, each ratio has its advantages and disadvantages so the choice between them will be guided by the purpose for which the measure is being used. The GNP ratio is the more comprehensive as it includes both private as well as public education expenditures and relates them to all other expenditures or income in the economy. The latter represents the best single indicator of what the economy can afford to spend. For international comparison, the GNP is therefore a better measure than the budgetary ratio for two reasons. First, it is more comprehensive. Second, unlike the budgetary ratio, its magnitude or size is not affected by the relative importance of private and public expenditures in education (i.e. the numerator of the ratio) or by the relative importance of public and private expenditures in the economy as a whole. The budgetary ratio on the other hand, will not accurately represent education spending in a country where private spending constitutes a substantial portion of total education expenditures.

However, budgetary ratios are more revealing indicators of public policy than GNP ratios because the latter include within them a significant proportion of expenditure which occurs within the private sector and is therefore beyond the control of government.

In addition, since data on public spending are more reliable than those on private spending, the budgetary ratio, which is based entirely on public expenditure, is more accurate than the GNP ratio which includes private expenditures. This is particularly so in most African countries, where the statistical base, as in many countries of the Third World, is weak.

The scale of public education expenditure in Africa

As outlined in the historical evolution of educational finance in the preceding section, the levels of public expenditure in African countries have been the result of a process of almost continuous growth. This has been particularly the case in the post-independence period, as illustrated by the trend of public expenditure on education as a percentage of GNP and of all public or government expenditure as shown in Table 14.3.

The table shows that the levels of GNP expenditure within the continent vary with the natural endowments of individual countries in terms of economic resources. For example, the percentage of GNP expenditure on education for Algeria (an oil producer) ranged from 4.0 per cent in 1965 to 7.8 per cent in 1980, whereas the figures for Niger, a comparatively poor country, ranged from 1.1 per cent to 3.1 per cent over the same period. Similar differences are also observed between the figures for Côte d'Ivoire and the relatively poorer countries like the Sudan and Tanzania. On the whole, however, the trend for all countries is one of an increasing rise in GNP expenditure on education, particularly between 1965 to 1975. By 1980, however, the decline in the economies of most countries resulting from the worldwide depression was having a serious impact as shown by either a dramatic decrease in GNP expenditure on education or at best a levelling off of expenditure. This fact is best illustrated by the figures for Nigeria and Ghana. Thus whereas in 1975 Ghana devoted 5.9 per cent of its GNP to education, by 1980 there was a drastic drop to only 3.1% although this has slightly increased to 3.6 per cent by 1988. In the case of Nigeria, the earlier increase in GNP expenditure levelled off going from 2.1 per cent in 1965 to 4.3 per cent in 1975 and then 5.5 per cent in 1980, dropping to 3.1% by 1988.

Turning to the consideration of educational expenditure in relation to total government or public expenditure, it becomes immediately obvious that education consumes a large share of overall expenditure. For example, in Kenya the consumption was 20.6, 17.6, 19.4, 18.1 and 27.0 per cent respectively in 1965, 1970, 1975, 1980 and 1988. Similarly, the figures for Algeria in the years 1964, 1970, 1975, 1980 and 1988 were 14.8, 31.6, 23.0, 24.3 and 27.0 per cent

Table 14.3 Trend of public expenditure on education in Africa: total as % of GNP and of all public expenditure

Country	1965		1970		1975		1980		1988	
	As % of GNP	As % total government expenditure	As % of GNP	As % total government expenditure	As % of GNP	As % total government expenditure	As % of GNP	As % total government expenditure	As % of GNP	As % total government expenditure
Algeria	4.0	14.8	7.8	31.6	7.1	23.0	7.8	24.3	9.9	27.0
Tunisia	6.5	–	6.9	23.2	5.1	16.4	5.4	16.4	6.3	14.8
Botswana	–	–	5.2	13.3	7.2	13.9	7.8	16.1	8.3	15.9
Zambia	–	–	4.7	10.9	6.7	11.9	4.5	7.6	–	–
Sudan	2.7	15.8	3.9	12.6	5.5	14.8	4.8	9.1	–	–
Egypt	4.8	–	4.8	15.8	5.0	–	5.7	9.4	5.2	10.1
Nigeria	2.4	23.0	–	–	4.3	16.5 (1976)	5.5	24.7	–	–
Ghana	4.5	17.7	4.3	19.6.	5.9	21.5	3.1	17.1	3.6	25.7
Senegal	3.5	19.6	3.8	21.3	–	–	4.5	23.5	3.7	–
Côte d'Ivoire (Ivory Coast)	5.4	20.6	5.4	19.3	6.3	19.0	7.0	22.6	–	–
Niger	1.1	11.3	2.0	17.7	3.8	18.7	3.1	22.9	–	–
Burkina Faso (Upper Volta)	2.1	–	–	–	–	–	3.0	19.8	2.9	14.9
Kenya	4.6	20.6	5.0	17.6	6.3	19.4	6.9	18.1	6.3	27.0
Tanzania	3.3	23.7	4.5	16.0	5.4	17.8	4.4	11.2	4.0	9.1

Source: UNESCO Statistical Year Book, 1975, 1983, 1991

• 1954

– = figures not available

Table 14.4 Trend of public expenditure on education in Africa: at current market prices 1965–1989

Country	1965 (000)	1970 (000)	YEARS 1975 (000)	1980 (000)	1989 (000)
Algeria (Dinar)	583,552[1]	1,854,400	4,080,500	12,354,500	32,826,00
Nigeria (Naira)	76,428	192,732	1,157,389 (1976)	7,551,600 (1979)	1,170,060
Tunisia (Dinar)	29,765 (1964)	51,429 (1971)	87,533	192,258	420,995 (1986)
Zambia (Kwacha)	36,086	56,063	98,020	126,637	246,706 (1984)
Tanzania (Shillings)	202,851	407,900	1,029,100	2,144,049 (1979)	13,997,000
Sudan (Pounds)	13,112	27,102	68,257	187,005	–

Note:[1] UNESCO Statistical Year Book 1975.
Source: UNESCO Statistical Year Book 1983, 1991.

respectively. In short, therefore, both the GNP and public expenditure figures demonstrate quite clearly that education consumes a large proportion of national revenues in almost all African countries. When the figures for the actual amounts are presented as in Table 14.4, then the magnitude of the monetary expenditures involved becomes even clearer. A significant fact which this brings out is that whereas educational expenditure as a proportion of GNP or of total government budgetary expenditure may fall, it is not necessarily accompanied by a fall in the actual amount spent on education as is shown by the comparison of the figures for Tanzania in Tables 14.3 and 14.4.

To comprehend this phenomenon requires the calculation of the real increase as opposed to money expenditure, for the difference between the two becomes important whenever the general level is changing as, for example, in a period of sustained inflation. Real expenditure is usually expressed in terms of the prices prevailing at a certain date, these prices are then taken as a baseline for comparison. For instance, it is generally accepted that there was a price rise (inflation) between 1970 and 1975 and between the latter and 1980. Hence applying the 1980 prices to the goods and services purchased in 1970 and 1975 we can calculate what the prices in those years would have been in 1980. In this way we can compare the prices prevailing in real terms in those three years. The values we then obtain are the 1970 and 1975 expenditures at the 1980 prices. Similar calculations can be made for the 1989 figures. In this way, it can be shown that spending on a part of the education system may rise in money terms while falling in real terms. It is, however, not possible to demonstrate this in the case of the figures in Table 13.4 since the actual prices of individual goods and services purchased in education are not available to us. Table 14.4 does show, however, the dramatic increase in expenditure by Tanzania and Algeria and the equally dramatic decrease by Nigeria in 1989.

Composition of education spending

The composition of the financing of education can be considered in the following ways:

1 Current versus capital spending.
2 Types of institutions spent on.
3 Types of goods and services purchased.
4 The spending authority.

Capital expenditure

In general, capital expenditure invariably forms a small proportion of total education outlay. This is because the resultant recurrent implication a few years later always far exceeds the initial capital expenditure. Thus in Table 14.5, the general pattern is that recurrent expenditure far exceeds capital expenditure. The only possible exception to this is in a situation of rapid expansion of the educational system as a result of rapid increases accruing from the sale of high demand commodities such as, for example, crude oil in the early 1970s. This explains the high rate of capital expenditure in relation to recurrent expenditure in Algeria and Nigeria. In the latter case, capital expenditure was 49 per cent as opposed to 51 per cent for recurrent in 1975 at the height of the oil boom in the country. The present difficulties of financing education in Nigeria can partly be explained by the very high level of capital expenditure on education in the mid-1970s. The lesson to be derived from this is that it is important always to bear in mind the likely recurrent implications of any capital developments in education from a few years hence. In the uncertain situation of steady revenue earning ability of a developing country, it is wise to tailor capital developments to the ability of meeting their recurrent demands in the future.

Table 14.5   Trend of recurrent v. capital educational expenditure in selected African countries

	EXPENDITURE					
	1970		1975		1980	
Country	Recurrent	Capital	Recurrent	Capital	Recurrent	Capital
Algeria	61.4	38.6	72.3	27.7	66.9	33.1
Zambia	79.2	20.8	76.9	23.1	95.1	4.9
Nigeria	–	–	51.0	49.0 (76)	65.8	34.2 (79)
Sudan	93.4	6.6	89.6	10.4 (74)	92.2	7.8
Niger	93.8	6.2	87.0	13.0	47.0	53.0
Kenya	93.9	6.1	95.4	4.6	91.5	8.5 (79)

Source: UNESCO Statistical Year Book 1983.

Recurrent expenditure

Recurrent spending in education characteristically accounts for a larger share of educational finance. Thus Table 14.5 shows that on average 80 per cent of total educational outlay is expended as recurrent expenditure. When we turn to Table 14.5, it is observed that recurrent educational expenditure forms quite a large proportion of total governmental current expenditure. For example in 1970, it ranged from 14.2 per cent to 26.4 per cent in the six selected countries. Moreover, the figures also tend to show that there is a correlation between government expenditure as a whole and current educational spending. This is best illustrated by the figures for Nigeria and Kenya where increases in recurrent educational expenditure closely follow their share in total government expenditure. For example, in Kenya whereas current education expenditure was 4.7 per cent, 6.0 per cent and 5.9 per cent of total government expenditure in 1970, 1975 and 1979, its share of current government expenditure was 17.6 per cent, 19.4 per cent and 18.1 per cent for the same respective years (Table 14.3).

Public current education expenditure by purpose is divided in Table 14.6 as follows:

1 Administration: enrolments of administration staff and other expenditure of the central and local administration.
2 Enrolment of teachers: salaries and all additional benefits paid to teachers as well as to all other auxiliary teaching staff.
3 Teaching materials: expenditure directly related to instructional activities, e.g. purchase of textbooks and other scholastic supplies.
4 Scholarships: scholarships and all other financial assistance granted to students for studies in the country or abroad.
5 Welfare: boarding costs, school meals, transport, medical services, etc.
6 Not distributed: expenditure which cannot be classified in one of the categories above.

Figure 14.1 shows the ratio of educational spending on the different levels of the education system in the sample countries. From this, it is clear that primary education in all countries enjoys the highest proportion of expenditure, followed by institutions at the second and third levels. Other aspects of education such as adult education and administration each enjoys a small share of the overall expenditure. It is, however, important to note that when we consider the student populations involved at the different levels of the system, then the small size of enrolments at the third level enjoys a greatly dispropor-

Table 14.6 Public current expenditure on education by purpose

Country	Year	Administration	Teachers' emoluments	Teaching materials	Scholarships	Welfare services	Not distributed
Algeria	1967	7.3	77.1	3.8	8.0	3.2	13.1
	1974	4.4	79.1	3.0	8.8	5.2	–
	1979	10.1	57.2	0.2	9.7	0.5	22.3
	1980	–	63.6	0.3	8.9	3.0	24.3
Botswana	1965	–	73.8	5.1	9.4	6.6	–
	1970	2.2	64.9	–	10.4	5.6	16.8
	1975	6.5	52.8	–	14.9	7.0	18.7
	1978	3.5	75.1	11.7	5.8	–	4.0
	1979	5.6	57.6	–	14.2	3.5	19.2
Niger	1965	–	59.2	–	15.4	–	25.3
	1970	10.5	64.5	–	11.8	–	13.1
	1975	–	51.5	24.9	13.9	–	9.8
	1977	–	55.1	24.2	10.7	–	10.0
	1980	–	68.2	13.1	9.4	9.4	–
Burkina Faso	1970	1.9	62.4	–	7.1	8.3	20.3
	1975	2.2	56.3	5.1	29.6	6.1	0.3
	1979	–	51.5	10.3	37.7	0.5	–
	1980	–	61.0	0.4	29.9	0.8	1.8
Zambia	1971	15.1	62.5	9.8	0.6	7.8	4.2
	1970	14.1	63.7	6.9	0.5	8.5	6.2
	1975	10.2	66.1	3.3	2.2	7.1	11.2
	1980	17.1	63.3	2.6	2.0	5.5	9.6

Source: UNESCO Statistical Year Book 1983.

tionate share of total educational outlay. This is followed by the second level with the first level coming last.

Table 14.7, which really contains the elaborations of the statistics presented in Figure 14.1, shows that at the second level, general secondary expends the largest share of education expenditure. An interesting contrast, however, emerged between Anglophone and Francophone countries at this level in the distribution of expenditure on teacher training and vocational education. The table shows that in both Ghana and Tanzania (Anglophone countries) expenditure on teacher training until 1980 was consistently higher than that on vocational education, whereas in the Congo and Madagascar (Francophone) the contrary was the case. This may have been a reflection of their different colonial traditions, for example, in the British colonies, trade or technical schools were always regarded as third rate. Since 1980, however, in Ghana, there has been a dramatic decrease in the percentage so it is now either equal or less than that spent on vocational education.

When we turn to a consideration of current educational spending according to purpose, the first pattern that emerges common to all countries is that teacher emoluments (salaries and associated benefits) consume by far the largest proportion of total recurrent expenditure (Table 14.6). A second common feature is the gradual reduction in spending on teaching materials, scholarships and welfare service in more recent years; an indication of the depressed state of African economies.

Thus, what emerges on the whole, is that about 90 per cent of current spending in African countries is devoted to salaries and wages of those employed in the education services, with 70 per cent being spent on the teachers alone. Therefore in Africa, as elsewhere, education is a truly labour-intensive industry.

In terms of spending authorities tertiary education is generally a national or central government concern. In the case of secondary or second level education, the practice differs, depending on constitutional arrangements. In federal structures, such as Nigeria and the Sudan to some extent, secondary education is on the concurrent list, that is, both federal and state governments have the right to organise them. Thus in Nigeria, apart from the state secondary schools, there are federal secondary schools, commonly referred to as federal colleges, located in each state (one each for boys and girls), recruitment into which is based on federal character. In the Sudan, secondary schools are run by state or regional governments, but there are no central government secondary schools as in Nigeria. In most other

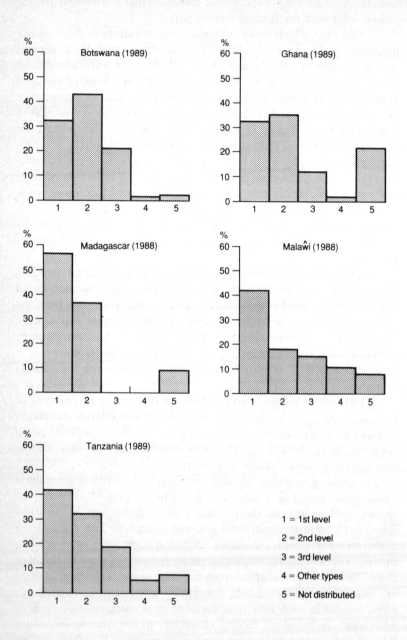

Fig 14.1   Composition of recurrent educational expenditure in countries of Africa (UNESCO Statistical Year Book, 1992)

Table 14.7 Public current expenditure on education by level of education (percentages)

Country	Year	Pre-primary	1st level	Second level				3rd level	Other types	Not distributed
				Total	General	Teacher training	Vocational			
Botswana	1970	–	57.6	29.8	17.5	4.7	7.6	8.8	–	3.9*
	1979	–	52.1	29.2	23.3	2.8	3.0	13.2	–	5.6
	1989	0.3	32.5	43.8	34.1	3.7	6.0	20.1	1.1	2.2
Congo	1970	0.2	48.7	36.3	21.6	4.1	10.6	9.6	0.4	4.8
	1979	–	31.9	34.2	24.4	1.8	8.0	23.8	0.1	9.9
	1984	–	30.0	35.6	–	–	–	34.4	–	–
Ethiopia	1976	–	38.6	40.9	35.8	2.6	2.5	14.6	1.7	4.2
	1980	–	42.2	29.9	26.0	2.6	1.3	19.1	4.0	4.8
	1987	–	52.8	27.6	25.5	1.0	1.1	13.3	–	6.3
Ghana	1970	–	39.2	27.8	14.7	10.6	2.4	25.1	–	7.9
	1980	–	29.3	38.7	31.5	4.7	2.5	1.8	0.9	21.3
	1989	–	32.0	33.4	29.9	1.5	2.0	12.1	1.0	21.4
Madagascar	1970	–	48.5	19.3	11.5	3.5	4.2	25.0	1.6	5.7
	1980	–	58.9	31.0	20.8	1.5	8.6	–	1.6	8.5
	1988	–	55.1	35.7	–	–	–	–	–	9.2
Malaŵi	1970	–	42.3	24.5	18.1	4.4	2.0	25.5	1.8	6.0
	1979	–	42.6	16.4	14.9	–	1.5	28.0	0.7	12.3
	1988	–	43.6	18.5	11.9	4.9	1.7	16.6	11.6	9.7

Table 14.7 (cont'd)

Country	Year	Pre-primary	1st level	Second level					3rd level	Other types	Not distributed
				Total	General	Teacher training	Vocational				
Tanzania	1970	–	41.5	22.5	17.2	5.3	–		12.0	16.8	7.2
	1979	–	45.0	13.6	7.4	3.6	2.5		26.7	1.6	13.1
	1989	–	41.6	32.1	20.0	8.6	3.5		17.1	3.4	5.8
Zambia	1970	–	44.2	30.3	27.3	3.0	–		13.0	–	12.5
	1980	–	45.3	25.5	18.8	3.1	3.6		18.0	0.2	11.0
	1984	–	44.2	36.0	27.7	2.7	5.6		12.1	0.3	7.3
Zimbabwe	1970	–	47.6	34.4	–	–	–		6.5	0.0	11.5
	1980	–	66.5	24.1	21.4	2.7	–		4.8	0.1	4.4
	1989	–	62.7	32.5	32.5	–	–		–	0.3	4.5

Source: UNESCO Statistical Year Book 1983, 1992.
* Includes expenditure for administration which is not shown here by level.

countries, the practice is for secondary schools to be organised and administered from the centre while primary schools are the responsibility of provincial/district authorities.

Sources of funds in educational financing in Africa

The sources of finance for educational provision in Africa are basically three, viz: the public authorities; the users of education and self-generated income.

Both public and private educational institutions may derive funds from all three sources. As has been shown elsewhere in the chapter, some privately-owned and managed schools receive government subventions, whilst some state school systems charge fees at some levels. The latter trend is becoming increasingly widespread throughout the continent. For example, whereas in Kenya fees have always been charged at secondary and post-secondary levels, in Nigeria fees were re-introduced in 1984 at all levels, for the first time in some states in thirty years. Both government and private institutions may meet a small fraction of their annual expenditure from their own resources in the form of accumulated savings or endowments, from fund-raising activities or from farming produce or craft activities.

As we have seen (Table 14.3), the GNP and the budgetary ratios spent on education rose fairly steadily in most African countries in the decades of the 1960s and 1970s. By the early-1980s, however, there were indications which pointed to a slow-down in this trend. The rapid increase in educational expansion can be attributed to an equally underrated increase in school-age populations and increasing enrolment ratios at all levels of the educational system, especially following the Addis Ababa Conference of 1961. The continuing increases in teacher salaries have also added to increased educational expenditures.

Public resources for education in most African countries are raised in three ways: taxation, foreign loans and grants. Taxation is normally raised for the general purposes of government and funds for education are shared from a general pool of public revenue.

Starting in the period immediately leading to independence and since, there has been a large expansion in the administrative system and in economic activities in almost all African countries. The result has been increased growth in tax receipts accruing from fairly steady increases in GNP, providing more income and more sales of goods and services to be taxed. This by itself would have produced an automatic increase in tax receipts even without any increases in the tax rates or even the imposition of new taxes. In fact, however, many African governments did take this latter action as well. Both actions thus contributed to the further growth of total tax receipts. This general increase in the GNP and national income also enabled the private sector, whether families or organisations, to spend more on education.

But enlarging total tax receipts through higher taxes and new taxes has its political limits. There is similarly an obvious limit to financing the growth of education expenditures by raising education's share of total public expenditures. Where then is the additional source of finance to come from? Three possible sources suggest themselves: foreign loans and grants from national and international organisations, or loans from domestic organisations; taxes earmarked for education; and financing by the private sector. Before considering the characteristics and consequences of these methods, it is useful to describe the main criteria for assessing different techniques for generating additional resources.

The three general criteria applied to any fiscal action intended to generate funds for public services are financial yield (i.e. how much money the action produces); equity (i.e. what segments of the population will bear the cost and who will receive its benefits); and administrative feasibility of the fiscal action. In addition, in the case of eduction, there are two other criteria: the impact on the quality of education and efficiency (i.e. the unit cost of producing the education). It is important to note, however, that the five criteria are not equally important for education financing.

Loans and grants

During the first decade of independence most African governments tended to rely heavily on bilateral (largely from the former colonial power) and multi-lateral loan grants. But it soon became clear that this source was rather a marginal and unreliable means of financing. Besides the economic burden arising from the need to repay the loans in foreign exchange, there were usually distasteful political conditions attached to the loans and grants. Moreover, by borrowing abroad for education, the government would be using up its limited borrowing capacity on education at the expense of other public sectors. Similar arguments apply to borrowing from domestic sources such as banks (private or public) and insurance companies. It is, in fact, argued that non-revenue producing projects or social services such as education, should not be financed through borrowing. As regards grants or foreign aid, it is nowadays largely confined to the offer of scholarships for specialised training, particularly at the graduate level outside the country. It may also take the form of technical assistance.

The huge expenditures on education (Table 14.4) have resulted in the users of education being more and more required to meet a part of the expenses of their education, foremost through the payment of fees. These may be levied in respect of tuition (full or partial depending on whether the school is government or private). Besides this basic tuition, fees may be charged in a number of ways: for those parts of the curriculum involving student use of materials (woodwork, domestic science), or for using expensive equipment (sports, music, domestic science); and travel on school expeditions. In addition, students are, with increasing frequency, being required to buy their own books and materials for use in the class and since these are required for learning, these purchases really amount to tuition fees, only called by another name. It is the same case with admission, registration and examination fees. It is also not uncommon for schools to demand deposits against the possibility of damage to school property or even against good behaviour in the form of causation money. Fixed contributions may also be demanded for each child towards the school development fund. Even if all such additional contributions do not represent income to the institution, they nevertheless represent a cost to parents and students which is tantamount to fee payment. Thus although fees may rank high as a reliable and potentially large producer of funds for education, they nevertheless rank low in terms of equity because the people who need education most are least able to pay. Hence tuition fees at primary and secondary levels would prevent the children of disadvantaged or low-income families from attending (Jallade, 1974). Generally, the intention of government taxation and spending is to reduce inequalities in income distributions by shifting resources from those fairly well-off to low-income segments of the population. But the poor tax collection systems in most African countries have actually meant that traders, businessmen and businesses that earn more, pay lower rates of tax than civil servants on fixed incomes.

One way to cope with the inequitable effects of uniform school fees, is for a structure of fees to be worked out in accordance with family ability to pay. But it is generally difficult to determine the financial capacity of most families because of the difficulty of ascertaining their income, which is often in kind and unstable. Moreover, the financial obligations of the head of the family are often unclear, because of the extended family system. Consequently, it is hard to design a fee structure that would both produce enough money and meet the conditions of equity. The result is that whenever African governments have applied tuition fees to relieve financial pressures on the education sector, this has often been at the expense of equity. The introduction of fees at all levels by most state governments in Nigeria in FY 1985 provides a clear illustration. In several other countries fees have been charged at the primary level where the low-income groups are heavily represented, while financing at post-secondary education is entirely out of government budget. Yet unit costs are highest at the latter level and representation of low-income families is generally low, particularly in countries with a long-established and well-developed education system.

Local government taxes

In almost all African countries the great bulk of public expenditure for education is financed directly out of the central government budget. Even in cases such as Nigeria, where state and local governments exercise a good deal of financial administrative power, most of the funds for education ultimately emanate from central government revenue.

In those African countries where central governments predominate in the financing and administration of public education, governments are moving towards decentralisation for three reasons:

1 Relieving the heavy financial pressures on their budgets.
2 Improving educational administration.
3 Making the educational system more responsive to the needs and desires of different segments of the population.

These are some of the reasons that have prompted the introduction of administrative decentralisation in Tanzania, and regional governments in Sudan. Decentralisation of educational administration provides financial relief to the central government if state or local governments are required to finance an increasing share of education costs out of their own budgets. The traditional sources of revenue for these lower tiers of government are taxes on property (residential and commercial) and sales taxes. The amount of revenue produced (financial yield) is therefore dependent on the tax base (amount of property and sales available for taxing) and the tax rates (Sirkin, 1979).

But the tax base and rates, and hence the financial yield, of state and local taxes tend to vary rather widely between states or local jurisdiction, especially in such large-sized countries like Sudan, Algeria, Egypt, Nigeria, Tanzania, Ethiopia and Zaïre, leading to regional disparities in income and wealth. Moreover, the tendency to concentrate industries in certain localities, which is a common feature of African industrial location practices, would tend to exacerbate these differences in the earning power of some few localities, over the majority. In the Sudan, for example, Khartoum province has the highest concentration of industries in the country; Lagos state enjoys a similar advantage in Nigeria. Consequently, even where state and local taxes could produce substantial revenues for the country as a whole, and thereby make a significant contribution to education financing, the unequal distribution in the amount and quality of educational inputs (equipment, books, learning materials, teachers, etc.) resulting from the linkage of these inputs to state and local tax revenues, would tend to accelerate inequalities in the distribution of educational opportunities and quality among different regions of the country (Sirkin, 1979).

Nevertheless, greater reliance on local government financing of education could, under appropriate conditions, produce a substantial increase in the total supply of funds for education. This might also provide an incentive to encourage greater community participation in the formulation and implementation of educational policies. Thus, whether state and local government taxation can make a significant contribution to the financing of education, will depend on whether the tax base is big enough to produce an acceptable amount of revenue, and also on whether the state and local government machinery can adequately collect the taxes and administer the expenditure of funds. Even if such local financing proves feasible, the problem of inequalities resulting from regional disparities in the distribution of income and wealth will still pose their own problems.

Earmarked taxes

In the discussion of funding for education, it has often been suggested that general tax revenues should be supplemented by special taxes whose proceeds would be earmarked partly or entirely to finance education expenditure. Tuition fees for public education and local taxes whose proceeds are used to finance education are examples of earmarked taxes. According to Sirkin (1979), there are three main advantages of financing educational growth through such taxation:

1   Earmarked taxes are likely to be more acceptable to taxpayers than additional taxes for general purposes because of the overlap between taxpayers and beneficiaries.

2   Financing that depends on earmarked taxes is likely to be more reliable than general revenue financing because it is not subjected to the uncertainties of the annual budgetary process.
3   The coincidence between taxpayers and the recipients of the education services to be financed by their taxes is likely to produce education whose quality and efficiency is more responsive to their needs and desires. This, of course, assumes that the taxpayers are in a position to judge the suitability of the educational provision, which is not always the case in African countries.

However, the first objection to this method of financing is that it runs counter to a basic objective of public finance, which is to transfer income from the rich or relatively well-off to the poor. This is undertaken by requiring the rich to pay a relatively large proportion of the taxes but giving the poor a relatively larger proportion of the benefits of the proceeds. Thus, for example, the lowest 40 per cent of income recipients might pay 20 per cent of the taxes but receive 60 per cent of the benefits of public expenditure through earmarked taxes. In African countries, the modern sector invariably grows faster than the rest of the economy. Hence, if the national payroll, which is highly correlated with the modern sector, grows faster than the financial requirements of the programmes, wasteful expenditures are likely: earmarked usually means that the funds cannot be spent in another sector, nor can such expenditures be deferred for very long after the funds are collected. The result is that if the earmarked taxes produce more money than can be effectively spent on the sector, the administrators of the education system may be tempted to make unnecessarily lavish or low-priority expenditures. Thus inherent inefficiency is built into programmes that are financed through earmarked taxes.

Private financing of education

It is important to state from the outset that in almost all countries in Africa, by far the vast majority of educational institutions are financed by the state. Hence the relative importance of private education and the running of the educational institutions in a particular country are, like its entire education, dependent on popular desires.

Wherever they operate, private institutions provide some of the best and some of the worst education offered in the country. In view of the wide range of sponsors of private institutions, varying from voluntary agencies such as churches and other non-profit-making institutions with strong social motivations to pure profit-making bodies or individuals, this is to be expected. However, viewed purely in terms of education finance, the financial yield of private education would be the cost of providing an equivalent amount of public education. Therefore, in so far as private education is a substitute for public education, it relieves the public sector of a financial burden which can be measured in terms of what it would cost to convert the private institutions into public ones and to support entirely the future growth in enrolment in government schools.

Nevertheless, in terms of equity, private education has both advantages and disadvantages. If the students attracted to the institutions are from higher-income families, the resources that would be required to provide them with public education can be saved and used to provide education or some other public services for low-income families. Hence, by partial or complete payment for the education of their children in private schools, the rich and higher-income groups release resources that can be applied to the benefit of lower-income groups and thus help promote greater equity. The actualisation of this scheme is, however, dependent on the fiscal policies of the particular government.

In a situation where the enrolment in private institutions is from low-income families, then the cost of the schooling of such groups imposes on them what appears to be an unfair financial burden. This, however, depends on how their education would be financed in the first place. If it were financed entirely through higher taxation on the low-income groups, then public education would be more equitable than private education.

In countries with substantial numbers of private schools, such as in Uganda and Kenya at the secondary level, many of the schools are of poor quality and the worst tend to be those whose enrolments consist largely of students from low-income/poor families. Various reasons can be given to explain why these groups of students attend such schools. Firstly, because they have no access to public schools; secondly, they cannot afford to pay for the higher tuition in the better schools; third, they are not able to meet the admission requirements of the better private schools; fourth, because students consider the education offered at such schools quite acceptable; and finally, because they receive a certificate which allegedly gives them a certain status.

Two alternatives are open to the government in such a situation: either to issue regulations to assure minimum standards of educational quality in the private institutions, which generally never proves effective, or a takeover of the private schools by the government which soon imposes an unmanageable financial burden on the public sector, as the recent experience of Nigeria has demonstrated. An alternative approach, which was in common usage in colonial Africa, was the institution of a system of selective subsidies to private schools, which in turn entailed a strict enforcement through a system of inspection and of minimum standards of education. Such subsidies would be selective in two respects. First, they would be enjoyed only by those institutions that need financial assistance to raise the quality of their educational provision to required standards. Second, the subsidies would finance only the costs of inputs such as higher salaries for better-qualified teachers, or more books and teaching materials that would be required to improve educational quality. The main advantage of a subsidy program is that in spite of the additional financial burden it would impose on the government it would cost much less than a complete takeover of the subsidised institutions. Thus, the overall benefit would be a marked improvement in educational quality for students from low-income families without adding significantly to their financial burden, depending, of course, on how the costs of the subsidy were financed.

At the higher education level the debate over private or public financing can be summarised as follows. Advocates of private financing claim that education yields private, or individual, as well as social returns. This is particularly the case with higher education. In addition, higher education has a priviledged clientele drawing on tax revenue paid by society at large. Consequently, public finances are much better spent on primary and secondary levels. Furthermore, beyond the issues of equity, multiple-income sources, it is claimed, insure university autonomy, efficiency and responsiveness and client choice and client responsibility. Principal sources of income for privately-financed higher education would include student payments (tuition and fees) and donations from companies/foundations and individuals. State support would be in the form of government subsides to the institution or through student grants or the provision of low-interest loans and tax exemptions.

Advocates of public funding, on the other hand, argue that all education is a state responsibility. The benefits, both economic and non-economic, make higher education mostly a public good, but only state public funding can guarantee equal access. Moreover, in African countries, the absence of well-funded foundations that are the main sources of finance for the privately financed higher education institutions in the developed capitalist countries such as the USA, leaves the government, as is the case with the other sectors of education, as the main source. This then brings us to the issue of student loans.

Student loans

It has to be stated from the outset that the predominant pattern in African financing is for total government funding. Nevertheless, there is a continuing debate about the feasibility of introducing loan schemes at university level in one African country or another. In one country, Ghana, the scheme was in fact introduced but later abandoned. A number of arguments have been advanced in favour of student loans. First, the unit costs of higher education are much higher than for primary and secondary education. Second, within the last decade or so, enrolment in higher education has been expanding at a faster rate than either primary or secondary education in most countries. Thus, student loans would provide relief to governments to avoid imposing a financial burden on qualified low-income students that would prevent them from enjoying university education. Nevertheless, in the African situation where governments have traditionally provided free university education, together with board and lodging, loans represent a hardening of financial terms.

Furthermore, providing loan schemes for specific types of courses can serve to influence or orient students towards particular areas of high priority to government. Where students have to make a choice between having to pay tuition or to receive loans, many would opt for the latter. The rationale for introducing student loans can be briefly stated as follows. Although only a very small proportion of the population of university age receives a university education, government expenditure on higher education accounts for a substantial proportion of total education expenditures. Moreover, university graduates receive not only more services in the form of education than do most people, they also tend to earn substantially higher incomes than they would have earned without their university education. It is therefore only reasonable that they should bear some of the costs of their education by repaying student loans out of their incomes, rather than imposing the burden on taxpayers who have not had the direct private benefits of this education (Sirkin, 1979; Woodhall, 1969; Woodhall, in Baxter *et al.*, 1977). It is arguments such as these that various African governments have used in reducing financial support towards university students. However, any African government contemplating the introduction of a student loan scheme has to consider how to collect the loans once the student completes his studies, especially in a situation where no system of hire purchase is in operation, and also the terms of repayments. Other issues to be considered would include financial yields, equity, efficiency and administrative feasibility.

Exercises

1   Trace the evolution of educational financing in your country.

2   Compare the financing policies of education of any two African countries you know.

3   a) Distinguish between GNP ratio and budgetary ratio.

     b) With the aid of Appendix I, discuss:

        i)   The relationship between total educational expenditure of the Congo, Kenya and Botswana.

       ii)   Total educational expenditure and current educational expenditure in Algeria, Mauritius, Nigeria and Zimbabwe, or of any four countries of your choice.

4   Using Table 14.6 discuss the pattern of current public expenditure on education by purpose in 1980 in any three countries.

5   With the aid of Table 14.7 and using the latest figures, which of the following countries shows the best distribution of expenditure on the different levels of education – Botswana, Ethiopia, Ghana and Zambia. Using earlier figures as well, attempt an explanation of the observed trend.

PART IV
CONCLUSION

In the three preceding sections we have tried to show: first the relation between education and national development; second, we have discussed the various theories underlying the planning of education as well as the methodologies and techniques used in the application of the theories in practice; third, we have also shown the principles on which the financing of education is based and the various techniques used in education finance. What, however, became apparent in the process of doing so is that for education to succeed in the decades of the 1990s and beyond, the involvement of the parents and local community will become increasingly crucial as few African governments and economies are in a position to shoulder the entire responsibility for the financing of education without the involvement of the direct beneficiaries.

In addition, various measures within the education systems need to be taken in order to prop the systems up in the decades to come. These measures consist of a wide range of strategies that could be implemented quite independently of the rest of the national economy. Suggested strategies might include: cost-recovery initiatives, e.g. the introduction of some level of community financing as pursued in Kenya; the use of expenditure reduction policies, e.g. rationalising and combining training programmes for several sectors of development; improved resources management, e.g. more flexible use of school buildings out of school hours; and greater decentralisation, particularly of supervision which could lead to reduction in expenses incurred by officers travelling to and from the centre.

The measures being suggested do not in fact constitute a radical departure from those already being applied in many other developing countries. They are, however, particularly relevant to those countries of Africa where educational provision has continued to be heavily subsidised, particularly at the post-primary levels.

Appendix I: Basic indicators

	Total population (millions) 1990	GNP per capita (US$) 1989	Life expectancy at birth (years) 1990	Total adult literacy rate 1990	% of age group enrolled in primary school Total 1986–1989
Very high U5MR countries (over 140)					
Median	1536T	290	50	35	63
Mozambique	15.7	80	48	33	68
Angola	10.0	610	46	42	93
Mali	9.2	270	45	32	23
Sierra Leone	4.2	220	42	21	53
Malaŵi	8.8	180	48		72
Guinea-Bissau	1.0	180	43		53
Guinea	5.8	430	44	24	30
Burkina Faso	9.0	320	48	18	32
Niger	7.7	290	46	28	30
Ethiopia	49.2	120	46		36
Chad	5.7	190	47	30	51
Somalia	7.5	170	46	17	15
Mauritania	2.0	500	47	34	52
Liberia	2.6	450	54	40	34
Rwanda	7.2	320	50	50	67
Cambodia	8.2		50	35	
Burundi	5.5	220	49	50	59
Senegal	7.3	650	48	38	59
Madagascar	12.0	230	55	80	97
Sudan	25.2	420	51	27	49
Tanzania	27.3	130	54	91	66
Central African Rep	3.0	390	50	38	67
Namibia	1.8	1030	58		
Nigeria	108.5	250	52	51	66
Gabon	1.2	2960	53	61	
Uganda	18.8	250	52	48	77
Cameroon	11.8	1000	54	54	111
Benin	4.6	380	47	23	63
Togo	3.5	390	54	43	101

Source: The State of the World's Children (UNICEF) 1992.

364

	Total population (millions) 1990	GNP per capita (US$) 1989	Life expectancy at birth (years) 1990	Total adult literacy rate 1990	% of age group enrolled in primary school Total 1986–1989
High U5MR countries (71–140)					
Median	793T	885	62	68	97
Ghana	15.0	390	55	60	73
Côte d'Ivoire	12.0	790	53	54	70
Zaire	35.6	260	53	72	76
Lesotho	1.8	470	57		112
Zambia	8.5	390	54	73	97
Libyan Arab Jamahiriya	4.5	5310	62	64	
Morocco	25.1	880	62	50	67
Congo	2.3	940	54	57	
Kenya	24.0	360	60	69	93
Algeria	25.0	2230	65	57	96
South Africa	35.3	2470	62		
Zimbabwe	9.7	650	60	67	128
Egypt	52.4	640	60	48	90
Botswana	1.3	1600	60	74	117
Middle U5MR countries (21–70)					
Median	241	1775	70	88	105
Tunisia	8.2	1260	67	65	113

Appendix 2: Education

	Adult literacy rate 1990		Primary school enrolment ratio 1986–89 (gross)		% of grade 1 enrolment reaching final grade of primary school 1985–87	Secondary school enrolment ratio 1986–89 (gross)	
	male	female	male	female		male	female
Very high U5MR countries (over 140)							
Median	49	24	70	50	50	19	9
Mozambique	45	21	76	59	34	7	4
Angola	56	29	101	85	24	17	9
Mali	41	24	29	17	40	9	4
Sierra Leone	31	11	65	40		23	11
Malaŵi			79	65	31	5	3
Guinea-Bissau	50	24	69	37	19	9	3
Guinea	35	13	42	19	43	13	4
Burkina Faso	28	9	41	24	68	8	4
Niger	40	17	38	21	75	8	3
Ethiopia			44	28	50	18	12
Chad	42	18	73	29	78	10	2
Somalia	27	9	20	10	33		
Mauritania	47	21	61	43	78	23	10
Liberia	50	29	43	24			
Rwanda	64	37	67	64	46	7	5
Cambodia	48	22			50	45	20
Burundi	61	40	68	50	87	6	3
Senegal	52	25	70	49	85	19	10
Madagascar	88	73	99	95	48	23	19
Sudan	43	12	58	41	76	23	17
Tanzania	93	88	67	66	71	5	3
Central African Rep	52	25	83	51	56	17	6
Namibia							
Nigeria	62	40	68	63	63	28	18
Gabon	74	49			44		
Uganda	62	35	76	63	76	16	9
Cameroon	66	43	119	102	70	32	21
Benin	32	16	83	43	36	23	9
Togo	56	31	124	78	52	36	12

Source: The State of the World's Children (UNICEF) 1992

	Adult literacy rate 1990		Primary school enrolment ratio 1986–89 (gross)		% of grade 1 enrolment reaching final grade of primary school 1985–87	Secondary school enrolment ratio 1986–89 (gross)	
	male	female	male	female		male	female
High U5MR countreis (71–140)							
Median	76	60	100	92	67	35	35
Mozambique	45	21	76	59	34	7	4
Ghana	70	51	81	66		49	30
Côte d'Ivoire	67	40	82	58	73	26	12
Zaire	84	61	86	65	60	32	14
Lesotho			101	123	52	20	30
Zambia	81	65	102	92	80		
Libyan Arab Jamahiriya	75	50			82		
Morocco	61	38	80	53	67	43	30
Congo	70	44			71	37	14
Kenya	80	59	95	91	51	27	19
Algeria	70	46	105	87	90	61	53
South Africa							
Zimbabwe	74	60	130	126	74	49	42
Egypt	63	34	100	79	95	79	58
Botswana	84	65	114	120	89	31	36
Middle U5MR countries (21–70)							
Median	90	86	106	104	87	57	58
Tunisia	74	56	121	105	72	46	38

Appendix 3   Africa: demographic indicators

	Population (millions) 1990 under 16	Population (millions) 1990 under 5	Population annual growth 1965–80	Population annual growth 1980–90	Crude death rate 1960	Crude death rate 1990	Crude birth rate 1960	Crude birth rate 1990	Life expectancy 1960	Life expectancy 1990	Total fertility rate 1990	% population urbanised 1990	Average annual growth rate of urban population (%) 1965–80	Average annual growth rate of urban population (%) 1980–90
1 Mozambique	7.2	2.8	2.5	2.6	26	18	47	45	37	48	6.3	27	11.8	9.7
2 Angola	4.7	1.8	2.8	2.6	31	19	50	47	33	46	6.4	28	6.4	5.6
3 Mali	4.5	1.8	2.1	2.9	29	20	52	51	35	45	7.1	19	4.9	4.0
4 Sierra Leone	1.9	0.8	2.0	2.4	33	23	48	48	32	42	6.5	32	4.3	5.1
5 Malawi	4.4	1.8	2.9	3.5	28	20	54	56	38	48	7.6	12	7.8	6.0
6 Guinea-Bissau	0.4	0.2	1.2	1.9	29	22	40	43	34	43	5.8	20	1.7	3.5
7 Guinea	2.8	1.1	1.9	2.5	31	21	53	51	34	44	7.0	26	6.6	5.5
8 Burkina Faso	4.2	1.6	2.0	2.6	28	18	52	47	36	48	6.5	9	3.4	5.1
9 Niger	3.9	1.5	2.7	3.2	29	20	53	52	35	46	7.1	19	6.9	7.1
10 Ethiopia	23.5	9.3	2.7	2.4	28	20	51	49	36	46	68	13	6.6	4.5
11 Chad	2.6	1.0	2.0	2.4	30	19	46	44	35	47	5.8	30	9.2	6.2
12 Somalia	3.7	1.4	2.7	3.4	28	19	49	49	36	46	6.6	36	6.1	5.7
13 Mauritania	0.9	0.4	2.3	2.7	28	18	48	46	35	47	6.5	37	12.4	7.4
14 Liberia	1.2	0.5	3.0	3.2	25	15	50	47	41	54	6.8	46	6.2	5.9

	Population (millions) 1990		Population annual growth		Crude death rate		Crude birth rate		Life expectancy		Total fertility rate	% population urbanised	Average annual growth rate of urban population (%)	
	under 16	under 5	1965–80	1980–90	1960	1990	1960	1990	1960	1990	1990	1990	1965–80	1980–90
15 Rwanda	3.7	1.5	3.3	3.4	22	16	50	51	42	50	8.1	8	6.3	7.7
16 Burundi	2.6	1.0	1.9	2.8	23	17	46	47	41	49	6.8	6	1.8	5.4
17 Senegal	3.5	1.3	2.5	2.8	27	17	50	45	37	48	6.3	38	4.1	3.7
18 Madagascar	5.7	2.2	2.5	3.1	24	13	48	45	41	55	6.6	24	5.7	5.8
19 Sudan	11.9	4.5	3.0	3.0	25	15	47	44	39	51	6.4	22	5.1	4.1
20 Tanzania	14.0	5.6	3.3	3.7	24	13	51	50	41	54	7.1	33	8.7	10.6
21 Central African Republic	1.4	0.4	1.8	2.7	26	17	43	45	39	50	6.2	47	4.8	4.7
22 Namibia	0.9	0.3	1.0	3.1	23	11	46	43	42	58	5.9	28	1.9	5.1
23 Nigeria	53.8	21.1	2.5	3.2	25	15	52	48	40	52	6.8	35	4.8	5.9
24 Gabonn	0.4	0.2	3.5	3.7	24	16	31	41	41	53	5.2	46	4.2	6.2
25 Uganda	9.7	3.9	2.9	3.6	21	15	50	52	43	52	7.3	10	4.1	5.2
26 Cameroon	5.8	2.3	2.7	3.1	25	14	44	47	39	54	6.9	41	8.1	5.8
27 Benin	2.3	0.9	2.7	2.9	33	19	47	49	35	47	7.1	38	10.2	4.7
28 Togo	1.7	0.6	3.0	3.0	26	13	48	45	39	54	6.6	26	7.2	6.2
29 Ghana	7.1	2.8	2.2	3.4	19	13	48	44	45	55	6.3	33	3.4	4.1

	Population (millions) 1990		Population annual growth		Crude death rate		Crude birth rate		Life expectancy		Total fertility rate 1990	% population urbanised 1990	Average annual growth rate of urban population (%)	
	under 16	under 5	1965–80	1980–90	1960	1990	1960	1990	1960	1990	1990	1990	1965–80	1980–90
30 Côte d'Ivoire	6.0	2.4	4.2	3.8	25	14	53	50	39	53	7.4	40	8.7	5.3
31 Zaïre	17.2	6.6	2.8	3.0	23	14	47	46	41	53	6.1	39	7.2	4.5
32 Lesotho	0.8	0.3	2.3	2.8	24	12	43	41	42	57	5.8	20	14.6	6.8
33 Zambia	4.3	1.8	3.1	3.9	23	13	50	51	42	54	7.2	50	7.1	6.1
34 Libyan Arab Jamahiriya	2.2	0.8	4.6	4.0	19	9	49	44	47	62	6.8	70	9.7	6.2
35 Morocco	10.7	3.8	2.5	2.6	21	9	50	34	47	62	4.5	48	4.2	4.1
36 Congo	1.1	0.4	2.7	3.1	23	14	45	46	42	54	6.3	40	3.5	4.3
37 Kenya	12.6	4.7	3.6	3.7	23	11	53	47	45	60	6.9	24	9.0	7.5
38 Algeria	11.5	3.8	3.1	2.9	20	8	51	35	47	65	5.1	52	3.8	4.6
39 South Africa	13.8	4.9	2.4	2.2	17	9	42	31	49	62	4.3	59	2.6	3.4
40 Zimbabwe	4.6	1.7	3.1	3.1	20	10	53	41	45	60	5.6	28	7.5	5.4
41 Egypt	21.7	7.6	2.4	2.5	21	10	45	33	46	60	4.3	47	2.9	3.1
42 Botswana	0.7	0.3	3.5	3.7	21	11	52	46	46	60	6.7	28	15.4	9.7

Source: The State of the World's Children (UNICEF) 1992.

Selected bibliography

Amond, Gabriel A. and Verba, Sidney (1965) *The Civic Culture: Political Attitudes and Democracy in Five Nations*, Boston: Little, Brown and Company.

Anderson, C. and Bowman, M.J. (1967) 'Theoretical Considerations in Education Planning', *World Year Book of Education*, London: Evans Brothers Ltd.

Anosike, Benji J.O. (1977) 'Education and Economic Development in Nigeria: The need for a new paradigm', *African Studies Review*, XX, No. 2 (September) pp. 27–51.

Anthony, Robert N. (1965) *Planning and Control System: A Framework for Analysis*, Boston: Harvard University Press.

Apter, David E. (1965) *The Politics of Modernization*, Chicago: UCP.

Armer, Michael and Youtz, Robert (1971) 'Formal Education and Individual Modernity in An African Society', *American Journal of Sociology*, 4, pp. 604–26.

Armer, Michael (1977) 'Education and Social Change: An examination of the modernity thesis', *Studies in Comparative International Development*, X11 (Fall) pp. 86–99.

Armitage, P. (1973) 'An Introduction to some Educational Models and their Application', in Fowler, G. *et al.* (ed.) *Decision-making in British Education*, Milton Keynes: OUP.

Baldridge, J.V. and Tierney, M.L. (1979) *New Approaches to Management*, San Francisco, California: Jossey-Bass.

Batten, J.D. (1966) *Beyond Management by Objectives*, New York: American Management Association.

Becker, G.S. (1964) *A Theoretical and Empirical Analysis, with Special Reference to Education*, New York: Columbia University Press.

Beeby, C.E. (ed.) (1968) *The Quality of Education in Developing Countries*, Cambridge, Massachusetts: Harvard University Press.

Bell, Terrel H. (1974) *A Performance Accountability System for School Administrators*, Englewood Cliff, N.J.: Parker Publishing.

Berg, Ivar (1971) *Education and Jobs: The Great Training Robbery*, Boston: Beacon Press.

Beshir, M.O. (1969) *Educational Development in the Sudan*, Oxford: Clarendon Press.

Black, C.E. (1966) *The Dynamics of Modernization*, New York: Harper and Row.

Blackmore, Kenneth and Cooksey, Brian (1969) *A Sociology of Education for Africa*, London: George Allen and Unwin.

Blaug, Mark (1980) 'Common Assumptions about Education and Employment', in Simmons, John (ed.) *The Education Dilemma*, New York: Pergamon Press.

Bock, J. and Papagianis, G. (1976) 'The Demystification of Non-formal Education: A Critique and Suggestions for a New Research Direction', *Issues in Non-Formal Education*, No. 1, Amherst, Mass: Center for International Education.

Bourdieu, Pierre (1973) 'Cultural Reproduction and Social Reproduction', in Brown, Richard (ed.) *Knowledge, Education and Cultural Change*, London: Tavistock.

Bowles, Samuel (1971) 'Cuban Education and the Revolutionary Ideology', *Harvard Educational Review*, 41(4), pp. 472–500.

Bowles, Samuel and Gintis, Herbert (1972) 'IQ in the US Class structure', *Social Policy*, 3 (November–December), pp. 65–96.

371

Bown, Lalage (1974) *Education and the Employment Problem in Developing Countries*, Geneva: International Labour Office.

—— (1980) 'Implementing a Coherent Non-Formal Education Programme: The Development of an Appropriate Institutional Framework', in Rasheed, Sadiq and Sandell, Terry (eds) *Non-Formal Education and Development in the Sudan*, Khartoum, Development Studies Research Centre, University of Khartoum.

Bray, Mark, Clarke, Peter B. and Stephens, David (1986) *Education and Society in Africa*, London: Edward Arnold.

Brimer, N.A. and Pauli, L. (1971) *Wastage in Education: A World Problem*, Paris-Geneva: UNESCO, International Bureau of Education.

Bronfenbrenner, Urie (1974) *Two Worlds of Childhood*, Harmondsworth, England: Penguin.

Brown, Godfrey, N. (1976) 'A Strategy for Lifelong Education', *Prospects*, Vol. VI, No. 2, UNESCO.

Cardenal, Fernando S.J. and Miller, V. (1981) 'Nicaragua 1980: The Battle of the ABCs', *Harvard Educational Review*, 51(1), pp. 1–56.

Carnoy, Martin (1974) *Education and Cultural Imperialism*, New York: David McKay.

—— (1980) 'Can Education alone solve the problem of unemployment?' in Simmons, John (ed.) *The Education Dilemma*, New York: Pergamon Press.

Carnoy, Martin and Werthein, Jorge (1977) 'Socialist Ideology and the Transformation of Cuban Education' in Karabel, Jerome and Halsey, A.H. (eds) *Power and Ideology in Education*, New York: Oxford University Press.

Chanan, G. and Gilchrist, L. (1974) *What School is For*, London: Methuen.

Chukunta, N.K. Onucha (1978) 'Education and National Integration in Africa: A Case Study of Nigeria', *African Studies Review*, XXI(2), pp. 67–76.

Christian Council of Kenya (1966) *After School What? Further Education, Training and Employment of Primary School Leavers*, Nairobi: CCK and Christian Church Educational Association.

Cohen, Yehudi A. (1970) 'Schools and Civilizational States' in Fischer, Joseph (ed.) *The Social Sciences and the Comparative Study of Educational Systems*, Scranton: International Textbooks Company.

Coleman, James S. (ed.) (1965) *Education and Political Development*, Princeton, N.J.: Princeton University Press.

Coleman, James S. and Ndolamb, Ngokwey (1983) 'Zaire: The State and the University' in Murray, Thomas R. (ed.) *Politics and Education*, Pergamon Press.

Coombs, P.H. (1968) *The World Educational Crisis: A Systems Analysis*, London: Oxford University Press.

—— (1985) *The World Crisis in Education: The View from the Eighties*, Oxford: Oxford University Press.

Coombs, P.H. and Hallak, J. (1972) *Managing Educational Costs*, London: Oxford University Press.

Coombs, Philip, Prosser, Roy and Ahmed, Manzoor (1973) *New Paths to Learning for Rural Children*, New York: International Council for Educational Development.

Court, David (1976) 'The education system as a response to inequality in Tanzania and Kenya', *Journal of Modern African Studies*, 14 (4), pp. 661–90.

Court, D. and Prewitt, K. (1974) 'Nation versus Region in Kenya: A Note on Political Learning', *British Journal of Political Science*, 4, pp. 109–20.

Cunningham, William G. (1982) *Systematic Planning for Educational Change*, Paulo Alto, California: Mayfield Publishing Company.

Delacroix, Jacquires and Ragin, Charles (1978) 'Modernizing Institutions, Mobilization and Third World Development: A Cross-national Study', *American Journal of Sociology*, 84 (1) (July), pp. 123–50.

Denison, Edward F. (1962) 'Education, economic growth and gaps in information', *Journal of Political Economy*, supplement, Oct. LXX.

Dobson, Richard B. (1977) 'Social Status and Inequality of Access to Higher Education in the USSR' in Karabel, Jerome and Halsey, A.H. (eds) *Power and Ideology in Education*, New York: Oxford University Press.

Dore, Ronald (1976) *The Diploma Disease*, London: Allen and Unwin.

—— (1980) 'The Future of Formal Education in Developing Countries' in Simmons, John (ed.) *The Education Dilemma*, New York: Pergamon Press.

Dror, G.Y. (1963) 'The Planning Process: A Facet Design' *The International Review of Administrative Sciences*, Vol. XXIX, No. 1, pp. 46–58.

Drucker, Peter (1954) *Practice of Management*, New York: Harper and Row.

—— (1974) *Management Tasks, Responsibilities and Practices*, New York: Harper and Row.

Edstrom, J. (1975) 'Education Finance, Expenditure and Unit Costs', IBRD Working Paper, prepared for the Education Review of Sierra Leone.

Eisenstadt, S.N. (1970) 'Breakdowns of Modernization' in Eisenstadt, S.N. (ed.) *Readings in Social Evolution and Development*, Oxford: Pergamon Press.

El-Ghannan, M.A. (1970) *Politics in Educational Planning*, IIEP Occasional Papers No. 19, Paris: UNESCO-IIEP.

Evans, D.R. (1981) 'The Planning of Non-Formal Education', *The Fundamental of Educational Planning Series*, No. 30, Paris: UNESCO-IIEP.

Evans, Emmit B. Jr (1975) 'Secondary Education, Unemployment, and Crime in Kenya', *The Journal of Modern African Studies*, **13**, pp. 55–66.

—— (1977) 'Sources of Socio-political Instability in an African state: The Case of Kenya's Educated Unemployed', *African Studies Review*, **XX** (1), pp. 37–52.

Fägerlind and Saha (1983) *Education and National Development: A Comparative Perspective*, Pergamon Press.

Fajana, A. (1978) *Education in Nigeria 1842–1939: An Historical Analysis*, Nigeria: Longman.

Federal Republic of Nigeria (1975) *Third National Development Plan*, Lagos: Government Printers.

—— (1977/1981) *National Policy on Education*, Lagos: Federal Ministry of Information, Printing Division.

Fields, Gary S. (1965) 'Private and Social Returns to Education in Labour Surplus Economies', *East African Economic Review*.

—— (1980) *Poverty, Inequality and Development*, Cambridge: CUP.

Forojalla, S.B. (1975) 'The Southern Sudan: Educational Evolution and New Strategy for Rural Education for Development,' unpublished M.A. (Ed.) dissertation, University of London, Institute of Education.

Foster, Philip (1965) 'The Vocational School Fallacy in Development Planning' in Anderson, C. Arnold and Bowman, Mary Jean (eds) *Education and Economic Development*, Chicago: Aldine Publishing Company.

Foster-Carter, A. (1985) *The Sociology of Development*, Ormskirk: Causeway Books.

Frey, Frederick W. (1970) 'Political Science, Education and Development', in Fischer, Joseph (ed.) *The Social Sciences and the Comparative Study of Educational Systems*, Scranton: International Textbook Company.

Furtado, Celson (1977) 'Development', *International Social Science Journal*, **XXIX** (4), pp. 628–50.

Garvey-Williams, F.H. and Mills, L.R. (1976) *Education in the Southern Sudan*, Juba: Regional Ministry of Education.

Gould, William, T.S. (1978) *Guidelines for School Location Planning*, Washington D.C.: IBRD.

Graham, Sonia F. (1966) *Government and Mission Education in Northern Nigeria 1900–1919*, Nigeria: Ibadan University Press.

Granger, Robert L. (1971) *Educational Leadership: An Interdisciplinery Perspective*, Scranton, Pean: Intext Educational Publishers.

Gurunge, Ananda W.P. (1969) *A Functional Analysis of Educational Administration in Relation to Educational Planning*, IIEP Occ. Papers No. 16, Paris: UNESCO-IIEP.

—— (1970) 'Functional Analysis of Educational Planning: The Internal Division of Functions and Administrative Organisation within the Ministry of Education', in *Administrative Aspects of Educational Planning*, Paris: UNESCO-IIEP.

Gusfield, Joseph R. (1967) 'Tradition and Modernity: Misplaced Polarities in the Study of Social Change', *American Journal of Sociology*, 72 (4), pp. 351–62.

Hallak, J. (1970) *The Role of Budgeting in Educational Planning, in Administrative Aspects of Educational Planning*, An IIEP Seminar, Paris: UNESCO-IIEP.

—— (1977) *Planning the Location of Schools: An Instrument of Educational Policy*, Paris: UNESCO-IIEP.

Hanson, John, W. (1974) *Report on the Supply of Secondary Level Teachers in Africa: Shifting the Locus Focus to Africa*, (summary volume), Michigan State University, East Lancing: Instit. for International Studies, Education and African Studies Center.

Harbison, Frederick, H. (1973) *Human Resources as the Wealth of Nations*, New York: Oxford University Press.

—— (1976) 'Human Resources and Development', in UNESCO, *Economic and Social Aspects of Educational Planning*, Paris: UNESCO-IIEP.

Harbison F. and Meyers, C.A. (1964) *Education, Manpower and Economic Growth*, New York: McGraw-Hill.

Hawes, H.W.R. (1979) *Curriculum and Reality in African Primary Schools*, Longman.

Hawes, H.W.R. and Stephens, D.G. (1990) *Questions of Quality: Primary Education and Development*, Harlow: Longman.

Hicks, Herbert G. (1972) *The Management of Organisations: A Systems and Human Resources Approach*, (2nd ed.), New York: McGraw Hill Book Company.

Hobsbawn, E.J. (1969) *Industry and Empire*, London: Penguin.

—— (1977) *The Age of Revolutions: Europe 1789–1848*, Abacus Edition.

Hoogvelt, Ankie M.M. (1976) *The Sociology of Developing Societies*, London: Macmillan.

Hostrop, R.W. (1975) *Managing Education for Results*, Palm Springs, California: An ETC Publication.

ILO (1971) *Matching Employment Opportunities, A Programme of Action for Ceylon*, Report, Geneva: International Labour Office.

Ilunga, K. (1978) 'Some Thoughts on the National University of Zaire and the Zairian Political Dynamic' (unpublished).

Implementation Committee for the National Policy on Education (1978/79), Blue Print, Lagos: Federal Ministry of Education.

Inkeles, Alex and Smith, David H. (1974) *Becoming Modern*, London: Heinemann Education Books.

Jallade, J.P. (1977) 'Basic education and income inequality in Brazil: The long term view', *Staff Working Paper*, No. 268, Washington D.C.: World Bank.

Jencks, C. et al. (1972) *Inequality: A Reassessment of the Effect of Family and Schooling in America*, Basic Books.

Jolly, A.R. (1969) *Employment, Wage Levels and Incentive in Manpower Aspects of Educational Planning, Problems for the Future*, Paris: UNESCO-IIEP.

Jolly, A.R. (ed.) (1969) *Education in Africa: Research in Action*, Nairobi: East African Publishing House. For the African Studies Association of the UK. Papers presented at the biannual Conference of the Association at the University of Sussex, 1968.

Jolly, A.E. and Colclough, C. (1972) 'African Manpower Plans: An Evaluation', in *International Labour Review*, pp. 247–8.

Kahl, Joseph A. (1968) *The Measurement of Modernism: A Study of Values in Brazil and Mexico*, Austin: University of Texas Press.

Kano State, Nigeria (1980) *The Reorganisation of the State Ministry of Education*, Kano: Government Printers.

—— (1985) *Kano State Statistical Year Book, 1984/85*, Kano: Government Printers

Kassam, Y. O. (1977) 'Formal Education and Social Justice', *Prospects*, Vol. VII, No. 2.

Kaufman, Roger A. (1972) *Educational Systems Planning*, Palm Springs, California: Prentice-Hall Inc.

Kindervatter, Suzanne (1979) *Non-Formal Education as an Empowering Process*, Centre for International Education, Amherst, Massachusetts.

King, R.W. and Cleland, D.I. (1978) *Strategic Planning and Policy*, New York: Van Nostrand Reinholt Company.

Knezevich, Stephen J. (1973) *Program Budgeting*, Berkeley, California: McCutchan Publishing.

Kuhun, Thomas (1962) *The Structure of Scientific Revolutions*, Chicago: UCP.

Labelle, T.J. (1976) *Non-Formal Education and Social Change in Latin America*, Los Angeles, California: Latin American Centre, UCLA.

Landers, Thomas, J. and Myers, Judith G. (1977) *Essentials of School Management*.

—— *Time share, The computer in Educational Decision-Making: An Introduction and Guide for School Administrators*.

Le Loup, Lance T. and Moreland, William B. (1978) 'Agency Strategies and Executive Review: The Hidden Politics of Budgeting', *Public Administration Review*, May/June.

Lewin, K.M. (1981) *Qualifications and Selection in Educational Systems*, Sussex: Institute of Development Studies, University of Sussex.

Little, Angela (1978) *The Occupational and Educational Expectation of Students in Developed and Less-Developed Countries*, Education Report 3, Sussex: IDS.

Lyden, Fremont J. (1975) 'Control, Management and Planning: An Empirical Examination', *Public Administration Review*, November/December.

Lyons, Ramond F. (1968) *Requirements and Supply of Teachers*, Lecture Discussion Series, No. 25, Paris: UNESCO-IIEP.

McClelland, David C. (1961) *The Achieving Society*, New York: The Free Press.

McFarland, Dalton E. (1979) *Management: Foundations and Practices*, (5th ed.), London: Collier and Macmillan Publishers.

McGregor, Douglas (1960) *The Human Side of Enterprise*, New York: McGraw-Hill.

Mann, Dale (1975) *Policy Decision-making in Education*, New York: Teachers College Press.

Massialas, B. G. (1969) *Education and the Political System*, Boston: Addison-Wesley.

Meyer, J. and Rubinson, R. (1975) 'Education and Political Development' in Kerlinger, F. (ed.) *Review of Research in Education*, (Vol. 3), Itasca, Illinois: Peacock Publishers.

Milkias, Pauls (1976) 'Traditional Institutions and Political elites: The Role of Education in the Ethiopian body-politic, *African Studies Review*, **XXIX** (5), pp. 79–93.

Moore, Wilbert E. (1979) *World Modernisation: The Limits of Convergence*, New York: Elsevier Press.

Morales, Abel Prieto (1981) 'The Literacy Campaign in Cuba', *Harvard Educational Review*, **Vol. 51**, No. 3, Feb.

Newsweek Magazine Special Report, 26 October 1981.

Nyerere, Julius K. (1967) *Education for Self-Reliance*, Dar-es-Salaam: Oxford University Press.

—— (1968) *Ujaama: Essays on Socialism*, Dar-es-Salaam: Oxford University Press.

Odiorne, George S. (1965) *Management by Objectives*, Belmont, California: Pitman Learning.

O'Donoghue, Martin (1971) *Economic Dimensions in Education*, Milton Keynes: The Open University Press, Gill and Macmillan.

OECD (1973) *A Framework for Educational Indicators to Guide Government Decisions*, Paris: OECD.

Open University Press (1976) *Planning Models in Education*, Milton Keynes, England: The Open University Press.

—— (1979) *Providing the Teachers*, Milton Keynes, England: The Open University Press.

Palsay, Alan (1981) *Organisation and Management in Schools*, London: Longman.

Pandit, H.N. (1980) 'International and National Trends in Forecasting Manpower Requirements for Economic Development', Seminar Paper presented at the Department of Guidance and Counselling, University of Ibadan, Nigeria.

Parnes, H.S. (ed.) (1962) *Forecasting Educational Needs for Economic and Social Development*, Paris: OECD.

Papadopoulos, G. (1970) *Educational Structures in Educational Policies for the 1970s*, Paris: OECD.

Phan-Thuy, B. (1985) 'Employment and training schemes for rural youth: learning from experience', *International Labour Review*, **Vol. 124**, No. 4. July–August 1985.

Portes, Alejandro (1973) 'Modernity and Development: A critique', *Studies in Comparative International Development*, VIII (3), pp. 247–79.

Portes, Alejandro and Ross, Adreian A. (1979) 'Modernization for Emigration: The Medical Brain Drain from Argentina', *Journal of Inter-American Studies and World Affairs*, 18 (4), pp. 395–422.

Prest, R. and Turvey, R. (1965) 'Cost Benefit Analysis: A survey', *Economic Journal*, Vol. 75, No. 300.

Psacharopoulos, George (1980) 'Returns to Education: An Updated International Comparison', in King, Timothy (ed.) *Education and Income*, World Bank Staff Working Papers No. 402, Washington D.C.: World Bank.

Pyhrr, Peter A. (1970) 'Zero-Base Budgeting', *Harvard Business Review*, Nov/Dec.

—— (1976) 'Zero-Base Budgeting: Where to Use it and How to Begin', *S.A.M. Advanced Management Journal*, Summer.

Reddin, W.J. (1971) *Effective Management by Objectives*, New York: McGraw-Hill.

Rensburg, R.V. (1967) *Education and Development in an Emerging Country*, Uppsala: The Scandinavian Institute of African studies.

Rostow, W.W. (1960) *The Stages of Economic Growth: A Non-Communist Manifesto*, Cambridge: CUP.

Ruscoe, G.L. (1969) *Conditions for Success in Educational Planning*, Fundamentals of Educational Planning Series, Paris: UNESCO-IIEP.

Sanderson, M.S. (1981) *Education, Religion and Politics in Southern Sudan 1899–1964*, London: Ithaca Press.

Schultz, Theodore W. (1963) *The Economic Value of Education*, New York: Columbia University Press.

Sergiovanni, Thomas J. and Carver, Fred (1975) *The New School Executive: A Theory of Administration*, New York: Dodd Mead.

Shamshul, Huq M. (1965) *Education and Development Strategy in South and South-East Asia*, Honolulu: East-West Center Press.

—— (1975) *Education, Manpower and Development in South and South-East Asia*, New York: Praeger Publishers Inc.

Shash, B.B. (1971) 'Application of PERT/CPM to Educational Programmes and Schemes' in *Modern Management Techniques in Educational Administration*, New Delhi: Asian Institute of Educational Planning and Administration.

Sheffield, James and Deijomah, Victor (eds) (1972) *Non-Formal Education in African Development*, New York: African-American Institute.

Shipman, M.D. (1971) *Education and Modernization*, London: Faber and Faber.

Simkins, T. (1978) 'Planning Non-formal Education: Strategies and Constraints, *Prospects*, Vol. VII, No. 2, 1978.

Sirkin, Irving A. (ed.) (1979) *Education Programmes and Projects: Analytical Techniques, Case Studies and Exercises*, IBRD.

Sjöström, Margareta and Sjöström, Rolf (1982) *Literacy and Development*, Limea: Limea University, Pedagogiska Institutionen.

Sokorov, G. (1968) 'Highlights of the Symposium' and 'The Absorptive Capacity of the Economy' in *Manpower Aspects of Educational Planning*, Paris: UNESCO-IIEP.

Stephens, D.G. (1985) 'Decentralisation of Education in N. Nigeria, a case of continuing in-direct rule?' in Lauglo, J. and McLean, M. (eds) *Control versus Decentralised Control in Education and International Perspectives*, London: Heinemann.

Stone, L. (1970) 'Japan and England: A comparative study', in Musgrave, P.W. (ed.) *Society, History and Education*, London: Hutchinson.

Sutchcliff, Claud R. (1978) 'The predictive power of measures of individual modernity: A critique of the paradigm of modernization', *Comparative Political Studies*, 11(1), (April), pp. 128–36.

Swatman, J.E.D. (1972) 'Factors which have influenced the distribution of educational institutions in mainland Tanzania' in *Teacher Education in New Countries*, Vol. 12, No. 3.

Ta Ngac Chau and Calloids, (1975) *Educational Policy and its Financial Implications in Tanzania*, Paris: UNESCO-IIEP.

Taiwo, C.O. (1980) *The Nigerian Education System: Past, Present and Future*, Thomas Nelson (Nigeria) Limited.

Thias, H. and Carnoy, M. (1972) *Cost-Benefit Analysis in Education: A Case Study of Kenya*, World Bank Staff Occ. Paper, No. 14, IBRD, Johns Hopkins Press, pp. 2–7.

Todare, Michael, P. (1977) *Economic Development in the Third World*, New York: Longman.

Torney, Judith V., Oppenheim, A.N. and Farnen, Russel F. (1975) *Civic Education in Ten Countries*, Stockholm: Almqvist and Wiksell.

UNESCO (1961) UNESCO/ED/180 Final Report, Conference of African States on the Development of Education in Africa, Addis Ababa, 15–25 May 1961.

—— (1964) *Economic and Social Aspects of Educational Planning*, Paris: UNESCO.

—— (1971) *World Survey of Education*, Vol. 5, Educational Policy, Legislations and Administrations, Paris: UNESCO.

—— (1980) *Wastage in Primary and General Education: A Statistical Study of Trends and Patterns in Repetition and Dropout*, CBR-E-37, Paris: UNESCO.

UNESCO-IBE (1972) *A Statistical Study of Wastage at School*, Paris: Geneva.

UNESCO-IIEP (1968) *Educational Development in Africa: II Costing and Financing*, Paris.

Vaizy, John *et al.*, (1977) *The Political Economy of Education*, London: Duckworth.

Vasudevan, Mullath (1976) *Criteria and Methods for Educational Research Reforms and Planning*, New York: Vantage Press.

Wacaster, C.T. (1979) 'Jackson County: Local Norms, Federal Initiatives and Administrator Performance' in Herrieth, Robert E. and Gross, Neil (eds) *The Dynamics of Planned Educational Change*, Berkeley, Calif.: McCutchan Publishing.

Wagaw, Teshome G. (1979) *Education in Ethiopia: Prospects and Retrospect*, Ann Arbor: University of Michigan Press.

Wass, Peter (1980) 'The Role of Non-Formal Education in Rural Development: Its Potential and Limitations', in Rasheed, S. and Sandell, T. (eds) *Non-Formal Education and Development in the Sudan*, Development Studies Research Centre, University of Khartoum.

Westoby, Adam (1976) *Costs in Education: University Examples*, Milton Keynes: The Open University Press.

Williams, Gareth A. (1976) 'Educational Planning and Manpower', in Ledj, Dobson L. *et al.*, *Management in Education: Some Techniques and Systems*, OUP; and Armitage P. 'An Introduction to some Educational Models and their application', (1973) in Fowler G. *et al.* (ed.) *Decision-making in British Education*, OU Press.

Williams, P.R.C. (1974) 'Cost-benefit Analysis and Rate of Return Analysis', mimeo, University of London Institute of Education.

—— (1975) 'Education Planning and the Evolution of Education Systems', mimeo, University of London Institute of Education.

—— (1979) 'Planning Teacher Demand and Supply', Fundamentals of Educational Planning Series, No. 27, Paris: UNESCO-IIEP.

Williamson, W. (1979) *Education, Social Structure and Development: A Comparative Analysis*, London: Macmillan.

Woodhall, Maureen (1970) *Cost-benefit Analysis in Educational Planning*, Fundamentals of Educational Planning Series, 13, Paris: UNESCO-IIEP, pp. 25–34.

The World Bank (1974) *World Development Report*, Washington D.C.

—— (1974) *Education Sector Working Paper*, Washington D.C.

—— (1980) *Education Sector Policy Paper*, Washington D.C.

—— (1980) *World Development Report*, Washington D.C.

—— (1991) *World Development Report*, Washington D.C.

Zeigler, Harmon and Peak, Wayne (1971) 'The Political Function of the Educational System' in Hopper, East (ed.) *Readings in the Theory of Educational Systems*, London: Hutchinson and Co.

Index

378